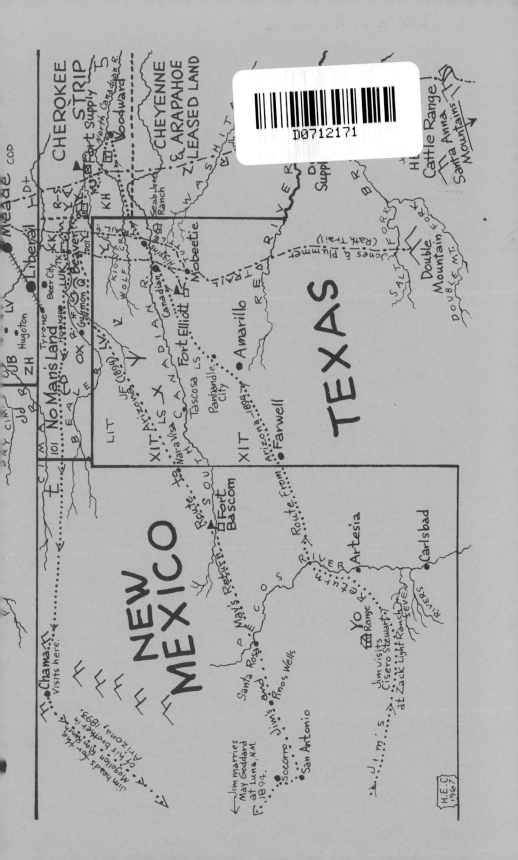

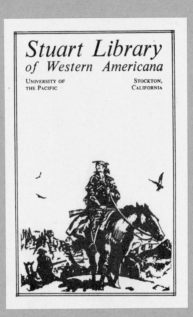

FIFTY YEARS ON
THE OWL HOOT TRAIL

TK
TXA
DOT
—O
MAY

OTHER BOOKS BY
HARRY E. CHRISMAN:

Lost Trails of the Cimarron, 1961,
1964.

*The Ladder of Rivers, the Story of I.P.
(Print) Olive,* 1962, 1964.

Chariot of the Sun (with Catherine
Ward Allen), 1964.

*Butcher's History of Custer County,
Nebraska,* ed. by Harry E. Chrisman,
revised 2nd Edition, 1965.

*When You and I Were Young,
Nebraska!* (with Berna Hunter
Chrisman), 1968.

The Fighting Railroad Mayor, by Earl
Walker (ed. by Harry E. Chrisman),
1968.

*Boss Neff in the Texas and Oklahoma
Panhandle,* by Boss Neff (ed. by
Harry E. Chrisman, 2nd Edition),
1968.

FIFTY YEARS ON
THE OWL HOOT TRAIL

JIM HERRON

THE FIRST SHERIFF OF NO MAN'S LAND, OKLAHOMA TERRITORY

by HARRY E. CHRISMAN

from an
Original Manuscript by Jim Herron

Introduction by EDWARD EVERETT DALE

SAGE BOOKS
CHICAGO

First Edition

Sage Books are published by
The Swallow Press Incorporated
1139 South Wabash Avenue
Chicago, Illinois 60605

LIBRARY OF CONGRESS CATALOG CARD NUMBER 73-75735

DEDICATED TO TWO GENERATIONS
OF WRANGLERS AND COWBOYS:

First, those Range Cattle Men of my father's and
Jim Herron's time, of whom I caught only a nostalgic
glimpse before they passed over the Great Divide, and

Second, a younger generation with whom I spent my
own boyhood years—and who now wear plenty of frost
in their own hair!

H.E.C.

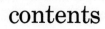

contents

INTRODUCTION: by Edward Everett Dale   xiii
PREFACE   xvii
ACKNOWLEDGMENTS   xxi

PART I

CHAPTER I (1880): Going Up the Texas Trail   3

CHAPTER II (1880-1884): Public Land Strip or "No Man's
Land" • YL Ranch • Cattle Growers Association •
Healy Brothers Ranch   15

CHAPTER III (1884-1886): Roundup • Law and Order   30

CHAPTER IV (1886-1890): Election • Cimarron
Territory • Sheriff Herron   46

CHAPTER V (1886-1888): Cattle Business in the Strip •
Daily Life in the Strip • Herron's Marriage •
Rodeo • Blizzard of '88   65

CHAPTER VI (1888-1890): Outlaws and Lawmen
in the Strip   101

CHAPTER VII (1890-1893): Herron as Cattleman • Alice
Herron's Death • Herron Charged with Cattle
Theft   116

CHAPTER VIII (1893-1894): The Trial • Escape   130

PART II

CHAPTER IX (1893-1894): The Owl Hoot Trail •
Payson, Arizona   145

CHAPTER X (1894): Return to No Man's Land •
Departure with May Goddard • Marriage in
Luna, New Mexico   164

CHAPTER XI (1894-1899): Payson, Arizona • Pearce,
Arizona • La Morita and Naco, Mexico • Herron
Charged with Horse Smuggling   180

CHAPTER XII (1899): "The Naco War"   215

CHAPTER XIII (1899): The Troubles and the Trial •
Naco, Arizona   227

CHAPTER XIV (1897-1901): Entertainment Along the
Border • Outlaw Gangs in Southern Arizona   243

CHAPTER XV (1900-1913): Return to No Man's Land •
Tombstone, Arizona • May Herron's Death •
Herron's Third Marriage • Courtland, Arizona •
Herron Charged with Cattle Theft •
The Trial and Sentence   258

CHAPTER XVI (1913-1915): Mexican Cattle Buying
and the Revolution   267

CHAPTER XVII (1915-1949): Return to No Man's Land •
Herron's Final Attempts to Clear His Name   286

APPENDIX: Story of the Original Manuscript   301
NOTES   305
BIBLIOGRAPHY AND SOURCES   335
PHOTO CREDITS   342
INDEX   345

illustrations

PART I

Map   front endpapers

Jim Herron, Al Dixon, F. M. (Jack) Rhodes, and
    John (Irish) McGovern, cowboys, 1891   73

Irish McGovern and Jack Rhodes   73

Longhorns   74

Young boy picking out his horse from *remuda*   74

Chuckwagons and roundup men at noon meal   75

JJ outfit on Cimarron roundup   75

Cowboys of George Littlefield's LIT Ranch   76

Remuda of JJ outfit on roundup   76

Hardesty Brothers Quartercircle S outfit   77

1887 roundup   77

"Sandhill" Johnson, bonehauler   78

Mills and Garvey Saloon, Beaver City, about 1887   78

"Red Alex" Foltz and Sam McLane, Cimarron cowboys, 1887   79

Beaver City, No Man's Land   79

Beaver City residents, about 1887   80

Beaver City main street, about 1890   80

The Territorial Advocate newspaper, Beaver, Oklahoma
    Territory, 1891   81

Fred Taintor's ranchhouse 82

Beer City, No Man's Land, 1888 82

"Big soddy" at Secoro Ranch 83

Shade's Well, No Man's Land 83

Issuing cattle on Rosebud Reservation, South Dakota 84

Beaver, Oklahoma, about 1907 84

The Beaver Advocate newspaper, 1893 85

Jim Herron and daughter, Ollie Dot, about 1893 86

Jim Herron's homestead claim validation and document
    of his sale of the land to John Over, 1893 87

School group, Beaver, 1894 88

Jim Herron and Jack Rhodes, 1893 88

PART II

Map rear endpapers

Jim Herron and his second wife, May Goddard, 1894 193

La Morita-Nacozari Stage and La Morita, Sonora, Mexico
    Customs House, 1900 194

Customs buildings, Naco, Sonora, Mexico, about 1923 194

Greene Consolidated Copper Company Office, Naco,
    Arizona, about 1900 195

William Greene's house, Hereford, Arizona, 1920 195

Jim Herron's Cow Ranch Saloon, Naco, Arizona, about 1903 196

Jim Herron and Charley Sanders with pack outfit 196

Colonel Emilio Kosterlitzky, about 1899 197

Arizona Rangers and Colonel Kosterlitzky 198

Colonel Kosterlitzky, his *cordada*, and Colonel Fenokio 198

William (Black Jack) Christian, outlaw 199

Burt Alvord, outlaw/lawman 199

Billy Stiles, outlaw/lawman 199

Modoc Stage and Hotel Nobles, Tombstone, Arizona 200

Jim Herron and his daughter, Rita, at his Hotel La Rita,
about 1906 200

Hotel La Rita, Tombstone, Arizona, about 1905 201

Grave marker for Jim Herron's second wife, May 202

Jim Herron, his son, "Sam," and friends, about 1906 202

Captain Francisco (Pancho) Villa, 1910 203

Pancho Villa and soldiers 203

Mexican rebel army train 204

Mexican soldiers 204

General Jose Inez Salazar and colleagues 205

Mexican "Red Flaggers" 205

Jim Herron's son and daughter, Thomas D. (Sam) and Rita 206

Jim Herron's daughter, Millie 206

The Jim Herron-May Goddard family, about 1930 206

Jim Herron, 1940 207

Jim Herron and other pioneers of No Man's Land, 1946 207

Jim Herron's grave marker 208

introduction

by Edward Everett Dale

This book is the story of a man's life. It is a remarkable story because its author, Jim Herron, was a remarkable man. This was not due to the fact that after serving for some years as Sheriff and Deputy United States Marshal he was convicted of crime and for the rest of his life was a "wanted man" with a reward offered for his arrest and imprisonment.

This alone would not be unusual on the American frontier, because from the close of the Civil War to the end of the century, and some years after, there were a number of men who had served as peace officers but ended life as outlaws and not a few who in their younger days had lived outside the law but eventually repented of their earlier sins, became good citizens, and were elected or appointed to the office of Sheriff or Marshal.

Conspicuous examples are Bob and Gratton Dalton who were both Deputy United States Marshals, and Joe Beckham who served two terms as Sheriff of Motley County, Texas. Defeated for a third term after a bitter contest, he met his opponent, G. W. Cook, on the railway platform at Seymour, Texas, and killed him. His career of crime was short, for he was killed by Texas Rangers within a year after becoming an outlaw. Also, Frank Canton, born Joe Horner, became a wanted man in Texas while quite young but eventually received pardon for past offenses, served two terms as Sheriff of Johnson County, Wyoming, was United States Deputy Marshal in Oklahoma, Wyoming, and Alaska, and eventually became Adjutant General of the National Guard of Oklahoma. While these are given as examples, there were scores of men on the American frontier who had lived for years on both sides of the law. None, to my knowledge, had a more colorful and adventurous life than the author of this book.

Jim Herron was born in what is now Ellis County, Texas, in 1866. His mother had died when he was only two years old so he did not know the exact date of his birth but when he grew older he placed it at December 25, so he could celebrate his birthday and Christmas on the same day.

It seems possible that Jim's future life was affected by the fact that he had never known a mother's love and care. There were comparatively few women in that great pastoral empire called the "Cow Country" and any good woman was regarded with respect closely akin to reverence. Many a cowhand, noted among his fellow range riders for his gay conversation and clever jokes, reverted to what seemed a stuttering, stammering moron in the presence of a girl that he had just met.

Certainly Jim Herron, like many other motherless boys, seems to have grown up starved for affection, yet so shy as to admit that he would never have had the courage to woo and win his first wife, Alice Groves, had not her parents helped him by giving him and Alice opportunities to be together a great deal. This was not difficult as her parents operated the hotel at the little town of Benton, not far west of the hundredth meridian which was the western boundary of the Cherokee Outlet and the eastern boundary of the Neutral Strip, known at that time as "No Man's Land."

No matter how shy Jim Herron was with women, however, he was anything but shy with men or in his business ventures. Evidently he was a born ranchman for his father had been a cowman in the future Ellis County when Texas was a part of Mexico. Like most Texas boys of his time, Jim yearned to be a real cowboy and ranchman.

Moreover, he started very early to achieve that ambition for he was only thirteen when his father sent him with two of his older cousins to drive a large herd of cattle from the Ellis County area west to what is now Coleman County. This was doubtless because pasturage in the Ellis County range had become short from over grazing. This new range was near the western trail to Dodge City, Kansas, which had become a great shipping point for Texas cattle to Kansas City, although some Texas ranchmen continued the drive to Ogallala, Nebraska; or if the herd was largely made of yearling and two-year-old steers, the drive might be continued to Dakota or Montana.

Seeing these herds of 2,500 or 3,000 head pass by so fired the heart of the adventurous young Jim Herron that after a year of helping his older cousins with the prosaic task of looking after his father's cattle he resolved to seek a job with some short-handed outfit going up the trail.

He did not have to wait long. In the early spring of 1880 a herd of 3,000 yearlings and two-year-olds came past at noon near the Herron's cabin. Jim rode out to the wagon where most of the men were eating and asked the foreman if he could use another good man. When the foreman, whose name was Quinlan, inquired as to where this "good man" was, Jim patted himself on the breast and replied, "Right here, sir. If I don't prove myself a good man you can fire me any day."

Quinlan pointed out the hardships and difficulties of driving cattle on the trail but was so short of men that he at last agreed to add Jim to the crew and soon found that the lad was an excellent hand.

Quinlan, as was customary for a foreman, rode ahead of the herd to study the trail, test the river crossings, and note if the next herd on the trail was far enough ahead of his own as to avoid any danger of a "mix up". While still in Texas, Quinlan was drowned in the Wichita River and Jim helped dig a grave and bury the body beside the trail.

On this long drive from what is now Coleman County, Texas, to Ogallala, Nebraska, young Jim Herron won his spurs as a top cowhand for he seems to have met with about all the experiences and trials that any man driving cattle on the trail at that time could have.

After this drive north, Jim hired on as a cowhand with a British-owned ranch, "The YL," a big, new outfit at the west end of the Cherokee Strip.

One of Herron's ranch assignments was to cut the trail herds that moved north through the range of the Dodge City cattlemen. In cutting back local stock, Jim began to realize the value in gaining possession of and personally branding the lame cattle, the sick ones, and the mavericks. This he did, and fell afoul of the regulations set up by the cattlemen's association. Herron's act was to bring about later retaliation by the association: a charge, a trial, and a conviction which caused him to flee to Arizona.

There and in Mexico he spent the remaining years of his life, making several journeys back to the Oklahoma haunts of his youth in futile attempts to persuade the court to set aside the charges against him.

In Arizona and Mexico Herron found a new life and became a successful hotel owner and a noted international cattleman. Though he was never able to officially clear his name, he never lost his old friends or failed to make new ones wherever he went.

It would not be fair to reveal more to the reader, yet it is proper to state that while the story of Jim Herron's life is packed with action and thrilling adventures, this book is far more than that. It gives to the reader a more authentic understanding of ranch life and the *social history* of the American frontier than he is likely ever to get from fiction or so-called "Westerns."

preface

As one of that pioneering band who helped formulate our image of The Cowboy, The Lawman, and The Outlaw, Jim Herron's unique story deserves attention, for he and his kind did much to establish Western mores. His personal observations of that brawling and brash civilization that was being molded simultaneously across the west from Oklahoma Territory to the Territory of Arizona should make its own contribution to our history of the great Southwest.

This old cowman spent fifty-six of his eighty-three years riding "The Owl Hoot Trail." Yet he married four times, raised good and law-abiding families, and entered into his community's social and economic life wherever he lived. Through it all he kept what was called "a good name." But his life story details the furtive existence a person lives who is wanted by the Law. In many ways it provides a true insight into the problems of the Wanted Man, the man who may prefer to go straight and return to polite society but who is never able to make that difficult transition from the Crooked Trail back to the Straight and Narrow Path. Such men generally refuse to accept the punishment society exacts in return for their eventual freedom.

Jim Herron's greatest mistake, second only to his original break with the Law, was the curious hope he held to the bitter end that he might trade the transient freedom he won for a more enduring one, a permanent freedom, guaranteed by the very Law against which he had transgressed. This was, of course, a swap that no court could make with him, even a friendly court, for he had been convicted and had evaded his sentence by flight. Yet his plight points up society's real problem in dealing with criminals: should we try *rehabilitation* of the individuals who have fallen afoul of the law, or is apprehension and *punishment*—or endless pursuit—the better method?

Herron would have agreed with Captain Thomas H. Rynning of the Arizona Rangers, and later Superintendent of the Arizona State Prison. Rynning was largely responsible for the creation of the new prison at Florence, Arizona, and the abandonment of the vile old Territorial Prison at Yuma. Rynning once wrote:

> If all prisoners could work their way out of prison, their days of hopelessness would be over, for the hopeless prisoner is always the one who leads the bad outbreaks.

Jim Herron was never allowed to "work his way out" of the position in which he had placed himself that fall day in '93 when he made his quick bid for freedom from the Kansas Sheriff. So Jim found the outlaw trail easier to take than to leave.

In his story it is interesting to observe that affinity which existed between the Lawless element of our society and the Lawmen of that time. To some extent it survives to this day. Many officers like Billy Stiles, Burt Alvord, Henry Brown—and Jim Herron—stepped back and forth across that invisible line which defines the Lawful from the Lawless, yet they were not significantly changed by the experience. It was as though a higher law had ordained that those men who made good Officers made good Outlaws, and *vice versa*.

The significance of this, if there is any, appears to be that the constant association with each other, and attention to their common problems, made for a better understanding between them. Yet the general public seems never to share with either group that sympathetic bond that exists between them. Frontier lawmen and lawbreakers, much alike in background and breeding, became most tolerant and understanding of each other, and this rapport seems to live on today among some of their successors.

This is probably why Jim Herron was so indulgent of lawbreakers. He was, like them, an archetype of frontier tolerance. In his attitude toward Law and Order we find a man almost unconscious of the wickedness and sin all about him, a being much as Adam must have been before The Fall. Though Jim Herron despised the hypocritical Mexican officials who attempted "legally" to steal his horses, he seems to otherwise regard theft, fornication, murder, drinking, and gambling as matters of personal taste. Certainly there was nothing of the Puritan in him, for at times he could indulge himself without remorse in a bit of brand-changing or cow larceny, if it were to his own advantage!

But we must not judge the Jim Herrons too harshly, nor be overly critical of their contemporary society. For there is a little of this amorality in each of us who was foaled in the West, and who brags of his Pioneer ancestry. Perhaps life was a bit too hard for our people on the Old Frontier—and pleasures too far between. If a little larceny of the moment relieved the stress of economic pressure on one's family, then could it be such a gross crime to purloin the property of a more fortunate member of one's community?

In this frontier society in which Jim Herron grew to young manhood he fit well, and even made a niche for himself. Old cowmen who had known him in his youth told of his warm, friendly, fun-loving personality, and of his ambitions and his loyalties. That one or two of his acquaintances betrayed him is hardly worth noting, for most of the men who knew him well spoke of him as *Mi Amigo*.

While rewriting this book from his manuscript notes, I have found it necessary in maintaining continuity to include many additional incidents provided me by family members and old friends. In some places I have found it helpful to the reader to interpolate, for in a few of the rich historical areas of his story he seemed to lack the curiosity we have today for historical detail. Jim Herron's role in life was not that of passive scribe. He was a man of action and decision, and it is to his credit that he thought to dictate the notes to a teenage granddaughter and to others when he was stone blind and a man in his twilight years.[1] But since he failed at times to set down his thoughts, as they must have related to his actions, some interpretation has been needed to give historical breadth and depth to his outlines. So it has been the writer's purpose only to clarify the materials as they came along, to depict the Pioneer era as it was during Jim Herron's life span. While I have tried hard to bring out the thoughts that may have impelled many of Herron's actions, my principal effort has been toward leaving just as much of the real Jim Herron in his story as is possible to do.

In but one place in his manuscript has Mr. Herron been less than candid with his readers. That is the portion which deals with his market operations in Pearce and Courtland, Arizona. The material did not appear in his manuscript notes, and it is not difficult to understand why he glossed over that unhappy time. A grandfather, stone blind and dictating his life story to a granddaughter of high school age, is more apt to consider the sparing of his granddaughter's feelings more important in choosing to conceal a part of his life which he knows is a matter of legal record. So that section of his story has been supplied by the undersigned as, I believe, Jim Herron would want it, not to pander to sensational tastes, nor to excuse his actions, but rather to provide a logical explanation for what happened to him.

In checking and verifying facts in his notes, one cannot help but be impressed with the few discrepancies found among them. Where oral tradition has been the chief preserving medium, and where, because of his blindness, the dictated material could not be easily checked by himself, it is amazing how well the facts substantiate this old cowman's memory. There are the usual misspellings of names and places, and a few incorrect dates, some of which may have eluded the undersigned as well. There have been times when his chronology broke down and where he would indulge in a flashback technique to rectify it, much as a mother does when relating a story to her children. The chronology has been straightened up as well as it is possible to do in the rewriting of this autobiography.

For the greater part, Jim Herron's story is the honest recounting of events in a life that was lived out in a time that has gone and can never be again—that historical era when the lands of the great Southwest were being discovered and settled, and when their rich cover of grasses and depths of minerals were being exploited for the first time. His story is rich in both romance and adventure, and contains a great store of intimate detail that I believe the reader will find entertaining and most interesting.

Harry E. Chrisman
10245 West 14th Avenue
Denver, Colorado

acknowledgments

It is impossible in this limited space to acknowledge the help of everyone who contributed to a better understanding of the principal character of this book, Jim Herron. But to all who provided bits and pieces of information that have served to clarify and add interest to his personal story, I extend my thanks.

The complications resulting from Herron's four marriages, three of which were with issue, can be readily understood by most readers. Happily, the members of the Herron families have been most considerate, and have provided their detailed knowledge of his family life to add greater depth and interest to his adventurous life.

Jim Herron's first wife, Alice (Groves) Herron, was the mother of their one daughter, Ollie Dot. This daughter married Carleton H. Stratton, an Oklahoma banker. Their son, J. L. Stratton, Stillwater, Oklahoma, is to be thanked for his contribution of information concerning his mother's life with the Ansel Groves and the Dyke Ballinger families who raised Ollie Dot, after her father fled to Arizona. Judge Ballinger and his wife were uncle and aunt to Ollie Dot, since Mrs. Della (Groves) Ballinger was a sister of Alice (Groves) Herron.

A third Groves daughter, Bertha, married Robert H. Loofbourrow, later a Justice of the Oklahoma Supreme Court. Judge Loofbourrow remained until death a valued friend and counselor to Jim Herron. To the three sons of Judge Loofbourrow—Hale J. Loofbourrow, Merced, California; and Robert H. and Wade H. Loofbourrow, both of Boise City, Oklahoma—the undersigned is indebted for much information of a legal nature concerning Jim Herron's troubles in Kansas.

Jim Herron's second marriage to Anna May Goddard produced three children: Thomas D., or "Sam"; Mrs. Rita McGrew, now of Superior, Arizona, the sole survivor of this family; and Jim, jr. The help of Mrs. McGrew and her daughters, Mrs. Jean Jeffrey, Post Falls, Idaho and Mrs. Edith Killion, Georgetown, California, all of whom read and helped correct the manuscript, is deeply appreciated.

Herron's third marriage, to Mary Valencia, produced one daughter, Mrs. Millie Borba, now of Newman, California. Mrs. Borba deserves great credit for her helpfulness in producing the manuscript notes dictated by her father, and from which this book is written. While living with Mrs. Borba at her home in California, Jim Herron, then eighty-three years of age, died and was interred at Newman in the Hills Ferry Cemetery.

In the course of rewriting Herron's story, the writer and his wife made a trip to Arizona. There, under the Mogollon Rim near Payson, and down in the Cochise country at the towns of Pearce, Courtland, Tombstone, Naco, and over in Sonora, Mexico at the old town of La Morita which once pulsed with the social and economic life of the border country, we visited the many places known to Jim Herron. There we interviewed many people, as we had previously done in old No Man's Land, and we found many who knew and talked of the exploits and adventures of Jim Herron.

At Luna, New Mexico, where Jim Herron and May Goddard were married, we interviewed Bert Laney and his wife. Mr. Laney, then eighty-three, told us much about John and Toles Cosper, the latter the Justice of the Peace who had married the young couple when they were en route to Arizona.

Near Pearce, Arizona, Harvey Cartmell, a resident of that area for nearly sixty years, gave us his candid estimate of Jim Herron, whom he had known there many years ago. In Pearce, Mrs. Gladys (Huddy) McLeod, postmistress there for many years, provided much information on the Herron families. At Bisbee, we were permitted to study the old files of the *Bisbee Daily Review* in which Herron's exploits were recounted.

At Naco, Arizona, we met and had a rewarding visit with Fred Valenzuela, Director of the Port of Entry, and who has been with U.S. Customs for many years. Himself a writer of history, Fred revealed much of the border lore of that section, and introduced us to Charles Sanders, then ninety-four, an old and close friend of Jim Herron. Mr. Sanders, though burdened by the infirmities of his years, had a clear and retentive mind and revealed to us much of the material concerning Herron's mis-adventures along the border.

Prior to their deaths, several old friends of Jim Herron who lived in Kansas and Oklahoma had told the writer much about Herron's early life. To these men—Bernard Lemert, Burris Wright, and Lee Larrabee, all of Liberal, Kansas—Herron was well-known as a cowman and Sheriff in No Man's Land.

Special thanks are extended to many with whom I corresponded; their names will be found in the "Letters" section of the Bibliography and Sources.

The aid of historical societies is always necessary to an honest treatment of such biographical efforts as this one, and I gratefully acknowledge the assistance given me by the State Historical Societies of Kansas, Oklahoma, and Colorado, and the help from the friendly staffs of the Arizona Pioneers Historical Society and Museum at Tucson, and the Western Division of the Public Library at Denver. To those who provided illustrative material, my thanks.

Dr. Edward E. Dale, eminent historian and author, of the Department of History, University of Oklahoma, deserves special thanks for taking time from a busy life to read and evaluate the completed manuscript for me, a task that was undoubtedly a great burden to him, but a tremendous help to me.

Warm appreciation is extended to Durrett Wagner, of the Swallow Press, who has labored diligently upon the manuscript and who has been most helpful to me in many ways in bringing forth Jim Herron's interesting life story.

To my wife, Catherine, go my deepest thanks for her assistance in organizing the material, and for her constant help and advice and her patience.

H.E.C.

FIFTY YEARS ON
THE OWL HOOT TRAIL

part I

There has been stealing since the world began, and it will probably go on to the end. On the range it was easy, somewhat pleasant work, to appropriate your neighbor's goods or chattels. In the old Texas days, when might was right and the big owners covered their vast tracts of land, sweeping up everything before them, their cowboys had a bad example. Their morals were corrupted, and many of the men, coming up on the trail with the idea that a horse or a cow was a sort of public property, soon commenced to put their ideas into action.

John Clay
My Life on the Range

chapter I

1880

GOING UP THE TEXAS TRAIL

Before 1880, the Southwest frontier I knew was populated only by Indians, vast herds of buffalo, large bands of antelope, wild deer, much small game, and prairie fowl. After 1880 most of the Plains Indians had been settled on Government Reservations, although there were still bands of young braves of tribal mixtures rambling around and causing depredations. The buffalo were almost gone, shot off by the hide men, and the once heavily-grazed Great Plains region was beginning to produce the thickest carpet of short grass the West had ever seen, for the end of the massive buffalo herds gave several years of almost complete rest to the land. The grasses were mostly tight, woolly buffalo grass, the sedge grass, and bunch grasses, the gramas and bluestems, and now their root systems deepened and doubled. This vast buffalo range across the sweeping plains of the Texas Panhandle, old No Man's Land to the north, and the Cherokee Strip to the east, was now wide open for cattle grazing. And it didn't take them Texas men long to jump in.

After the successful, initial years of free-range grazing, the profits seemed big enough to lure capital investments from far across the seas. Along with the Texas men now came the Scotch and English investors, organized into Ranche companies to cash in on this free range, and paying no taxes for the privilege. Them big cattle companies needed ranch foremen and cowboys to care for their herds, men who understood the business. So that's where I came into the picture.

I was born in 1866 in central Texas, south of Dallas, in what is now known as Ellis County.[1] I never knew what day or what

3

month I was born, so I took the Lord's Day as my birthday, December 25. My mother had died when I was two years old. My father was among the pioneer cowmen when Texas was still a part of Old Mexico, and he and others like him helped to make Texas one of the truly great states of our nation. His people had been O'Herrons, but dropped the O after reaching America.

In 1879 papa moved some of his cattle from Ellis County to the Santa Anna mountain range in Coleman County, some distance west of our old ranch. This new area was at that time still frontier country. Papa left me on the new range with some cousins to help take care of our cattle. Then he went back home. I was then somewhere past thirteen years of age. Our work was typical cow work. We gathered cattle in the roundups, doctored them for screw worms, grass bloat, itch, heel flies. We branded and castrated the bull calves and spayed some of the very poorest heifers. We treated our saddlehorses for fistulas and setfasts, caused by the poor saddles and hard riding through thorny brush. We cooked in the open much of the time, slept on the ground, and lived like all the Texas cowboys lived. It was not an easy life, for we rode in all sorts of weather, winter and summer.

I had always wanted to be a real cowboy, for that was the dream of every Texas boy of my time from the hour we snagged our first hen or rooster with a twine loop, imitating our fathers. But just staying there on the ranch, working with cattle like we had to do, didn't seem to be very romantic or adventurous to me. The new Texas Cattle Trail, or "Western Trail," as they were beginning to call it, for it was some distance west from the older Chisholm Trail, passed through Santa Anna Gap, west of Brownwood and close to the range where we held father's cattle. Many big herds passed that way daily in the summer months. They were all Longhorn cattle, all colors, all sizes.

The young men we saw with these herds looked more like the real cowboys than we saw in our daily work, and naturally we all wanted to "go up the trail." Well, I did. And I never regretted it.

Toward the spring of 1880, when the first big herds of 2,500 and 3,000 head began passing by, I couldn't stand it any longer. Talking with the cowboys at the chuckwagons and hearing such names as Yellerstone, Piney Ridge, Ogallalie, and Powder River set my heels to itching in my boots. I had never heard of these faraway places before, and I knew that I must see some of them.

One day a herd of 3,000 yearlings and two-year old steers came swinging into sight where I was camped that night with another boy. They made their bedground nearby, and we rode over for a visit with the men. I learned that this herd was heading for the Black Hills in Dakota. The outfit was owned by a Major Garth of St. Joseph, Missouri. The men all looked clean and good to me and I asked what the boss' name was. They told me "Quinlan," and I rode out to where he was setting his horse with two of his men.

When I rode up I asked, "You need a good man?"

The boss stood up high in his stirrups and shaded his eyes with one hand, all the while looking across the prairie, like he was studying the country for miles around, and looking right through me. He was a tall, lanky galoot who carried a big wad of tobacco in his cheek that made him look lop-sided. After gazing for a while he turned to me.

"Wheah is this man?" he asked. "I sho don't see him." The two men with him howled with laughter.

I stuck my thumb into my chest. "Right here in this saddle," I answered him, sitting as tall as I could manage.

Quinlan now laughed, and I saw his blue eyes twinkle and a lot of laugh-wrinkles formed at the corners of his eyes. He slapped his chaps with his quirt, all the while looking down at me, a freckled fourteen-year old kid.

"Well, son," he said in a kindly way, "I guess you'll do to ride the rivers with—'specially since I'm so god-damned shawt-handed."

Quinlan talked with me for a spell, and he sounded like papa, for he warned me against following the cattle trails and leaving home. It was hard work, he told me, just hard work and nothing else. Even growed men nearly died for lack of sleep, he said. He asked if I could ride well.

"I can do anything on a hoss that your men can do," I told him. The men again chuckled at my confidence, or brave front.

5

"Some Injun may lift youh haih, boy," one of them remarked. It was true that we would pass through Indian Territory, and the thought of Indians made the fuzz on the back of my neck stand up, but I put up a brave front. "I'm bound to be a cowboy," I said, "even if I have to be a bald-headed one without a scalp." This time Quinlan joined in the laughter.

"Wa'al, if yo' don't mind losin' them curly locks son, then come along," he said. I rode back to our camp, picked up my gear, told my friend to report me gone to Dakota with a trail herd, and joined Quinlan's outfit.

I was assigned eight horses from the *remuda*, just like the other men had, for we changed two and three times each day. I was the proudest boy in Texas, and I swore to myself that I would make a good hand, make Quinlan and the boys proud of me, come hell or high water.

We headed north the next morning, me riding the drag, that is at the rear of the herd, bringing up "the leppies, the lamies, and the lazies," as we called the young cattle, the cripples and foot-sore, and the tired ones. This was the worst job with a trail herd because of the thick dust and the amount of riding and shouting that had to be done to keep the slowest cattle moving, but I welcomed it.

Everything went well until we reached the Wichita River, north of where Seymour, Texas is today. That morning Quinlan rode on ahead, as was his practice. Sometimes he would stay to visit with neighbors on the trail, so we didn't think much of his failure to return until we saw his horse coming back later when the herd had almost reached the river. Quinlan's black gelding was dripping wet and lame. Pearl, the straw boss, called the herd off the trail and told us to water them in small bunches until he found Quinlan. Pearl came back later, without the boss. He had us throw the herd back from the trail to a grassy area along a dry creek. Then he and all the men but two guards went searching for the boss. I stayed with the herd.

We were at the river crossing for two days while they searched for Quinlan. The river had been high when we reached it, but was now subsiding. Then they found Quinlan's body. It was washed up on a sandbar three miles down the stream. But we never learned how or why he drowned.

We dug a grave on a little knoll a hundred yards south from the river, and there we buried our boss. They say cowboys are a hard lot, but I tell you I saw tears in most of them boys' eyes when Quinlan's body was lowered with their lariat ropes into that narrow grave there on the prairie. I never had time to know Quinlan well, though he was always friendly and pleasant to me, but from what them men who knew him said, he was a stouthearted and good man. The lesson I learned from his sad fate was that even a growed man could lose his life on the trail, and I thought about his death many a night as I set my horse doing night guard under the stars.

Pearl took charge of the outfit now, and we headed on north. We reached Red River at Doan's Store, a general merchandise and supply outfit that set on the south bank not far from the crossing. The river here was wide but not so deep, and the cattle herds had packed the sand so it was a safe crossing. In crossing all rivers it is difficult to get cattle to take to the water. It was no trouble for them Longhorns to swim the widest rivers, but it was hard to start them. They mostly wanted to drink, then get out, fall back and graze, or just stand and beller. But Quinlan had showed them boys how to drive the horse herd in first, and we had about seventy-five head in the *remuda*, then crowd in some of the lead cattle behind the horses. So rivers never stopped us, just slowed us down at times.

Not long after we crossed into Indian Territory we ran into our first Indians. They were Comanches or Kiowas, about a dozen of them. It was then I wished I had stayed home. I was on the drag, as usual, that day. My partner was fifty yards or so to the west of me, and in a tower of dust so thick I could hardly see him. I had rode off the trail a piece to bring back a bunch-quitting two-year-old steer. Suddenly, over a little bald knob to the east, came them Indians, all mounted on fast little speckled ponies and yipping like coyotes. They were almost on to me before I knew what had happened, and I heard one of them yell, "Take papoose home!"

7

That was enough for me and I turned Old Thunder, the big lumberwagon gelding I was riding, back toward the herd, kicking him up to as fast a gait as he could travel. But those young braves were beside me in a second and I felt one of their *lazos*, a regular lariat rope like we used, start to settle over my head. I threw off the loop before it tightened, but I didn't yell for help for I couldn't think fast enough, just spurred Old Thunder toward the nearest man I could see alongside the herd, Wes Standifer, who was riding right flank at the time.

Wes saw us all coming in a bunch, me not ten feet ahead of the braves. Out came his six-shooter. He fired twice. That was enough. The Indians turned tail and headed back to the bald knob. We didn't see them again until late afternoon when they popped up on a high hill to watch us, then disappeared for good. Wes teased me that night before all the men about my breakneck escape. He told everyone that the braves were young fellows and just having fun with me, laughing and cheering as they chased me swinging their ropes. He shot high in the air, he said, for he knew they were only having fun with me and he didn't want to have trouble with them while passing through their lands.

"What they really wanted was Delgadito," Wes laughed. Delgadito was the thin two-year-old I'd been chasing back to the herd. They called him that for the word means "thin" in Spanish, and the little steer was half sick and scouring. I told Wes that the next time Delgadito strayed a quarter-mile from the herd, the Injuns could have him. But that never happened, for Pearl, who cared little what the men ate, had the steer killed a day or two later and we had him for Sunday breakfast, dinner, and supper and for a day or two more. That sure agreed with me, for I had been running down a good horse every day getting that little *ladino* back into the herd.

Farther north of Red River a bunch of Indians rode right up to the lead cattle in the herd, turned them off the trail and held up ten fingers to Pearl, asking for "a-oh-a-wo-haw," or ten head of those best steers. These Indians were all Kiowas. Pearl argued with them for a spell, then ordered the point men to get the steers back on the trail. As the herd passed, Pearl stayed and talked with the braves. When we came up alongside I could hear Pearl protesting.

"No, no! Too many *wo-ha*. I give you two, no more!"

The Indians acted in a threatening manner, two of them rode right into the herd like they might cut out what they wanted. I could see Pearl was nervous, for there must have been thirty of them beggars collected around him now.

"Squaws and papooses hungry," a one-eyed brave said to Pearl, gesticulating with both hands.

"Git goin'," Pearl said. "Three *wo-has*, no more!"

I helped Pearl cut three lamies from the herd. The redskins left with them. But before dark that night they were back with demands for "more wo-ha," for they had seen that Pearl was an easy mark, in spite of his protests. And do you know, those Indians and others came back almost daily until we got within forty miles of Camp Supply, on the North Canadian River, or "Beaver Creek," as they call it upstream from the fort. If I remember right, Pearl gave them Indians nearly seventy-five head of steers! That made Wes and Pablo, a Mexican *vaquero* who rode left swing, right mad.

"I'd feed them sons-of-bitches some lead to eat if it was left to me," Wes said. I was inclined to agree with Wes and Pablo, for it was sure a high price to pay just to cross that strip of Indian Territory.

When we came to the Antelope Hills country, south from Camp Supply, we found different tribes of Indians. These were Cheyennes and Arapahoes, but just as hungry as the Kiowas and Comanches we had left behind, eating our seventy-five steers. These new Indians begged for *wo-ha* and more *wo-ha*, but Wes talked Pearl into standing pat this time and offering them a diet of lead if they got too rambunctious. So they quit annoying us.

The U.S. Government had a troop of colored cavalrymen at Camp Supply. Their job was to protect the people in that area and to keep the Indians on the Reservations. They were also supposed to stop the whites from selling firewater to the Indians. I don't know how much territory was covered by them Buffalo Soldiers, as they were called by the Indians because they wore

9

big, warm, buffalo-coats in winter, but the Indians seemed to know when to stop pestering the trail herds, at least twenty to thirty miles from Camp Supply.

This old Camp of Supply (they called it Fort Supply later when I was there) was built to support the soldiers in the Winter Campaign of 1868, when Custer wiped out Black Kettle's village. It was maintained for many years after that. A firm named Lee & Reynolds had a general store there under a concession from the Government. A stage line ran to Fort Dodge, up the old Military Trail, and big freight wagons plied back and forth carrying supplies into north Texas and bringing back buffalo hides. Lee & Reynolds also had a saloon there at the fort. One of the clerks had been a Union soldier during the War Between the States and he gave me a big-ear run-down on those times. His name was Sheridan, he said, and he was a brother of Gen. Phil Sheridan.[2]

After a day or two rubbering around the fort, we moved north again across the Cimarron River and into the big hill country between there and Dodge City. The cattle were moving along good, for we had given to the Indians or shot and eaten all the troublemakers in the herd, so within a week we were at Dodge, about a hundred miles north from Camp Supply.

We camped up the river from the town about five miles, as there were many herds already laying up there near the crossing and the grass was grazed down short. When we crossed the Arkansas, Pearl took a tally on the herd. His count was 2,965 head. Since we had given the Indians at least seventy-five head and butchered some on the trail, Pearl figured we should be short about eighty head. Actually, we counted short only forty-four head, which meant we had picked up some strays on the trail. I recall my partner turning in two head on the drag and I picked up three head near Red River, so the point and swing men must have got the rest.

At Dodge we stopped a few days to rest the herd and Pearl sent the wagon in for supplies. This gave all the men a few days to "see the elephant," as they called it, and I was one of them. I had always wondered what that expression meant, and when I saw the big elephant painted on the front of Ham Bell's stable and wagon yard I supposed it meant Dodge City. Nobody told me any different at that time, but later I learned the hard way what it really meant. There was a saying in them old days that a man "had seen the elephant and heard the owl holler." It meant that he had been around a lot and slept out, maybe hid out when he got tangled up with the Law a bit. If he was wanted real bad by the Law, we'd say he was "ridin' the Owl Hoot Trail."

I went into Dodge with Wes. He was an older man and had a father's instinct about me. There was all sorts of ways to spend your money there at Dodge and the town was full of wild women. Wes wouldn't let them women fool around with me very long at a time, though he didn't care how much tiger milk I lapped up at the saloons. But he said them women would give a boy something to remember them by that he wouldn't care much about recalling after a week or two in the saddle.

When we were rubbering around Dodge we talked with a boy who had ridden out with the Dodge posse to fight Dull Knife's Indians when they raided through that country two years before. We had come up the same trail Dull Knife and his Indians had followed and had seen some of the burned out ranch houses where they had stolen horses and killed some men, so Wes and I were interested in the fellow's talk. He said the posse men hoped they never saw an Indian, and I guess they didn't for the old Indian reached Nebraska in spite of the army and all the Dodge volunteers. Them Indians just wanted to go home was all. It just went to show that no Government should move people away from their homes, whether Indians or whites. For when they expected them Cheyennes to stay peacefully in Oklahoma and forget the Black Hills they were mighty disappointed.

In a few days we headed for Ogallalie, Nebraska. I had now been on the trail for over forty days, done a man's work and never asked a favor. It was mighty hard work for a boy of fourteen, but I knew another boy, Tom Judy, who came up the trail at the age of twelve! There had been only nine of us to handle this big herd after Quinlan's death. Each of us stood guard a quarter of the night and rode all day. During a few storms we rode all night too. But we only had two bad runs with the cattle, and soon milled

11

them and got them back on the bedground. But them stampedes were something frightful to see, and any man's knees will rattle when the big Longhorns start to run. There was nothing to do then but run with them, stay ahead of them if you could, and turn them into a tight mill when you got the chance, circle them until they was wound up as tight as an eight-day clock on Sunday. It took your best night horse to stay with them. Once we rode alongside the leaders for five miles, then gathered cattle over that five-mile stretch all the next day.

North from Dodge all went quiet and nice. Rance Whitcomb, another boy some older than me, decided to quit the herd when we reached Ogallalie. I decided to go with him. We each owned a fat horse and once we had seen Dodge we decided to go back and take a longer look. Wes tried to talk sense into my head, but I wouldn't listen to him. Before backtracking, we decided to look at Ogallalie, for it too was a wide-open cowtown.

When Pearl paid us off we left the herd and rode into the little town alongside the Union Pacific tracks. It was just a collection of board shacks along a dusty street, but to us boys it had all the glamor of Paris. We tied our horses to a hitch rack in front of a saloon and Rance went into a boot shop to get a boot sewed up. This place was the Crystal Palace, and while I waited on Rance I went rubbering into this saloon. I didn't go far inside, for the bartenders didn't approve of a kid coming into a place unless a father or older brother or friend was along with him. While I was standing around I saw a man, not a cowman, who was making various plays with his short-barreled revolver. This fellow was making a spectacle of himself, twisting his gun around and spinning it and pointing it at various men along the bar. Now this was something that a man never did in Texas or Oklahoma unless he was asking for trouble.

Suddenly I heard a shot, and this gun-flashing fellow let out a squeal like a javelina. His gun flew out of his hand and went clattering off across the board floor, and as he grasped his hand in pain I could see he was minus a perfectly good finger, for a bullet had hit him in his gun hand. A small fellow walked over from a card table, blew smoke away from his own revolver, and spoke sharply to the injured man. I could not help but stare at this fellow from the card table, for he was a real little dandy, and dressed the part. Later, a man told me that his name was Ben Thompson, and that he was a well-known gambler and gunfighter. It appeared that Thompson had tired of this guntwirler's sport, for he said later he had no intention of killing him. But he was suspicious that the fellow might turn the gun on him, just to make himself a record. "I just wanted to slow him down a bit before he got himself into real trouble," Thompson had told this man. Well, it wasn't a way to win a friend, say what you will!

This man Thompson was later City Marshal in Austin, Texas. His name was associated with that of another gunman, John King Fisher. The pair of them was bushwhacked in the old Vaudeville Theater in San Antonio by three men said to be Joe Foster, Billy Simms, and a policeman named Coy. There was something mysterious about the murder of these two men, and several stories were told how it happened. But all agreed that Thompson and Fisher were dead when the smoke cleared away. They had both been bad ones in their time, so few tears were wasted over their end.

We left Ogallalie after a few days, coming right back down the Texas Cattle Trail to Dodge. I found Dodge just as interesting as Ogallalie now that I was not under Wes' restraining influence, and it wasn't long until I was stone broke.

Rance left Dodge in a few days, going on back to Camp Supply where he had found work. It was my intention to sell my horse and take my saddle with me on the train and go back to papa's ranch in Texas. But I didn't have carfare left, so that changed my plans. It is strange how the course of a man's life is changed by such a small thing as the lack of a few dollars to pay carfare home. I worked for Ham Bell for a few days to catch up my horse's board bill, then I rode down the Texas Trail where Mr. Bell had told me I could find work on a ranch. Before I got to Camp Supply I met some cowboys who were hiring out to a new ranch that held range both in the Indian Territory and in what they called the Neutral Strip, to the west, as well as range in North Texas. It was a big outfit, well financed, so a boy would be sure of his pay, they said. I joined them and we all rode to Camp Supply, where the foreman was said to be doing the hiring.

This new outfit was an English concern, called Cattle Ranche & Land Company.[3] We called it after its brand, The YL, as was the custom on the range. The foreman was Alex Young, and I soon found out after he hired me that he was a genuine Texas cowboy. They paid us by check every thirty days.

I had learned to ride in Texas, and it was a good thing I did, for the YL had some of the meanest horses on the range. Most of us were new boys, and it was up to us to break them. We would just catch the horse, tie up a leg, and throw on a saddle. Or maybe sometimes we had to throw the horse and roll him into the saddle. When we couldn't get him to open his mouth to take the bit, we would pry open the mouth and open up the bridle and slip the bit in from the side. When the boy was set in the saddle we would let the horse up and pull the blindfold, and it was every-one for himself after that!

I was about a full-fledged cowboy by this time, I thought, for I could set any bronc, rope with the top men, and I had even learned to tell time by the stars. Old Wes had learned me that "the old peckerneck·star comes up near midnight in the low east; time for the second guard—about two o'clock—the Horseshoe kicks up with its five stars in a circle corral." We never carried watches nor compasses, for they broke too easily, so we were guided by the stars at night. I figured I knew as much as them other YL boys, but I soon learned that old Alex Young had a lot of tricks in his warbag to teach me. But I was young and eager, and I learned fast.

chapter II

1880-1884

PUBLIC LAND STRIP OR "NO MAN'S LAND" • YL RANCH
CATTLE GROWERS ASSOCIATION • HEALY BROTHERS RANCH

That fall of 1880 I rode my first roundup for the YL along Kiowa and Beaver Creeks, the northeast Texas Panhandle, the western end of the Cherokee Strip, and old No Man's Land.

I can remember on that roundup, and several others, hearing the men talk around the chuckwagon, wondering what country we were in. The fact that we were working for an English company added to our confusion. None of them men seemed to know anything about American history, nor had I ever heard about this country. There were no laws whatever here where we had found ourselves, so it was all a big mystery to us. I was all ears, listening, trying to learn, to be a good cowboy, so there was not much said that I didn't hear.

I gradually learned that this *Public Land Strip*, or "Neutral Strip," which we called No Man's Land, was bordered on the south by the Texas Panhandle, on the east by the Cherokee Strip, on the north by Kansas, and on the west end by the Territory of New Mexico. It was a strip of land 168 miles east to west, and 34½ miles north to south.[1] The Cherokees and other Indians used it as a passageway west to the mountains during their fall hunts. They could be seen late in the fall on the old River Trail, north of the Beaver, heading west, just about the time fall roundup started. They would hunt, dry their meat and make jerky, then trail back through anywhere from November through December. They traveled by tribes, men, women, and children, their spotted ponies dragging *travois*, just two lodgepoles, one on either side of the horse, and on these poles they tied their gear and the meat from the hunts.

15

These Indians were peaceful, but they were great beggars. They wouldn't go near a ranch in a body, for I don't suppose they were supposed to be off their Reservations. But they would appear in ones and twos and beg fearfully for *wo-ha* or other stuff they saw lying around they could use. The cattlemen were not hard on them, and we often let them have a beef when the hunt was bad, for they didn't cause much trouble, either coming or going.

Well, we got along fine, believing that this strip of land where we ran cattle was a part of Indian Territory. Eventually we got a sort of mail service through there from Dodge to Zulu, Texas. We had one from Camp Supply to Fort Elliott, and the mail ran on to Adobe Walls and Fort Bascom, but the service was rotten. One editor once wrote:

> Had the mail service been in the same condition in ancient days that it now is in this country, Paul's Epistles to Titus and others would have never been received in time for publication in the Bible.

This "Star Mail Service" eventually got into big trouble with the Federal Government, for it was costing a premium to deliver one letter in that country.[2] But someone else will have to tell that story.

When the Western Cattle Trail from Texas came through the land in 1876, the cowmen from Texas and elsewhere began to see the advantages of holding range in that area. They had started leasing land from the individual Cherokees in the Cherokee Strip, to the east of us, but since no one had any title to this land of the Public Land Strip they just turned their cattle loose there to graze for free. One of the first ranches, I am told, was the old Chain C's. This was the Cimarron & Crooked Creek Cattle Co., with C. T. Herring as one of the principals. This group later used the Crooked L name and brand, conceived after the shape that Crooked Creek made on the map there in Kansas and into the Strip. Bob Steele was its manager.

Another outfit, the Prairie Cattle Co., had made such an impressive record of profits that it was not long before Scotch and English money, like behind my company, the YL, began to flow into that Southwest country. Some of these companies claimed range as wide as forty miles in extent. The company men often had disputes over range and boundaries. On Little Wolf Creek, for example, while working on the roundup on Saturday, September 1st, 1883, Al Thurman, foreman of the KH, which lay to our southeast, killed G. C. Smith, the foreman of the Box T, an adjoining ranch. This dispute, though range entered into it, was really over branding maverick cattle.

There was a sort of range law that at roundup time you branded every calf in the brand worn by its mother. However, many times calves were overlooked when a yearling or coming-two showed up "slick," that is wearing no brand at all and not following its mother. Well, the man that was handiest with his iron usually claimed that one, and slapped his brand on that little dogie. This was a range rule, understand, and everyone did it.

But no individual cowboy was supposed to do this for himself. The ranch owners kept such privileges for themselves and they expected their boys who were getting their $30 a month to use their ranch brand. It was really unfair to rely upon young cowboys to go straight while asking them to steal in this manner for their employers. But most of us had growed up doing it and it was the way of life that had emerged through the years, so none of us knew enough to question the sense of it. Well, even today many employees are still expected to steal *for* their employers, but not *from* them.

This murder of Smith was the first real trouble we had there on the range, and that's when we found there were no laws down there, and no law officers to act against the murderer. Smith's folks were Texas people, where feuding was a common practice, and they were not about to let his murder go without a reprisal. They wanted to prosecute Thurman, as did Smith's employer, and make Thurman and the men who were with him pay the price. Thurman's case was taken to the courts at Wichita, Kansas; at Fort Smith, Arkansas; and to Graham and Paris, Texas. But the courts turned it down for one reason and another, none accepting the jurisdiction, and I don't rightly recall what happened with it.

It wasn't long after I got there that men with lurid reputations began drifting in and out of the Strip, knowing that no law would

17

bother them there. One cowboy feller I knew called No Man's Land his "King's X." For he likened it to a children's game he had played in Virginia where you crossed your fingers and said the magic words "King's X," and no one could bother you. I know that one common question we used to ask one another on early acquaintance was "What did you do, John?"

There was another class of people drifting into the Strip, some of them good people, men with families, who were trying to establish themselves on dry land claims. These folks were called "squatters," but they were just as entitled to the land as the big ranchers, for nobody could own land there where there was no law behind the title. So there were neither fences nor Herd Laws in No Man's Land. The cowmen had come early, and based their claims to range on right of discovery, exploration—and seniority. But shucks, if that was right the Indians or the buffalo hunters both held prior claim.

To protect their holdings, the cattlemen met at Dodge City in the spring of 1882, I believe it was, and organized the Dodge City Cattle Growers Association, a branch of the Fort Worth (Texas) association. The Dodge group came to be called The Western Kansas Cattle Growers Association, though most of the members like Col. R. J. Hardesty and Ed Hardesty, Sim Holstein, Bake and Tom Hungate, Fred Taintor, R. E. Steele, A. H. McCoy, W. I. Harwood, Wash Mussett, and others ran cattle in the Public Land Strip and the Cherokee Strip as well as western Kansas. It was estimated that the ninety-four members of the Association in 1884 owned 425,000 head of cattle valued at a cool $12,750,000. Now cowmen are always great overestimators of the number of cattle on the range, but it was true that there was a lot of money and power behind this group, and they weren't ready to let anyone get a penny away from them under the range laws they passed at their organizational meeting.

"The Association," as they were collectively called, passed, in their great wisdom, many resolutions. Amongst others, all general managers, foremen, and wagon bosses were instructed not to encourage immigration of grangers into No Man's Land or any other part of the southwestern country. The Association claimed farmers were a detriment to their cattle industry. During this first con-

18

vention nothing was ever said in actual print, so far as I recall, as to what the cowboys should say or do to the newcomers who moved in. But it seemed plain enough that if we should find some of the granger's livestock far from his home, we would make no effort to tell him about the stock or get it back where it belonged.

Here is where I could not agree with The Association, for I felt the grangers had as much right to that land as did the cattle companies, especially since several of the companies were not even American companies, but English and Scotch concerns whose members never lived on the land, just hired us boys to run things and make big money for them. The older cowmen, the managers and foremen, to whom The Association members paid good wages and gave extra presents for running their outfits, kept advising The Association that it was wrong to oppose the grangers. For they knew that the cowboys were friendly by nature to the grangers, and looked to them for the courtship of their pretty daughters on an otherwise womanless range. We cowboys were young men, many of us just boys, and lonely as could be for womenfolk. So a settler's daughter or a charming schoolma'am looked mighty good to our eyes after what we had seen at the end of the annual beef drive to Dodge City. Most of the settlers were hospitable and treated us boys as though they thought there was yet a chance we would be good citizens one day. This treatment gave us a chance to learn some of the social graces by mixing around with worthwhile people.

One of the most aggravating actions of The Association was a paragraph in their by-laws that forbade anyone employed by The Association members to accumulate his own cattle. There was hardly a cowboy or a foreman that didn't look forward to owning a small herd hisself some day, and this action irked all of them. It was this rule that eventually got me in bad with The Association.

The Association decided to keep better track of the pilgrim cattle coming up from Texas, so they ordered two of their cowboys who knew all the Texas and local brands to cut those Texas herds as they came up the Western Trail and the Tuttle Trail. I was chosen to be one of these boys and with another young fellow I was posted on the Western Trail to cut out all range brands belonging to our Association members that were picked up in the through trail herds. We were also instructed to cut and hold any improper brands. I knew most all brands from Red River to the Platte, so Alex Young gave me a high recommendation when he put me on this job.

Together with my partner, Harry Reas, we set up in a small log cabin they built for us alongside the Western Trail, the same trail I came north on in 1880, near the Beaver River. The cabin was made from thick cedar logs and had a wood roof. On the roof they had put ten inches of sod for protection against Indians' burning arrows and also to keep the cabin cooler in the heat of the summer.

This little cabin was quite comfortable, and we had but one run-in with Indians, when they sneaked up one night and took our two saddle horses and gathered our other loose horses, leaving us afoot. We had been instructed not to follow any Indians away from our cabin, so we just set tight until a trail boss came by the following morning. He sent one of his men to the Fort and they sent out a squad of cavalrymen. Within a few days the cavalrymen came back with all of our horses. But them damned Indians had notched the ears and pulled out some of their tails until a white man would not want to be seen on them.

There were white men who also stole horses, and we were prepared to give them a fight if they tried to rob us. I always hated a horse thief, so I never had much use for a fellow, Charlie Stevens, who used to hang around that area. He was called "Wash," and some of the men told me he had run with the Chitwoods, who were also notorious horse thieves. Jim Chitwood and his brothers, however, had some good qualities. But Wash Stevens had none. Once, when a Kansas farmer appeared at the Chitwoods to claim a horse, the Chitwood boys threatened to hang him, for they hadn't stolen his horse. Wash Stevens rode by, and he agreed to give the farmer one of his own horses if the farmer would promise to stay in Kansas and not bother them any more. The Chitwoods never knew, but Wash just returned the horse he had stolen from the farmer!

Wash and a fellow named Hudson stole thirty head in New Mexico, then drove them east to the Chickasaw Nation. Tobe (Red) Odem and some U.S. Deputy Marshals caught Hudson. Wash told me later how he had escaped, walked for four days and nights, sustained only by green ears of corn, straight back to Odem's ranch. There he stole Odem's best saddle mare and made his way back to No Man's Land! He was surely a tough one.

There was a third fellow who ran with them, named Kid York. He stole cattle and horses all over the Strip. Northwest from our range, up on Crooked Creek, Laben Lemert found a wagon load of his own butchered beef turned over in a canyon when he had pressed the thieves too close. Lemert and a posse caught Kid York and his men at the Figure 4 Ranch and a hanging party followed, four of them thieves gracing a cottonwood limb.

The main duties Harry and I had there on the trail was to see that our own range cattle didn't get mixed up in the trail herds and driven on to Dodge. Those herds of 2,000 to 3,000 cattle would be strung out sometimes a mile in length. Harry would take one side, I would ride on the other, and we would scan those herds, cutting out anything we didn't think belonged in it. These cattle we would throw back a mile or two away from the trail to graze. We made a tally on all cattle cut out.

At the peak of the season, June and July, as many as twelve herds would pass by daily at our inspection point. We often found what was called "give-out cattle," little leppies, some yearlings, and others that were not able to travel farther up the trail. Some would have sore feet, some were sick or crippled. These cattle would be eventually left along the trail anyway, so I began to dicker the trail bosses out of them. I bought them cheap, and had the trail boss write me a bill of sale on whatever paper we had handy in our pockets, an old envelope or the back of a letter, the edge of a newspaper or magazine or the blank pages torn from the front and back of a brand book.

After branding these cattle with my own brand, I would throw them back in a little valley I knew where there was a spring and the grass was good, not too far from the YL Ranch. When I started

21

up my own brand, I had to be careful, for I wanted no trouble on the range with Association members or others. A new brand had to be unlike any others nearby on the range, so I made a careful study, eliminated all similar marks, and picked the brand TK. The Dominion Cattle Company range bordered the YL on the southeast and used a Box T, the T within the box and also an OK Connected. So there was no likeness there. The New York Cattle Company used a KH. So I could never be accused of working on top of their mark. The same applied to other brands, like Hi Kollar's CY, and the Half Circle Reverse J to the north, another brand of Hi Kollar's, or the R Bar S of Word & Byler to the east.

In cutting these herds, Harry and I would sometimes find other Texas brands on these give-out cattle. Knowing that these cattle would never catch up with their herd I felt that it would be good business to take care of them too, even if I didn't have a bill of sale. So my enterprise grew, and I was soon initiated into that mystic economic system by which cattlemen made money appropriating livestock on the range, a practice that was carried out through their hired help. The only difference I could see was that I was doing my own work, riding for cattle like they did in the early days in the brush of south Texas, after the Civil War. My activities were similar in every way to those of The Association members, and I, too, was prospering through my own initiative.

My pal, Harry Reas, was a good fellow, but he would not take a part with me in branding these cattle or buying them. Yet he did everything he could to help me along with my enterprise, and he cast no criticism. He knew as well as I did that at roundup time, when those cattle of mine showed up in the herds and I claimed them, my popularity with The Association members would soon fade. Harry said he expected me to lose my job with the YL, but I just laughed at him, for Alex Young was my friend and I knew he would stand behind me. Harry was about my own age. He was New York-born, but had come west when he was sixteen and was now a first-rate cowboy. He later married Maggie Ong, a popular girl of the Strip, and he worked for the Hitch outfit for several years. Harry was a rough customer when he wanted to be, and he could whip almost anybody. I used to scuffle around our little log cabin with Harry, and wrestle out on the grass with him, just to give him exercise. For he was always spoiling to wrestle or box. But I was no match for him, and he always treated me gently. Once he whipped another rough fellow, Sam McCord, at a dance. Sam had made some remark in front of Maggie that Harry didn't like. A friend of Harry's, George Sprowl, stood up beside Harry that night and nearly got shot for his trouble, for McCord also had friends.

By the end of September the southern herds had all passed up the trail, for after that it would be too cold to take unacclimated herds into the frozen north. There being few herds to handle, Harry and I returned to our respective ranches for the winter. I told my boss, Alex Young, about my project of buying cattle. He just shook his head. He said that while he didn't approve of my activities, neither did he blame me for trying to make a dollar for myself. As I look back from this distance, I realize that Mr. Young was just trying to warn me of the trail I was blazing for myself to follow. But his tone was kindly.

"You know that your actions are contrary to the rules of The Association, Jim," he told me. "This may lead to your getting fired or laid off by the company. I'm not sure you're doing the right thing this time."

I had wanted to take a layoff anyway, I told him. But I asked him not to fire me, for that would hurt my chances of getting another job. I had the reputation of being a good cow hand, and I didn't want to jeopardize it. Besides, Mr. Young had taken me in as a boy and taught me everything I knew about the cow business and I felt toward him almost as I did toward my own father. I had not wanted to hurt his feelings or cause him grief in any way.

Mr. Young assured me that he would not fire me unless forced to do so by company officials. He told me of a new ranch that was starting up to the west of us. It was the M Bar, the principals being a Mr. McKinney, John Over, and the old Dodge policeman, Joe Mason, a silent partner. Earlier this was called the B A D Ranch. Mr. Young said that this new company would need some good she stuff to start their herds and it would be a good place to turn my recently acquired cattle if I wanted to sell. So I rode over and talked with Mr. Over. I found him a pleasant man to deal with, and a man who appeared to understand the cattle business. The upshot of the talk was that he bought my she stock for his company and gave me a check for $1,800. This money, together with my paychecks which I had saved over a long period of time, gave me a nice little stake. Now, with my resolutions reinforced with cash money, I asked Mr. Young to let me resign. He did so. There was no bad feeling between us, at that time or later.

I had wanted to see father and the old home ranch, so I bought a ticket to Ellis County, Texas. To my surprise father was glad to see me again, even though I had abandoned his cattle in the Santa Anna Mountains when I left. I had hoped he would be tolerant of me, and he was, even after my running off that way. I missed seeing one older brother who was now ranching on the Brazos River, near Round Timbers. He had taken a wagon just before I arrived and left on the roundup.

Father asked if I planned to return north. I told him I probably would, since I had a good job and Mr. Young had invited me to return for spring roundup work. We had a long talk and I told father of my experiences getting into the cattle business in the Strip. He offered me some good advice, and as things turned out I wished I had taken advantage of it.

"Son," he said, stroking his mustache, "I want you to listen carefully to what I say. For I won't repeat it. You tell me you have been very successful in getting hold of cattle and then selling them. You have more money now than I ever had at your age. But what you have done is to take a bold chance to get it. This will lead to your taking even greater chances. Now if you're not careful, you may wind up at the end of a rope, for such actions as this are a long ways short of being legal.

"I know that the big cattle companies do business in a different way than they want the small man to do. But you must not pattern after them. They make the laws. They have the laws on their side, written to protect them and their property. You no doubt got away with this only because you were in such a lawless country."

24

What father told me was not what I wanted to hear. But I listened to him, more out of respect than because I intended to be guided by what he said. Yet I knew that he was right.

"When you get through sowing your wild oats," father concluded, "I want you to come back here to stay. I want you to have your fair share of my cattle here and on the Brazos, even if you didn't show enough sense of responsibility to stay with them and care for them. They're rightly part yours, and it's my hope you'll return and claim them."

Father was not angry, but from his voice I knew that he was leveling with me. Though I thought then I should and would return one day and take up my claim to the cattle, it was not to be.[3] I stayed around Ellis County for two weeks, meeting old friends. Then I took a trip to San Antonio. I had some interesting experiences and met some real characters, but it is not my purpose to amuse you or worry you with the various stunts we pulled off while I was visiting in Texas. I did have an enjoyable time, and anyone who has witnessed a cowboy off duty several months enjoying himself will tell you that no one is more competent to create bad jokes and foolish stunts for his and others' entertainment than a footloose cowboy with plenty of green stuff in his pockets.

In April, 1884, when the grass was greening, I had the urge to go back up the trail. This time I landed in Dodge City on April 15. Dodge was about the liveliest of the cowtowns then, for the Western Trail was still bringing cattle in there and the Jones & Plummer Trail and the Tuttle Trail were bringing in the New Mexico and north Texas herds. Not yet had the settlements of the grangers pushed the great trails westward out of the state. More than 300,000 head of cattle reached Dodge that year, more than a hundred big herds with all their cowboys, cooks, ramrods, and wranglers.

Kansas was legally dry at that time, but Dodge always had whiskey, even when they sold it at the drug stores. They used to say, "There's no law west of Wichita, and no God west of Dodge." All the big cattlemen were gathered here at this time for the annual convention of The Western Kansas Cattle Growers Association. The Dodge papers were blowing about it, and they appeared about like the old *Fort Worth Livestock Growers Journal*, a front page with some news and the rest estray notices and imprints of brands and market information.

Once again the granger situation was being discussed and I listened at length to many long, drawn-out speeches about the matter. One speaker told of the maneuvers the grangers were making to establish themselves on the cattle range and the methods the stockmen must take to dislodge them. The owners implied that their foremen, wagon bosses, and cowboys must try in every way to discourage the grangers from settling on the "free range." But again, some of the older cowmen like John Over, George and Frank Healy, Tom Hungate, and my old boss, Alex Young, advised The Association to leave the grangers alone.

"Nobody owns this Government range in the Strip," I heard one old cowman argue. "If you start pressing them until they use guns to defend their personal property, then we'll all have hell to pay. I say it's best to help them, not to fight them. Then the range will still be free for our cattle to range outside the small crop areas."

But all efforts to make compromise with the grangers was opposed by the bigger companies in The Association, many of them with absentee ownership and with stockholders who had never seen the cattle range. I talked with Alex Young at the convention and he seemed glad to see me. Over a couple of beers he told me that his company, the YL, was dead set against giving me employment again. But he had learned that Healy Brothers were looking for a man to take charge of their ranch. George Healy was in Dodge and I talked with him. Upon Mr. Young's recommendation, I got the job.

The Cattlemen's Convention ended with a big ball, and I left Dodge with the fixed purpose in mind to be a loyal employee and a top foreman for Healy Brothers, for I was extremely glad not to be blackballed from all the ranches in the Strip.

Healy Brothers had a good range on the Beaver River, not far west from the YL range, at the mouth of Cottonwood Creek. I started to work there about April 20, 1884. They branded a KK

26

on either shoulder of all their increase, and also had an H brand, an AH Connected, and a Double Quartercircle. We cropped the right ears and undersloped the left. George and Frank Healy were Boston men who had been in the Texas Panhandle since 1878, so were no tenderfeet to that country when I met them. Both were fine men and good employers. I did most of my business with George, for he was the ranch manager. He later operated a store at Alpine, east of Beaver City on Duck Pond Creek. George later studied law and became a lawyer. Frank served a term or two as Sheriff of Beaver County later on. Both men were well-respected in the Strip.

The main equipment of a good cow outfit was its saddle stock. Healy Brothers had a fine *remuda*. I began at once feeding the horses grain to get them in top condition for the hard roundup work that would soon start. Grant Perkins, Charley Smith, and others who worked for Healy helped me. Grant later married a daughter of Dr. E. B. N. Strong, an old neighbor on Horse Creek, and he became foreman of Healy's spread and she cooked for the ranch. They were a fine couple.

We usually began gathering the cattle about May 10, so I had twenty days to get my wagons greased, the grub ordered, the horses cleaned up, the leather stuff repaired, and the outfit ready to ride. I was mighty proud to be running a wagon, for I was the youngest wagon boss in the Strip, just eighteen years old.

Healy Brothers, and the M Bar, on Timber Creek, held range close together, shared it as a fact, east of the Jones & Plummer Trail. Between them they claimed range from Beaver City east to the Cherokee Strip, a distance of about forty miles in length and fifteen to twenty miles in width. The Beaver River flowed through this range. Its tributaries from the south, such as Cottonwood Creek, Clear Creek, Camp Creek, Duck Pond Creek, and others, and those from the north like Pinto Creek, Cavia and Timber Creeks made it the best-watered range in the Strip.

One day while we were riding on the roundup, I saw that the land was becoming dotted with sod dugouts and tents of the new grangers. At one place, about four miles east of our headquarters ranch, a little town was starting up. It was later named Benton,

27

and was between Mexico and Duck Pond Creeks. The whole eastern end of the Strip appeared to be booming. A few days later on a little creek we ran across a large whiskey distillery, secreted in a big cave, with a logged-over roof. It was owned and operated by a man who introduced himself as "Judge L. M. Hubbard." He headed up one group of Vigilantes, he said. He handed us tin cups and told us to make ourselves at home.

After we had drunk about all we should, he showed us the complete still. The big cooking apparatus was built back into the bank of a hillside alongside the small stream, Hog Creek. The roof was covered over with large cedar logs and earth. There were twenty large barrels setting back there; he called them "hogsheads," and each held about four times as much as an ordinary vinegar or cracker barrel. While I had seen a lot of booze in saloons, and had drunk my share for my age, this was the first time I had ever seen a place where it was being manufactured and I was properly impressed by the size of this man's distillery operation. It would have been a credit to the Sunnybrook or Old Crow distilleries!

This "Judge" Hubbard produced the liquor we bought over the drug counters and in the saloons at Dodge City, Englewood, Ashland, and Protection as well as in towns like Garden City and others as far as a hundred miles distant. In Benton and Beaver City this booze sold at a price all could afford to pay, for there were no Federal or State taxes of any kind on it. Only at Camp Supply, where the Government concession sold whiskey could you buy "legal" booze, but at a much higher price.

The liquor in us made us all talkative, and I asked this man Sutter, for that was his real name, if he paid Uncle Sam any taxes. He drew himself up and answered "No." He went on to explain the ways of the law to us boys, for he was a lawyer by training, he said. Since Uncle Sam ignored this land and nobody claimed any jurisdiction there, it was not necessary to pay taxes on anything, he told us. The "Judge" used a lot of big words and showed off his learning to us, telling us that it was his intention to establish what he called "Organic Law" in that region, and to make it a fit place for people to live in.

Now I had already lived there for several years, and I thought it a good land, and that we had good people to live among already. So his talk roused me, for he was using a lot of words which do not belong in the cowboy language. All his talk about "Organic Law" was Greek to me, but I did gather that it was his intention to establish a new country there called "Cimarron Territory." This Strip we called No Man's Land would be divided into five parts, or counties. Benton, for example, would be the county seat for the eastern end, or "Benton County." Well, as a matter of fact, the Strip was later divided into seven counties, called Benton, Beaver, Shade, Springer, Turner, Kilgore, and Sunset. But I will go into that later.

My pals and I left Sutter's cave pretty wobbly on our feet, but with our heads buzzing with learning. And I was to see more of old "Judge" Hubbard and his still at a later date.[4]

chapter III

1884-1886

ROUNDUP • LAW AND ORDER

Range cows in the early days started dropping their calves in April and the calffall continued through May and into June. On May 10th we started on the roundup. I took a KK wagon and three boys and drove down to Packsaddle Creek on the South Canadian. Our groups were to work up the Canadian to the Texas line, then cross over the divide to the head of Wolf Creek. From there we moved across the flat to where the creek emptied into the Beaver River, close by Camp Supply, in the Cherokee Strip.

The general roundup in that area usually started at Cantonement and worked west up the Beaver. Another group would be working up the Cimarron River. The outfits from the east planned to meet at the YJ Connected fence, on Hi Kollar's ranch. Whichever bunch arrived first would wait a day or two for the other to get there. Both outfits would then move up the Cimarron and Beaver valleys, the Cimarron wagons quitting the work at the Harwood Ranch (the O Bar L Connected brand) near Fargo Springs. These big springs were on the north side of the river, near the Garden City stage ford.

The Beaver River wagons then worked west toward the headwaters of the Beaver, crossed over at Point of Rocks on Beatty Brothers range, then turned down the river and back to the O Bar L.

My wagon was assigned to work up Wolf Creek to Sixteenmile and Buffalo Creeks. There had been some bad grass fires down there on the Washita and the cattle had drifted out of the country. We found a lot of them with the gather along Wolf Creek, for the winds were predominantly from the south in that area and the livestock had drifted north and west up the streams, ahead of the fires.

The Cimarron Division had by this time finished the work along Kiowa, Bluff, and Sand Creeks. The outfits to the northwest on the Arkansas waited until the Cimarron Division groups reached the O Bar L, then joined with them, working down the Arkansas River eastward from the Colorado line. There were smaller, isolated sections that were rounded up separately, like a little group that started at Pat Ryan's on May 5, ahead of the rest of us. They worked this range, also Adam Telfer's and Bob Wright's Quartercircle W range, so they would be through before the general roundup started.

The general roundup started when grass was greening in Texas and moved north with the weather, like the wheat harvest now does as the grain ripens. It was the biggest and most fun- and work-filled period of the year, and there was always a wave of expectancy from the first of April until we got started. We would be up early those preceding days, feeding our saddle horses and taking care of their feet, shoeing some and currying off the accumulation of winter hair. We oiled and greased our gear, patched our clothes if they needed it, and shined our boots with lamp black, for the range cowboy was a proud cuss and wanted to appear his best when he met the other boys from the far-flung range country. We had great pride in our outfit, and like an army group wanted it to appear the very best when the wagons gathered for the work in the spring.

The fall beef roundup was somewhat different. The men had been on the range all summer, so it was not like getting out early in the spring when the weather warmed. The beef gather looked forward mainly to seeing Old Tyrone or Dodge City when we trailed the beef to the railheads. But the spring work was action, good and friendly feelings, and lots of hard riding and roping, for the calves had to be branded, the bull calves castrated, and every animal carefully scrutinized for screwworms and other disease, for there was lots of pleuro-pneumonia among some cattle in the Eighties and always the fear of blackleg.

The men who captained these roundups were fellows like Sim Holstein and John DeLong, both of whom ranched on Wolf Creek; Tom Hungate, Hardesty's foreman; Wash Mussett, an old

Texas cowman; Alex Young, my old boss at the YL; and other such responsible and capable cowmen. They were selected by The Association's Roundup Committee at the annual convention. Each Captain drew extra pay, but the real honor came in being chosen Captain of their particular area. Every man obeyed the orders of the roundup Captain to the letter, even when working on your own range.

These Captains were exceptional men who had no fear and could handle any situation that came up. I recall one smart young cowboy who rode in from New Mexico to work the roundup. He soon made his brag as to what he would and could do when he rode into the gather. One morning he rode into the herd to rope a yearling calf, but he made so much fuss the cattle started running. Sim Holstein was Captain at this point. He watched the boy for a spell, then without even waiting to shout a warning he took down a length of his lariat, doubled it, and started after that cowboy. The boy by this time had got his loop on the calf. Sim rode alongside the calf, pulled his Bowie knife, and cut the boy's string. Then he rode over to that young fellow and started lashing him over the head and hat with that double length of rope. The boy turned his horse and rode out of the herd as fast as he could travel. But Sim's horse was faster, and he kept alongside thrashing that fellow over the back with that rope as far as we could see them.

Sim apparently told that boy never to come back, for another boy called for his bedroll that night. I never saw that fool cowboy on the range again. And Sim's prompt action taught the rest of us boys a good lesson—that the roundup Captain was Boss!

On this particular work there were nine wagons that I can recall: The Crooked L's, with Bob Steele, the boss, coming down from Meade, Kansas, in a top buggy. Steele was an attractive man, a Virginian, and a good judge of cattle. Dave Mackey was his foreman. The Crooked L's had eight men on the roundup, Alex Foltz, later their foreman, Bill Shouse, Bernie Lemert, Jim Martz, Charley Haggenbach, and Sealy, a boy from New York, a nephew of Deerdorf, one of the previous owners of the ranch when it was called the Chain C's.

Then there was my old outfit, the YL wagon, with Alex

Young as the wagon boss. Beverly Brothers had a wagon down from Dodge City; McCoy Brothers, the Eks-I-Eleven as we called them, were there with Steve Rupe running their show, and Al Lapham, Matt and Tom Brennan, Emmet Powers, Dick Nave, Lengthy John Halford, Alex McCaire, Charlie Boone, and Adolph Peters, their cook. The Figure 4 Ranch of Cooper and Givens had an outfit there with Dirkson, their wagon boss. Col. Hardesty was down from Dodge for a few days, and Tom Hungate captained the work in their section of the range along Palo Duro Creek. Old Doc Ross was the Hardesty cook. Fred Harvey, the famous chain restaurant owner, had his XY wagon there. His foreman was John Lute, or Dutch John, as we called him. Harwood had a wagon there, and John O'Loughlin's Pigpen joined us near Fulton Creek.

For the benefit of those who have never seen an old-time roundup I will give just a few sketches of how the work was done on a large range like ours. The Captain would get all the outfits together, then take the wagon bosses aside for a talk. He would explain what country was to be worked, then assign each wagon boss to work a certain part of that range. For example, he might tell the Crooked L foreman, "Dave, you're an older man and know that country in between Timber Creek and the Jones and Plummer Trail, so I'm going to ask you to take charge of the circle there." That would mean that although the Crooked L man was off his own range, he would take charge of the big circle in west of the Healy Brothers range, and would be boss during the roundup over Healy's foreman and cowboys. This way the work got done better, putting the best men in the right place. Generally the wagon boss took charge on his own range, but this example is just to show that a roundup Captain could handle the work the way he felt best.

When the Captain had selected the areas to be worked by the various wagon bosses, each would go to his own wagon and on the following morning he would get his men up, fed, and mounted. Then he would gather them around him, all mounted up, and "tell them off." This was what we called it when he directed each man where to ride for cattle, what streams to follow, what hills or canyons to look among. When he had finished he would generally

33

ask, "Any questions?" If none came he would say, "Ride off!" It was the practice on the range for every man to then leave the Captain in a high lope in the direction he had been assigned, just like cavalrymen do when receiving an order from a superior officer. I believe this custom came from having old Union and Confederate Army men giving and taking orders during the early roundups, for it showed that the man giving the order expected immediate obedience, and that the man taking the order was prepared to carry it out to the letter. I have had cowboys who worked in Montana and the Dakotas tell me that they followed this same practice.

The cowboys would ride out in a big circle covering many square miles of range, searching each ravine and canyon and every thicket along the streams for cattle. Each man would start driving his gather toward a central point that had been selected previously: near water, usually a good level area where there was an abundance of grass. For here was where they would work the herd.

When the roundup herd was gathered, there might be several thousand, perhaps 5,000, head of all kinds of cattle. Some of the wagon bosses or their top men would then ride slowly into the herd on their best cutting horses and begin the process of separating each owner's cattle from the mixed herd. They worked easily and without talking or exciting the cattle, for to chouse up the wild cattle might start a stampede. In cutting out, the calves and their mothers were always taken first, then the steers. After the various smaller herds of different brands had been made up, they would be moved farther away from the big herd by each ranch owners' hands. Each outfit would take its "cut" back to its home range and there pick a suitable spot to brand the calves and castrate the bull calves. They would look their own cattle over at this time for ticks, screwworm, blackleg, pleuro-pneumonia, or any other disease. Meanwhile, the Captain and the rest of the wagons would move on to the next range where the same performance would be repeated. There were always wagons and outfits joining up and dropping off as the roundup worked over the area. Representatives, or "reps," who worked alone and represented distant ranches, would ride a few days with one wagon or another of his choice. They usually picked up a few of their drift cattle that had wandered in the storms.

One young fellow I recall on the roundup one time was Sandiford, who repped for an outfit in the Cherokee Strip, in the Medicine Lodge country. Sandiford's night horse was a fine animal, but with an inclination to buck when he first set him. One night his partner called Sandiford for second guard, and teasing him, he put Sandiford's saddle on his own back and jumped up and down, pretending he was Sandiford's night horse bucking. As Sandiford crawled out of his soogan, watching the performance, he shook his head doubtfully.

"I'm shore gettin' shy o' that night hoss o' mine," Sandiford admitted.

Everybody got such a laugh out of that boy's remark that they called him "Shy" Sandiford after that.

Nicknames like that stuck to everybody in the range country. One feller was called Pock because he had the marks of smallpox on his face. Yet no one thought it unkindly, it was just our way. Another boy was called Bur-head, because he had a bristly head of hair and whiskers like sandburs. "Handshaker" was a cowboy from the east who made it a practice to introduce himself and shake hands, like the businessmen in the east would do, with every man in camp. This was not the way we usually did, especially while working on the range. "Pack-rat" was a fellow who kept a special warbag in which he collected junk. He had everything anyone would ever need in this sack—cough syrup, iodine, toothpicks, razor blades, bandages, talcum powder, arnica, two or three pairs of drug store spectacles, a small sad iron, needles and thread, and God knows what all—stuff never carried by cowboys. But everyone borrowed from Pack-rat, and no one ever paid him back. His forethought earned him nothing but this crazy name, yet we all liked Pack-rat Davis.

There was the widest assortment of men in the Strip who had nicknames. "Hooker" Threlkeld was one, a good cowman and a top roper. "Bake" Hungate was another, but how he got his name I never knew. Everyone thought "Boss" was a nickname, so we called Boss Neff by his *right name* for years, and never knew the difference! Why I never collected a nickname I'll never know. I suppose it was because "Jim" was about as short as they could make a name, so everyone was satisfied with it.

But animals got funny names, too. A steer on the Healy ranch that had a particularly fierce look in his eye we named Thunderbolt. Apple Blossom was a fine cow that brought a good bull calf every year for John Over. We named her because of her color. I once owned a dry cow that the men named Tin Horn, because she had a crumpled horn that glistened in the sun like a new tin can. Old Bunt was a muley cow with a red frizzle top. She used her head like a ramrod to push other cows out of her way. And there were many names to fit the colors of the Longhorn cattle—Blue, Roan, Red, Streak, and scores of others, usually with the word Old ahead of them.

And so it went. At roundup time we learned the new names or helped make them up for the cattle that were gathered on the range, and for the men who came to us as strangers but were soon "Shorty" or "Fleaball" by nickname. The cook usually nicknamed the cowboys, but the cowboys pinned the names on the cattle.

Hooker Threlkeld, after whom the town of Hooker, Oklahoma, got its name, once told us a story about two of his cowboys who about 1888 discovered an old granger living in a sod dugout with two pretty daughters, both wearing homespun. These boys loaded the old fellow with tales about buffalo, and told him they could ride north a few miles and rope one and fetch him back for fresh meat. Now there were no buffalo in that country by that time, but the old fellow, an Arkansawyer, thought that would just be fine, for he and his girls had eaten nothing but jackrabbits and prairie dogs for weeks. The two boys appeared the next day when the old fellow was occupied sharpening his grasshopper plow. They each put a comely daughter on behind their saddles and headed for "buffalo country," to rope some fresh meat. Late that evening the boys and girls returned, but without a sign of a buffalo! The old man grieved so much about not getting the promised fresh meat that the boys rode off about three miles from his dugout, shot a maverick steer, carved off two hind-quarters and delivered

36

them back to the dugout, telling him they had unexpectedly come on a young buffalo bull across the hills while on the way back to the ranch. The old man was most grateful to them, and told them how much different the buffalo meat tasted from ordinary fresh beef! That must have put them in right with the old fellow, for both of them boys soon married his daughters and set to work farming dry land claims!

In 1884-85 there were still a few buffalo on our cattle range and west of us. There were not many, for the large herds were all shot off, but on the roundups we occasionally ran across a scattered band of forty or fifty head in the west end of the country. We also saw an occasional small group of old bulls, three to eight head, grazing in the rough breaks near the streams where few men were to be seen. Once I ran across an old bull with the stub of an Indian lance still in his shoulder. We ran him down, shot him, and found the wound, though healed over, was still draining, with the lance point rusted in it.

There were beginning to be stacks of sun-bleached buffalo bones at different locations where the grangers had piled them up for freighting to Dodge, the nearest point on the railroad. They got $8 a ton for them at the railroad. Some of the bone haulers drove ox-teams, harnessed like horses with the collars upside down and using a jerkline like the big freight outfits did with their seven-mule-team wagons on the Jones and Plummer Trail. From a distance these bone piles, standing there in the glare of the sun, resembled the buildings of a city: white, stately, and throwing off a mirage into the sky. Many a cowboy rode off toward them bone piles thinking they had found a town, only to learn on their arrival they were looking at a six-foot-high stack of old bones. I made that fool mistake once myself.

After the spring roundup is ended there is always something going on in the little towns to keep up interest. One day a friend and I were riding into Benton to look around. We were on my own range, on Mexico Creek, when we saw a group of men and women gathered around two forked cottonwood logs they had set up near a bend in the creek. They had laid a third log across the tops of the forked logs and I could tell, as we came nearer, they had been

37

fixing up a hanging scaffold, a gallows. An elderly man was slumped on a keg beneath the gallows while a red-muzzled fellow was tying a hanging knot in the rope. By the time we rode up to the circle the rope had been tossed over the log and several men had a hold of it and were beginning to hoist the old man up. He started kicking and crying out, for they hadn't tied his legs together and he had no gag on his mouth.

They lowered him as we rode into the bunch, and I then noticed that there were several women and children in the crowd. I hardly knew what to say, and after a few uneasy seconds my pal said to them, "Looks like you-all fixin' to hang this ole fella?" The men said nothing, just stared up at us. My pal turned to me.

"You better talk to them, Jim. You got a bosses job and I'm just an ordinary cowhand and they might not listen to me."

I looked into some of the men's faces. They were all dirty, needed shaves, and were ragged. One of them spoke to me.

"Jim, youah th' boss on this range, an' we want you to he'p us hang this ole geezer."

"What's he done?" I asked.

"Why he's a damn old drunkard an' he's bin feedin' them outlaws," the red-muzzled man with the rope end answered me, banging the old man across the legs with the loose end. I could see they were going to hang him up to dry out for good if something wasn't done soon. But my pal rode in closer and saved me the trouble of acting.

"You got a bosses job, Jim, but I got nothin' to lose talkin' to these galoots." I could see by his looks, and the old man's (whose name I later learned was Fowler), that they knew one another. So I nodded for my friend to go ahead, and he spoke right up.

"Now listen to me, you damned greasy coyotes," he addressed the mob, "you're not going to hang anyone!" He looked down at the redhead holding the rope. "The first man that tugs on that rope is going to find it cut in two with a forty-five bullet from my gun." He patted his revolver in its holster. There was a pause, and I added my bit.

"I don't think we have a right to hang any man," I said, for I wanted them to continue on friendly with me. "What's more, I

38

can't go along with any of you men who try it." I patted my own Peacemaker as a suggestion that I might use it. The men began to act now like they felt someone besides the old man would get hurt if they insisted on a hanging and the redhead started to argue about it. My pal quickly drew his revolver, cocked it, and shoved it into the fellow's face.

"Now take off that damned loop," and the red-beard scrambled to get the noose off the old man's neck. "Now knock down this damned scaffold," my friend said, motioning with the gun barrel to the posts.

The crowd lifted the posts out of the ground. I noticed the women in the mob looked relieved, and one of them smiled and nodded to us. I don't believe many in that crowd wanted to see a man die, however worthless he may have been. I stuck down a paw and helped the old man get on the horse behind my saddle. We rode off down the creek, leaving the Vigilantes staring at us.

This was just one example of what went on in No Man's Land when I was a boy. Them Vigilante groups that organized to "maintain law and order" got as bad as the outlaws. For example, on another occasion when five of us boys from Over's and Healy's ranches were riding across the country on roundup, we came to Judge Sutter's—or Hubbard's—distillery. We rode into the ravine just to be sociable and have a friendly drink together. When we had dismounted and walked into the hole where his hogsheads set in rows on each side of the cave, we almost bumped into two men's bodies that was hanging from the ridgepole. They were young men, both dead of course, their necks stretched like they had strangled to death in the rope nooses. There were two cracker boxes lying near, like they had been kicked from under the men. Their boot toes didn't lack more than four inches from reaching the dirt floor, and the ropes were snubbed off close to the ridgepole. I studied the faces but I had never seen either of them before.

Old Judge Sutter looked surprised—and guilty—and started to explain. He had sold a shipment of whiskey and received a substantial sum of money in gold and silver coin, he said. Them two boys, both strangers, had boasted in Beaver City that they would rob him and hijack the rest of his booze. So the Judge called up his

Vigilance Committee. Some of them testified they had heard the boys make their brag. The Committee sentenced them to hang. It was as simple and easy as that. What we had stumbled onto was the result of this decision the Committeemen had made.

I never knew if the Judge or the Committee did that hanging, but it was as certain as anything could be that them two strangers hadn't stepped up on them cracker boxes, tied a noose around their own necks, and stretched hemp just for the fun of it.

This Committee of Judge Sutters' got quite active about this time. They would drop around to the various cow outfits in the Strip and tell their ranch foremen and range bosses how the ranches should be run in the future. The ranchers, they said, must not allow any strangers to eat or sleep at the ranches or their line camps unless they obtained full information about the newcomer, who he was, where he came from, and so forth. Well, this just wasn't the way it was done on the open range, and it is to the cow-men's credit that they didn't hold a meeting themselves and go out and hang all them Vigilantes to the same wagon tongues they talked so much about hanging other men on.

There is no question in my mind but what this Committee, and several others in the Strip, intended to keep order in that country, and especially around the distillery where we got our drinking whiskey. But I have often wondered if they used much wisdom in the way they went about keeping order. In the first place, they were all self-appointed, for nobody elected them to any offices. They just took it upon themselves, as most busy-bodies do, to adjust other peoples' affairs to suit their own fancy. They were, for the most part, high-minded people, but they missed their mark, for sometimes they would see bad in other people, then lose their heads like a bunch of locoed bronchos or stampeding steers. They wouldn't know where they were going, but they headed for trouble just the same. They would do something worse to right a simple wrong, like hanging a drunk man, just to teach him he shouldn't drink so much. Them Vigilantes reminded me of a Wichita, Kansas, woman who, about 1888, took an axe and chopped down thirty-one doors in a saloon building to get to where they had her husband locked up in the bullpen, drunk. She slapped him sober again, broke up everything she could find with her axe, horse-whipped the man, and drove him home in their buggy. I believe he quit drinking not long after that. This woman's name was Mary Elmer. I give it because many might think it was just another stunt of the crazy woman, named Carrie Nation, who broke out saloon windows.

It seemed to me that some folks had an idea like a preacher who once told a friend of mine in Beaver City, "We'll convert you and make you a Christian, by God, if we have to hang you!" The Vigilantes were like them old-time fundamentalists, ready to go to any end to make men conform to their own ways. They set up organizations all over the Strip, some good, some bad.

In spite of these facts, there were many peace-loving and respectable people in the Strip who only wanted to build a good home for themselves and their families. The total absence of law there put them at a disadvantage, like an unarmed but honest man walking the streets where all the thieves and murderers carry guns. There were many men in No Man's Land who were wanted elsewhere and "Law" was sorely needed, but not this Vigilante kind. Beaver City had proved by several cold-blooded murders that this Vigilante justice was not right or good for a town. Benton was little better, for there, and within a score of miles of the place, there had been several lynchings and murders. Most of the killings were over personal grievances, usually associated with cattle theft and quarrels over range and water. For example, one fellow named Rice thought another fellow, Kinsley, was killing his cattle for beef. (Someone had shot several of Rice's cows without using the meat or taking the hides.) Anyway, Rice killed Kinsley in cold blood. Among the cowboys, we thought maybe some Association cowboy had done the dirt to get the grangers fighting and running each other off the cattle range.

There were two Germans killed on Kid Creek, but I never learned the particulars. Josh Daniels was nearly hanged by a Vigilante group, but like old man Fowler, someone showed up to save his hide by telling the Vigilantes how much his family needed him. Ben and Bob Cavius stopped another Vigilante lynching on Mexico Creek by that same mob we run into. Old Man Gilbert, a sheepman, was forced to clear out by threats against his life by both cowmen and the grangers. His boy, Mack, went back after a crippled ewe and some fool shot and killed the boy. Old Man Gilbert then returned to the Strip on a foray and searched out the fellow who shot his son and killed him. There were three others involved in killing the boy, but they cleared out when they learned his father was back in the Strip and on the prod.

D. S. Johns was a rancher east in the Strip. He fenced some rough land on his ranch and threw some cattle into that pasture. A granger passed through there one day and left his gate open. Christ Dobie, one of Johns' men, saw this and quirted the granger all the way back to the gate and made him close it. This granger was no coward, so he armed himself with a Winchester 45-70 and made it known he was going to kill Dobie on sight. Mr. Johns was a peaceful man, so he asked Christ to quit and leave the country so the feud could end on his range. So Dobie left, went to the Oklahoma lands as a sooner. Another granger, Ol Nelson, once got his dander up and ran half them Vigilantes in Beaver City out of the Strip before he finished. Then there was the Eldridges and the Johnsons who shot it out over pasture differences. Charlie Johnson was killed and Si Eldridge, too, both of them twenty-year-old boys. The Vigilantes ran both families out of the Strip and took their cattle. But the people got together and petitioned the Eldridges back. So the Vigilantes lost that round.

Bill Bridgeford was a gambler, and a wild one. He was shot at Neutral City the summer of '86 by Buck Davis. Charlie Rocknole, or Rockford, a bartender, was also wounded in this shoot-out; and a boy, Boone, was badly cut up when leaving: he ran his horse into a barbed wire fence in the dark. Doc Douglas, a YL cowboy I knew, was hit in the arm.

Up north of Neutral City this same fellow, Rocknole, later killed Frank Vanderlip after Frank had gone with the Vigilantes to hang Rocknole for fighting with a neighbor, Bender. They rode up on Rocknole's soddy, ordered him to come out. He refused. Vanderlip then crawled on top of the soddy and soaked the frame roof with some kerosene, fixing to burn him out. Vanderlip made one mistake—he let a piece of himself show at a window for a split second when he dropped down from the roof. That peek was all

Rocknole, a dead shot, needed and he blasted Frank to Kingdom Come. The fire on the roof drove Rocknole out, and the Vigilantes shot him twice before he mounted his horse. But he got on and made his getaway. I knew him at Kiowa later, after all this happened.

There was a Mr. Carter hanged by the Vigilantes. Another old man, Kingston, was horsewhipped and run out. He had started a boom town, Fairview, south of Knoles, where he would sell whiskey. But it was a temperance area and some of them blue noses on the Vigilante Committee nearby gave him a beating. Word then came back from the Texas Panhandle that he was later murdered down there for his money.

Collier, a merchant at Alpine, shot a saloonkeeper there. His trial was held at Benton, in the Grove Hotel. Collier was freed. There was quite a bit of agitation about whiskey. Many of the people didn't want it sold, especially the grangers coming in who expected the Strip after 1886 to be dry, like Kansas. But most of us cowmen, and a few of the grangers, liked a sociable drink and didn't want to be penalized for a few drunkards who should have left the stuff alone, since they couldn't handle it at all. We didn't like drunkenness then any more than folks do now, but neither did we like the hypocritical way the Kansas people voted dry then drank wet at their drug stores. There was a lot of that bootlegging going on, and it made it hard to get a drink of good whiskey when we took the beef herds to Dodge in the fall. About the only town that didn't sell some sort of whiskey at some time was Slapout. But that place came by its name because the storekeeper there was always apologizing to his customers, "I'm sorry but we're slap-out of that." And it applied to about everything a person needed, flour, bacon, beans, sugar—and whiskey.

There were many other ruckuses in No Man's Land from 1880, when I got there, on up through the years. Chance Fish, or Fisk as he was called, Smith Ellis, and Charley and Lyman Parson once had a shoot-out. I have heard that Jim Chitwood was in it too, but I wasn't there at that time. The Chitwoods stole horses and caused a commotion for a while, but they were later run out by the Vigilantes. Then there was Bob Smith who disappeared on Mexico Creek. His saddle and gear showed up in Dodge. Charley Sebra, who had the saddle, claimed he bought it off a stranger. Charley got the name "Sugarfoot" out of the deal, for he said he only knew the stranger by that nickname. Charley was later sent to the pen for something or other, cattle theft, I believe. Yet he was a good cowboy, and when I knew him he worked for Bob Wright on the Quartercircle W and was as reliable as any man on the range.

It would be difficult for anyone to relate all the beatings, horse-whippings, lynchings, and shootings in that land. There were too many, though folks tried to minimize the violence when we were attempting to bring organized law to that region. Many shallow, unmarked graves have been dug in No Man's Land, the bones of which have showed up later with the buffalo skulls in heavy rain-storms when the land eroded away. So it was high time for some sort of Law to be welcomed into the Public Land Strip; and usually when a large enough body of Americans want something they find a way to get it. This was the way with the so-called "Organic Act" which I first heard about from old Judge Sutter's lips, the old whiskey-maker on Hog Creek whom I have referred to before.

About this time handbills began to show up in all those little towns in the eastern part of the Strip, announcing that Judge Hubbard, as he called himself, would address the citizens, including cattle company officers and owners, cowboys, settlers, and the businessmen of Benton. The roundup being over at that time, we could all be present for the occasion. I attended, and there was a large crowd to hear him that day. He spoke from the porch of the Grove Hotel, and we stood in the street, listening to him. I heard that address of his, and though he was an eloquent speaker, I could not digest all that he said. It was my first public meeting where a real lawyer, a trained talker, swayed the crowd like an organist controls that instrument by pulling and pushing on the various stops. I had heard that there were herds of these lawyer fellows in the cities, and I had been lucky this far in not having any of them either prosecuting me or defending me. But I realized that if I judged all lawyers by this man Sutter, I would give them all a bad name. For whatever had brought a man of his talents and fine appearance to No Man's Land, I knew it could be nothing trivial.

44

The "Judge" began his talk by telling of a distant "some place" which he never mentioned by any other name, where "cattle barons sought to exterminate the new settlers." Them grangers, he said, introduced to that land what he called an "Organic Act" for their own protection. They called for an election of officers, the same as they did in all states of the Union. The Judge talked at length about this Act, not much of which I, or the others, understood very well. From what he said, it was a new way by which we could initiate Law and Order into the Strip. We liked that.

In concluding his oratory, the Judge asked, "Where are these eastern cattle barons who were invited to attend this meeting? They do not live here. It is not their purpose to make a good life for their families here on these plains. Those foreign people have always contested our republican form of government. It is not their plan to work toward democracy. Why, these English cattle companies have no more legal right to this land we stand upon than any other foreigner—a Chinaman, say, from Hong Kong! They are here to make profits only!"

This was pretty heady stuff for us cowboys and grangers to listen to. Now I had come to this land as a boy of fourteen to work for this English company, the YL, or Cattle Ranche and Land Company, as it was known. I had been taught the work of a cowboy by their top foreman and range boss, Alex Young, and he had always treated me right. So I was not anti-cattle companies, and neither was I ag'in the grangers. So such talk as the Judge made didn't set too well with me. Yet I, like the others, could not help but be impressed by his strong argument for Law and Order. We all knew that we needed it. So as the Judge made them speeches all over No Man's Land he created such a movement for this Organic Law which he talked so elegantly about that we all began to sort of accept it. In order to have government, he said, we must create our own. This sounded right, even to me. But he was so bitter against the cattlemen that I knew I could never go along with him. For I knew we would have to make some sort of compromise if the grangers and the cattlemen lived in peace together, in spite of all of Judge Hubbard's big talk.[1]

chapter IV

1886-1890

ELECTION • CIMARRON TERRITORY • SHERIFF HERRON

One evening as four of us were riding back to the ranch from Benton, all liquored up a bit, we saw several covered wagons, drawn with horse and mule teams, coming up the River Trail. Many such wagon trains were heading for western Kansas and Colorado at that time, for this was about 1885 or '86, and the land boom was on in full blast in that area. As we watched, one wagon, followed by a lighter rig, turned off the main trail, like they might be looking for a night camp, or a place to squat. One of our boys, about fifteen, who didn't have any use for grangers, rode ahead to see why the wagon had quit the trail right on our range. It was rough country along them ravines on the north side of the Beaver, and when the rest of us came down to where the other boy had intercepted the granger's wagon we rode alongside. The man and his wife and two small girls were in the larger Studebaker wagon with a jet top over them. In the smaller spring wagon, which also had a little canvas top rigged over it, sat a very lovely young girl, dressed in a pink gingham frock and wearing a pink sunbonnet. Beside her sat a small, wide-eyed boy, her brother. Our young friend, who was "going to give that granger a piece of my mind," sat alongside the spring wagon looking goose-eyed and silly.

I rode up to the old man's wagon, tipped my hat to his missus, and asked if we could be of any help to them. He told me his name was A. K. Goddard, and he introduced his wife, his daughter May, and son John, in the little rig, and the two little girls on his wagon, Belle and Bertha. May was certainly a beautiful child, about twelve or thirteen years old, and we boys surely gawked at her. His wagon was heavily loaded, and he was stuck in the sand. He asked if we could help him get out.

We all took down our ropes, tied on to the wagon tongue and the front axle. Mr. Goddard urged the team on again, and with our help we broke the wagon loose from the sand and got it on top of a low-lying hill with hard sod, north of the river. The girl's team made it on their own, though I secretly hoped her rig would stick, too, so we could rescue her. But no such luck.

We visited with the Goddard family for a while, and the old gentleman told us that he was looking for a place to settle and bring out some cattle he had in Arkansas. He liked that area there near the river.

"We've been almost everywhere within fifty miles of here," he said, "but there's Indians one place, rustlers another, dry salt lakes, or mean cattlemen on the rest of the land. We've just about exhausted our supplies and have nothing yet in sight."

Mrs. Goddard looked dejected, and I could see the family was about done in from traveling, fighting dust, heat, and bad trails. There was a place I had picked out for my own ranch while on a roundup two years earlier. It was at a bend in the river where some hardwood trees grew near a good spring. The river bend had caught the silt and good soil that had washed down in the old floods and there was at least fifty acres there that could be irrigated with river water. I had sort of kept it in the back of my mind, but now that there was someone who had immediate need for a home I pointed it out to Mr. Goddard. Then I led him down into the river bottom on an old buffalo trail that was hard-packed after centuries of use. We could see the grass was real green down there and when we came to the spring it was flowing good water at quite a good capacity.

"Does anyone claim this land?" Mr. Goddard asked at once when he had seen the spring and surrounding land.

"Yes," I answered truthfully, "it's on cattle range, and the cowmen who use it will probably tell you to get off. But this is actually U.S. Government land, and the Government, I am told, has recognized squatter's rights. So if you tell the cattlemen this, and tell them you are determined to live here and be a good neighbor, there's nothing they can do legally to make you move.

But my advice is to try and live and let live, for there's already too much violence in this Strip. To do this you will have to fence your crop land, for cattle feed all over this range, and they must get down here to the river to water. You can't stop them from that."

"Could I fence this spring, to use for my family's water," he asked me.

"Yes," I told him, "but don't molest the cattle when they come to the river to drink."

The Goddards were grateful for our help and most happy to locate such a good place on the Beaver River. I felt like I had lost the place when I rode back to the ranch, and actually I was never able afterward to locate such a good place for myself. But that good couple, those three nice little girls in their gingham frocks, and the round-eyed boy always came to my mind when I thought of that pet location of mine; I was later to become mighty well acquainted with that fine family.

That year when the fall roundup came was a pleasant time for me. I had enjoyed being Healy's foreman, and had earned the goodwill of the range men. Healy Brothers were beginning to breed up their stock and acquire better bulls and stocker cattle. But there were still lots of long horned cattle and my, they were wild ones to work with! I was always a coward about wild cattle when I was afoot, as most range men were, for those Longhorn bulls, or a choused up cow, would worry even a man on horseback.

One fellow, William Evans, a Baptist preacher of Richfield, over across the western Kansas line, was loaned a longhorn cow to furnish milk for his family. He decided, with the owner's permission, to de-horn the cow, to render her less dangerous. He tied the cow to a loaded freight wagon and started to saw off a horn. That cow fought like a tiger and caught the preacher in the neck with a horn before he could get one sawed off. He bled to death. I learned of another fellow who tied a Longhorn cow down and tried to chop off a horn with an axe. The first lick the axe bounced back and struck him in the forehead. When he regained consciousness he told his boys to untie the cow and forget about dehorning her. Those brittle old horns didn't come off a live cow very easily!

When we returned from the fall roundup we found that the election under the Organic Act had already been called to create what they said would be called Cimarron Territory. This would be the whole Neutral Strip. The election was to be held February 22, 1887. The folks up the river at Beaver City were deciding most things at that time, so the bosses and us cowboys got together and talked over the situation. We did not approve the tactics of Sutter and his Vigilantes nor the Vigilantes at Beaver City, but we all agreed that something should be done to bring us Law and Order.

Now I knew less than nothing about politics or civil government; didn't even know whether I was a Democrat or a Republican. I did recall that my father was a staunch Democrat, so I figured that must be what I was. And, after all, that is the way most people select a political party to affiliate with. Since nobody else knew any more than I did about elections and voting we decided to get some advice from someone who did, that is besides Judge Hubbard and old Doc Chase at Beaver City. They appointed me to go over and talk to John Savage, the storekeeper at Benton who was well-respected as a businessman and who also ran the A Dot cattle brand. We thought he would know how to approach the political fires that were starting without getting scorched.

"John," I greeted him, laying my cards face up on his counter, "we want to know how to hold a proper election and to learn if this Judge Hubbard and his people are the sort who should represent us in this political roundup. Most of us don't like his notions, but we don't know what to do."

Mr. Savage first explained to me that this "organic law" that Judge Hubbard was proposing would have to fall. "Such a law has no foundation to support it," he said. "To establish a system of Law and Order, Jim, you must have some precedent, and this so-called 'organic law' proposed by Judge Hubbard will not stand by itself as a legal instrument. This land is U. S. Government land. Any laws that are established here will have to conform within the system of American law, not what Judge Hubbard and others think is law by their terms. Now, if the grangers who are hostile to the cattle interests carry this election, it may lead from what is already bad to something worse. Inasmuch as the more evenly balanced settlers who have come here to make their homes, not just speculate on land values as Judge Hubbard and others have done, are already friendly to the cattlemen, you folks should think about putting up your own political ticket."

I pondered that one for a minute, then asked, "But who in hell among us knows enough about politics to run for an office, much less fill it if we won?"

"Put up your most level-headed cattlemen, cowboys, and settlers," John answered, "men who are ready to adjust their differences and not look for things to quarrel about. This will make you a strong political ticket among both settlers and cowmen. And I feel certain that businessmen like myself will support you."

That was good advice. Mr. Savage had been a Justice of the Peace before coming to No Man's Land and through his guidance I began to see what politics should mean there in the Strip, the representation of *all* the people living there, not just one class or group. We held several get-togethers there at the ranches and two meetings at the Groves Hotel in Benton, and I relayed John Savage's thoughts to the people. At each meeting there was agreement that we should meet this threat to our unity as cowmen and grangers by making up our own ticket. A Committee was appointed to draft a slate of candidates. The Committee named John Savage for Judge; Ansel Groves, who ran the hotel, for Clerk of the Court; and other offices that I cannot readily recall, though I remember campaigning with Tom Judy, so he was undoubtedly a candidate for some office. I was named to run for Sheriff.

Tom Judy and I took a two-week buckboard trip through the Strip and delivered ballot boxes to various polling places. I did most of my politicking shaking hands and calling on the ranchers of the west end of the Strip, for I was no speaker. I had much to learn about politics and about getting voters to support me. In politics you will find that if you ever pushed a little

50

chicken into the creek or showed a blind tumble-bug the wrong road home, your opponent will tell all the voters about it and even enlarge upon your crimes. As I campaigned, I knew that some of the big cattle outfits had already left the Strip and that while I could have been certain of their votes, being a cowman myself, I couldn't count on the grangers' votes. At this time about seventy-five percent of the voters would be grangers, and a lot of them ex-Union soldiers.

I was a Democrat candidate. My opponent was an ex-soldier of the Union Army, and he rode all over the country with the Stars and Stripes draped over his buggy seat and the American flag fluttering from its shaft which was stuck into his whip socket. He told people I was a Texas man, a Confederate, and that the cattle companies had raised and groomed me for this one political job.

But I had friends, too. Mr. Goddard, the granger, campaigned for me. He told them, "I was stuck in the sandhills and Jim Herron and his cowboys came and pulled me out. I was without a home or land, and Jim showed me the very spot he had selected for his own ranch and invited me to live there. I don't give a tarnation what influence the cattlemen think they have with Jim Herron, for I'm still living on the good land he pointed out to me on his own cattle range. I was desperate and in need. He helped me. That's enough!" He was stretching the story for all it was worth, of course, but it won many grangers' votes for me.

The election went over with a bang for all people in the Strip. Our ticket won in our area. However, once the election was over, we were confronted with the real problem. Judge Savage carefully pointed out to us the same things he had said of Judge Hubbard's high-falutin' plans: namely, we had no precedent in law, no legal basis for the election, no place to turn now to qualify for our respective offices. Judge Savage had remained silent about this during the campaign, for he didn't want to discourage our voters from going to the polls and expressing their wishes in the matter. But now, he warned us, we must consider our every action, for though we were elected by popular vote of the people, the offices we held were actually illegal!

Here was a sobering thought. If Uncle Sam, at some later date, decided to inquire into our objectives and purposes, how could we explain away what we had done? How could we bring other men before the bar of justice, judge them, pass sentence on them, maybe imprison or execute them, and then be able to explain in legal terms to some higher court, possibly the Supreme Court, about our actions and show where we received our authority?

I didn't know just what to do. I had been elected Sheriff of Beaver County, which included all of the Public Land Strip we called "No Man's Land." It ran from the Cherokee Strip to New Mexico. There were approximately fifty villages there with a population that was judged at near 10,000 persons; it was as heavily populated at that time as it would be for many years to come, for after the Oklahoma Indian lands were thrown open for settlement, in 1889, a general exodus from the Strip followed.

In our elections Thomas B. Braidwood had been elected "Senator," but of course was not recognized when he went to Washington. Judge O. G. Chase of Beaver City, with a beard like an Angora goat, was named Representative to Congress from Cimarron Territory, and met the same fate as Braidwood in Washington. Judge Sutter-Hubbard was defeated, but a couple of years later popped up with the title of "Attorney General," proving that you can't keep a good lawyer out of public office.

In July of 1887 a group of dissidents met at Rothwell, up the river from Beaver City, and elected John Dale to represent them in Congress, seeing Judge Chase wasn't so popular in the nation's capital. Dale soon left for Washington and was about as welcome there as a coyote on the range at calving time. When Braidwood, Dale, and Chase all gave it up as a bad deal, one in which their fingers were not going to touch any of the money in the pot, old Judge Hubbard dealt himself a hand in the game. But nothing came of that, either.[1]

In spite of the failure of all of these men to personally capitalize on the creation of "Cimarron Territory," the attention of the nation was drawn to our peoples' need for permanent Law and Order in No Man's Land. We needed something more than law based on jawbone, the use of a distillery ridgepole, or the report of a shotgun or Winchester in the night. Our political campaigns, as badly as they were conducted, and as hopeless as was our case, were, at times, an education for the people in the democratic process. So I allow that our people there in the Strip did profit from our activities toward self-government, say what they may about it. I know I learned a lot about politics and about people while participating in that campaign. But I had a lot more to learn when I began to conduct my office as "Sheriff."

That following Christmas we had a big dance at Benton. When the dance was over, most of the boys went to the saloons where they played poker the rest of the night. About sunup that morning a man came riding into town, his horse lathered and breathing hard. He stopped at the saloon and asked for me. I went to the door and saw from his appearance that something mighty bad had happened, for he looked gray in the face and his nerve was shot. He told me his name was Broadhearst. He was a granger who lived a few miles out from town.

"I have just shot and killed Bill Maine," he told me. "Now you are Sheriff of Beaver County, so I came to ask your protection."

I knew of both Broadhearst and Maine. They were grangers, and I suppose good enough men, though I never learned anything about either of them later which would have earned them a commendation. Both of them had families. But I sure didn't want a murder case to deal with, even if I had been elected Sheriff. So I stalled.

"I haven't been legally qualified to act as your Sheriff," I told Broadhearst. "Besides, I know very little about the duties of a Sheriff, and further, I don't want to take sides in you grangers' quarrels."

"Well—what do you expect me to do?" Broadhearst begged me. "I just killed a man. Now I come to the only law we got around here to get justice."

"Look," I told him, "you better quit talking about 'justice' or you just might get it. Now listen to me: you got a good horse, and a head start on anyone that comes after you. Why don't you just get back on that horse and move on—fast—and show anyone who follows you a lot of new country."

"But I've got a family here," he argued. "If Bill Maine's friends overtake me they'll string me to the first wagon-tongue they come on to and ask questions later. There was fear written all over him. I talked with three or four boys inside the saloon who hadn't been drinking heavily. I told them that I presumed it was my duty to protect this boy and see that he got a fair trial, not to let another lynching take place. They all agreed, and offered to back my play. At one of the tables was a fellow we called "Dogie John," who was married to Bill Maine's sister. Being a brother-in-law of the slain man, I counseled with him to see what his position would be. I told him all I knew about the murder.

"See here, Jim," he answered me, "the only member of that family I am interested in is the girl I married. Besides, I'm busy in this here poker game, and winning at this time. You do what you think is right. I won't interfere."

I felt relieved that the one person who should be taking up the feud was more interested in the outcome of the poker game than in a brother-in-law's fate and was glad to have the other boys backing me. I went out and tied Broadhearst's horse to the hitchrack in front of the saloon and then took him to the Benton Hotel where all the ladies were staying after the dance of the night before. I set up a cot for him in the lobby, for we had no jail.

"If you go out on that street, or make any scrap with anyone else, I will have nothing more to do with your case," I warned him. "On the other hand, I will not allow any reasonable number of grangers to come riding in here, exciting the ladies, and taking you out to hang you." I had no trouble keeping Broadhearst in the building.

By the time I returned to the saloon, a posse of settlers came riding down the main street. They saw Broadhearst's horse tied before the saloon and went inside. When I entered, they all turned to me, asking where Broadhearst was and telling me how he had murdered Bill Maine in cold blood and they were there to string him up for his crime. I heard them out. Then I told them I wanted to say a word or two.

"You boys all step up and have a drink on me," I said. "Then I want you to listen closely to what I say. I am holding a murderer in custody. He has admitted his crime, and is waiting to stand trial."

"Thanks, Sheriff," a couple of them busted in. "Now bring him out to us and we'll get the trial over in a few minutes."

I was amazed at their attitude, for these fellows had just recently held elections in their district, and had elected me Sheriff. I guess they now thought I was working for them.

"See here, you fellows," I said, "You are the ones who rigged up this new 'organic law,' or this kangaroo court idea here in the Strip. Now maybe none of you voted for me for Sheriff, but you all know who won. Since you wanted Law and Order so damned bad, you are going to be the first to have a taste of it. We have a new Judge here, too, John Savage. You all elected him to preside over your court affairs. So this man Broadhearst is going to get a fair trial before a jury of men selected from the likes of you. So don't start any funny business. Now enjoy yourselves in town, then get back to your homes, and leave the Law and Order business to them you elected to do it."

There was some grumbling, but most agreed that the man deserved "a fair trial before he is hanged." Since Judge Savage was out of town, they would have to wait, I told them. I slept rather poorly in what little time remained of that night, propped up in a chair in the lobby, my shotgun in my lap.

When Judge Savage opened the door of his store that following morning, I was there to greet him, leaving one of my boys to guard the prisoner. I related what had happened. The Judge shook his head slowly from side to side, and I could see he took this matter very seriously.

"I would like to try this case, Jim," he told me, "but I seriously doubt our right to do so. Further, do you feel that you can keep order in a court where all these friends of the deceased man will be waiting just to find retribution?"

I told him I could get plenty of men to help me.

55

"Yes, I know you will have help. But should you have to kill some other person or persons maintaining order we might be in one hell of a fix. Some day Uncle Sam will take over here in our lawless land. Then he will start asking questions. The first question he would ask us would be how come we chose to be so officious here?"

I assured the Judge that I would do everything in my power to avoid another murder. "I will ask all the cowboys at the KK, the YL, and the M Bar to ride in for the trial, then get them to stand behind me. That will discourage the grangers," I said.

"All right, Jim. We'll give Mr. Broadhearst a fair trial," the Judge said.

There was a little sod schoolhouse at Benton that was built by the people. This was to also serve as our court room. Judge Hubbard, the moonshiner, was appointed to serve as counsel for the prosecution. They sent to Ashland, Kansas, for a qualified lawyer to defend Broadhearst. When the court was called, Judge Savage asked all the spectators to leave their arms in the little vestibule, for only officers could carry arms in the court room. I had three deputies, which gave us an edge on any trouble-makers that should show up. I was instructed to maintain order in the court room, to see that no loud or boistrous language was used while the court was in session.

My deputies did not know any more about this sort of thing than I did, but they were willing to learn. One of them had been in the Strip but a short time. He had come to the Healy ranch looking for a job. He went by the name of Sam. I let him winter with us, then put him to work on spring roundup. Outside of that I knew nothing about him. It had actually never seemed reasonable to me that he was looking for work in the cattle business, but I had learned not to ask too many questions. The young fellow had taken a liking to me and was now anxious to help me out.

One day before the trial he said, "Jim, I'm pleased to help you keep the peace, just for the fun I get out of it. When I told you I would help you pull off this rough stuff for the amusement

I get out of it, I meant all that and then some. Now in case we have to fight these nesters, remember this: Use every effort to make it appear that they drew first, that we drew only to protect ourselves. Make it self-defense. That puts all the blame on them. Even if they just bat an eye and we kill them for it, that's self-defense, according to law."

I had to caution this boy, and tell him that was not what was meant by keeping the peace. "Some day Uncle Sam may throw a big loop over the whole country here. There will be real law then to replace this organic stuff. When that roundup comes, we'll be asked to explain how we acted to keep the peace. So don't start any rough stuff. Just tip-toe around with me until this damned trial is over with." The boy didn't like the idea, but agreed to go along with it just to help me.

Plenty of grangers and cowmen came to this trial. There were many, like myself, who had never heard a witness testify under oath. But there seemed to be others who knew all about murder trials, some, I think, who had fled other places to avoid any more contacts with juries and judges!

Two days were used up selecting a jury. Some jurors knew too much, some too little. A few wouldn't have anything to do with the trial, just wanted to watch and be entertained by it. When one lawyer liked a juror, another didn't and scratched his name off the list. By the time the list was about exhausted, a jury had been picked. Both lawyers then got up and explained the case to the jury.

This Judge Hubbard—or Sutter—was an eloquent cuss, and his account of the murder was most convincing. It didn't take long to see he had been in many courtrooms and knew his way around. He told in detail just how the murder had occurred, as though he had been present at the time. When he was through I would have voted a conviction myself.

Then the defense lawyer stated his side of the case. Though he was not so positive in his approach, he began to toss so much dust on the trail that the jury could hardly follow the herd. Not many in the Strip really liked Judge Hubbard, and it wasn't long until the defense lawyer had put Judge Hubbard on trial, and the jury began to want to vote against the prosecution, rather than against the man who did the killing. At this time my sympathies began to run pretty much for Broadhearst.

Then they called a lot more witnesses and both lawyers talked a lot. The defense lawyer made some clear gains with me when he jumped on the jury. "There are some of you people, like the learned Judge Hubbard here, who came to No Man's Land because you could not, or were afraid to, raise hell in the United States of America. Some of you have been run out of the States. It is too bad your people have so few worthy men down here, men like Mr. Broadhearst, who could put the fear of God into you. It would be better for all concerned." Everybody in the court liked that.

Broadhearst was painted as a "good, decent, God-fearing man who puts the welfare of others ahead of his own. He is a man given to prayer and meditation, and to the principle of saving other men from themselves." Well, the only times those who knew Broadhearst ever heard him speak of God was when he would say "God damn!"

I couldn't fancy a man talking to a jury like that, but I suspected that he was trying to make the jurymen feel a kinship with the accused man. I personally knew two or three men on that jury who had come riding down the Owl Hoot Trail to No Man's Land and who had become good citizens there. I also knew two others on the jury who were psalm-singing hypocrites, so I presumed the God part of his speech was intended to rope them in.

None of the witnesses had actually seen the murder so there was a lot of objections made by both lawyers to this and that. The trial ran six or seven days in that little school building. The main evidence finally led to one conclusion: Broadhearst had killed Maine. It seemed that the two men lived neighbors and had families on adjoining claims. The two men were too tough and violent to live peacefully, side by side. They had quarreled about livestock and other things.

Mr. Maine, on the morning of his death, had gone on foot to

58

bring in his milk cows. As he passed Broadhearst's barn, Broadhearst stepped from the building and mowed him down with a shotgun. The lawyers tried to introduce a lot of background talk about the previous difficulties, and the defense attorney did manage to get some facts across, though it was "stricken from the record." These facts were that a cow, on a previous morning, had returned to Broadhearst's barn with a pitchfork belonging to Maine stuck in her back. The cow had been grazing in Maine's pasture. This act had angered Broadhearst until he decided to kill Maine. What should have been discussed in a neighborly manner, or at least left to the decision of other neighbors, had brought tragedy to both families.

After the final pleas were made to the jury, Judge Savage instructed me to remove the prisoner from the courtroom and take him back to the hotel to await the verdict. Then he instructed the jury and left them in possession of the sod school building until they reached their verdict. It took the jury about an hour to reach a decision, then they rang the school bell to call the Judge back to hear it. I took Broadhearst back to the building, which was now jammed to the vestibule with a crowd outside.

The clerk read the verdict which said, "We, the jury empaneled . . ." and a lot more stuff, and wound up saying they had found the prisoner "guilty as charged." This meant a legal hanging.

In event of a conviction, Judge Savage had instructed me what to say before the court. This was to the effect that I wanted to tender my resignation as Sheriff of No Man's Land. But of course I had forgotten all of my speech except to tell them I was resigning the office. I mentioned that I had acted in that capacity for some time but without any legal authority and at the risk of my neck, all without any substantial financial remuneration. I concluded by telling them, "If my actions as Sheriff have in any way helped to civilize some of you people, it was worth my taking the chance." This last brought whoops and hollers from the men.

It was the nature of these people in the Strip to take a real hiding about their characters with humor and good sense. For them that didn't deserve it knew that most of us did, so we all went along with such jokes just for a laugh.

Judge Savage then addressed the courtroom. Since No Man's Land had no jails, he said, and Beaver City, the largest town in the Strip had been able to afford only a steer hide under which their prisoners were pegged down for brief periods, weather permitting, Benton could be excused for inflicting the death penalty for murder and thereby relieving the county of the trouble and cost of building a jail. "However," the Judge continued, after the shock of his words had worn off, "this court is in no legal position to inflict the death penalty upon any man, even one convicted of a murder charge. Consequently, I feel that my resignation is also in order at this time, and I herewith tender it to the people as of this day."

The unexpectedness of both their Sheriff's and their Judge's resignations threw the people into a state of excitement. Broadhearst, sitting beside me, now pleaded, "For God's sake, Jim, don't turn me loose here or they'll hang me for sure." The court was adjourned, and I took the prisoner back to the Benton Hotel with me, the pack of grangers from his neighborhood following on my heels like a wolf pack ready for the kill and all grumbling and growling.

This sudden and complete collapse of our "organic law" now placed me in the position of having no right either in law or outside the law of defending the prisoner from the lynch mob. That talk had already started. I didn't want to bear the responsibility for Broadhearst's safety, but neither did I want to see the mob hang him while he was in my care. But fate has a pleasant way of sometimes taking care of unpleasant matters and removing them from one's hands. The following morning Broadhearst did not appear for breakfast at the hotel. During the night he had vamoosed. Soon afterward his family left No Man's Land to join him.

Several years later when I happened to be walking down the street in Kingfisher, Oklahoma, I heard a voice call my name. I turned to see Mr. Broadhearst approaching me, holding out his hand. He was well-dressed in a dark business suit, wearing shiny black boots and a good, soft western hat.

"Remember me, Jim?" he asked.

"How in hell do you ever think I could forget you," I laughed, shaking his paw.

"Jim," he said, "that trial in No Man's Land made a Christian out of me. When I left the hotel that night I rode to Kansas on a stolen horse at a high run and never slowed down until I crossed the line. But I left the horse with a man with instructions to return him to his rightful owner. Then I joined up with Captain Payne and Pawnee Bill and waited for the opening of the Unassigned Lands, later got myself a good place here in Kingfisher. I'm getting along fine."

Mr. Broadhearst invited me to take supper with him at his home, but I told him it was impossible as I was leaving that evening.

"I have one more favor to ask of you, Jim," he said. "You are the only person who can help me. The U.S. Marshal has had me before the U.S. Commissioner because of that trouble with Bill Maine. Anything you can say in my behalf now before him will surely be appreciated and a great help to me."

During his trial in Benton I had become very well acquainted with Broadhearst. He was not really a bad man at heart, but when he saw his cow, upon which his family depended for milk, with that pitchfork driven into its back, he could not control himself. He decided then and there to kill Maine for doing such a cruel thing to a dumb animal. Knowing his better side, I told Broadhearst I would stay over until the following day and say a few things before the Commissioner.

Broadhearst arranged an appointment for me to talk with the Commissioner and I made my appearance the following day. I was questioned at length about my part in the "trial" of Broadhearst, and I explained, as best I could, of our attempt to establish "organic law" in that land, and how we had failed because of legal precedent and the lack of proper authority. The Commissioner was interested, but asked that I tell him why I had accepted the office of Sheriff.

"Mr. Commissioner," I said, "I knew when I was acting as Sheriff of No Man's Land that I lacked the legal right to that office. Mr. John Savage had made that clear to me and that is what brought about our resignations when we faced the fact that we could not properly bring criminals to trial and pass judgment on them. That is also why Mr. Broadhearst escaped with his life. But we who were elected to office at that time hoped that it would restore peace and order to the Strip, which it did, in part, simply by our presence as elected officials. Now, it was impossible to bring Bill Maine back to life. And Mr. Broadhearst, too, had a family dependent upon him, so we all felt he deserved a fair trial. We brought about the trial to save him from the lynch mob."

The Commissioner had listened patiently to me, then he asked, "What sort of a man do you judge Mr. Broadhearst to be?"

"Well, at the time of the murder, both Broadhearst and the man he killed, Maine, were sorry sights," I volunteered. "But today Mr. Broadhearst is raising a good, law-abiding family and he is a good citizen. He has helped build up this section of the country and I feel that he has a promising future. In any decision that is made about him, I believe it is well to consider the lawlessness that has marked the settlement of this whole southwestern country."

The Commissioner must have agreed with me, for he removed the charge against Broadhearst and never bothered him again.

While talking with the Commissioner I had learned that they performed somewhat like a Justice of the Peace. They simply investigated cases where the matter of jurisdiction was doubtful and if they found sufficient evidence to warrant a prosecution, then they turned the case over to some Federal Court. In them days when no court wanted to have jurisdiction over No Man's Land, I suppose that Commissioner was happy to end Broadhearst's trouble.

There were many crimes committed, and many dramatic and interesting events during those lawless years. A book could be filled with them. That condition changed only when Congress, during the administration of President Benjamin Harrison, on May 2, 1890, annexed the Neutral or Public Land Strip (No

Man's Land) to the new Oklahoma Territory. The Strip then became the Territory's seventh county. Later, when the Territorial Legislature met at Guthrie, the entire Strip became Beaver County, and remained under that name until Oklahoma's admission to the Union as a sovereign State, on November 16, 1907.

When this newly created Oklahoma Territory held its first election, in August 1890, I filed for Sheriff of No Man's Land and was again elected, legally this time. George Healy was one of my bondsmen. We newly elected officers took our oaths of office January 1, 1891.[2]

When Judge Burford came to open court at Beaver City, he brought Chris Madsen, the Deputy U.S. Marshal, with him to keep the peace. We held court in Beaver City at that time above a saloon, and when some tough nut down in the saloon decided he might take over the Judge's functions, Judge Burford would send Chris down to stop the noise and restore order in the saloon. On one occasion there proved to be three really rough troublemakers and Madsen, after a brief scuffle over one of the men's guns, shot one fellow through the hand and beat the others over the head with his gun barrel. He then marched the three culprits upstairs to Burford's court.

"Jedge," he reported to the court, "Yo rebellion is oveh now. What disposition should I make of these prisoners?"

Watching Chris Madsen and some of those other U.S. Marshals and their deputies taught me two valuable things any officer must learn: First, if you really have to act, act fast and decisively. Second, most men can be persuaded to behave themselves if you use a friendly smile and a little kindly talk. Not long after this I was myself appointed a Deputy U.S. Marshal and helped Chris and others keep peace in the Strip.[3] My travels took me the length and breadth of the land and I became well-acquainted with new settlers and all the old cattlemen in the western end that I had never met before.

Being Sheriff and Deputy Marshal put a lot of responsibility on my shoulders. It wasn't like being a ranch foreman, for I grew up on the cattle range and knew every angle of the trade. This law and police business was all new to me. Like the first time I was asked by the District Court Judge to open the court for him. We were all standing there before his desk, the crowd in the sod building was noisy and shuffling chairs and benches around to accommodate them for seats. The judge suddenly turned to me.

"Mr. Sheriff, you may open the court," he said, taking his seat.

I moved over closer to him and whispered, "I don't know just what you say or do to open a court, Judge." He just smiled up at me and wiped off his spectacles.

"Do you have a gun on your person, Mr. Sheriff?" he asked.

"Yes," I answered, patting my six-shooter which hung in a holster at my hip.

"Then take your gun, go to the front door and fire a few shots into the air," the Judge said. "Just be careful not to hit anyone. From the noise, the townsfolk will know that something's going to happen here—and maybe they will quiet down."

chapter V

CATTLE BUSINESS IN THE STRIP
DAILY LIFE IN THE STRIP • HERRON'S MARRIAGE
RODEO • BLIZZARD OF '88

In order to tell all this law business, and about the court trials, I have had to run ahead of my story. But I would like to tell more about the people of that area and about the range cattle business there, and the reasons for its downfall, for I have not seen much written about that country.

Through those thirteen years I was in the Strip, from 1880 to 1893, the cattlemen generally enjoyed success if you will except two periods of storms, the storms of 1885-86 and the Blizzard of '88 when they lost many cattle. The land was free, there was good grass most years, and we had a well-watered range. Cattle prices were up and the grangers were raising good crops of corn, castor beans, and sorghum by 1885-86. We had a dry year in 1887, and there was a money panic, but our people were not greatly affected, for we had little money anyway. The killing of cattle by grangers eventually led to cattlemen killing a beef on Saturdays and sharing it with their nearest granger families. That ended the indiscriminate and unauthorized slaughter of beef cattle on the range. In 1888-89 we had good years, but in 1890-91 the grass was short. Many cattle were sold to the settlers on long terms, as low as $9 a head, and this often incuded cows with calves at their side.

None of the big cattle companies had bought land in the early years, for no land there could be bought or sold legally. Neither did they pay taxes on it, nor on the cattle they held there in the Strip. Their only expenses were for horses and equipment, for food for their men, and for their wages, about $30 a month for good hands. A company that held 40,000-50,000 head of cattle would employ thirty to forty cowboys in busy seasons. Some of those big companies made money so fast in the earlier years that they began to get the idea that they owned the land and everything on it, and that their cowboys had the job of holding the property for them.

One of the sillier rules that was passed by The Association forbade grangers, who might own a few head of cattle on the range, from working with the wagons of Association members. This created ill-feeling between the two groups[1]. There was one granger family located on the Cimarron that had brought in about 400 head of Arkansas cattle. These cattle were soon scattered all over the range. The family had two half-grown boys, fourteen and sixteen years of age. The younger of the two came to the Healy ranch and told me his father had sent him to work on the roundup. He asked if he could eat at our wagon. He stayed overnight with us and I learned that his brother had been allowed to work with the M Bar wagon by John Over, their ranch manager, who, though an Association member, was no stickler for all of their foolish rules and regulations.

The M Bar range adjoined Healy Brothers on the east. George Healy was a charter member of The Association, and he was all wrapped up in its affairs. But George was a good man, a fair man at heart, and he understood that we should maintain good relationships with the settlers for our own good. When John Over and I had put our own personal cattle on the Healy range and the M Bar range, George made no objection, and he told us that it would not bother their operations. So I was relieved when I asked George whether the boy should go with our wagon or not and he nodded his head.

That fall when we shipped the beef herd I went along with them, for I had two carloads of my own grassed-out steers on that train. Healy Brothers, John Over, and I all shipped to the same Commission House at Kansas City—Offett, Elmore & Cooper Company. I knew Frank Cooper, one of the executives, pretty well and he told me there were 400 head of big steers in the Texas Panhandle that I could buy worth the money. He even made me a loan, and I got possession of those steers.

That winter, when we returned from market, I spent quite

a bit of my time watching over these cattle on the range, and visiting in the town of Benton. It was beginning to be a lively little town. There were two saloons, one owned by Tom Parker, a friend of mine. George Healy always ordered his whiskey through him. John Dix operated a still near there, and since George wouldn't drink white whiskey because of its moonshine appearance, Tom thoughtfully boiled dried peaches, strained off the juice and mixed it with the white liquor to produce a beautiful, amber-colored and fancy-flavored drink with a sweet, cordial taste. Tom Parker didn't drink, but his brother Bill drank enough for both of them. Bill, George Healy, and I frequently tipped the jug together, and we were often joined by "Irish" McGovern, Jack Rhodes, Al Dixon, and other cowboys of that area who were all good friends. We didn't get hog-drunk, and none of us were alcoholics, just a bunch of young men out to enjoy life and have a good time.

In Benton, E. L. Gay was editor of the *Benton County Banner*, our first and only newspaper[1a]. He was a good man, intelligent and a fine writer, and he worked hard to make our town a leader in the area. My pal John (Irish) McGovern ran the livery stable for a while, when he tried to quit punching cows. He was the best bronc rider in the neighborhood, though to look him over you wouldn't guess he could ride out alone and bring in the milk cows. But he was all for fun. Old James (Medicine) Steadman, the father of Ben and Stella, was a town character who had earned his nickname when he prescribed some physic pills for a sick Indian a wandering tribe had left in Benton. Before leaving, the Indian's friends administered the entire package of pills Steadman had sold them, and the brave nearly died. After three days sitting in the sod john, back of Tom Parker's saloon, the brave left, following the trail of his friends. "White man heap run'em, stink'em, kill'em sick Injun," he told Tom, who had let him sleep in the saloon's bullpen. "Me go die with good Injun friends."

Belle Perkins was our first school ma'am, and she was highly respected by all in Benton. She was paid $1 a month per child, and taught a four-month term in the little sod schoolhouse. She had students who were growed men and women. At that time Healy Brothers had a middle-aged cowboy named Jack Larsman—some called him Landsman—who came from Texas. He was a lanky bronc rider who often rode the rough strings. Jack started riding into Benton and back to the ranch daily to learn to read and write. It was such a long ride that Healy couldn't get any work out of Jack, so he told him to stay in town during the school term and just return Saturdays and Sundays to the ranch for work. George even paid his board and room in town while he was learning, for George admired education and was himself reading law books to become a lawyer. So Jack stayed at the Benton Hotel and attended school with the children.

This arrangement worked fine. In just a term or two Jack learned to "read and write and cipher to the rule of three," as he once told me. But he was no good as a cowboy after that, for he wanted then to teach school. He left there not long afterward, and someone said he taught a school at the head of Palo Duro. But I never learned what happened to him.

Mr. and Mrs. Ansel Groves operated the Benton Hotel, and they had three charming daughters, Alice, Della, and Bertha. I had made the acquaintance of Miss Alice Groves during the trial of Broadhearst, for I stayed at the hotel, and now that I had some jingle in my pockets and good prospects ahead I began to think about marriage. So I paid much attention to Alice during that period and in the course of my courtship I made George Healy acquainted with Lydia Savage, the pretty daughter of Judge John Savage. When George and I had both been successful in persuading the girls to say Yes, we decided a double wedding would be the thing and set the date. For some reason or other George and Lydia decided to wait, but Alice and I went ahead with our plans and engaged a minister from Meade, Kansas, to come down to the Strip and tie the knot. I believe this must have been one of the first, if not the first wedding, in No Man's Land, in 1886.

A wedding in them days was an important event, and we invited practically everyone in the Strip and from north Texas to attend. And most of them came! Following the ceremony, we

68

had a dance every night and a feast every day for three days and nights. The Groves family kept the tables loaded with food; the men visited at the saloons at regular intervals to brighten themselves up. I saw to it that there was plenty of free liquor and beer to drink.

One old boy, Thunder Thompson, would often ride into Benton, get soused, and pay Mr. Gay for a subscription to his newspaper. Gay said Thunder did this so often that within a year he had his subscription paid up to the year 1996. Thunder failed to attend my wedding and I later asked him why. He told me, "That man Gay already has nineteen papers coming to my ranch every week, and damned if I want twenty!"

How different those dances were to these of today! The boys in them days enjoyed a drink just as they do now. But we never would have thought of taking the ladies into a bar or saloon with us, and they would have slapped the face of any boy suggesting such a thing. We bought cloves, and chewed parched coffee, to keep the girls—and particularly their Ma-mas—from knowing we had taken a drink! Yet if any cowboy or granger had tried to raise a disturbance in the room where we were dancing, we would have hog-tied him like a choused up steer to keep him silent.

Our wedding was a wonderful, a beautiful, and an unforgettable experience for both Alice and me. We had never known such attention before, and were flattered by it and our hearts warmed by these friendships so openly expressed during this time. It was also the only occasion at which I ever saw the mothers of babes give their children laudanum to make them sleep, then coffee, a few hours later to awaken them! Later, about 1890, George Healy and Lydia married, and we repeated the performance, but not on quite such a grand scale.

My wife proved to be all that any man can expect in a woman. She was a slim, lovely brunette with deep brown eyes and a creamy complexion, with soft skin and a most loving disposition. I had never courted a girl before, and had not Alice's parents, with great understanding of my shyness, made many meetings possible for the two of us and encouraged me in

69

every way to come and visit their daughter, I would never have won her attention, for I was but one of the many swains attracted to her.

The Groves family was from Indiana, and they were fine people. They not only cared for their own, but had taken a small orphan boy to raise. His name was Elery Cooper, and he later was a printer and also taught school on the Coldwater, where he had to whip several of the toughest young fighters in the neighborhood to maintain control over his schoolroom. For Elery wouldn't tolerate any foolishness where he taught. Once he had trouble with two male parents who upheld their sons in their orneriness. Elery just took off his coat and vest, laid them on a desk and told the two fathers, "If I have to discipline fathers, too, we may as well begin right here. Which of you two wants to be first?" That ended the matter, for neither parent wanted to test Elery's mettle that day. Elery later started up the *Santa Rosa Star*, a newspaper in Santa Rosa, New Mexico, when the Rock Island Railroad built down through there in 1903. He earned a reputation there of being a "fighting editor."[2]

In the first few weeks following our marriage, I divided my time between the Healy ranch, where I worked, and the Benton Hotel, where Alice and I first stayed, for we had not yet decided where we would live. During these weeks George Healy and I had some heart-to-heart talks about the cattle business, and especially about my way of looking at it.

At that time in the cow country there was a custom which we cowboys called "playing even." It was a range rule that was fair enough for all owners concerned, and it helped keep down trouble over cattle. It worked this way: If you were a range foreman, as I was for the Healy spread, or were a ranch manager for a cattle company, and happened to get more mavericks —unbranded cattle—than really belonged to your outfit, you were considered to be just working honestly for your company, not stealing. That is, you were "playing even," as we called it. For the next time it was the natural run-of-luck that some other company would get and take the advantage. Seldom, if ever, would a range foreman or manager ever be questioned by officers of any other ranch or company for having extra calves or other cattle in his gather.

Likewise, if you sent one of your boys out to cut out a fat beef for the ranch table, that boy would never bring up, rope, or butcher an animal bearing his own ranch brand. He would look first for a maverick, and then probably settle for a beef wearing a neighboring ranch brand. Now that, too, was not considered stealing, or dishonest, for everyone did it. If you didn't do it, you would not be "playing even" for your employer, for you would be eating your own beef while everyone else was eating it, too. In them days if you wanted your own beef to eat, you took dinner at a neighbor's!

There was another simple expression that we all used on the range which I have never read about. We called it "getting some good stuff." This meant adding cattle to your own herd through some hook or crook that may not have looked very ethical but was not considered illegal. To "get some good stuff" you might buy when another man was selling because of drought on his range. Or you might catch a cattleman where the hair was short in a poker game and get some of his stock. Or a few head of trail cattle that could not keep up with a herd might be dropped off near your range, and you would just slap your brand on them. Oh, there were many ways of "getting some good stuff," and a man acted when opportunity knocked at his door. Many cowmen started in the business that way, and all the old Texas cowmen got theirs in the early-day cow-hunts when the Longhorns were running loose in the brush and thickets of Texas and wore no man's brand. A man soon learned that it was easier to "get some good stuff" than it was to wait nearly a year for a cow to have a calf.

Them big herds that came up the Western Trail and the Tuttle Trail from Texas made it possible for me to build up a small herd of she-stock from those little yearlings and leppies that got so footsore on the trail they couldn't walk any more. We called them "limpies" and "lamies." Some of the trail cattle that scoured bad and weakened also had to be left along the trail. There was a rule among the trail drivers that they would pick up the strays that got able to travel that had been dropped by earlier herds passing along. They then tallied them, shipped them, and settled with the former owners when they could find them. And they were pretty good about that, too. But we ranchers and cowboys *who lived near the cattle trails* soon learned that drovers would pick up our cattle from the range and make no tally of them and not effect any settlement whatever when the herd was sold. So we just did the same, and made their drop-off cattle feel right at home on our range, wearing *our* brands! This was some of the cattle we called "good stuff." For they cost nothing to raise, and you didn't even have to own a cow to get a calf. Likewise, the cattle that drifted in the storms on to our range became "good stuff" for us, if their reps didn't come down there and claim them.

The fact that I had acquired cattle this way, and the presence of the 400 head I had bought and which The Association members didn't know I had paid for, all running together on the Healy Brothers and M Bar range, made my views different from The Association members. I also was partial to the grangers, for I was under the influence of several granger families and married into one family. Though my background was all employment by cattlemen, The Association brought pressure on George Healy to get rid of me.

As I have previously said, and shall repeat, George Healy was a good and fair man, but he was under the influence of The Association members. One day when we had been talking about the two positions we held, George told me of the pressure that was being put on him by those men. He assured me that he would never fire me to please other cattlemen, so long as I did a good job for him, and that we would continue as good friends, come what would. I confided in George at that time that I felt the same friendship for him, but that I did not want to be the cause of criticism of him by other cattlemen. I had not done anything, I said, that the most respected cattleman in the organization had not done time after time—that is to "play even" and to watch out for some "good stuff" and my own best

Benton, Oklahoma Territory Dudes, 1891

Al Dixon

Jim Herron

F. M. (Jack) Rhodes

John (Irish) McGovern

Irish McGovern   Jack Rhodes

The type of Longhorns Jim Herron dealt with most of his life. Jim, aged fourteen, helped drive them north along the Texas Cattle Trail. Years later he himself shipped similar Longhorns to supply Indians of the Cheyenne and Rosebud Reservations in South Dakota, and was charged with cattle theft.

Boys of Jim Herron's age (twelve to fourteen) rode with the men in early days of cattle business in No Man's Land, 1880-1885. Note lad (center right, between two men) picking out his horse from *remuda* for the wrangler to rope.

Chuckwagons and roundup men at noon meal, southwest Kansas, about 1889.

The JJ outfit on the Cimarron roundup.

Cowboys of George Littlefield's LIT Ranch at roundup on the Canadian River in the Texas Panhandle. These men rode roundups with Jim Herron.

The *remuda* of the JJ outfit on the roundup, near Arkalon, Kansas about 1887-90. Note cattle train at left rear.

Hardesty Brothers Quartercircle S outfit in No Man's Land.

On the roundup in 1887. Jim Herron and his comrades of the saddle are shown here in the vicinity of Beaver City, No Man's Land.

"Sandhill" Johnson, who lived in the hills near Fargo Springs, Kansas, was one of the last of the bonehaulers, the bones being shipped from Liberal, Kansas in 1888-89. Here the hauler had a load of buffalo skulls, no doubt bringing them in to sell the horns which were prized for making knife handles.

The Mills and Garvey Saloon, Beaver City, No Man's Land, about 1887. Ban Kinder, Beaver pioneer, is the bartender.

Cimarron cowboys, October 22, 1887. "Red Alex" Foltz (left) and Sam McLane. Foltz was later a foreman for the Crooked L Ranch on Crooked Creek, Meade County, Kansas.

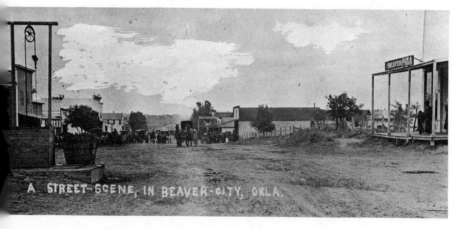

A STREET-SCENE, IN BEAVER-CITY, OKLA.

Towns such as Beaver City (above) and Benton sprang up all over No Man's Land in the period 1885-1900. Some were sod towns, the better ones "frame towns." Note the town well at left.

Beaver City residents, about 1887. Joe Hodge, the postmaster and general store operator, is shown in front of his place of business with other members of the Beaver City Vigilantes.

Main street, Beaver City, No Man's Land, about 1890. The roundup chuck-wagon had pulled into town for supplies. Ox teams at right freighted on the Jones and Plummer Trail which ran through the town.

Sample front page (partial) of *The Territorial Advocate,* Beaver, Oklahoma Territory, March 18, 1891. Earlier, without adequate newspaper coverage to spread the word about their Organic Act and the deliberations surrounding it, the Cimarron Territorial Council decided, in January 1889, to "trust the publication of the proceedings to the ladies." We can only assume they relied upon Woman's timeless talent for gossip!

81

The old Fred Taintor ranchhouse, No Man's Land. Taintor ran thousands of head of cattle on Taintor Creek northeast of Beaver City, north of the Healy Brothers and the John Over Ranches, where Jim Herron worked.

Beer City, No Man's Land. This prairie haven of rest and relaxation for the cowboys of the Oklahoma and Texas Panhandles was called "The Sodom and Gommorah of the Plains." Lew Bush, the town Marshal, who was shot-gunned to death by Madam Pussy Cat Nell, sits next to the standing fiddler. Photo taken in front of The Elephant Saloon on June 25, 1888.

The "big soddy" at the Secoro Ranch, Beaver County, Oklahoma Territory.

Shade's Well in No Man's Land. Trail herds from New Mexico and north Texas were watered here before being put on the railroad cars at Tyrone in the Strip. The big well and the watering facilities were installed in 1889 under the authority of J. V. Shade, livestock agent for the Rock Island Railroad. Zachariah Cain managed the operation for many years.

83

Issuing cattle on the Rosebud Reservation, South Dakota. The steers would be released one at a time from the pens onto the open prairie, and the name of an Indian family called out. The family member would then run the animal down, kill it with bullets or arrows or knives, and skin it and dress it out right where it fell.

Main street, west side, Beaver, Oklahoma, about 1907-10. Bulick & Co., general merchandise store, at left. Beaver County Abstract building just to the right of horse and wagon. Jim Herron's old hotel building at far right.

Sample page (partial) from *The Beaver Advocate,* February 1893. Jim Herron's Beaver City Hotel, which he owned prior to his fleeing Oklahoma Territory, is advertised; as is the Osgood Hotel, where Jack Rhodes died after his unsuccessful escape attempt with Herron. Note also the advertisement by Dyke Ballinger, Ollie Dot's uncle, who helped raise her.

Jim Herron with his daughter, Ollie Dot, by his first wife, Alice Groves Herron. Photo taken about 1893, when Herron fled Oklahoma Territory for Arizona.

The United States of America.

To all to whom these presents shall come: Greeting:

Homestead Certificate No. 25

Application 201 } Whereas there has been deposited in the general Land Office of the United States a certificate of the Register of the Land Office at Beaver Oklahoma Territory whereby it appears that, pursuant to the Act of Congress approved 20th May 1862. "To secure Homesteads to Actual Settlers on the Public Domain", and the acts supplemental thereto, the claim of James Herron has been established and duly consummated, in conformity to law, for the South east quarter of the North west quarter: the west half of the North East quarter and the south east quarter of the North East quarter of section twenty eight, in Township four North of Range twenty six East of Cimarron Meridian in Oklahoma Territory, containing one hundred and sixty acres, according to the official Plat of the Survey of the said Land, returned to the General Land Office by the Surveyor General:

Now Know ye, That there is, therefore, granted by the United States unto the said James Herron the tract of 2 tract ... [margin text]

This indenture, made the 17th day of August in the year eighteen hundred and ninety three (1893) James Herron of the first part and John E. Orr of the second part. Witnesseth, that the said party of the first part in consideration of the sum of four hundred and fifty dollars ($450.00) lawful money of the United States paid by the party of the second part, doth hereby release and grant unto the said party of the second part, his heirs and assigns forever all his right, title, and interest in and to the following described real estate situated in Beaver County Oklahoma Territory to-wit: S.E. ¼ of N.W. ¼ and ½ of N.E. ¼ and S.E. ¼ of N.E. ¼ Sec. 28, Town. 4 N. Range 26 E. of C.M. Beaver Co. Okla. Ter. Together with the improvements and all the estate and right of the first part in and to said premises.

James Herron.

Territory of Oklahoma }
Beaver County } ss.

These instruments established Jim Herron's homestead claim and conveyed it on August 17, 1893, for $450, to John Over of the M Bar Ranch.

School group, Beaver City, Oklahoma Territory, 1894. Dot Herron, Jim Herron's daughter, is number 24 in the first row. She was then about seven years old.

Jack Rhodes (left) and Jim Herron (on Rhodes' right) walk, handcuffed together, across the street, followed first by under-Sheriff Dick Buis and next by Deputy Sheriff Sam Givler; during the trial at Meade, Kansas, September 1893.

interests. But rather than put him on the spot, I said, I would hand in my resignation. George accepted it, and he gave me the very best recommendation so I would find work with another company if I wished to do so. George and I remained friends ever afterward.

Since I had no work at Healy's after that, I spent more time in Benton with Alice and her folks, riding out every few days to look over my own cattle on the range. One day while I was in town, my attention was drawn to two covered wagons drawn up on the street, their drivers engaged in a furious mouth-fight. A crowd had gathered and I walked over to see what the trouble was about. After rubbering around the scene for a bit I learned that one man claimed that the other owed him $10. Though they were traveling together, and both had wives and children on the two wagons, the men appeared ready to settle their quarrel then and there, with force if need be.

Almost as soon as I had arrived at the wagonside, my friends in the crowd began pointing toward me and asking if I wasn't going to stop the ruckus. I was no longer a lawman, having resigned as Sheriff; this was in between my first term and my re-election in 1891, so I told them I had no authority to step into anyone's personal quarrels. But the two men's wives, upon learning I had been Sheriff, petitioned me to render some decision that would settle their husbands' dispute once and forever. So I finally agreed to act as arbitrator in the matter. But I insisted that each man pay me $2.50 for my advice and time. They agreed, dug down into their greasy purses, and pulled out the cash.

With the $5 in my hand I waved them to the saloon, where I would hold court. They climbed off their perches, the women walking at a distance behind the crowd as we trailed over to the saloon. Inside, I ordered drinks for all the men, paying for them with the money I had collected, and sending out soft drinks to the women and children on the street. When I paid the bill I found my fee short, and had to dig into my own pocket to pay the bill. Then I opened court.

I asked each man to tell me his side of the story. They did. I learned they were heading for the Cheyenne and Arapahoe country which they thought would be opened for settlement in a year or two. Both were nearly broke, and the fee I charged them hadn't made them any richer. Their dispute had arisen because one man spent money that actually belonged to both of them. The money was now gone, only the quarrel remained. I decided that a few dollars to enrich them would reduce the virulence of their quarrel, so I passed the hat among the men now in the saloon, a goodly crowd.

"Contribute something to this good cause," I ordered them, "or if I ever get to be Sheriff again I'll make it plenty hard on the non-contributors."

Everyone in the saloon caught on to the spirit of the fun, and there was nearly twenty dollars in the hat when I was back at the bar. I gave each of the disputants five dollars from the collection, then walked to the doorway and handed their women the balance. That seemed to settle their grievances, and they shook hands with each other and with the men in the crowd. Then they returned to their wagons, after buying a sack of candy for their children, boosted their wives onto the seats, and pulled off down the dusty trail to Indian Territory, laughing and waving back to us in the street at Benton. We never heard of them again.[3]

Once, after the beef roundup, a group of us were standing at the bar talking when someone mentioned the Wild West Shows of Buffalo Bill, popular at that time. One cowboy had ridden in Cody's show and he said there were just as good cowboys there on the Oklahoma range as in the show. That set us to thinking about putting on a Wild West Show of our own. We knew that we could put on a good program of bucking broncos, for the YL and Healy had some of the worst broncs on the range. We talked about having steer roping, some wild horse races, riding bareback, and maybe a wild cow-milking contest. We had some of the best cowboys in the business within fifty miles of Benton. The show would be mainly for the benefit of the grangers and especially for their pretty daughters, for the range men wanted to get better acquainted with them. Not too many cowmen would be interested in bucking horses, for after you have watched horses buck away from the chuckwagon for twenty years it is no entertainment. But them girls were beginning to play an important part in the boys' minds and we hoped that such a Wild West Show would entertain them and help enliven our friends' social life. It would also help compromise the differences between the cattlemen and the grangers was our hope.

An outdoor show had a good chance of succeeding since the weather in that country is usually delightful in the late fall, even up to Christmas, the bad storms and wind coming later. But you could never tell. We had a saying that "Only newcomers and damned fools predict weather here. Which are you?" As a matter of fact the weather was so changeable down there that there were lots of stories to illustrate its vagaries. For example, one story told of a cowboy who passed a granger's dugout on a warm December morning and saw the man skinning an ox. That evening as he again passed the granger's dugout on his way back to the ranch, the cowhand saw the granger skinning a second ox. "What happened?" the cowboy asked, "You run into some tick fever with your oxen?" The granger tossed the skinning knife on the ground and wiped the blood off his hands on his trousers. "Nope," he replied, lighting his pipe and sucking deep on it. Then he began. "This morning that blue ox died of sunstroke when we were bringing in cowchips from the flats. This roan ox died at just four o'clock when I was tryin' to git the wagon unloaded. Froze to death in that nawther." This was about true of our changeable weather.

But in spite of worry about the weather, we got the Wild West Show all talked up, charged each cowboy a fee and that money we used as prizes. We set up all the events, bronc and steer riding, steer roping, and so forth. We knew where the bad broncs were on that range, and we asked for a loan from the ranchers for the worst ones and for the biggest, wildest, longhorn steers we could rustle up. We had no pasture, so night-herded them near Benton.

Our first show day was bright and nice and the show was a great success. Folks showed up from Beaver City and as far east as Camp Supply. We had the best cowboys in the country there competing. The wild horse riding was about the funniest, for we made up teams of two bronc-busters each. We selected six two-man teams, all to ride at the same time. Each team was to rope a wild bronc from the horse herd, saddle him, and put on a bridle or make a hackamore from their lariat and then have one man mount him and ride him to a given line at the end of the field, about a hundred yards distant. It took some real doing to get a man on top of one of them broncs, and then a lot more doing to stay there and ride him out.

In the regular bronc riding contest Irish McGovern won with a good ride on a claybank mustang called Soda Biscuit. John George, later a banker and rancher in the Strip, was a fair rider and won second place. I recall that John, who was a short, stocky built man, asked Wes Chadwick, an older cowboy, to haze for him and catch the horse and take him off when the ride was over, "if I'm still atop the beggar." This prevented a horse from getting away with the saddle and bridle, for there were no fences around there at that time. Well, this horse that John rode was called "Chalkey," for he was a Chalk Beeson horse, off the COD range. "Chalkey" pulled every stunt in the book, sun-fished, rolled, and sunned his belly, backed and twisted like murder. But John stuck like a Devil's Claw to a heifer's tail.

When Wes picked John off, after a long, hard ride and a chase, John said, "You know, Wes, if my legs were four inches longer, I believe I could ride any horse in the Strip!"

Later we repeated our Wild West Show, but it turned cold and stormy and was not a great success. A few years later, in '91, we held a show at Hardesty, a sod town at the confluence of the Coldwater and the Beaver Rivers. A big crowd attended that one, too. That year Boss Neff came out on top in the roping contest, which we cowboys regarded as the highlight of the day. Maude Ashcraft[4] penned this poem about that match:

THE WINNERS

You never heard about the time,
When Boss and Pocket won
The roping match near Hardesty,
Back there in Ninety One?

Pomp James, a noted roper
And cowboy of that day,
Rode up the trail from Texas
To take the prize away.

Among the home-range cowboys
Who, too, the rope could swing,
Was Boss Neff, riding Pocket,
As sure as anything.

Say! Pocket knew his innings,
And Boss roped pretty well,
So when the match was over,
Not much was left to tell.

The keeper of the tallies
Made plain whose was the loss;
Pomp James coiled up his lariat
And doffed his hat to Boss.

Those Wild West Shows are today called "rodeos," and have caught the fancy of all the nation. Then they were just local entertainment that was got up on the spur of the moment, using the animals we had at hand, bucking horses, wild cows and steers, and cowboys who had learned to ride and rope on the open range. But believe me they were star performers!

All of the old timers who lived in the Strip through those hard winters of 1884-86 will recall the blizzards and remember the terrible cattle losses we suffered in the storms. They were the worst winters known to that section of the cattle range, and took a toll of human lives as well. Cattle simply froze to death in the bitter below-zero temperatures or were smothered by the fine, wind-driven snow that froze into big ice-balls on their soft, wet muzzles. Then two years later, in January of 1888, this same story was repeated in what came to be called "The Blizzard of '88."

It is my personal belief that many of the serious cattle losses came about because of an earlier decision made at their Convention by some of them cattlemen who didn't know what they were doing. In one of their early Conventions, they decided to build a "drift fence" from the New Mexico line and run it eastward across the divide between Wolf Creek and the Beaver River to the Cherokee Strip. The purpose of this barbed wire fence, as they gave it, was to keep their cattle from drifting off the range during the winter storms, for cattle always drifted with the wind and weather.

The resolution to build this fence met with much opposition from some range managers and from the old range men who were foremen. They knew and understood the danger of placing such an obstacle in front of animals who were doing the only thing they could do to survive cold weather and wind and storms—walking ahead of the storm, keeping their blood circulating and "weathering" the storm, as we called it. Most animals can out-walk a normal snowstorm or even a blizzard, providing they are free to "drift," that is stay ahead of the storm and keep themselves warm by exercising. True, they suffer, sometimes lose tails, and ears, and even horns, but they come through alive. Of course, southern cattle, fresh to the northern range, perish more easily in storms than do the seasoned stock on the range. But after bad storms on the range we would find cattle on the spring roundups that wore brands of the Arkansas, Republican, and even Platte River ranches. Those cattle survived by walking. So the resolution to build the drift fence was passed over the protests of the old range men who knew what would happen if we had really bad storms.

That drift fence was constructed across some 200 miles of prairie range, with strong cedar posts, and carried four strands of barbed wire, stapled to each post. It was said to have cost $300 a mile to build it. This was about the first barbed wire introduced onto our range. As it proved out, it would have been better had not a spool of that wire been unwound. Not only cattle and horses but antelope, deer, and other wild game suf-

94

fered and died on its barbed coils, for once the wire was broken, it would encircle and lacerate like so many razor blades. Animals had never experienced it before, nor could they see it, or realize it was there, especially in the darkness or in storms.

The weather that fall in 1887 had shown no inclination to give us a bad time. So the bitter cold weather and blizzard that struck us in December caught us by surprise. By New Year's Day, 1888, the worst of the cold spell had passed. That day I was in the store owned by George Healy at Alpine, a small boom town of no consequence that had sprung up on Duck Pond Creek. Lu Kramer, a German rancher who owned and operated the LUK and the Quartercircle Q with Frank and Charley Kramer on Home Creek, was standing there with us discussing the big Christmas Day losses and the death of Joe Cruse and his wife who froze in that storm. Lu said his loss would be so great they wouldn't know until spring thaws came. And true enough they lost so many cattle that they moved to Colorado, then on to Montana in '92 or '93, where they settled on the Big Dry country, east of the Musselshell.

George and I were more optimistic than Lu. So in the talk I proposed that I take a wagon and a few boys and ride down to the drift fence and see what had happened there. My personal pitch was that I would take all the hides we could skin for heading up the exploring party. I knew that the hides would bring $3 to $5 at Dodge City, so I could salvage something from the storm loss if it was as bad as Lu thought. Whichever way the cards fell I couldn't lose much but my time, and I had cattle on the range and was as interested in their fate as was Healy or Kramer. I thought that if we got there in time, we might be able to cut them through the drift fence and save many of them by letting them drift on into the breaks of the South Canadian where they would find grass and protection.

Both Healy and Kramer agreed to provide the men, wagon, and supplies and also get a clearance from The Association for me to take what hides we might find on the frozen cattle. We drank on it. Old Lu Kramer muttered as he sipped his drink,

95

"Dot Jeem Herron make more money from my cattle dis year dan I make!" He was about right, the way it turned out for the cattlemen that winter.

George warned me of the risks we would be taking should another bad storm come on, and he cautioned me to outfit so we would not run short of food, clothing, or bedding. I took great caution in putting our expedition together, because the weather was still running along below freezing. First, I selected my own boys with care, for I wanted no rannies along who wouldn't take orders. I picked three of Healy's boys and took one from Kramer's that Lu personally recommended and trusted. We took only a light wagon, for I knew the little mule teams could not draw a heavy wagon through the drifts in the ravines and canyons we would encounter. I did not plan to haul many hides back on the wagon, just peel them off, stack them, salt some so they would keep a while, then return for the rest of them when the weather moderated.

We packed as much dry prairie hay on the wagon as we could take and took several sacks of corn chops and oats for horse feed. We piled the bedrolls on top, along with bags of salt, the skinning knives, and other gear which I would need on this get-rich-quick scheme I had concocted. When we left Healy's I drove the wagon, my horse tied on behind, and the other boys rode their saddlehorses. It was thirty-five to forty miles to the drift fence, the way the crows fly, but it was more like seventy miles the way we drove it through them canyons and ravines and snow drifts.

We spent a cold and miserable night on the prairie in a dry camp that night. About noon of the second day we came within sight of the drift fence. At first it looked like a dark line skimming the horizon, reaching from a point on the east to where the fence dipped into a small arroyo on the west. As we pulled up closer within several rods of the fence, I stopped the mule teams and we all sat there for a few minutes, puzzling the sight ahead. When it penetrated our skulls that what we were staring at was not the drift fence but a long windrow of frozen cattle, one boy said, "Good God, Jim, let's go back!"

A man could have walked atop the bodies of them cattle piled along that drift fence two and three deep for a half mile. The bodies were frozen in every imaginable position, just as they had been when death took them. Some were lying on their sides, some were standing on four frozen legs, a few lay with all four feet in the air. One thing they all had in common: all were piled together as though they had been seeking warmth from each other's bodies in the evening of their lives. There was only a thin blanket of snow covering them, and it was wind-drifted so that their winter hair, horns, feet, and ribs stuck from it as though to better expose them to the icy wind from the northeast that still blew a gale.

A few of the cattle were half-way through the fence, but not many had tried the sharp barbs on the wire. Most of them had just walked along the length of the fence, bawling in their misery until death had claimed them. Then they had fallen and died where their strength had left them. At one place I counted 200 bodies, most of them calves and yearlings and coming two's. Some of the bodies on top showed that other cattle had crossed over the fence on the dead cattle, no doubt saving their own lives if they reached the Canadian.

I studied the brands as carefully as I could and found many of Healy's KK brand and quite a few Kramer cattle. But there were brands of all kinds, including my own, and I recognized two of my fine, big steers, one a roan and the other a four-year old muley I had picked from a Texas herd and wintered two seasons. They lay side by side, like twin brothers.

"Well," I said to the boys after we had all rubbered around in the chilly wind, "we don't start back yet, so we'll skin some of them this evening." I asked a Healy boy and Kramer's boy to keep a tally of their own brands that we skinned, as well as a total tally of what they found of their own dead cattle along the fence. For I wanted everyone to know what to expect. The rest of us started dragging the biggest steers from the pile and making a place where we could work. We melted some snow water for the mule teams and saddlehorses to drink from a washtub I fetched along filled with oats. Then we gave each of the animals a hatful of grain in the *morrals*. From the cedar posts along the fence line we built a good fire to warm up by, set on a pot of coffee, ate a lunch, and then started peeling off the hides.

We left one stout cedar post standing, where we could tie a dead steer's head with a lariat. When the head was tied solid to the bottom of the post we skinned the hide back from the neck, cut it loose from the legs, and slit it down the belly. We tied a rope around a knot of hide from the neck and hooked it on to the doubletrees of the little mule team. As the team pulled slowly, the skinners cut the hide loose from the frozen flesh underneath. Those little mules were naturally high strung and not used to smelling blood and seeing dead cattle all around them, so when they started pulling, and the hides started crackling and the skinning knives slicing away, they would lay back their ears and their tails would twitch something fearful. It was all I could do to hold them.

We skinned out forty beeves that afternoon and evening and stacked the hides with some salt on them. My boys were not professional skinners, so they left some pretty big knife holes in them frozen hides that would have amused an old-time buffalo hunter. But we got the hides off, which was what I set out to do.

As we were finishing up for the day, I noticed that the wind had shifted to the northwest and that a dark cloud was moving in on us. I began to realize that we might be in for another storm, and it set me thinking. The day was cold, but in our work we had hardly noticed it. Now, as we stopped our labor of skinning, we began to feel the chill from the north wind again. I had the boys pull up a good many of them cedar fence-posts and lay them where we would have them to burn. We pulled several hides from the stack and with lariats laced them to the fence and wagon to make a tent-like protection we could all sleep under. We took other hides, bent them to cover the horses and mules and tied them on, fur side to the animals' bodies. Then we spent one hell of a cold night trying to keep from freezing as another storm swept down from Canada, the worst I was ever out in.

By noon on the following day the storm had blown itself out and we crawled out of the drift. We had been careful to picket and hobble all of the livestock, so they hadn't drifted far. But we had tied some of them green cowhides over them, fur side down, for their protection from the wind and cold. Now them hides were frozen to their shape and so solid that we had trouble getting them loose. That was just a little more misery we hadn't expected. But we didn't lose an animal from the cold.

There was nothing more to do, so we hitched up and started back to the ranch. I had personally tallied 1,406 head of dead cattle along less than three miles of that drift fence. Most of them were cattle from the YL, many with the 777 brand, and Healy cattle. Kramer had some dead ones, too, but his loss was farther west from there. I found eight head of my own big steers in the piles, so I knew that most of my younger stock would all be gone. The Lord only knew what would be found in the piles of dead cattle, come spring roundup.

Before leaving the drift fence we had cut several wide holes, each a mile or so apart, along about ten miles of the fence, so the rest of the cattle could walk through. But it was no use, for the weakened cattle died right around the ranch houses and in the canyons in the weather that followed. The story was the same wherever we went. Fred Tracy told me that spring that Lu Kramer rounded up but 2,500 head of his estimated 20,000 cattle he had owned the previous fall. Lu lost all his calves and a lot of his she stock. Only the biggest, ruggedest steers survived. Healy's loss was not so heavy. He didn't have as many young cattle, and his range was partly north of the Beaver. The river froze solid, and the cattle didn't cross over the slick ice. The boys got in there and chopped holes in the ice for the cattle to drink from. My losses were small, for I owned only the 400 big steers and some stocker cattle I had picked up here and there. They were all north of the river, and most of them stayed there. I did find many of my cows and calves frozen along the river banks when spring came.

We traveled about twenty miles on the return trip from the drift fence that day and met some of Kramer's boys looking for cattle. "Go on back, boys," we told them, "Your cattle are all dead along the drift fence." It took some time before they believed us.[5]

We made it back to Kramer's the next day and stayed at his place on Home Creek that night. We were all in when we got there. That following night I was back at Benton with Alice and her folks. It was some change, and I was glad to be there.

Soon after this get-rich-quick trip, on January 8th, 1888, the stork delivered a fine baby girl at our house. Our baby girl weighed seven pounds on the grocer's borrowed scales, and Alice named her Olive Dorothy. She was always known as Ollie Dot.

Now I looked forward to a more pleasant and less strenuous future, for I was possessed of a good wife, a fine baby girl, a comfortable home at our ranch, and I still had some cattle left on the range.

chapter VI

In 1888 the Rock Island Railroad built down across the Cimarron River and angled southwest into the Public Land Strip where the track-laying ended for the time. At this railhead, which it was to be for the following fifteen years, they built a good-sized set of corrals with wide catch-wings to head the Longhorns into the pens. They constructed seven loading chutes alongside the tracks there and this place was called Tyrone. Back up the tracks about five miles, and on the Kansas side, another place called Liberal started up. Just south of Liberal, and across the line in the Strip, another town was started. We called it White City at first, for it was a tent town. This place had nothing to offer cowmen, for it was off the railroad and had no gathering yards or cattle pens. Its chief business was selling beer and whiskey at the saloons and dance halls, so the place soon was known as Beer City. Almost every saloon had a few girls to drink with the cowboys and practically every game of chance known to the trade was operated there.

Many of the Dodge girls were working at Beer City and Tyrone in shipping season, for old Dodge was in the doldrums when the Western Trail was pushed out of the state and Liberal became the trading point for the ranches of the Southwest. And there were a lot of new girls came in from the east, stayed at Liberal, and worked the trade at Beer City, for there was a hack that made regular runs between Liberal and Beer City. There was nothing slow about the Beer City businessmen; they believed in advertising and they gave free boxing and wrestling matches, horse races, dances, and even a Wild West Show. They sent brochures all over the country and paid for advertising in papers, inviting folks to move to "White City, the only town of its kind in the civilized world where there is absolutely no law." They had a blowout there in 1888 that rivaled Dodge City's famous bull fight.

The Beer City businessmen established their own self-appointed government to keep pickpockets, con men, and holdup men away from their own legitimate customers. A person coming there who was found unacceptable to the town's sporting fraternity was soon advised to depart—and usually did. When anyone became helplessly drunk in Beer City, the saloonkeeper would search him and take all his money and valuables and put them in the saloon safe. Then they would stuff the man—or woman—into the bullpen, a heavygauge wire enclosure that each saloon had at the rear of its building. There the drunk could sleep off his jag. This prevented thugs from "rolling" customers while around the saloons, and it made the drunks feel better to wake up and have something left beside a hangover.

At the end of one of their celebrations, Pussy Cat Nell, the Madam in charge of the house above the Yellow Snake Saloon, put a load of buckshot into the body of the town Marshal, Lew Bush, a Texas cowhand who had been active with the rustlers there in that region along the Cimarron.

While Tyrone, Liberal, and Beer City flourished and grew in importance, the towns west of there in Stevens County, off of any railroad, became involved in a most sanguine county seat war which didn't end until there had been a cold-blooded massacre of four men and a wounding of a fifth at Wild Horse Lake, a watering place in the western end of the Strip.

Wild Horse Lake lay on the divide between the Cimarron and the Beaver Rivers, and it was actually just a large basin that caught the run-off in wet years, yet I have seen it when you could swim a horse in it. But I have also seen it when you could trot a horse across the bottom of it and raise a dust! There was a wide area around the lake where the prairie grass grew thick and tall, and the neighboring ranchers and grangers in the summertime put up hay here. For this reason, the murders committed there were afterward referred to as "The Hay Meadow Massacre." The killings were an outgrowth of the county seat war that raged between

102

the towns of Hugo and Woodsdale, Kansas, and occurred in July 1888.

I shall not spell out the details of this fracas for it has been written up many times before, and it happened a bit off my range. The murders were committed by a posse of men from Hugo, or Hugoton, as they called it, headed up by their town Marshal. The murdered men were from Woodsdale, including the Stevens County Sheriff, John Cross, whom I knew quite well. The Woodsdale men were disarmed and shot in cold blood like dogs. It was a disgraceful act, and none of those who perpetrated the murders were properly punished for it.

Many of us younger cowboys had enjoyed the hospitality of the grangers around Hugoton and Woodsdale when we were on the roundup in that area. The settlers had many pretty daughters, and we were all hungering for social life, so the dances there attracted us like a lantern attracts millers. Few of us boys took part in the county seat wars, and those that did had no real interest, other than favoring the town where their pretty sweethearts lived and for the fun they got out of the excitement.

This far-western end of the Neutral Strip had for centuries been the hunting grounds of the Comanche and Kiowa Indians. The Cherokees drifted through there in the fall to hunt in the mountains. In them old days there were buffalo and deer and antelope there in bands of twenty to several hundred head, small game of many kinds, and wild fowl by the millions resting at those fresh water lakes in the wet seasons during their migratory flights.

I once stopped there at a granger's soddy and he had two hen turkeys. Each had picked up a brood of young quail to raise. I tell you it was some sight to see how proud them mother turkeys were of their adopted broods. Seemed to me there was a lesson there for human beings in getting along with other tribes.

In making my official trips out there when I was Sheriff, I came across hundreds of circular areas of buffalo bones, where hide hunters had killed as many as 600 and 800 head of buffalo in a space of less than two miles. At some of the spots alongside the prairie swales, where a fresh-water lake had been during that killing season, the bones would appear from a distance like someone

103

had chalkmarked the prairie at that spot. I once counted more than 300 skulls scattered along an old lakeside where a large stand had been killed. It looked like they had all been killed at one time. There were also hundreds of buffalo wallows dotting the plain where the buffs had rolled in the dust or mud, cleaning off the insect pests they had to endure.

Whenever I rode out that way I usually stuck close to the Beaver River, following the old Indian Trail on the north side that the immigrants had by then pounded into a fair wagon road. I sometimes cut across the ZH cattle range, owned by the Muscatine Cattle Company, along the Cimarron, then angled up toward Wild Horse Lake. There were some good springs at the headwaters of Goff Creek and Teepee Creek, where my buggy team or saddle horse could water.

On one trip I arrived at Wild Horse Lake late in the afternoon. I had driven my team on the buckboard nearly seventy miles that day. I planned on watering and feeding them at the lake, then resting there for the night. As I approached the lake I saw six men on the far shore. They had hobbled their saddle horses nearby and were camped at the edge of the water. It would never have done for me to camp across the lake without making myself known to them, for almost every stranger you met out there, unless he was a cowboy, was an outlaw or a lawman looking for outlaws. The place was so isolated that it made a good hide-out for outlaws between bank jobs or train robberies. I knew I must make myself known or get on the trail, and my team was wore out.

I watered the horses, and I could see that the men on the other shore were eying me. So I drove around to their camp. As I drew near, I saw that all the men were armed with side arms, and I also saw their Winchesters sticking out of the saddleboots, which were scattered around the camp. Two of the men walked over to my buggy as I pulled up. One fellow, a younger man, stuck out his paw.

"Howdy, Jim," he greeted me. "You come all the way out here to arrest me?" His beard was so heavy that I didn't recognize him at first.

104

"I can't say I did," I reassured him as I took his hand. "As a matter of fact, I wouldn't know who I was arresting behind all them whiskers." The men all laughed, then the second fellow spoke up.

"You remember me, Jim?" I studied him a moment or two, then I saw he was the boy, Sam, who assisted me at Broadhearst's trial.

"Hell yes, I remember you," I answered, as I shook his paw. "You're the boy who was ready to fight all the grangers at the trial of Broadhearst in Benton. If I'd known it was fellers like youall who were camped here I'd a' dodged this place for sure!" We all laughed and I shook hands all around. "Any objection to my camping here tonight, boys?"

"Hell no, c'mon in," they all invited, and I stepped down from the buggy and started unhitching the team, the boys helping me.

I was treated as their guest, and they were all most friendly. They were starved for news of what was happening over the cattle range and asked me some pointed questions about the activities of other lawmen in that region, particularly wanting to know the whereabouts of U.S. Marshals in Kansas and Indian Territory. This boy, Sam, who had acted as my deputy, told the others about our kangaroo court at Benton and how we gave Broadhearst a fair trial to save him from a lynch mob, then how the Judge and I resigned our offices after his conviction because we had no jail to throw him in and didn't want to be responsible for the hanging! Them boys all laughed long at the corner we had driven ourselves into by getting up the election in the first place. This story seemed to set so well with them I got the feeling that more than one of them had at some time faced a lynch mob. And though I denied it, none of them would believe that I had not aided Broadhearst in his escape. I didn't try too hard to convince them, for I felt this a sort of ace in the hole fortune had dealt me, and I soon realized that these boys were a part of the Dalton bank- and train-robbing gang. They had been in this vicinity for two weeks, having apparently pulled a holdup somewhere, or were getting ready for one. I knew there was probably a liberal reward on each one's head,

105

but a lone lawman would have been out of his mind trying to collect it. I have always believed it better to stay alive than to be the center of conversation about a dead hero. I spent an enjoyable night with them boys, eating some fine roast ribs of beef they had prepared over their campfire. A big ZH steerhide lay nearby which they had not even bothered to bury, and one boy was working up a rawhide strip to lace his stirrups with from the hide.

The next morning as I was preparing to leave, Sam, my former deputy, rummaged through his warbag and came up with a brand new .41 caliber Colt revolver. He handed me the gun.

"You know as well as I do that for your work, or mine, there is no better gun made. It's a little gift for you," he said, handing me the revolver. "I've got its mate," and he patted his hip.

I thanked him for the present. I carried that six-shooter for many years, and it saved my life on at least two occasions.

This western end of the Strip had been the stomping grounds for outlaws for many years. One really vicious and mean outfit that once hung out there was the Coe gang, in the Cimarron canyon. This was before my time, but I'm told they dressed up like Indians and massacred wagon trains in the early days. L. A. Allen, a Colorado Sheriff, and his Rangers knocked them out. Coe was lynched.

The Daltons and others holed up there at ranches and along the river. The cowmen never bothered them, for it was best to get along with them. Outlaws from Indian Territory drifted in and out. Frank James wintered there at Towers & Gudgel's OX Ranch headquarters when he had a bullet in his leg, acquired in a Dakota bank robbery. The fact that the outlaws dressed like most range men helped them to cover their tracks. Later these outlaws would meet at some prearranged spot and map out another bank robbery or train holdup.

I met two of the Dalton boys in the late 1880's, Bob and Gratt. Bob was just my age. He was fair-complected, had blue eyes, dressed well, and wore sixteen-inch top boots. The Dalton boys were related to the James boys, through the Youngers. Their mother, Adalene, was a half-sister to the Younger boys' father. When I knew them, Bob and Gratt were Deputy Marshals in Indian Territory and, strange enough, their job was to ride trains

and keep off robbers. They were also trying to keep whiskey ped-
dlers from selling booze to the Indians, but this was a hopeless job.
Later they were successful as train and bank robbers, and they
continued in their lawlessness longer than most got away with it.
Frank, their older brother, was a lawman, and a good one. I believe the other boys would have been good officers had they been
treated better. They were not murderers at heart, but made a
business of robbery, and they handled it in a nice, gentle way. It
was not their intention to kill anyone unless it became necessary.[1]

The first time I met Frank was in the early '80's when I was
on a trip back to Texas. While the train was passing through
Indian Territory, just before crossing Red River, Dalton came
aboard with two prisoners, handcuffed together. I had been at
Dodge City a few days before and had bought myself a new Colt
.45 revolver. When I took my seat in the chair car, I took off my
belt and holster and laid them on the baggage rack above. Dalton,
who was a tall drink of water, stepped over, reached up, and took
my gun from the holster and looked it over.

"You've got a pretty high-class gun here, kid," he said to me.

His tone was friendly enough, but a man in them days didn't
go around picking up another man's revolver unless he had a right
to do so, so I concluded he had this privilege. Although I hadn't
done anything wrong recently, my heart did some powerful jumping around inside my vest when he dropped my gun into his coat
pocket and pulled back the coat so I could read his badge. It said,
"U.S. Marshal." Then he started to question me.

He was keeping an eye open for some young fellow I resembled
and who had been doing some stick-up work along the railroad, he
said. He didn't believe I was the boy, but he was going to take
me into custody until he could check me out. When he asked me if
I wanted to go along peacefully, or did I want to hold hands with
his other two prisoners, I saw he was the boss. I told him I would
be ashamed to be handcuffed to a couple of woollies like he had
brought with him onto the train. He chuckled, and I then assured
him I would cause him no trouble.

When we arrived at Denison, Texas, he took me off the train
with the others. He locked them up, then we went to a Judge there
who, he thought, had seen this other boy and would recognize

him. The Judge asked a few more questions and I told him I was coming down from Dodge for a visit with my father in Ellis County. They wanted to know who I knew up at Dodge. I had met Bat Masterson, who was once a lawman there, so I mentioned him. I also mentioned Clark Hart, Robert Wright, the storekeeper Ham Bell, who ran the wagon yard; then when I began mentioning some of the cattlemen, many of them I knew or knew about, the Judge began to appear more friendly. But I was held there several hours while they checked up on me by telegraph wire; then they let me go, returning my gun to me. I had been uneasy, and I felt much better. Later I saw Frank Dalton several times around over the Territory and in the Strip and became quite friendly with him.

Occasionally I saw Bob and Gratt Dalton after they had gone into the holdup business and I knew some of their men. Bob told me one time after the Wharton train robbery in '91 that he and Gratt didn't follow the crooked trail from choice but because they had been treated badly when they worked as lawmen in the Territory. Bob claimed that they only drew $60 a month, plus a small fee for taking prisoners to Fort Smith. In addition to the poor pay, he said they were not paid for nearly a year's work, and they had spent a lot of their own money as peace officers, after Frank Dalton had been killed by a whiskey peddler and his woman. Bob and Gratt had been to California, robbing trains, but Gratt came so near prison they returned to Oklahoma Territory where it was safer for them. They never mentioned this to me, but I learned it later in my law work. Well, that was their story.

I also was acquainted with old Dick Broadwell who went out with them at Coffeyville. Dick had helped his father steal beef, but he was not a bad one. He got to running in fast company with them Starrs and Daltons though. And the Daltons got blamed for every train robbery in the Nations for years, and there were plenty to account for.

Eva Dalton was their sister, and she married J. N. Whipple. I met her quite frequently, for they lived at Meade, Kansas. Eva was a beautiful girl, and she was most friendly to me when she learned that I knew her brothers and didn't censure them too much. We often talked about them and the route they were following, which she and Whipple didn't like one bit.

Bat Masterson was an old buffalo hunter, as were his brothers. Bat had fought at the Battle of Adobe Walls, but I knew him when he was a Kansas lawman. He helped make the history of that country, and he promoted prize fights at Dodge. He was a splendid peace officer, never took it all too seriously, and when it looked like there would be real trouble he had what it took to stop it. He was a young man and seemed to get all the fun out of living that he could. Some of them boys were like that. Bat died in New York, a newspaperman, of all things!

I recall a little episode that took place at Dodge after my return from Ogallalie. It has no importance, but shows Bat's sense of fun. There was a bunch of cowboys standing on the board sidewalk on the north side of Front Street, a half-block from the station. They were drinking and talking fight, twelve or fifteen of them, and it made it difficult for women and others to pass along the street. The boys meant no harm to others, but were just boisterous like you get when you are drinking. The Marshal had told them to cut it out or get off the walk, for there were women and kids there, too, but they paid him no mind.

On one of the porch roofs directly above the cowboys' heads there were two big oak water barrels filled to the top, to be used in case of fire in the hotel lobby below. There was a twenty-foot length of two-inch hose attached to each barrel, and a spigot to turn the water off and on to empty the barrel. All you needed to do if fire broke out below was uncoil the hose, drop it off the porch, turn the spigot on the barrel and you had a little water to fight the fire. There was no pressure, just gravity fall. Other barrels on the street below had water buckets hung on the sides of them. It was little enough fire protection, but better than nothing, although it didn't keep that block of Front Street from burning to the ground a few years later.

Well, those rannies on the sidewalk were auguring and cussing and Bat, now above the hotel lobby, signaled me from a window to step up there. I went up the inside stairs and looked out the open window. Bat was on the porch, holding the hose end.

"Step out here and hold this hose," he told me, "I'm going to cool them woollies down a bit."

I stepped out and took the business end of the hose and uncoiled it so it reached the edge of the porch above them. Bat told me to wait until he was back down on the street and had given them a talk, then to open the spigot and pour the water on them from above. It looked like real fun to me, but I was afraid of the boys, and told him so.

"Leave them to me," he said, "They'll never blame you, for they know I'm in charge of the fire department."

Well, we broke up that meeting in a hurry, with them boys pouring stale water out of their hat brims, some pretending to drink it. I was scared and left through the back door, but when I came around to the front looking innocent-like they all slapped me on the back and told me how much they enjoyed the cool bath in such hot weather. That's the way the boys were, anything for a laugh.

Mentioning lawmen and their duties reminds me of one of the most distasteful jobs I was ever asked to perform while I was Sheriff of Beaver County, or County No. 7, as it was called in Oklahoma Territorial days. One of my friends was an R Bar S cowboy I'll call Fred. Fred couldn't help "playing even" and branding the good she stuff he found running loose on the range with his own brand. I had helped him out of two or three scrapes, but I couldn't do any more this time. He had been sentenced to five years, and since Oklahoma Territory didn't have a prison system he was to do it at Leavenworth, Kansas.

We had no railroad then at Beaver City, where he was tried, so I took this boy over to Meade, Kansas, to board the train. Sheriff A. J. Byrns of that county and I were good friends, as I had been with Sheriff Eckhart who had preceded him in office. Our two counties joined, so we helped each other on occasion. So I put my prisoner in his jail.

Fred was a real musician, mighty handy on fiddle, mouth harp, and organ. I had heard him fiddle on the roundup many times, for we always encouraged him to bring his instrument along, and he would play any tune a cowhand could whistle up for him.

110

When we left Beaver City I urged him to bring his fiddle along, for I knew it would help him over the rough spots ahead of him.

Now many of the young people at Meade knew this boy and had danced to his music. They were just then beginning to dance to this ragtime music and that boy could sure vibrate them strings! He had played several dances at Meade during shipping season and now his friends wanted him to play a dance for them. I could hardly turn them down when they came to the jail and talked about it, so I gave my consent for the prisoner to play. They got a hall and a piano player and some drummer and a banjo man and everything was ready.

This young R Bar S boy had what I would call an unconcerned mind or disposition. He was one of them happy-go-lucky fellers that worried less over going to the pen than most Sheriffs do about getting them there safe and alive. He tuned up and that little pick-up orchestra put out some real music. That boy played like he was on vacation instead of on his way to the pen. A couple of the other boys there changed off with him so he could have a dance now and then himself. All of the boys and girls knew of his destination, but instead of working against him it was all in his favor, for every girl wanted to dance with him and every boy wanted him to enjoy his final night of freedom. This dance was more in the nature of a going-away party than anything I ever seen.

I thoroughly enjoyed the dance myself, and never missed a set. It seemed to me that folks in them days were different than people today. They felt this boy had just made a mistake, was all, and they didn't seem to blame him for his behavior, just thought it was real bad luck that he got caught.

The dance lasted nearly all night, so I didn't have to take my prisoner back to jail. Everyone told us, as the dance broke up at daylight, what a good time they had, then most of us went to the hotel for breakfast together.[2]

When we arrived at Leavenworth, I delivered my prisoner to the Warden. I volunteered the information that this boy was a real good fellow but his luck had played out. "Any favor you can do him, sir," I told the Warden, "will be a favor to me."

"From the papers you have here, I take it this man was sent

here from No Man's Land?" he said. "I hear it's not absolutely necessary there to become a respectable businessman or a responsible cattleman?"

I explained to the Warden the type of law we had out there, and how hard it was to live in a land without any sort of Law or Order. He was a jolly fellow and was interested in our problems.

"We're all having to shake loose from our old habits," I told him, "and there's a mighty fine people out there, once you get to know them."

The Warden studied my prisoner for a few seconds. "Young man, you have heard what Sheriff Herron has said of you. Now if you will promise me, in his presence, that you will not attempt to escape, and that you will obey our rules and regulations, I shall try to be fair with you and help you in all ways."

"I shore promise you," my friend said.

"What is your occupation?" the Warden asked him. The boy looked at me, for I don't believe he understood the word.

"He's a cowboy," I offered. "And he's a damn good one."

Well, the Warden eventually found the boy a job of herding the town cattle, and he won his freedom by parole, with three years off for good behavior. The R Bar S cowboy came back to the Strip, married, and is today one of the best of the old-time cowmen left there, honest, a reliable citizen, and liked by all who know him. So any of you reading this who have a father or granddaddy that was a top-notch fiddler in the early days, ask him about this!

Another unpleasant task, to my way of thinking, after I had taken over my Sheriff's duties following the legal election of 1890, came from my appointment as a Deputy U.S. Marshal. This caused me to make additional long trips clear to the western end of the Strip, for it was all now called Beaver County and had not yet been divided into the three counties. These trips were to collect federal taxes arising from the bootleg distilleries that operated in the Strip. The government claimed that they should be paid $1.10 a gallon for every gallon of spirits produced in them stills.

My first visit to a distillery to force the collection of taxes was a visit to see old "Judge" Hubbard. I rode over to his still on the

112

creek one day and told him that he must either pay Uncle Sam the revenue or it would become my painful duty to dump the mash on the ground, break up the equipment, and put him out of business. He argued that it was impossible to pay such heavy taxes, since he could not compete with the big eastern distilleries where corn and other grains and essentials cost less and were more readily available. We had a drink or two together as he showed me the hogsheads in the cave, all lined up and looking mighty impressive. These big barrels held four times as much as an ordinary vinegar barrel, and they were all filled with mash. I could see it would cause a lot of work, just to dump the barrels.

"If you dumped this mash," he explained, "it would mean several thousand dollars of loss to me and my friends."

Now I had close personal friends who sold the whiskey from this mash all over the Strip and up in Kansas. This was about the only industry we had in the Strip at that time that brought in money from outside, besides the cattle business. I did not know whether I was right in the way I looked at it or not, for it would have taken the wisdom of Solomon to answer all the problems that dumping the mash and destroying the still would create. So in the end I agreed to let him process the balance of his mash, providing he would agree to pay Uncle Sam the taxes on what he had on hand and was about to make. This way I wouldn't be responsible for letting taxes kill an infant industry that brought cash money to us all. I meant to be firm about getting the proper taxes, but I knew that he could not pay all that he owed and I was in no position to maintain a check on his production. It seemed better to keep him half-honest than to knock him out of production and thereby deprive us all of a belt of whiskey when we wanted it.

There was a second really big still in the west end of the Strip that I knew about, almost as big as Judge Hubbard's. So I rode out there to have a talk with its proprietor. This fellow was a tough nut, had three guards with him when I arrived. He at once accused me of messing in his financial affairs. It was a free country, he said, "and no man can tell me how to run my business."

"Hell," he snorted, "I'm out here a hunert miles from nowhere while you people down there are makin' laws and holdin' elections.

No Man's Land got along well and good wit'out you people. We don't need no law out here. We'll make our own."

The guards with him agreed, nodding, and acted threateningly toward me. I didn't take to that. I had been elected Sheriff by these people and had been appointed a Deputy U.S. Marshal to attend to their affairs. I wasn't about to back down in my duty.

"Look here," I told him. "You're living thirty years behind the times and I'm going to bring you up to date if I have to send you to prison for a few years to do it. These people in the Strip voted to have the U.S. law when they made this the Territory of Oklahoma. Now I'm going to make myself damned clear, not only to you but to these three rannies standing here beside you. I am a Deputy U.S. Marshal and the Sheriff of this county. What I tell you to do, you are going to have to do, one way or another, for I am carrying out the will of the people. You can make it easy on yourself, paying the tax, or I'll tear this still up piece by piece and dump the mash on the ground. If it isn't me that does this, someone else will eventually make you woollies obey the law."

I gave them a few minutes to think on it, and he and his boys stepped off a few yards to talk. As they did so I checked my revolver and pulled my Winchester out of the saddleboot. When I threw a cartridge into the magazine, I guess they all thought I meant business, for the distilleryman turned around and said to me, "I'll be damned if I pay out good money for bad whiskey. You'll just have to tear up the still, that's all!"

"You're sure the hardest headed man I ever met," I told him. "I hate to see all this drinking whiskey and mash go to waste, but if you want it that way, that's the way it'll be."

There was an axe near his wood-pile, so I ordered one of his own men to take it and start chopping up the hogsheads. "Just cut a hole in the bottom as big as my head," I said. To the two other men I said, "Vamoose!" They left, sullen and mean.

I told the still-owner to take out ten gallons for himself, and I also let the woodchopper have five gallons for his work. Then the three of us fell to, tore up the still, bent the copper tubing, and broke up other things concerned with the manufacture of the booze.

114

Before I left, we had several drinks together. The man made fair whiskey, but nothing comparable to Judge Hubbard's. This stuff was hardly two weeks old. I warned the distiller if I caught him again making whiskey without paying Uncle Sam the tax, I would take him to court.

"I wouldn't want to see a distiller on a rock pile," I warned him. I believe this touched him, but I felt he would have that still back in operation within two weeks, the next time though in some ravine or canyon where I'd never find it.

While I was in the west end of the Strip on these trips, I would visit with the old fellows I knew and make it a point to meet the newcomers, for I was Sheriff and didn't know but what I would be running for office again soon.

At Kenton I would stop overnight. It was a booming cowtown, and one of the liveliest spots in that section. On the way back I would visit friends at Old Optima, near the OX Ranch headquarters. I stayed overnight sometimes at Boss Neff's place. He owned a good ranch near the confluence of the Coldwater and the Beaver, but later his place blew away in a cyclone. George Merchant had a good ranch in the central part of the Strip, and I always enjoyed visiting there. There were the Anchor D, and the Three C's, and Hardesty's place where I called. Billy Dixon, the old army scout and Indian fighter had a claim down at the Adobe Walls where the big fight with the Indians took place, and I rode down there one time and had a nice visit with him. Later he took a claim up in the Strip, I heard. These visits helped me make a wide acquaintance with the cowmen and the grangers, all of whom I regarded as good friends and fine people, with the exception of a few of The Association-trained men who were to later cause me great trouble. But for the most part I cultivated the good opinion of these ranchers and farmers, and in my old age I was to find that many of them remembered me and held an equally good opinion of me and my work there while I was their Sheriff.

chapter VII

1890-1893

HERRON AS CATTLEMAN • ALICE HERRON'S DEATH
HERRON CHARGED WITH CATTLE THEFT

The winter previous to taking up my Sheriff's duties was a bad one. The cattle loss to Association members was set at twenty-five percent of the total. The Brand Book of 1885 estimated that there were 200,000 head of cattle on the Beaver River range. Many owners had moved out and withdrawn from that range by 1890, but there were still a lot of cattle there, and that range was overgrazed. All of this great loss tended to bring cattle prices up in those succeeding years, and the cattlemen got more for their fat cattle in Kansas City and Chicago than they had been getting for years. Many of the cattlemen shipped all of their fat cattle, and that helped us all to "play even" on our heavy storm losses in those bad years. And it helped restore the grass roots by less grazing.

This condition set up, of course, a whole new situation. As the grass situation got better, cattlemen thought of getting more cattle on the range and, if prices held, we would all be in for better times.

John E. Over was now the manager of the M Bar. He had bought out his partners, C. F. McKenney and Joe Mason, the latter an old-time lawman from Dodge City and a Civil War veteran. Mr. Over shipped most of his cattle to market to pay off his partners' share and that left him with but a small stocker herd of cattle, a good *remuda*, and the right to the good, well-watered M Bar range, though he did not own the land, of course.

Mr. Over had a fine home there on a good spring, Skull Spring, I believe he called it. I had also located a fair spring near there that flowed in all kinds of weather and had built myself a cozy little ranch house of rock and timber. This was not out of order, for I was respected by Mr. Over and the other cattlemen like the Healy's who knew me well, and the whole country was wide-open for such squatter settlement. The land had never been surveyed in detail, so there was no knowing what section or township your property might be on until a survey was completed.

The summer of 1890, I believe it was, the cattlemen in New Mexico suffered a bad drought. There was no rain whatever to make grass for their livestock. Most of the streams quit flowing, and even the Pecos was dry in places. The cattlemen were going every direction to find grass for their remaining livestock and shipping them out of the drought area for the winter. The Westmoreland-Hitch Ranch, John George, and John Over bought some of those drought cattle. Mr. Over took 2,000 head of the Reynolds Cattle Company steers to winter, the stock coming from the LE ranch near Tascosa. We could buy all we wanted for $12 and $15 a head, and farther south get them for $10. We called them "Meskins": they were Longhorns but not the big-boned Texas Longhorns of an earlier day, for their horns were slimmer, their bodies lighter. They were cattle that had grown up on the thistles of an arid land and they had a genuine toughness for staying alive.

I didn't have either the money or the backing to spread out and take advantage of a situation like this, but I did lay claim to some range that fortunately, because of John Over's heavy cattle sales that year, wasn't overcrowded and had good grass. I got Mr. Over's approval and made a deal with a New Mexico man to receive and care for 3,000 head of his poor Meskin cattle, to winter them at $1.50 a head. I agreed to help deliver them back to his ranch in New Mexico the following spring after the general roundup.

That winter Mr. Over and I decided to fence some land for a joint horse pasture. When we were figuring the cost, he came up with the suggestion that we fence the entire M Bar range, which had been controlled by his company for the past ten years. He thought it would discourage other cattlemen from throwing their cattle into that area and would protect our own grass. Since my range was established on what would be inside this larger range fence, I could run my cattle right along with Mr. Over's stock.

Mr. Over and I saw the granger situation alike, and we wanted to treat all new settlers like friends and neighbors and to share this good free range with them and let them make good homes for their families on it, just so long as we could continue raising cattle, too. We decided to make an agreement with any settlers who came onto this land and made a claim to a quarter section within our fence. Their livestock would be permitted to run right along with ours and we would all live there in peace together. If they were able to fence their crop areas to keep the cattle out, so much the better. If they decided to fence their entire quarter section, we would not object, for we had plenty of range for all. When we killed a beef, we would share it with them. All they would have to do in return was to be peaceful and let us run our cattle business without trouble.

Mr. Over's plan sounded good, and I agreed to help him. The fence we erected ran from Benton east to the Cherokee Strip, a distance of twenty miles, then north and across the river for fifteen miles, then west twenty miles and back fifteen miles south to Benton. We estimated that we would have 300 square miles of the best cattle range in North America, for it was centrally watered by the Beaver River and its tributaries, flowing in from both north and south.

That fall when I shipped my beef to Kansas City I repaid the loan Mr. Cooper had made me. I now had a good herd of stocker cattle, mostly grade stuff but a few good bulls of Hereford breeding. I told Mr. Cooper of the good range I now shared with John Over, and he was very interested.

"Jim," he said to me, "our firm has an interest in a thousand head of big, rough Texas steers. They should have been on the market this year, but because of the drought conditions they are too thin to sell. They're near Fort Elliott, in the Texas Panhandle now, being held there on poor pasture. They're not doing well and I'd like to get them on better winter pasture, so they could be marketed next fall at least. Now you say you have all this good grass. Well, we have the cattle and the money to finance their sale if you want them and we'll carry the paper ourselves. They're yours if you want them—and I think they'll make you some money. It would also help us to help this Texas man get something out of them."

I was interested, though I had never thought of getting in the cattle business in such a way. Mr. Cooper set a price of $12.50 a head. I couldn't see how I could lose on such a deal.

When I returned to the ranch I took one of my boys with me together with our saddle horses, two pack horses, our bedrolls, and some cooking equipment and we rode down into Texas, a hundred miles south from my home range, to look at the steers. It was pretty late in the season to be moving cattle north, but we found the steers in good enough flesh to travel that distance if we took our time. I wired Mr. Cooper the count, 990 steers, and reaffirmed my wish to own them at $12.50 a head. I warned him the grass was very short there and the herd should be moved at once. Bud Hutson, his man in charge there, was helpful and signed a release on the stock and helped us get them started north after Mr. Cooper had wired him and said he would meet the herd at Higgins, Texas, where the trail crossed the railroad.

We met at Higgins as planned, and Mr. Cooper and I signed the papers. Bud left us there, and I picked up three Texas boys and with their help we started north up the Tuttle Trail to my range.[1]

The second afternoon out from Higgins we encountered one of them "nawthers" that are so unpopular with cowmen in that area. It came out of a gray cloud on the northwest horizon that was no bigger than a drover's hat and had laid there three days. My boy from the ranch and I were both clothed for winter riding, but we nearly froze to death because we had to share clothing and blankets with them Texans who had brought along little more than the wads of tobacco and the cigarettes in their mouths and them wide smiles that Texas cowboys always had on their faces.

When that storm first struck us we had to get off the trail and hold the cattle, for it was their impulse to drift south, and there is no holding big hungry steers like them when they decide to drift. But the grass here was so much better than what they had been on and the cattle so hungry that we spent our time just

119

milling them and letting them graze. I cooked a hot meal or two for the boys, and when the wind had subsided we drifted the herd on slowly north, letting them graze their fill all the way back to my range.

When we reached the Beaver River it was froze over solid, and we crossed on the ice, breaking through in only a few places. It had been an awfully tedious and cold trip, and I felt so good at doing so well I paid all them boys just twice the amount I had agreed to pay them at Fort Elliott, cutting my own man into the bargain along with the others.

That spring of 1891 I had purchased the Beaver City Hotel at Beaver, west of Benton. Alice's folks moved with us to Beaver and operated the hotel, which was now sometimes called the Groves Hotel.[2] Though I spent some time at the ranch and had my Sheriff's duties to perform we now enjoyed more time together than we had since our marriage.

That following winter Alice took sick. She failed to respond to treatment by a local doctor, and her mother and I took her to Kansas City where she underwent surgery for a ruptured appendix.

Alice had loved to ride with me and I had a saddle mare she kept at the ranch just for these excursions. But she had started to complain about a pain in her side and we had quit riding together. Now I knew what had affected her, and despite all the tender care and the best treatment known to medical science, she passed away two days after the surgery at the Sisters Hospital. Her mother and I shipped my wife's body back to Meade, Kansas by rail and from there on to Beaver City on a freight wagon. The trip from Meade down to Beaver City could not be made in a day, so we spent a sad and lonely night camped beside the wagon that bore her casket at the Busing Crossing on the Cimarron River, near the old Niles Post Office and store. The coyotes in the hills to the north and south wailed plaintively all night back and forth across the river and in the sandy wastes. I could never bear that place after that, and when crossing the river at that point would kick up my horse and make the passage as quickly as possible.

The following day we took Alice's body on to Beaver City, and the day after that we buried my darling on that high, wind-swept

120

hill that overlooks the little village from the southwest, near the old Jones and Plummer Trail. This was the year 1892.

I was left with only our lovely little five-year-old daughter, Ollie Dot. Since I was on the range a lot and taking care of my other duties I could not properly care for her so her care fell to her mother's parents, Mr. and Mrs. Ansel Groves. Later, Mrs. Dyke Ballinger, her aunt, helped care for her; she was the former Della Groves,[3] Alice's sister. Those families gave Ollie Dot the finest care and upbringing, for which I have always been grateful. She studied music at the Lynnsburg, Kansas Conservatory, graduated with a degree , and went on to make a fine marriage and have a good son. I continued to help out in a financial way, but the major credit for her upbringing must go to those two fine families who raised my daughter.[4]

I had adopted several cattle brands, a few of which I added to my original TK. One was a TXA, on the Texas steer herd, and another was a Bar O on the stocker cattle on the M Bar range. Now I registered a brand for Ollie Dot's future, so that she would have something if anything happened to me. The brand was DOT, and I put this brand on 300 head of good she stuff.[5]

In them days, after the buffalo had been exterminated as a source of food for the Reservation Indians, the U.S. Government bought beef for them on the hoof. The government liked big, mature beeves like my Texas steers, so that spring of 1893 I got in touch with a party who had a contract to supply beef for the Cheyenne and Rosebud Reservations in South Dakota. I soon made an agreement to furnish not less than 1,500 head, and I was obligated in the contract to make delivery by April 15 on part of them. This forced me to round up my cattle starting April 1, instead of May 10 with the usually scheduled roundup. This did not set well with the other cattlemen because The Association members did not like to have anyone out on the range gathering cattle by himself. They preferred to do it in a group, for that way every rancher was on hand to protect his own interests.

I knew how they felt, for I felt the same. So I sent word to my neighbors that I would have to round up early to meet my contractual obligations with the U.S. Government and get the cattle to the Reservations on the date set. I welcomed all cattlemen to

121

have a rep there to check my tallies and the brands and told them where I was loading the stock, at Meade, Kansas, and gave them the date. I went ahead and worked a few days on the Beaver River where my cattle were most numerous, and inside our range fence. Then I spent a few days gathering strays along the Cimarron. I ended up with approximately 900 head with my brands.

There were reps there from several cattle companies to look over the cattle at the ranch and help clean up the herd. The hair on the cattle was still winter-long, and some of the brands difficult to read. We cut back twelve or fifteen head, a few for sickness, and we roped six or eight head to study the brands on them and sent a few of them back. After we reached Meade with the herd, no one made any claim against any of the cattle in the shipment. I had set the date, ordered cars from the railroad to ship in, and there was nothing at all secret about this operation. Nearly everyone in the town interested in cattle was there the following morning to watch the loading when the cars were spotted along the chutes. The Association's inspector, who lived at Liberal, was there and he made no mention to me that there were any other brands than my own in the herd. The shipment made two trainloads, for we had only seventeen or eighteen head to the car since the big steers were in good flesh and I didn't want to crowd them on such a long trip on the slow freight trains that would take them via Kansas City, Omaha, and then to Valentine, Nebraska, where we would unload them and trail them to the Reservations.

I followed the shipment on a passenger train a day or two later and when I reached the Reservation was paid by U.S. Government check, then had the Valentine bank take out the freight and shipping charges. I sent a draft to the commission house and repaid the loan Mr. Cooper had made me. I made a tidy profit on that shipment, and still had eighty or ninety head of the big steers at the ranch. I felt the honest pride a man feels at making a successful business transaction, where he stakes his labor, time, money, and judgment on a deal that requires personal risk, and no government subsidy to prop him up. That bad storm, when we brought the steers north, had been a great risk; the hard riding in winter weather to see about them and keep off *lobos* took risk. So all of this gave me great satisfaction, and what followed about knocked me off my heels and caused me to lose faith in some of my fellow men.

It was a month or two after I returned home that friends brought me the word that one of them ambitious Dodge cattle inspectors, not the regular one at Liberal, had paid a visit to the Dakota range. He came back with the fantastic tale that he had found "two hundred head of steers wearing Association brands on that Dakota reservation range." He further claimed they had been shipped there with *my* cattle, and said he was prepared to prove it. He had brought back with him a tally sheet which very nearly resembled the old *Fort Worth Livestock Growers Journal*, for on his sheet were pictures and tallies of brands of all sorts that he dreamed he saw on the Indian Reservations in South Dakota. This inspector took his sheet to Mr. Cooper, my commission man, and told him this windy tale.

Mr. Cooper knew me pretty well through the years I had done business with them, and he did not swallow this story. Instead, he wrote me a letter. Among other things he wrote was that he did not believe me guilty and wanted to learn my side of the story. If I *was* guilty, he wrote, if I did happen to get some Association cattle mixed up in my shipment, I would understand that he could not fully support me or back me, in view of the fact that he and his firm depended largely on The Association members for their sales commissions; but if I was not guilty in any respect, then he would use all the influence he had to prove my innocence. He urged me not to worry about the matter, and just await developments.

I answered his letter, telling him I was not excited about the false charges, for they were not true and I knew no other brands were in that shipment. I agreed, however, that it was possible for cowboys to fail to read a brand properly, and that an inspector, too, familiar with those brands might make an error or two. But, I said, it was utterly inconceivable that all of us, experienced range men and cattle inspectors, would let 200 head of other men's brands creep into a shipment. Even when the hair was long, as it had been, and with those Texas cattle wearing two or three

123

brands, such a gross error in brand-reading was impossible, I told Mr. Cooper.

I made the suggestion that I go to the Reservations with that same inspector and that he show me the cattle he claimed I had shipped there and that were wearing other brands than my own. I promised Mr. Cooper that for every steer we found bearing another cowman's brand, I would then and there pay the inspector $50 in cash. But the inspector would have to prove by the U.S. Government men at the Reservation, and by the cowboys who had handled my shipment there, that the steer came *with my shipment, not another.*

So Mr. Cooper extended my invitation to the officers of The Association to meet with us both at Wichita, which was close to our cattle range, and there he would go over the matter with us and set a date to leave for the Reservations on the inspection tour. The Association officers agreed to meet with us. But, when Mr. Cooper and I showed up at Wichita, not an Association man could be found in the city! Mr. Cooper returned to Kansas City and I boarded a train for Englewood, Kansas, where I had left my team and buggy.

I was not surprised when the train conductor handed me a telegram from my friend Jack Rhodes, who happened to be at Englewood. The telegram read:

SHERIFF A. J. BYRNS OF MEADE COUNTY, KANSAS,
AND WALTER LYONS, ASSOCIATION CATTLE INSPECTOR,
WATCHING YOUR TEAM HERE AT ENGLEWOOD.
ADVISE YOU GET OFF AT ASHLAND IF YOU DO NOT
WANT TO MEET THEM AT THIS TIME.
J. R.

I had nothing to conceal, and I was certainly not going to let The Association bluff me out of riding a train through the state of Kansas, even though I knew they could not legally lay a finger on me if I stepped off the train at Ashland and took a rig into No Man's Land. But I knew that we were now coming to grips over the matter of cattle theft, and I was not going to lay down and take a licking when I was completely innocent of these charges. I realized that they were trying to make an example out of me for

124

my past operations and the fact that I was not friendly to their Association, especially when dealing with the incoming settlers. I could understand the officers of The Association being interested in uncovering the thieves on that range, for there were some. I had suffered losses myself, and I found beeves butchered on the range, their hides clumsily buried or hidden nearby, some Association beef, some mine. The officers were justified in looking for rustlers, and the annual Brand Books of the Association *had named some of them!* But to accuse a man as well-known as I was at that time of driving 200 head of other men's cattle fifty miles overland to a shipping point on the railroad in a county seat town, while scores of cowboys and half the town watched him as he loaded them, was just nonsense. That was stretching the rawhide too thin, and I was determined to fight all such charges to the end. It had rankled some of them Association men how I, an ordinary young cowboy, had established himself in the cattle business, and right on the public range they claimed as their own. Then, I think, to see me elected Sheriff on a range they dominated, but where most of them couldn't even vote, further angered them. For most of the owners lived in Dodge or farther to the east. I had established a naughty precedent before the eyes of their own cowboys, and they were determined to make me pay for my cheek.

When I stepped off the train at Englewood, Sheriff Byrns walked over to me and we shook hands, for we were well-acquainted from our law work together. Lyons, the cattlemen's agent, stood slightly behind the Sheriff, looking dourly at me, nor did he offer his hand.

"We've been waiting for you all evening, Jim," Byrns remarked with a smile. "Some thought you wouldn't stay on the train, including Mr. Lyons here," and he indicated with his thumb over his shoulder.

"Perhaps Mr. Lyons has misjudged me—and my intentions," I answered, looking at my watch. "Yes, we're just two hours late. I learned back a few miles that you would meet me, Sheriff," and I handed him Jack's telegram, with his initials at the bottom torn off. Sheriff Byrns read the wire, then handed it to Lyons. "Here, you should be interested," he told the inspector.

125

"I rode over horseback," Byrns said to me, "and I'm not accustomed to that sort of exercise, I'm about all in." I could see he was telling the truth, for he looked used up from his thirty-mile trip.

"Why not ride in my buggy?" I invited him. "We can lead your horse and it will give us time for a good visit." I knew that Sheriff Byrns must be planning to place me under arrest, for that was his job, but he made no mention of carrying a warrant for me. We walked to the hotel for supper. When we had finished eating we matched for the supper and he won. Then we matched to see who would buy a pint of whiskey for the trip to Meade, but he lost that time.

"I'm happy to ride with you, Jim," he told me as we got the team and buggy from the livery barn, "for I've a little business to take care of there." We both laughed, and I then understood without doubt the purpose of his trip: my apprehension and arrest.

After we were on the road an hour or more Sheriff Byrns admitted that he had a warrant for my arrest in his pocket. "I haven't served it, Jim, for I know you have money enough for the bail so I figure I can just take you in on your own recognizance and you can talk with the Judge and make some sort of settlement to this fool charge." Then Byrns told me he held warrants for all the cowboys who helped me gather and load the Indian Reservation stock I had shipped from Meade.

I told Byrns it was not necessary for him to go to all that trouble of going to No Man's Land, extradicting the boys and all that legal fuss. "I'll round them up and we'll come to Meade when you call us," I said. He agreed, and saved himself a long and tiresome trip and saved the state some money.

The cattlemen's inspector heard none of our conversation, for he was riding along half asleep a ways behind us.

It was early morning when we arrived at Meade. The Sheriff and I went directly from the livery stable to the hotel, followed by the inspector. When the Sheriff and I turned in, Lyons was still sitting up in a chair by the lobby stove, half asleep, but still on guard should I make a break from the clutches of the law.

"If you want to sit up and guard the Sheriff all night, it's perfectly all right with me," I told him as I started up the stairway. "But as for me I'm getting some rest."

"You better get some sleep, too," Byrns told him. "I'll be responsible for the prisoner."

At the preliminary hearing I asked the court for permission to return to the ranch, get in touch with the boys who had helped me with the cattle that spring, and make arrangements with the local inspector to testify in my behalf. I gave bond, which the court set very low. It was my hope to have a full and open hearing later, I told the court, for I felt sure that when my side of the matter had been presented, and all the witnesses testified, the charge would be dropped, since The Association would not be left a leg to stand on. One man's word against what I could muster as absolute proof of my innocence would surely not amount to much, and that inspector was apparently simply following some instruction given him by the officers of the cattlemen's association. Their hope, I told the court, was to continue to dominate the range country, keep settlers out, and run the show in the future as they had in the past.

The court granted me permission to return home. I engaged two able lawyers to handle my case, Edward Sample of Medicine Lodge, Kansas, and Harry Bone of Ashland.[6] The attorneys agreed to represent all the cowboys, as well as my personal interests. We all entered pleas of not guilty at the formal hearing, and I asked the court to exonerate all the boys who rode for me, for they were only working for wages and doing my bidding. I alone took responsibility for the shipment of cattle.

The Association lawyers tried their best to hold all of the boys they had charged with cattle theft, making several offers behind my back to set them scot-free if they would testify as state's witnesses. I am proud to say that not a boy I had hired turned against me. The Judge ruled at the hearing that there was not sufficient evidence to hold or try them, so all were released from the charges. Only Jack Rhodes, who had been held on a separate charge, remained charged with me, and his trial was to be apart from my own. Since Jack was a close personal friend, it was clear

127

to me that the court would stick him on any charge placed against him, however false it may be. They knew he would never testify against me, nor against any of my cowboys. So I felt unhappy about Jack, and regretted that his loyalty to me might bring trouble to him and his family.

After the hearing, my attorneys and I met to set up plans for my defense. Ed Sample, my head counsel, was one of the leading criminal lawyers in Kansas at that time. He also proved to be a genuine friend, as well as astute lawyer, at my trial. At this time he suggested that I make a trip to South Dakota to see if there were cattle on the Reservations wearing Association brands as was being charged. Everyone familiar with the range cattle business of that time knew that thousands of head of Texas steers as well as Meskin cattle were scattered over the Dakota range, many no doubt right from the Neutral Strip, where I had shipped. The Government beef business was a big one, and thousands of the animals were shipped there to feed the Indians, and they might kill a hundred at a time. Them cattle wore brands of every sort, and many would naturally have Association brands. Yet I was certainly not to blame for their presence on the Dakota range, and I warned Ed Sample about this point. So he switched his tactics and held a consultation with Mr. Cooper, my livestock commission member friend.

Following their conversations, Ed decided to issue a second invitation to the inspectors to meet with Mr. Cooper and me at Wichita, Kansas or Omaha, Nebraska, and at my expense. From one of these points we would continue on to the Reservations in Dakota, go out on the range, and look over the brands on those remaining cattle I had shipped. Surely, we reasoned to them, if as many as 200 steers wore Association brands, at least some of them would still remain with the remnant of the herd. The Association agreed to the plan and set Omaha as the meeting place. Mr. Sample made the arrangements, and decided to send Mr. Bone with me. So Harry and I made the trip together. He was then a young man about thirty years of age, and he was a fine traveling companion. I found him intelligent and well-read in law. Though he had just recently been admitted to the bar, I could see that he had the training and talent to become a fine lawyer.

Upon our arrival at Omaha we went to the Rome Hotel. While awaiting the arrival of the Association inspectors, Harry and I took in the city and had an enjoyable time. At the day and hour agreed upon, we were at the meeting place, but again no Association men showed up. We waited two full days and wired Mr. Sample and The Association. Neither he nor I could get any response out of them.

Harry and I talked and he advised me to continue on to Valentine by train, just in the event the others had gone direct to the Reservation. At Valentine we found no word from them, neither had the Government or hotel people seen or heard of them. We stayed at the Reservation one night, and at the town of Valentine two nights. By now we knew we were tracking down ghosts.

What remained of my cattle shipment were held nearby, so we studied them carefully with a Government man along who did some cattle buying. There were no brands but my own among them. Several of the boys who had moved the cattle from the railroad to the Reservation were there, and they told Harry Bone what they knew, and several agreed to return to Meade and testify at my trial.

When Harry and I got back to Meade we talked with Ed Sample. He now knew I was in real trouble, and they were after a conviction, not to find the truth. He issued subpoenas to some of the cowboys at the Reservation, and we found the trial date was set for the September term of court, 1893. I returned to No Man's Land, confident that everything would eventually turn out for the best, for I knew I was completely innocent of the charges.

The lawing was costing me a lot of money, more than I could afford to spend, but my cattle on the range looked good and the calf crop that spring had been a heavy one, so I felt I would not go broke. Yet this business of being called a cattle thief weighed heavily on my mind and I knew I would never feel right until it was completely disproved.

chapter VIII

1893-1894

THE TRIAL • ESCAPE

As the trial approached, my attorneys tried again to have the date set ahead on the calendar, for they had found it even more difficult to subpoena witnesses and to get them to Meade in time for the trial than they had anticipated. We had hoped to bring most of the cowboys from that northern range down to Kansas for the trial, but drifters, as many cowboys were, they were difficult to locate.

The Association was, of course, all prepared for their trial, so they would hear no arguments for postponement. The Hon. Samuel Cowan, attorney for the Fort Worth Stock Growers Association, was on hand for the prosecution, as well as two or three attorneys from Dodge City. Mr. Cowan was a fine gentleman, an expert lawyer with a charming personality and a steel trap brain. Before the trial was underway an hour I was convinced he was one of the ablest attorneys in my old home state of Texas.

The trial was held in the old court house at Meade, and the initial arguments between the attorneys were concerned with the testimony collected from the cowboys on the Dakota range, testimony which the prosecution found impossible to rule out. In lieu of their personal appearance, we had taken depositions from some of them boys who had helped me with the cattle to the Reservations. After a bitter fight, Judge Francis C. Price of Ashland, Kansas, the 31st District Court Judge, who presided, ruled that since the cowboys could not be present, and since their testimony was so important to my defense, he would allow the depositions to be entered as evidence. All of them boys testified to my honesty in dealing with them. They all stated that no other brands than mine were in that shipment, and since they moved the cattle forty miles they should have known.

130

I watched Louis Boehler, the court reporter, and Fred Fick, the Clerk of the District Court, as the trial progressed. They took shorthand notes of all of this palaver of them attorneys, and how they got it all down on paper is beyond my understanding, for them lawyers didn't spare the words.

During the trial I stayed at the Osgood Hotel, the best in Meade at that time. I was under bond, of course, but free to come and go. Most of the folks took their meals there, too, and there was always a friendly group around the Sheriff, myself, and my friend F. M. (Jack) Rhodes. Jack was a small rancher in the Strip. He had punched cows with me for years and was a close friend. He was married and had two small children. Jack was trying to make bail until his own case was tried, and I agreed to help him make it.

In the course of the long trial I made many friends at the hotel. I sensed that most of the spectators and several of the court officers held me in esteem and felt I was being railroaded by The Association. Many of these folks had known me personally as their Sheriff in No Man's Land, both in pre-Territorial days, before any legal status had been given us, and afterward, as their first Territorial Sheriff. I had also served them as a Deputy U.S. Marshal, and since boyhood had been riding the range as a working cowboy, loyal to my brand and proud of my trade. Though I had never known many of the niceties of life, and had no parents to guide me after the age of thirteen, I had been raised among and trained by some of the best cowmen in the Southwest, and I had always made a top hand wherever I worked.

When the trial was nearing its end and about to go to the jury, a period of seven days, both my attorneys told me I had less than a fifty-fifty chance to win. One fellow that the prosecution had dug up from the Texas penitentiary, and who I had never seen before in my life, gave some very damaging testimony against me. He claimed he knew me, had rode for me, stole for me, and a lot more such lies. But there was no way to refute such nonsense, and I suppose he gained a shorter sentence for saying them things.

The jurymen were all good and honorable men, mostly from

business houses in Meade or ranchers on the nearby ranches. The commercial men's ties to The Association there were strong ones, for the ranchers bought supplies from them and filled their cash boxes. The few grangers on the jury were little known to me, since they were from Kansas, and they could have no idea that I, a cowboy and cattle owner all my life, would be friendly toward them. I was standing trial in a court fifty miles from my home range, and in them horse and buggy days that made the difference between neighbors and total strangers. My lawyers had done all they could to keep The Association's members off that jury and had used up their privileges scratching some of the most biased of Association members from the jury list.

In the course of the trial, different lawyers of The Association had questioned Association members as follows:

> PROSECUTOR: Do you know the defendant, Jim Herron?
> WITNESS: Yes.
> PROSECUTOR: Do you represent these different brands of cattle? (Showing him a list of brands).
> WITNESS: Yes.
> PROSECUTOR: Did you authorize the defendant, Jim Herron, to ship any of these cattle that you represent?
> WITNESS: Well—may I answer—?
> PROSECUTOR: Answer Yes or No.
> WITNESS: Well—No.

This procedure was like asking a man, "Have you stopped beating your wife?" Whatever the answer, the answer made me guilty. During the cross-examination of these witnesses, my lawyers would ask:

> MY LAWYER: "Do you *know* that my client did ship out any of these brands of yours on this list prepared by the prosecutor?
> WITNESS: No.

This sort of testimony should have convinced any juryman that these men knew absolutely nothing detrimental to their interests brought about by me. The testimony was, however, given by members of The Association, ranging from vice-presidents to range managers and foremen. So I began to have the feeling that the jury was very likely to find me guilty.

132

The evening before the case went to the jury, Ed Sample stopped by the hotel for a chat. "What do you feel are your chances for acquittal, Jim?" he asked.

"All I can hope for now is a hung jury, Ed," I answered him. "Maybe get another trial later."

"The court has been fair with us all through the trial," he said, seating himself in a chair beside me. "I don't really know what grounds we could base a request for retrial on. But I'm afraid you've been double-crossed, Jim. I sense that Judge Price has that same feeling, though of course he has never intimated such a thing to me in any way."

I knew that some Association witnesses knew nothing about my cattle business, how hard I had worked to build up my herd, especially the big, rough steers that had gone to Dakota. I hoped the jury would see through their testimony and discount it for what it was, pure fabrication. But I knew of no "double-cross," so I asked Mr. Sample, "What information do you have on that?"

"I will say this, Jim," he told me, "I will have good reasons in my arguments for a retrial, reasons that I believe Judge Price will hear through, for he is a most fair man. But in event he does not—" he hesitated a moment, "—if he fails to give us a new trial —then you're stuck."

Mr. Sample's words gave me a shock, for it was his first admission of failure since the trial started. I knew that he understood all these legal niceties like I knew cattle, so I was grateful for his frankness, even though it made me despondent. I instantly blurted out my deepest feelings.

"Ed, I'm not going to spend ten or twenty years of my life in prison if I can avoid it—not while I have a gambling chance to make a scratch. I have a good horse at the stable and my bondsman won't give a damn if I travel back to the ranch." I was well able to pay my bondsman, that I knew.

"Jim," the lawyer said, "I'd prefer you wait and hear the verdict. The case will soon go to the jury. If you've got the nerve —hang on."

"I'm not going to let the damned Association lawyers ruin me, especially when I have good friends who are members of that outfit and who know I'm not guilty. They want to make me Exhibit Number 1, not because of my guilt but because they need an example to show the real cow thieves—the ones their inspectors can't catch." I was out of breath from so much talk, but kept right on. "I've ruffled The Association's feathers in the past in taking up the grangers' cause, but it isn't fair to treat me this way now. I got in the cow business just like a lot of Association members. They can't stick me without sticking themselves, too!"[1]

Ed Sample didn't answer me for a few moments. But I could see that he realized then that I wasn't going to stay hitched to The Association's bone wagon and be turned in with the bones. He arose to go and stood before me, beating his pearl gray hat on his thigh.

"I will say only one more thing, Jim, and I give it to you as both your personal friend and as your legal counsel. True to my oath as an attorney, I must caution you to not take this escape route. Don't run. If you do, you will always regret it." Ed left, leaving me to ponder his words.

The next morning as I passed through the lobby of the hotel into the dining room I tried to appear as jolly and unconcerned as ever, but there was a qualm running through me. I visited with one of the waitresses as I ordered my breakfast and to confirm my previous anxieties I learned that Earl Spencer, an Association man—a vice-president, I believe—had made the remark in the dining room that I was certain to be convicted. Spencer was an Englishman, the head of the YL company, my old outfit, and one of the biggest figures on the cattle range then. What he said was important. The girl told me his remarks.

"When Jim Herron came to our company as a small boy," she said Spencer had remarked to all in the room at that time, "we never dreamed this would happen to him. I could never have believed that he would be sentenced to a long prison term for stealing our own cattle, but he is surely going to be put away."

A friend of mine happened to be in the room and challenged Spencer. "How in hell can you be so certain he is stuck?" he asked the Englishman. "The jury hasn't brought in a verdict—yet—and no red-muzzled son-of-a-bitch of an Englishman is going to tell me that he knows what an American jury is going to decide before they have even reached the jury room to work out a verdict!"

The girl told me that Spencer had then turned to another waitress and said to her, rather plaintively, "I must say, old girl, this is a rather distressing description of me. In England, most describe my coloring as a 'beautiful blond'."

My friend answered him, "Well, you may be that in bally old Hengland, Spencer, but here in this country you're just a damned, red-muzzled puke!"

My cowboy friend's opinion of Spencer was a good one, for Spencer and Drew, and the others who were later the officers of the YL company, took out big salaries for themselves, lived in splendor, and finally ended up bankrupting that company. They cleaned the stockholders out of thousands of dollars. They were not cattlemen in any sense of the word, just promoters. The West was full of them big talkers in the Eighties, and they were in railroad speculation, land booms, cattle ranches, and everything else. The country could have done better without them.

After breakfast, which I hardly touched, I walked down to the Buis Livery Stable where I talked with a wrangler, a colored boy who was working for me at that time. He had come up from Ellis County, Texas the previous year. In slave days, his people had been owned by my father and grandfather. Bob was a good cowboy, and as loyal to me as his family had been to mine in them old days, for father was a kindly man and treated slaves with respect, never whipped or punished, and always rewarded good work with some favor. Bob liked me so well he would actually been hung in my place. As I came to the barn he whispered to me that he had two horses ready and he and I could make a break *pronto* if I so ordered. I told Bob to sit tight, keep the horses ready, for I was going to sit and hear the verdict before making any other plans. Then I walked over to the drug store.

The jury had been out since nine o'clock that morning. I found Cape Willingham and P. Doyle sitting in front of the drug store on a bench.[2] Drug stores at that time in Kansas were popular places for drinking men to obtain liquor, for the state had been dry since 1881, and only the druggists had permission to sell bonded whiskey, which they sold on prescription; they also sold raw alcohol, which they compounded with "medicines."

As I walked up to the men, Doyle spoke to me. "Sit down, Jimmy, we were just talking about you." I leaned against a porch pillar.

"You know that you're going to be convicted, don't you?" Cape said. His statement was so positive that it took me aback for an instant.

"The jury's not in yet, so I'm entitled to hope, ain't I?" I answered. I could not understand why they were so certain I was stuck, even though these two men were big names in the area and represented the largest cattle companies in the Southwest and their opinions should hold some weight.

"Cape and I can get you out of this scrape yet," Doyle said. "But you'll have to do exactly what we tell you to do." Their offer had a hook attached to it, that I could see, but I was interested in hearing any plan to clear me.

"I don't want to be railroaded to the pen, that's a fact," I told them. "I'll listen to anything that is half-right and that will get me loose."

"Listen to me, then," Cape Willingham said, and he motioned for me to sit between them. I sat down and listened. "Now you come back to the courthouse with us," Cape said, "and before Judge Price pronounces sentence on you, you stand before him with us and tell him you are guilty of all charges against you. Tell him everything you know about cattle rustling on this range, how you do it, where you and the others sell your beef and the hides, how you get this 'good stuff.' You do this, Jim, and we'll not only get you off scot-free, but you'll get a good job with The Association again."

As soon as Cape had finished, Doyle took up the talk. "You're a boy raised right here on the range with us, Jim. I would put up my own money to help you out if I could do any good."

I saw it was a pure and simple effort to get me to turn state's witness, to tell everything I heard on the grub lines and make up a lot more to save my own skin. They intended to make me involve many of the grangers who were my friends, as well as the cowboys who occasionally put up what we called a "winter job," that is left a few big steers on roundup where they could find them and sell them in the winter months instead of riding the grubline. Them two men, both old Texas cowmen like my own father, would have liked to help me. I knew that. Down in their hearts they hated to see The Association, of which they were members, get the best of me and give me a long term in prison. But their deal sounded so ugly to me that I stood up and turned to face them.

"I know nothing against the cowboys, or the grangers, either," I answered them. "And you both know that I wouldn't out with it if I did know. If I turn state's witness, I would have to lie to implicate innocent men like myself. That ain't fair. No, I won't be a party to such a deal."

At my answer, Mr. Willingham turned to Mr. Doyle. "I told you that Jimmy wouldn't go for it." I knew then that it had been Doyle's plan.

The three of us went into the drug store and got a drink. Then we walked to the courthouse together. It was then about one o'clock, and the jury had been out just nine hours. There were many of my old friends from the Oklahoma Panhandle and the Cherokee Strip there to hear the verdict when I was taken in to the court room. As I walked down the aisle, many shook my hand and wished me the best of luck. I needed it, and it touched me to see my friends stand by me so loyally.

When everyone had taken his seat, Judge Price entered the courtroom and the bailiff called the court to order. The jury then piled in and took their seats. Since my talk with Willingham and Doyle I felt little hope for a favorable decision, for I knew that they had some inside information that had never reached me, though it had reached my lawyers. When the jury foreman handed his slip of paper to the clerk, I listened to their decision with no great surprise. The clerk read:

> We, the jury, duly and legally empaneled and qualified, find the defendent guilty as charged.

There was a little moan went down through the courtroom as my friends heard the verdict. Ed Sample had expected just such a verdict, and he now arose with a bill of exceptions which the court heard without comment. To his request, Judge Price stated that he would hear his plea for a new trial and pronounce sentence that afternoon at two o'clock. Then the Judge dismissed court.

I had another unpleasant surprise coming, for I was expecting my bond to hold good until the motion for a new trial was heard. This was not to be the case, and the Judge placed me in the custody of the Sheriff.[3] The Sheriff was absent at the time, so Dick Buis, the under-Sheriff, and Sam Givler, the latter an owl-headed deputy, took me in charge. I was put in jail where Jack Rhodes, my friend, was sitting playing solitaire.

Jack now asked me what was the status of my case, for he had not yet heard of the verdict. The two law officers stood nearby while Jack and I talked, but we held our voices low so they could not overhear us. I told Jack I had lost the case, and that I was going to try and make a break for freedom before two o'clock, but that I would try and help him make bond before I skipped. Jack begged me to leave Bob, the colored boy behind, since he was free anyway, and not in any trouble, and to take him instead on the second horse. I advised Jack to wait and stand trial, for I thought he would be acquitted. I knew Jack should not hook up with me now, even though we were fast friends, for he had a wife and two children to think about and no record against himself. But I couldn't shake him from the notion of leaving with me, and when he revealed to me that he had a .41 caliber Colt concealed in a leather money belt he was wearing, I began to think about dealing him in to my escape plan.

I told Jack that we could make the scratch if he would act unconcerned and let me plan it. I would arrange to have only the one deputy with us when the time came. I would then ask this deputy for his gun, and on that cue Jack would pull his Colt, get the drop on the deputy while I took his gun. This way we would hurt no one, and we would not get shot ourselves, for I wanted no one hurt because of me. Since that day I have heard the story that one or the other of us wanted to kill the deputy and the other kept him from it. That is false. Jack agreed to use my plan and to go out with me.

The deputies, Jack, and I ate at the hotel. When it came time to return to the courtroom to hear sentence pronounced, I asked Sam Givler if one of them would step over to Mr. Smokies' residence and tell him I wished to see him about making bond for Jack Rhodes. I would sign as his bondsman, I said. Sam directed Buis to go and get Mr. Smokie, leaving only Givler with Jack and me. I then suggested to Givler that we have a cigar, to which he agreed, and we walked to the drug store. It was only a few steps from the drug store to the livery stable where Bob waited with the horses all ready to ride. I asked Givler, after lighting the cigars, to allow me to step into the barn to relieve myself, and he sauntered along behind with Jack as I crossed the street. Meeting Bob at the smaller entrance door, where foot traffic entered the barn, I noted that the big door was closed within six inches. This would give us trouble, I thought to myself as Bob whispered to me, "They's all ready to go." I whispered back, "Don't you take any part in what follows. Just stand clear of the door." For I knew he would be left alone and on foot, and I wanted him to play no further part which would entangle him with the law. The boy was smart, and walked away as Givler and Rhodes entered the stable. I turned to Sam and said, "Sam, it's best that I leave you here. Hand me your gun."

I reached out to take Sam's gun, but Rhodes stood there without drawing on him. I repeated, and looked to Rhodes, "Loan me your gun, Sam." But Jack never acted, so we three just stood there for a second or two looking at each other. Then Sam spoke up, for he knew something was wrong.

"I'll do anything I can to help you, Jim, but just don't try to leave town," Sam said, and I could see he meant business. I believe I was as nervous as he was, but I took my horse's reins and paying little attention to the deputy, mounted. Out of the corner of my eye I saw that Jack mounted the other horse.

"If I'm not to ride again for years, believe I'll see how it feels to fit in a saddle again," I remarked to the deputy.

"Jim, you move that horse one step and try to leave town and I'll be obliged to shoot you," Sam said to me, laying his hand on the butt of his revolver and flicking his coattail back for business. I turned again to Rhodes.

"Jack, make him give up that gun or one of us is apt to get

139

hurt," I said. But Jack made no move to draw on the deputy, who never suspected that Jack Rhodes was carrying a revolver.

Well, the element of surprise had passed. There was no hope for me to get Sam's gun, mounted as I was on the gelding. I saw a choice of two things to do: dismount and give up, or get going through that little door and take my chances. This smaller door opened out onto the plank sidewalk, which was a step or two up from the barn floor. It was risky, but this smaller doorway was our only chance, and the best bet we had if the deputy drew and started firing. I kicked the big gelding in the ribs as hard as I could boot him, shouted back to Jack, "Follow me!"

The gelding and I went through that little doorway like a bolt of lightning. Fortunately he didn't stumble when he hit the plank sidewalk and pile us both up on the street, though I lost a good Stetson hat going through the doorway. I heard Jack behind me as he booted his horse and yelled "He-e-e-yah!" Then we were both on the street, riding east hell bent for election down the main street of Meade.

This stable was across the street from the Osgood Hotel where I stayed during the trial. The girls at the hotel had expected something to happen, and had gathered on the porch. When my horse landed on that board sidewalk with a crash, as I came streaking out of the barn, I caught a glimpse of the waitresses waving and heard them shout, "Goodbye, Jimmy!"

Jack and I had hardly cleared the doorway before I heard the shooting start, five shots, as I counted them, from Sam Givler's revolver. When I reached Crooked Creek, a small stream east of the town a quarter of a mile or so, I looked back and saw Jack weaving in the saddle, and I knew he had been hit. He was bent over low, as though in great pain, and hanging on to the saddlehorn. I drew up until his horse came alongside of mine, reached out and steadied him in the saddle as we made a run for it to the south, along the stream, where the old Jones & Plummer Trail headed into No Man's Land. As we rode along at a dead run I could see Jack was white in the face and gasping, his lips drawn back in pain, and it was all I could do to support him upright in the saddle. I pulled up the horses, dismounted, helped him down

140

and laid him in the grass alongside the trail. He could not move, though his eyes were open, and he spoke to me. He had been hit twice, once in the shoulder and once low in the back.

"I'm done for, Jim," he gasped out "Take Barney, my horse, he's the best of the two. Make it if you can—no use both us getting killed—go see my wife—tell her what happened . . ."

Those were the last words I ever heard spoken by my friend. I took the gun from his pocket, more so they would never know he had it than because I felt a need for it. It was fully loaded. As I glanced back down the trail I could see men on horses coming fast toward us. I was surprised to see several of my friends in the lead. I bid Jack a hasty farewell, took his hat and mounted. I waved to the boys coming, for I knew that they would take care of Jack, pulled Jack's hat down over my ears and headed for No Man's Land as fast as Barney could run.

I was about fifteen miles south of Meade and had recovered from the first shock of the excitement when I felt a burning sensation across my stomach. I stopped and took time to investigate. A bullet had pierced my shirt in two places and left a long, red welt across my stomach with a furrow about an eighth of an inch deep at one end. The groove was now red and swollen, and very sore.

I rode to the M Bar Ranch and there got a fresh horse. Since a posse might soon be after me at Jack's place, I rode over to Tom Runyon's ranch about four miles from where Jack lived and sent one of Runyon's boys over to tell Mrs. Rhodes what had happened. She immediately drove to Meade. Jack lived three days, just long enough to wind up his affairs and tell his wife and baby goodbye.

I heard later that Judge Price gave Sam Givler a tongue-lashing for shooting Jack. "When those boys made that break, you should have let them go," he said. "You had no call to murder them. They would have been picked up later." The Sheriff asked for Sam Givler's resignation. At the hearing over Rhodes' death, Givler testified he had fired three shots at me as I sailed out the barn door and two shots at Rhodes after he got on down the street. So he had almost missed me at close range, but he had hit my friend twice at fifty to seventy-five yards distance. Though I never liked Givler, I could not understand the criticism of him. He had only been doing his duty. He was later elected Sheriff of Meade County.

In the years that followed I had many friends tell me that they were glad I made the scratch. But we were all deeply sorry that the break caused Jack Rhodes' death, for he was a good man.[4]

part II

There was a saying in them old days that a man "had seen the elephant and heard the owl holler." It meant that he had been around a lot and slept out, maybe hid out when he got tangled up with the Law a bit. If he was wanted real bad by the Law, we'd say he was "ridin' the Owl Hoot Trail."

Jim Herron

part II

chapter IX

1893-1894

THE OWL HOOT TRAIL • PAYSON, ARIZONA

I was now twenty-eight years old, a widower with a small girl-child, but strangest of all to what I had expected of my life, I was now an outlaw. I had known outlaws, had arrested some of them and brought them to the bar of justice, but it just didn't seem real to me that I was now a part of their fraternity.

I returned to No Man's Land, where I had lived since the age of fourteen among my cowboy friends. Though The Association had posted a reward for me, and a fat one, none of the local lawmen or those from adjoining Kansas or Texas attempted to apprehend me. But I soon began to receive information from various sources that The Association was now really out to get me. I also knew that some of them so-called "inspectors" were actually just gunmen, what we called blood, or bounty, hunters. There were others anxious to make a "rep" for themselves by capturing or killing me, for though I was not known as a gunman I had made my enemies among that type of man.

My life at this point was changing. I became uneasy, slept with one eye open, as the saying was, and jumped at sudden noises. I began the practice of sitting always facing the door or the windows of a house, and I had an uncontrollable desire to keep looking behind me when I rode, like Billy Dixon told me he always did when riding in Indian country. I was not happy as I began to see such changes come over myself, for I had always been open-handed, hail-fellow-well-met, a man who cherished friendships and never talked about others' mistakes. Now I was studying every new face I met, looking for the worst in men, not the best. I didn't like myself too well this way.

Although I had quite a few cattle there on the range at that time, and owned the Hotel in Beaver, I had earlier realized that

145

if the verdict at my trial went against me, then I would need cash money to clear that country in a hurry. So that previous August, 1893, I had concluded a deal with John Over to buy my homestead which, as heretofore mentioned, was within the M Bar fence we had built. This sale had given me $450 in cash jingle in my pockets, and it was to come in mighty handy for I soon had to travel fast.[1]

Several weeks had passed since the trial and my break-away, and I realized that I must look for a new home, regret it as I did. I did not particularly grieve about leaving that country, but I did regret having to leave my old friends, especially the Goddard family—and May Goddard in particular. I had known them since they came to No Man's Land, and they were like my own family after Alice's death. Mr. Goddard ran 700 head of cattle, and his older girls were real cowgirls. I had grown up near them, and rode with them. Both rode "clothespin style," as they called it, and threw a rope as well as most cowboys. When the roundup was far from their range, we boys brought their cattle home with the throwback, but if the range work was close at hand, say within fifteen miles of their own ranch, May and Belle would work with the regular roundup, gather their cattle, and cut out their own stock.

Before the trial, while I was still under bond, I accompanied May to a picnic on the Beaver River, a popular recreational area at that time. The families all went along then, taking big baskets and boxes of food with them. We would select a nice grassy and shady place, such as the Red Rocks, or the fishing pools on Sharps Creek, where the old Adobe Walls Trail crossed the stream at Fulkerson's Ranch, and would stay two or three days at a time. Usually these summer affairs were to celebrate the Fourth of July or some other such occasion, or to pick wild plums for canning. At Sharps Creek we had constructed a platform under some cottonwood trees where we danced. Young and old danced, and we all had great fun. The music was provided by local fiddlers, harmonica players, guitarists, or banjo players, and occasionally an organ would be hauled by team and wagon for fifteen or twenty miles if the circumstances warranted it. The songs we danced to and sang were such tunes as *After The Ball, Barney McCoy, The Old Folks at Home, The Yellow Rose of Texas,* and *White Wings.* There were many waltzes played in them days, and *The Bowery* was another favorite to sing.

On this particular picnic, May and I were sitting in my top buggy near the stream, talking. She told me that she hoped very much that I would win this lawsuit, for she knew I was innocent of the charges against me. I asked her why she wanted so much for me to win. She answered with a question, "Don't you know?"

Now May had been a dear friend of my first wife, Alice, and she had helped us take care of Alice in her last illness. Though I knew May before I met Alice, neither May nor I had ever expressed any feelings of endearment for we were just close friends. And May was merely a child when I had first met her family—ten years my junior. But now, as we sat side by side in the seat, talking, I suddenly wondered why this had been so. May was now seventeen, and a most attractive young woman. I recalled one day when Alice was so ill and had asked me to sit by the bedside. May had been talking with her and comforting her, and had just left.

"Jim," Alice said to me, "if anything happens to me I would want you to marry again and be happy." As I shushed her, telling her that all would be well when we went to the specialists at Kansas City, she blurted out, "May would make you a wonderful wife!"

I had not thought of Alice's words since she uttered them, but now as I sat there in the shade of the big cottonwood trees with May beside me, the words came to me as a revelation. I took May's hands in mine and told her I was very happy that she cared about the outcome of the trial. "Whatever happens at the trial, May, you will always be uppermost in my mind," I pledged her.

"Whatever the outcome, Jim, I will be waiting at my home for you when it is over," she said, squeezing my hands.

I had remembered her words at Meade as I sat waiting to hear the verdict, and I realized then I had fallen deeply in love with her. When her father learned of our feelings, he spoke frankly to May and me.

147

"I don't hold anything against you, Jim, I want you to know this. I have never thought you guilty of The Association's charges. Neither do I object to your courting of my daughter. But Jim, it will be better for everyone concerned if you do not call on her at my ranch. The inspectors will surely watch you closely now. I do not want to have trouble with them here." Then he expressed to me his concern for May.

"You both must realize that if you marry now and try to ride out of here on your horses, that would be very dangerous. You must be careful, Jim, lest you leave May a widow."

I well understood what he meant, for he knew the bounty hunt was on for me. I would have to move most carefully. I thought at the time that May's father's attitude, although it curbed us from being together more, was completely right and totally justified. Since then I have helped raise three daughters of my own, and for that reason I know that Mr. Goddard was absolutely right.

Following his good advice, I would sometimes meet May at a little country schoolhouse where she taught, about a mile and a half from her home. There I had a clear view, and no bounty men could get in a position to surprise me. Frequently May and I would ride over to some neighboring ranch or granger's home and spend the evening with them. We visited the Healys and John Over on several occasions during this time, and on all of these trips tried to further our plans.

Mrs. Goddard's views of our affection for each other was different. One Saturday May's father had gone to town. There being no school that day, Mrs. Goddard asked May to go and find me, for she wanted to talk to both of us. May found me at Over's ranch and I quickly saddled up and rode back to Goddard's place with her. Mrs. Goddard greeted me in a friendly manner and served us some coffee and cake. As we sat at the table visiting, Mrs. Goddard told me of her attitude about us.

"As much as I regret it, Jim, I am aware of your love for each other," she began. "But I wonder if you are also aware of the consequences—or of the chances you are both taking? I want you to be conscious not only of the danger to your own life in staying here, but of May's reputation as well. Now I want you both to promise me that you will not leave the country together as I believe you have planned to do. If you do, you will surely be caught and it will simply ruin May's reputation. She is only seventeen, Jim. You are twenty-eight. You are old enough to think carefully about this."

I confessed that we had talked about leaving the Strip together. "But we have already abandoned that plan because of what would be said about May should we be caught," I told May's mother. "But now I am planning to leave—alone. I am going to establish myself on a ranch someplace, then return for May—and without any public announcement or marriage until we get out of the Strip and where folks don't know us. We'll have a quiet marriage someplace, and I'll take May to my ranch. Will we have your blessing then, Mrs. Goddard?"

Mrs. Goddard then gave her word that we would both have her consent and blessing if we did this the proper way. After this talk we all felt better, for it cleared the tension in their home and it gave us a sensible solution to our common problem.

That night May wrote down on a ruled sheet of writing paper the verses of an old song we had sung together many times. It was titled *The Queen of Hearts*, but this is the way she wrote it:

> To the Queen of Hearts is the Ace of Sorrow,
> Here today, Jim, gone tomorrow.
> I love my father, I love my mother,
> I love my sisters, I love my brother.
> I love my friends, and kinfolk, too,
> But I'll foresake them all *to go with you.*

May had underlined the last four words. I kept that little slip of paper in my warbag until it was wore out completely, with only the last line visible, "I'll forsake them all *to go with you.*" I learned the little verse by heart, the way she put it, and it was always a source of contentment to me in troublous times just to repeat it, to hum the tune, to recall May's lovely features, and to know she was waiting for me.

149

That following evening I rode up to John Over's ranch and had a long talk with him and revealed our plans. I made arrangements with Mr. Over to look after my affairs until he heard from me, for I had taken in a partner on some of my cattle there on the open range and I felt that this new partner might bear watching. After leaving John's place I hunted up a young man the next day who wanted to go west with me. I shall not tell his name, just refer to him as "Buck," for he was leaving there under a cloud to make a new life for himself, which he did. We took my two best saddle horses the following day and headed toward New Mexico.

We rode straight west 300 miles from my ranch without hardly seeing a man. Horsemen in them days were inconspicuous, especially if just traveling the trails without any special outfit. We followed up the Cimarron Canyon on the old Indian Trail, past Black Mesa, avoiding all towns and ranches. We passed through Kenton one night, calling the attention of only a half dozen barking dogs. When our horses became footsore and jaded we stopped at Chama, New Mexico, a lively little town on a narrow-gauge railroad high in the mountains where you cross the Continental Divide. The elevation there was 8,000 feet, the air crisp and cold. At a livery stable I swapped an old man for two fresh horses. I took a beating in the trade, but I was in no position to haggle. Then we pulled out in about three days for Globe, Arizona, singing a tune we had learned in a local dance hall:

> It's a little painted cottage,
> But far from it I roam,
> I'll trade my hoss and saddle just
> To be at Home Sweet Home!

I had a brother, Frank, who lived at Globe. He also operated a cattle ranch under the Mogollon Rim, east of Pine, and near Payson, which was sixty to eighty miles northwest of Globe. Frank later ran a hotel at Winslow and was pretty well known around Arizona. I did not know but what the inspectors might lay a trap to catch me at Globe, but Frank was a good friend of the Sheriff of his county, Henry Thompson, and he had written me that he thought the Sheriff would let him know if it got too hot for me there.

When I reached Globe, Frank and I went to talk with Sheriff Thompson. When Frank introduced me, the Sheriff laughed.

"Yes, Frank, I know all about this young man. I have his photograph and description." The Sheriff reached into a case and handed us the dodger with my photo on it and the charges of The Association. The reward was stamped in bold, black type "RE-WARD $2,000." I was grateful to see it didn't say "Dead or Alive," but I tell you it is some experience to stand in a Sheriff's office looking at your own picture and reading the amount of the reward!

"I'm not looking for blood money or bounty," the Sheriff said to Frank. "You just make sure your brother behaves himself and is a good fellow and he can stay right here and never be bothered. Should anything happen, we'll arrange it so he can move on."

Sheriff Thompson was so friendly that I was greatly relieved to know there was some place in the country where I could lay down at night and sleep with both eyes closed. Yet that feeling underneath that I was a "wanted man" would not leave me, and I was to learn to live with this most of my life as I traveled down the Owl Hoot Trail.

While the trial in Meade County, Kansas, had been in progress, a friend of mine, who was living at that time in Minneapolis, was back to the cattle country on a visit. He had worked as a cowboy for the Healys and later married one of our local girls. He was a French-Canadian, and we dubbed him "Frenchy." After he married, he took his bride back to Minnesota, for his parents were wealthy and needed him in their various business enterprises. When Frenchy learned of my trial he came up there and testified as a character witness for me. He told me at that time that if I left the country unexpectedly, and still wanted to keep in touch with my friends, to mail my letters through his Minneapolis address; he would then re-mail them for me. That way I just enclosed the pre-dated letter in an envelope addressed to Frenchy and he would take it out and post it for me. My return mail came the same route.

All the while this was going on, the inspectors and bounty hunters were watching Miss Goddard's mail, and some of them

151

went to Minneapolis, but returned sadly disappointed. May sent me a newspaper clipping about this time which told another version of my disappearance and present whereabouts:

This story was, of course, pure nonsense, and the bit of news didn't worry May or her folks, for they knew where I was hiding out and that I had promised both her mother and father that I was going absolutely straight. At that time the Jennings brothers and their family lived not far from the old YL ranch on Kiowa Creek. They were highly respected when I knew them and the boys were practicing law at Woodward, Oklahoma. Later, Al got to running with some boys led by a worthless character called "Little Dick," and they set up a shake-down operation in Oklahoma Territory, pretending they were U.S. Deputy Marshals and making the cattle drovers pay so much a head to trail cattle through the country. But that didn't last long, and Al and his friends tried robbing banks. Al got a life sentence for that. After serving a few years he was given a Citizen's Pardon, which restored to him his freedom and his vote. Later, Al ran for Governor of Oklahoma in the Democratic primaries and got beat.

Temple Houston, the son of old General Sam Houston, was another lawyer in Woodward who cut quite a wide swath. He was a good defense lawyer, a flamboyant fellow who wore his hair down around his shoulders and sometimes dressed in buckskin to have his picture taken. In October, 1894, Jack Love, an Oklahoma rancher, had a lawsuit and hired Houston as counsel. I wasn't there at the time, but Burris Wright,[2] a young feller who rode with me in Arizona later, and whose father was the Beaver County attorney about that time, told me afterward at Naco what had happened.

One of the Jennings brothers, Ed or John, Burris said, called Temple Houston a liar, or what amounted to it, about something

152

that had happened at the trial. Temple and his client were having a friendly drink that evening at the saloon when Ed and John Jennings entered. Then the ball started. Ed got himself killed and John was wounded. There was a question as to whether Temple Houston did all the shooting, but he got all the credit for it. Anyone who would call a Houston a liar to his face was a fool anyway.

Old Al Jennings was around California for years, stuffing dudes with nonsense and telling them wild yarns about himself in the early days. But the point is, I never did travel with any of them Jennings boys.

I stayed in Globe for three months, freighted with a sixteen-mule team between there and the Grand Prize Mine at Payson, hauling ore one way and supplies on the return. On this job I met a boy who was a store clerk, George W. P. Hunt, who was later to be governor of Arizona, and my life-long friend. After that I went up to my brother Frank's ranch near Payson where he and his wife Molly lived with their two children, Francis and May. Francis was later killed in World War I; May married John Lazar. The town of Payson was in a very isolated location, under the Mogollon Rim, which they pronounced like it was spelled "Mokie-owns." The cowboys who rode in from the north when asked by another for the makins' for a cigarette would tell him "Smoke-y'-owns!" The western story writer, Zane Gray, hadn't arrived there yet, so this land of prickly pear and pine trees, hills and lovely streams was yet a primitive area, known only to the miners and cattlemen and a few loggers. Flagstaff, the county seat town of Coconino County, was almost a hundred miles to the north over a twisty mountain trail.

The people at Payson in them days were working people like I was used to knowing, cowboys and miners and such. I took to them like a thirsty man takes to good bourbon whiskey. They just accepted strangers there for what you were. They were unconcerned as to *who* you were or where you came from, and they treated you just like you were born the minute they first laid eyes on you, like you had no past, no background, and had never done wrong. They seemed to accept me as a pretty good fellow, and that was all the introduction I needed.

The couple who ran the hotel there in Payson was typical of

the type of folks that lived there. They had come from Texas, and had four pretty daughters who waited on tables in the dining-room. One evening at the supper table, when I was still new there, the mother of these girls stopped by my table and we had a nice visit. She asked me where I came from, since I talked like a Texas man. I didn't want her to know I had fled from Kansas or Okla-homa Territory, so I just answered that I was a "native of Texas." When I told her my name was Jim Herron she became very inter-ested, and put me through a third degree. After a lot of question-ing she established that we were *cousins!* Imagine that!

This was a surprise to me, for I didn't know I had any relation except Frank and his family there. Her father and my father were brothers, and her father had been killed in the Confederate Army, so my father raised her. She was older than I, and all this hap-pened when I was too young to remember it. So the fact that the four pretty girls at the hotel were related to me helped us all get better acquainted, and though I stayed at Frank's ranch, by spring I had made many friends both in town and on the range. I was considered "one of the crowd" and we had real good times, riding them mountain trails ten and fifteen miles to attend a dance or social of some sort.

I did not tell these cousins of mine, or anyone else, of my re-cent troubles. I had made up my mind that if I could get back home to my ranch, straighten out my business affairs, and get May Goddard to return with me, we would marry and make the beautiful forested Mogollon Rim our home. I realized it would be most dangerous to return to Oklahoma Territory, for I had been on this crooked trail an outlaw must ride for several months now. But as spring came to central Arizona and the soft rains brought fresh and colorful wild flowers from the warmed earth, my mind turned, as do all young men's thoughts, to "the girl I left behind me." I had never forgotten May for an instant, nor my promise to her and to her folks, so I began to lay my plans for a careful trip back to old No Man's Land, where I had left my heart.

I knew it would be unwise to ride the trains, for every railroad detective would have a copy of my picture in his pocket. That closed the fastest and most comfortable route for me. I decided then that the safest way to return would be by horseback. I would leave Payson on my best saddle horse that spring of '94, going by way of the Valley of the Seven Rivers in New Mexico, across the Pecos, then in between Carlsbad and Artesia, north to Roswell, and over into the Texas Panhandle by way of Farwell. By this route I could avoid all lawmen on the trails. I would stop at ranches near Globe and Safford, in Arizona, and at other ranches near Deming and Las Cruces, in New Mexico. I would make no unnecessary delay at any point, would stay out of towns and eat my own cooking. I could carry a few handsful of grain in a saddlebag for my horse, but he would have to make out grazing on whatever grass he could find on the way. I would head for Zack Light's ranch, 400 miles distant from Payson, where I knew several of the cowboys and particularly M. C. Stewart,[3] an old friend of mine who was the ranch foreman and was later Sheriff of Eddy County, New Mexico for eighteen years. He was called "Sis," or Cicero.

Everything worked out as I had planned it, and when I reached Light's Ranch and hunted up Cicero he greeted me warmly. We had worked on the roundups together as young boys, and I was happy to see someone I had known before and to get filled in on the range news of that area.

"You bin on this Owl Hoot Trail near a year now?" Cicero asked, after we had visited a while.

"Yes," I answered, "and almost two thousand miles of that trail is enough for any man. I'm trying to get off it, Sis, but it's like leaving a mountain path in the Mogollons—a damned sight harder to ride back up than it was to come down for the dance!"

Cicero laughed, for he knew I wasn't cut out by nature to be an outlaw. I always liked every man I met, unless he did me dirt. I was always friendly to strangers, easy-going. I enjoyed being in a crowd, I liked cards, I enjoyed drinking with friends and acquaintances. A man like that just don't cotton to the lonely and secret life an outlaw must live.

"Knowing you, I have the feelin' that you'll get back on the straight and narrow again," Cicero told me. "You'll get a good woman and that'll help settle you down." I grinned back. But I didn't mention May, for at the time I was wondering if May—or any woman—could ever replace Alice in my feelings. I missed her and the baby a lot while riding the rimrocks above Payson and I

155

was to always feel a hole in my heart when I remembered her.

I arranged with Cicero for a change of horses, for mine was done in after the long, hard miles on them desert and mountain trails I had been riding. For the first time since leaving Payson I felt secure at Cicero's and the YO Ranch, so I stayed a week to rest up.

While I was there who should ride in one evening but my old pal from Benton, John (Irish) McGovern. He had been riding the rough string at the LFD nearby. Irish and I had met first at Dodge City when he was seventeen, fresh from New York state. He had never seen a cow outfit. I took him to Healy's ranch with me and, if I do say it, I made a real cowboy out of him. But he was the one who furnished the nerve and the staying qualities that a bronc stomper needs. He had sand, but he was the kind who gentle-broke his horses so that when he turned them to the boys to work cattle, that's what they did, not just buck. The horses Irish broke for a *remuda* were always worth ten dollars a head more than others for that reason. When he left Healy's he went to work for John Over. Later he was John's foreman. Irish still talked with a touch of his father's brogue from the "owled counthry," though I believe he was born on this side of the ocean. He was a boy you could tie to in any circumstance.

When Irish learned that I was on my way back to No Man's Land, he immediately decided to return with me. He also had a girl at Beaver City and wanted to see her again. He was broke so I loaned him $50 to make the trip back with me. Irish insisted on making out an IOU for the amount. His IOU was among more than $4,000 worth that I burned in a campfire when I left No Man's Land that summer. I had collected a lot of them at poker games, and I had made many loans to friends and acquaintances. I always gave away money when I had it, and with little thought of ever getting any of it back again.[4] I figured such small amounts are actually an investment in making better men and shouldn't be considered as a banker looks at loaning money, to make money. For you make such loans as I did only to friends anyway, not strangers. When a friend is down and out and needs some jingle, he should be helped by them that know him best. I always lent to any man I considered worthwhile and a lot of them—most of them—paid me back in some fashion. Many repaid me after I had burned their IOU's. Irish was one of them.

I got Irish a better horse at Cicero's, but I warned him it was going to be dangerous to travel with me, especially from the New Mexico line across the Texas Panhandle and to my old range in the Strip. Once we reached my range, I had little to fear from lawmen, for we would be among friends again and I would be planning my next get-away. Irish laughed at my new business of dodging the law, for he had known me as a lawman and he saw how out of character my new role was for me to play. But I had begun to get used to it, so I laughed with him. We were such good friends that nothing could ever have come between us.

By the time we reached Panhandle City, Texas, our horses were beginning to play out and it was still a hundred miles to Higgins, where I had friends. I asked Irish to ride on ahead into Panhandle City, leave his horse at the stable and take the train to Higgins. From there I suggested he go to Seab Jones' ranch, about three miles from Higgins on Commission Creek. There he could talk to Seab, who was an old friend of mine, and get a fresh horse and bring it back to me near Canadian City. I would meet him at the river breaks, four miles west from the town, near a flat, open area we both knew, where we had gathered cattle on the roundup at different times.

I rode on from there alone, my horse now so weary that I was afraid someone with a fresh horse might take in after me and botch my plans. I kept off the main road and stayed on a back trail until I reached the flat on the river, where I had a good view of the road. I watched and waited there all that day.

The next morning I saw the Irishman coming along leading the fresh horse. I was surprised to see that the horse he had borrowed was Jim, a running horse that belonged to the old YL. Charley Rynearson, the manager of the YL at that time, had been at Seab's when Irish arrived.

"Here—tell Jim to take my race horse," Charley said when he learned what Irish was after. "This hoss can outrun anything in the country," Charley said, meaning of course a Sheriff's posse.

I later learned that the horse had been named after me! Such is the notoriety when a man has to run from the law.

Since every road into Canadian City at that time was a section line road, we waited until night, for section-line fences criss-crossed the country and it was impossible to ride around the town. I saddled Jim and turned the other horse loose, where Seab's men would pick him up the following day.

The Canadian City officers had suspected something was amiss when they saw Irish leading Jim down the street earlier in the day. So when they saw us just after sundown skulking down the side streets, they must have decided to inquire into our movements. By the time we reached the river again, and got to the other bank, I could see the officers coming. It took all our nerve to hold our horses back and not start running, but Irish's horse was in no condition to make a run from the law, nor could he have kept up with Jim. I remembered that wild ride that Jack Rhodes and I had taken, too, and didn't want to make that mistake twice and involve Irish in my troubles, so we just kept enough distance between us and the lawmen so their rifles were of no use to them.

It is eighteen miles from Canadian City to Higgins, and we could see the officers following for about half that distance before darkness fell. I assumed that they had then returned to Canadian City, and breathed a little easier. When we reached Higgins it was good and dark, and I dismounted at the stock yards, in the darkest corner, near the edge of town. I had learned that Jack Rhodes' widow was then running the Higgins Hotel and I asked Irish to ride in and tell her I wanted to visit with her. Irish rode into town and stayed a while, but Mrs. Rhodes came at once, bringing me a good lunch and a cold bottle of beer.

After greeting her I asked about her family, and as we stood there chatting my horse nickered. Out of the darkness, along the road we could see dimly the three figures who had been following us. I hoped they would pass in the dark without seeing us, but they were too close to miss us and so near to us that I could hear every word they spoke.

"That's those fellows over there," I heard a bass voice say, and I heard the click of a hammer as a revolver was cocked, then the lever-action of a rifle as another threw a cartridge into the breech of his Winchester. My heart was doing double time and my throat got so dry I had to take a swallow of beer to wet it. It looked like real trouble ahead, and I was calculating how to avoid pulling Mrs. Rhodes into it as I had pulled her husband into his casket over that old trouble of mine. Then another voice whispered loud and clear.

"If that's them, George, I wouldn't try to take 'em in that dark corner." That struck me as good advice.

Mrs. Rhodes was a very large woman and she happened to be wearing a white dress. I suppose they could see this white object plainly there in the corrals and they talked about it, wondering what it could be. One said, "That's a white horse." Another whispered, "It wouldn't pay to bet on that." But when one of the three lit a cigarette it gave me the feeling that they had decided not to make a fight of it. They must have let the white dress lead them to believe it was a white horse, and since we had been riding bays it no doubt threw them off my trail, for they all soon rode away.

While I could have had the best of it in that dark corner, I had no intention of fighting officers of the law and had already taken my rifle from the scabbard with the thought of turning my horse loose to keep Seab Jones' and Charley Rynearson's names from coming into the talk if I were captured. I knew that the officers would not hurt Mrs. Rhodes, and that I could get through that wooden plank fence quickly and make myself scarce. I had friends nearby where I could borrow another horse before morning.

I learned eventually that when the three officers found Irish in town, they arrested him for "being in bad company." He didn't tell them who he was riding with, and pretended he didn't know my name. He said I was just another cowboy from New Mexico, so they turned him loose a few days later.

After them officers left the corrals, I told Mrs. Rhodes I was heading for Seab's ranch. She said Seab was in town, and that she would tell him to meet me at his ranch the next day. When I reached his ranch that night, I was surprised to find Billy Hill, "the Texas Hill Kid," as he was locally known, at the ranch. I had met Billy in No Man's Land when he was about seventeen.

He lived there with his mother and his two brothers, John and Alley. I met Mrs. Hill a time or two, and she was a real nice woman, but was having a difficult time on the frontier, raising a family alone. I once shot a young steer so she could have meat on the table. Billy, her son, was now about twenty or twenty-one, and he had become a hard, tough puncher who gave others a bad time. They called him a hard case, but he seemed to want to be friendly and helpful to me. So we had a talk.

I asked Billy to accompany me as far as Woodward, O.T., where I wanted to talk with my lawyer, Ed Sample, who I had learned would be there. Billy agreed to accompany me, but he told me that Seab wouldn't be there until the following morning, and that since the law was looking for me, we had better take a position away from the ranch house to await Seab's arrival. So we each took a couple of blankets from the house and rode over to a hill about a quarter of a mile or less from the ranch but which overlooked the ranch yard and the road approaching it. There we slept until the next morning.

I had a pair of field glasses, and when we awakened early that morning I took a look through them at the ranch. I saw dust arising on the road, and saw that Seab was coming but was accompanied by the same three men who had followed me from Canadian City. They stayed at the ranch but a short while, then all left, including Seab. I had wanted to talk with him, but I had no business with those other men so I stayed put on the hill. I figured that Seab had come out with them just to prove to them I was not at the ranch, then returned with them so they wouldn't be suspicious and also so he might keep an eye on them for a while.

When they had disappeared down the road and all was quiet again we noticed Jones' big Negro cook in the ranch yard. He was hoeing in the little garden patch, south of the house near a little pool of water they kept for irrigation purposes. The Hill Kid squinted through the glasses at him.

"I'm going to scare that old boy a bit before we leave," Billy said. He picked up my rifle which lay beside us. It was a Winchester 40.82, a good gun at that time.

"Now be careful, Billy, and don't hit him," I warned, laying my hand on the rifle barrel, for I didn't want the murder of an innocent Negro on my hands.

"Oh, I'm not going to hit him," Billy assured me, "I'm just goin' to scare him back into the house. Besides, he's bin workin' too hard anyhow." With that he put the rifle to his shoulder, took careful aim, and fired.

The bullet struck in the water, within ten feet of the colored boy, splashing water from the little pool almost on his feet. I handed Billy the glasses and took the rifle from him, then tried a shot into the pool of water myself. When I next squinted through the field glasses, the cook had disappeared from the garden, only to reappear at the window on the second floor of the ranch house, peeping out from behind the curtains.

"That's enough, Billy," I said. We mounted our horses, moved eastward behind the crest of the hill so the Negro couldn't see where we had been in hiding, then approached the ranch house from the road on its blind side. When we came to the house we called to the cook, asking him if he could prepare us a lunch, but never mentioning the shooting.

"Dey's bin someone shootin' at me," the cook said, his eyes wide with fright. "Ahm shouh leavin' dis place." He was plainly disturbed.

"Did they hit you?" we asked, hoping now to undo the damage we had done and reassure the cook.

"No sah, but they shouh knocked watah fum dat little pond," he said, pointing. He had looked, but couldn't find a dead body, he said, so no one had been killed there—yet. He fixed our lunch and we left. A few days later I saw Seab and mentioned our prank. He said, "Damn it, Jim, you boys cost me a good cook. You shouldn't act that way." His cook had quit.

That same night Billy and I rode to Woodward, and I learned at the livery stable and wagon yard that Ed Sample had already arrived in town as I had expected. It was late, but Billy knew where the saloonkeeper lived and we walked over to his home, for I wanted him to take the message to Mr. Sample. The saloonman agreed to deliver the message and arrange a meeting for us.

The following morning Mr. Sample met me at the saloonkeep-

er's house. Temple Houston was with him. I told them of my
hopes to obtain a new trial. I would accept whatever medicine the
court prescribed, I told them, then return to No Man's Land to
live after my term was served. For that was where I most wanted
to be. Mr. Sample was skeptical of my chances to win another
trial, but he agreed to intercede with Judge Price and see if he
would agree to a new trial.

I waited there at Woodward for four days while Ed Sample
went to Ashland and talked with Judge Price. When he returned
he said, "It's hopeless, Jim. The Judge takes a firm stand against
a new trial for you. We asked him to spell it out for us, and he did.
Here's his judicial opinion, insofar as your case is concerned."
With that, Ed handed me a sheet of legal paper on which the
Judge had sketched his thoughts something like this:

TO: Counsel for Jim Herron
FROM: Judge Francis Price
SUBJECT: Appeal for New Trial Etc.

In The Matter of Jim Herron vs the State of Kansas:
TO WIT:

If Jim Herron had not adjourned my
Court so abruptly at that time:
And had he not at that time stood convicted of grand larceny:
The court may have been pleased to
grant him a new trial.
However: Jim Herron has never served
a day of a sentence that the court would
have made as lenient as possible; so he has
small grounds upon which to plead for a
new trial.
As a personal note, let me state:
Jim is still a young fellow and can go
away to some other country and start all
over again. It may be that he will perform
some great miracle in this world's history
that will forever establish him as a worthy
man—and I wish him luck in his endeavors.
But if Jim thinks he can ever come back
here and live in peace, and without worry
about past transgressions, then he had
better think again.
I would like to be more obliging, Coun-
selors, but this is the way it must be.

162

I was sorely disappointed, and the whole thing had a comic touch that the Judge had purposely given it, no doubt because I, as he had pointed out, "adjourned his court so abruptly," that day at Meade.

"I'll bet that Judge Price asked you to give this to me to read," I said, shaking the paper before the attorneys.

"He did," Ed Sample said, nodding, his eyes twinkling.

"Then that means I must make some different plans," I said. But I knew damn well I was not going back and serve an unjust prison term while there was any free choice left to me.

chapter X

RETURN TO NO MAN'S LAND
DEPARTURE WITH MAY GODDARD
MARRIAGE IN LUNA, NEW MEXICO

It was forty miles from Woodward to the M Bar Ranch but the Texas Hill Kid and I made it in record time. May met me at the ranch the following morning and she was just as lovely as I had her pictured in my mind's eye. After we had become reacquainted, she took from her purse a newspaper clipping she had saved, and handed it to me. The story announced in bold headlines that "Jim Herron is back in the country and riding an Association-branded horse." It also mentioned that the Texas Hill Kid ". . . is riding now with Herron." This hand-out was evidently sent to the newspapers by some Association member, for every word was written to blacken my character. Jim, the race horse I had been loaned by Charley Rynearson, was indeed a YL-branded horse. But the story made it seem that I had stolen the horse, and the thought flittered through my mind that maybe Charley had made the loan, then gave the story to the newspapers. But I trusted Charley, and the fact he had nerve enough to lend me his horse, a common enough favor between friends at that time, kept me from tying his name up with the story for long. Associating my name with that of Billy Hill was designed to make us both look worse, for Billy did have a bad name. He used to keep his mother broke buying cartridges for his revolver that he used to kill wild game for their table—and an occasional maverick he found on the range. Billy had learned to draw exceptionally fast, and he was the best two-handed shot in the Strip when I knew him.

Billy Hill was not actually a bad boy, though he was very high-spirited and looking for adventure. He never showed any desire to kill a man just for the sake of killing like some of the fast gunmen did. But everyone knew of his cool nerve, and he had held his own with some of the toughs that inhabited No Man's Land without having to kill them. So he had their respect, if not their affection.[1]

While Billy was with me he did nothing that was wrong, other than playing the prank to scare the Negro cook at Seab Jones' ranch. And this sort of stuff we regarded as cowboy play in them days. I always felt that as long as the Hill Kid was traveling with me that the bounty hunters and The Association gunmen would think twice before tackling me. So I kept Billy close around me all the time I was straightening out my tangled affairs and waiting to get out of No Man's Land again. Billy became known as my bodyguard at that time, yet I had told him that all I wanted of him was to help me get out of the Strip without any more trouble. And he did.

I dealt what cattle and horses I had left to Mr. Over of the M Bar Ranch, and also sold him my interest in the pasture. I had left another good bunch of steers in which I held half-interest with a partner whom, for the purpose of this story, I shall just call "Tex," though that was not even his nickname. This Tex had sold our cattle to Seab Jones while I was gone. That was why I wanted to see Seab when I returned, for I had learned of the sale while yet in Arizona, and I wanted to know what the price had been that was paid for them. Seab gave me the exact figure he had paid Tex. Tex was now avoiding me, but I learned he was in the Panhandle of Texas and rode down to Higgins to see him. I guessed that he knew there was a price on my head, that if he could lure me to Higgins, have me arrested, then he would be free to spend the money from our cattle. He might even be thinking of the reward for himself.

When I told the Hill Kid about this business he was all for going after Tex with his gun, but I cautioned him about involving either of us in a murder charge. All I wanted from Tex was my share of money from the cattle. Furthermore, I was leery of just riding into Higgins and asking for Tex, for I might get myself bushwhacked by him or a cowman's posse, for that was an easy way to collect a reward. But nevertheless Billy and I rode down

165

to Higgins to figure out some way of collecting my money.

While we were camped a few miles out of the town, a couple of men rode up horseback and I immediately recognized one of them as Jim Barnes, a friend of the old days. He informed Billy and me that we were at the right spot at the right time, for he had seen Tex in town. Billy at once offered to ride in and get him for me, and I could see that was the only way I would ever lay a hand on my money again. So I agreed to let Billy go after him.

"But remember this, Billy," I cautioned him, "I want this man brought here without any violence of any kind. He'll bluff, if you act tough. But don't let him bluff you into drawing on him and starting trouble, for he'll have the whole town behind him then." I ordered Billy to carry only one revolver, no rifle, no knife, which he always wore on his belt. "Just look and act as peaceful as you can, but be stern with him."

Billy saddled up and mounted. As he rode off he grinned and called back over his shoulder, "Jim, I'll bring that old partner of yours out here or I'll bring his scalp!" I shook my fist at Billy.

"I don't want his scalp," I shouted after him. "I just want my money, you damned Injun!"

"You're too old to get shot, Jim," Billy shouted. "Besides you're planning on getting married!" I worried all the time Billy was gone, for I did not trust his temper.

I had never felt that I needed to watch or check up on friends and partners, and I was hurt by Tex's treachery. The amount due me would be in the neighborhood of five thousand dollars, too much to just let slip away. Yet men had been killed for far less than that, I knew. I hoped Billy would return without trouble, but I knew inside me I would make Tex very unhappy if he didn't return with Billy and talk to me.

In town, Billy soon found Tex standing along the sidewalk visiting with some other cattlemen. Billy called him aside, told him to make no effort to get back into the crowd or into the building or he would kill him then and there. He told Tex that his old partner, Jim Herron, wanted to talk with him and to get on his horse and they would ride away from town like brothers. Tex

166

understood this sort of lingo and went willingly with Billy and without challenge from the other men and they soon rode into our camp.

I greeted Tex as cordially as I could under the circumstances, for it is difficult for me to lose an old friend or be betrayed by him. Tex tried to make it appear that he had been looking for me and I let it go at that, just told him I was there to divide the money from the cattle sale.

"I'm not going to tell you how much money I'm expecting, Tex," I said to him, "for you know that better than I do. Take out the expenses you have been put to in keeping them since I left; then divide." I never mentioned the figure Seab Jones gave me on the amount of the sale, but I let it slip that I had talked with Seab. I then handed him a checkbook on the Higgins bank where he had deposited the money. "Just figure it up here on the back of this," I suggested to him.

Tex took the checkbook and started figuring. He had all the figures well in his head and in a few seconds he handed the book back to me. My share was noted as $4,894.89. There had been some money paid to grangers for damage to garden and fields and haystacks, together with other incidentals which he had a right to deduct. I handed the book back to him.

"Make out the check," I said, "I have no quarrel with these figures." Tex made out the check. I endorsed it right there and turned to Jim Barnes, who had remained in camp with me. I asked him if he would ride in and get me the cash. Jim remarked that it would make him nervous to be carrying so much money alone.

"I'll have Billy ride in with you, if you wish," I told him. So Billy accompanied Jim back to town. Tex, at my request, waited with me.

Jim returned with the money in paper bills, none larger than a twenty. They almost filled a saddlebag. That night, after handing Jim a twenty for his trouble and saying goodbye to him and his partner, Billy and I rode back to the M Bar Ranch. I was now ready to leave all my problems behind me, since I couldn't resolve them anyway short of going to prison for ten or twenty years. I never did believe that locking a man up in prison helped either the man or society. It just makes the man worse, then when he does get out society has a really bad problem with him as an ex-convict, for prison sentences teach men all the bad tricks of the trade and it then takes ten more lawmen to keep track of one more lawbreaker. Only the soft-headed believe in punishment stopping crime; if that were so, then after all the misery that has been dealt out in the world's past history, why is there still crime?

The next day I talked with May about the best way for us to leave the Strip and how we would get married once we were away from there. Once our plans were laid, we both felt better about it. I would leave on the following Sunday morning. I would arrange with Irish McGovern, who had again joined me after his three days in the Higgins jail, for him and his girl to take May to meet the train at a flag station on the railroad the following Sunday, a week after I left. That would give me an eight-day start on her. I gave May plenty of money for expenses, and the carfare to return home in event something happened that we hadn't planned on. We agreed to meet at San Antonio, New Mexico, the first small town on the Rio Grande south of Socorro, and on the railroad.

When we revealed to May's mother our plans to leave she did not think it safe, but she promised not to interfere.

"I only want you to be good to May, and to marry her, Jim," she said to me. Then she turned to May and said, "And I want you, May, to be a good wife to Jim and a good mother to your children. If you do that, you shall always have my blessing." May and I both rejoiced that her mother approved, for we would neither have wanted May to leave had it been otherwise.

When I had previously sold my cattle and horses, I kept back ten head of the best horses in the *remuda*, and they were really top cow horses, good young ones. I found a cowboy working for the Healys, Gene Hopper, who wanted to go southwest to work cattle. He agreed to take care of the horses, ride one, pack two others, and trail the rest. He would change off from time to time to rest the horses. His job was to follow along the dim roads and trails, as all cowboys did in them times when going to the roundup, so no one would think much about his string and the packs. I in-

168

structed him to stop along where there were settlements and pick up what provisions we needed. We packed our supplies on the pack horses, and always kept along a little grain for them, too. I wanted every horse in good condition when we reached Arizona, still 900 miles ahead of us.

The Hill Kid and I rode off the roads and trails a ways to avoid meeting anyone or letting anyone know we were traveling with this boy and his string. We stayed away from cow ranches this trip, for I wanted no trail for lawmen to follow. When we stopped at noon, or night, I would take my field glasses and sweep the area with them. If the way were clear, we would then ride down out of the hills to join the wrangler at night. We always camped before dark, and ate supper in some secluded spot, preferably one near a spring or stream where we had water for the animals. We'd find them a good spot for grazing and hobble them every night. Then Billy and I would pull off a quarter of a mile with our two horses picketed on the lasso rope and saddled for a quick get-away if necessary. Next morning we would throw those "night" horses into the herd and take two fresh ones for the first part of the day, for a horse don't graze well at the end of a rope, and with a saddle on all night.

We all changed horses every day and frequently we would change two or three times a day if the trails were rough or steep. I wanted no saddlesores or sore feet in my *remuda*. I had shod all the horses before leaving, for it would be dangerous to need to trade off a horse, or leave one with my brand on him behind, just because he went lame on us. They all carried either my Bar O or DOT brand, and a favorite saddle horse of May's that I took along I had branded MAY. I used this brand later on many horses and cattle in Arizona.

When we awoke each morning I would again scan the country with my glasses, then look over the camp. If the wrangler had out the "red signal," his red drawers tied to the saddlehorn or hanging on a bush, we would stay away, for he was indicating danger. But if it was his white shirt hanging there, we would know all was right and we would then ride into the camp for fresh morning horses and breakfast. I did most of the cooking, for like most cowmen, I had cooked since I was a boy on the roundup and sub-

169

stituted for ranch cooks who quit. I could whip up the best sour-dough biscuits, fry bacon, make good coffee and even a fair SOB stew, just like the old-time range cooks did. But I stopped cooking when I got married!

We made every effort to make this trip without incident of any sort, for I had promised to meet May, and I wanted no hitch in our plans. Only once did we entertain trouble, when six horse thieves rode down upon our wrangler from some nearby hills and started to unhobble and run off the horses. This was south from Gallinas Peak, in Lincoln County, New Mexico, where Billy the Kid and his gang once thieved and plundered. Apparently the law there hadn't rid the country of all them outlaws, for this outfit of five Mexicans and one Indian acted like they expected no trouble, taking ten good horses from this lone cowboy. But Billy and I had watched them through the glasses from the hill country opposite, and we knew they were following Gene but were unable to tell whether they were lawmen or just some curious cowhands who worked nearby. Only when they started unhobbling the horses and stood Gene off with a rifle did we begin to realize they were the real McCoy.

Billy and I worked our way down through the rocks and pines to get a better point from which to fight them off, for they were still out of rifle range. For some reason they left the wrangler mounted on his horse, after throwing his guns in the bushes. This gave Billy and me a better chance, for when they started away from the camp, driving the saddlehorses ahead of them we knew Gene was safe and spurred up our horses and made a run on them.

They probably thought a Sheriff's posse was behind them, for they put up only a short pretense of a fight. Gene quickly got his rifle and joined us. We stretched one of them across his horse and the rest pulled out, holding their friend on his saddle.

The gunfire made me very nervous, for I knew it could bring others to the location. We got out of there as fast as we could, and traveled late into the night. We made a camp on a dry arroyo that night, then I rode back on our trail for three or four miles in the dark. But no one was following, and no one came that night. It was the last we saw of any horse thieves on the trip.

170

I did worry about gunfire attracting others to us, for Billy practiced shooting the heads off rattlesnakes whenever we ran across one. He shot about equally well with either hand. I was not such a bad shot with my right hand, for I had practiced most of my life with a six-gun, and when rabbits, antelopes, prairie dogs, and coyotes would pop up, I would blast right along with Billy. But I usually did it when we were in wild country, and not near ranches or villages. Sometimes I hit my targets, but Billy never missed. There was something uncanny about the way he could handle those guns, nothing fancy, no twirling or tossing, but just draw fast and fire. Billy had even broke his saddle horses so that they never flinched when he drew and fired. My own horse, of course, would flinch, and sometimes the one I happened to be riding would pitch a few licks and try to spill me.

Billy shot much of the time with his right hand, and from the hip position, without apparent aiming of the gun. Nine times out of ten he would get a perfect hit on his target. But when he aimed, he never missed. One day he had aimed and killed a prairie dog that sat barking at us—something that a skilled rifleman will tell you is hard to do. Those dogs, of course, hadn't seen many men, probably never had been shot at, and didn't jump in the hole at the sight of a man on horseback. But it was a long, careful, and skillful shot. I asked Billy at that time that if he had to kill a man, would he aim or just shoot fast from the hip.

"Jim, you always aim, even when you shoot from the hip," he explained to me. "Like pointing your finger. You can learn to aim a gun, just like you aim your finger, to point at any target in any direction. It's just as fast, faster, for me to fire from the hip than from eye level."

"But aren't you more accurate when you aim from eye level?"

"Yes," Billy said, "if it's a real long shot. But less than sixty feet I shoot from the hip," He fired two or three times at a prickly pear cactus to show me how he could hit the same spot several times, firing from the hip. Then he aimed at eye level and shot through one leaf of the cactus three times. I could see it would have made little difference to him in a gun fight, for he put every bullet in the space of a man's hat band.

I had purposely avoided the country down around White Oaks and Carrizozo, for too many men knew me down there. That was quite a hangout for men who came from the Neutral Strip. We left the main road southwest of Santa Rosa and I started cutting across country near the salt lakes at Pinos Wells, depending on my compass to get us through the mountains. That is all rough country: rocks, junipers, and piney trees, and we didn't join up again with the main trails until we came south from Chupadera Mesa, near where Bingham, New Mexico, is today. There we were only thirty to forty miles from San Antonio, where I was to meet May.

When we approached the town, I sent the Hill Kid ahead to scout for me, and he found May without trouble. She had arrived there on the scheduled day and started looking for us. When I didn't ride in on the pre-arranged day she began looking in the nearby towns, hiring a livery rig to take her around. She had arrived almost a week before we got there, for that mountain trip had slowed us down some, but she had not worried for May had a lot of faith in me. She was just returning from a trip to Socorro when Billy found her. No one had been watching her movements, she said, so she and Billy attended a show that night in Socorro. As they sat watching the show, Billy said to May, "Old Jim would be eating his scarf tonight if he could see what a good time we're having!" Billy was in his early twenties at that time, and he was full of Old Ned and sure enjoyed good times.

May bought a buckboard the next morning and a good driving team, as I had instructed her to do. Then she and Billy drove east on the trail to meet us, leading Billy's horse. We met a few miles east of San Antonio and I tossed my cack into the rig and changed places with Billy. From that point we drove northwest across the flats, forded the Rio Grande south of Socorro, by-passed the town, and took off up the road to Magdalena. This was a lively little cow town near the Magdalena Mountain, so named because of the image of a woman on the north side of the mountain. We stayed on the main trail and crossed the plains to Augustine, with the Datil Mountains showing to the northwest. We spent a night at Horse Springs and the next morning crossed the Mangus range

172

near Aragon, dropping down to Apache Creek, where we camped for a night. We had begun to get into rough country and had slowed down. May now told me she understood why I had insisted she buy a sturdy wagon with a spring seat, for the mountain driving was rough even on this little heavy-tired wagon we had.

As we approached Luna Valley, a rich, forested, and hilly area covered with thick black grama and wheat grass in the meadows, we met up with a traveling cowboy. I immediately recognized him as Scott Reed, an old school chum of mine who was from Fort Worth, Texas. We pulled in under some ponderosa timber, camped in the pine cones and there had a fine visit. Scott had worked for the Spur outfit, he told us. His job had come to be more that of a gunman than a cowman, he said, for there was much trouble between the cattlemen and the grangers in that country where he had worked. The company expected him and the other boys to run the settlers out of the country, just as the Dodge Association had wanted us to do. Scott balked at such business and they fired him. If the Spurs hadn't fired him he would have quit anyway, he told me, for he wouldn't use a gun for a cowboy's wage. Billy agreed he was right on this point, and so did I.

"You know as well as anyone, Jim, that I don't mind gun-fightin'," Scott told us, "but I don't mean to harm folks that ain't hurtin' me. Them settlers is like my folks, and they got as much right there as cowmen." Scott talked with that familiar Texas drawl that I'd forgotten I once used, and here, away from everyone I knew back home where we were born, it gave me a feeling of homesickness, and made me feel right close to him.

Scott's folks had a ranch twenty miles northwest of Magdalena, and he was riding home for a visit. The place was only a small one, he said, but his father needed someone to care for it. Scott had been working on ranches and trail drives since a boy, and he relished the idea of being his own man for a while.

I told Scott my plans, and asked him if he knew of a minister in the country, one who could keep his mouth shut.

"Ah don't know a preacher," Scott said, "but I know just the old boy for youall. He's a Justice of the Peace sort of minister, an old cowboy that can legally tie your knot for you."

"Who is he?" I asked, "and where is he?"

"Name's Toles Cosper, and he lives right ahead in the little village—Luna, they call it. It's a Mormon settlement," Scott said.[2]

When we reached the valley we drove in from the east where the trail dropped down over the ridge almost into the town. At the Judge's home I asked if he would perform the ceremony, but not mail in the papers to Socorro, the county seat, for a week or so. He was a wise old fellow, understanding, and agreed there was no great hurry on his part to mail in the certificate. I gave him my most recent address, telling him we had come from San Antonio, New Mexico, and he duly recorded that on our marriage certificate. Well, it was true; just not *all* the truth.

The Judge called his wife, May and I, and Scott and Billy Hill into the little parlor of his home. There my dear little May and I stood before him and were placed in the "bonds" of matrimony, which are not really bonds at all but one of life's greatest privileges and deepest satisfactions.

The people of the village and Luna Valley were mostly Mormons, and though we were not of their faith they gave a little dance that evening in our honor. There were several of the range men present, but the only man I had ever known before was Scott Reed, though he knew several of the others. We always recalled that evening as a most pleasant one, for we were among both old friends and newly made ones.

Scott headed back to Magdalena the next day. Some time later I learned that he entered into an argument with another boy over a poker game. An eyewitness to this sad affair told me that the two boys both drew their revolvers and fired at the same time, killing each other. I felt very bad to lose this old friend, for Scott was a good boy and meant well.

We stayed on one more day at Luna, getting supplies and learning about the trails to the west through the mountains to Payson. This trip ahead would be the toughest we had made, so in spite of the fact May had purchased a good spring wagon, I traded it in on a mountain wagon with heavy tires and sturdy running gear over the body of which I spread a good twenty-ounce tarp for protection. I made up a four-horse hitch to pull it. Billy stayed with us while we outfitted. But he wanted to return to Oklahoma Territory the worst way, and it showed on him. He had a grievance with some boy, he said, and wanted to get it settled. I begged Billy to forget it, to come on with me, and start a new life. I offered to stake him in a small cow outfit, or to take him into whatever business I entered in Arizona, but this trouble on his mind kept him from thinking straight, and my offer had no appeal to him.

It was sometime before I heard of this Texas Hill Kid again, after he left us there in the San Francisco Mountains. News then was always four months late and a lie when it started. But the story came to me, and pretty straight, that he had gathered some of the old boys there in the Strip and set out in the get-rich-quick robbery business. Those sort of boys always seemed to blame someone besides themselves for their troubles, and wanted to "get even," just as Billy felt when he left me. Sometime later I read in the *San Francisco Examiner* about the Hill Kid and some others being surprised by a posse at the Gamble Ranch, in the west end of the Strip.[3] All were arrested but Billy. His five men were at the corral when the posse surrounded them. All surrendered. Billy was on the porch of the ranch house talking to a girl. He saw at once that he must get out of there, so he walked down the hill to a canyon below, almost in plain view of the lawmen. He called up to them, "You've got all of my men and our horses —now be satisfied."

The posse men knew Billy's prowess with his guns, but one of them cut loose at Billy. Billy turned, fired but twice and wounded two of the officers. That seemed to convince them that they wanted no shoot-out with the Texas Hill Kid, so they made no effort to follow him.

Most people admired Billy's nerve. And some of the posse men knew Billy personally, no doubt. So I am inclined to believe the officers preferred to take what they had, and as Billy told them, "be satisfied."

This Hill Kid was one of the few who took the crooked trail and quit the game without being locked up or killed. He is today

(1935) a well-respected citizen living under another name and has a fine and large family. Billy is still small in stature, and usually has a benign expression on his face, smiling and friendly. His wife and children would never suspect that behind that mask once rode one of the really few "two-gun" men of the frontier, a hip-shooting expert. I feel sure that his grandchildren would look at him from a new angle should they learn of his tempestuous past, and of the several men he had dropped with those revolvers he carried. But they will never know, for he left that life behind many years ago. I shall always remember Billy with a feeling of warmth and with gratitude, for he rode beside me at a time when there was a price on my head and gave me protection from the bounty hunters that wanted to collect it.

While I am on this subject, I shall mention another boy who was as lucky as the Hill Kid in getting out of the robbery business with a whole skin. You have all heard of Sam Bass, who held up the Union Pacific train and took off a load of gold coins. This was a highly successful robbery by a group of half-trained amateurs, and they were lucky to get away with it to begin with. But Sam Bass was eventually betrayed by one of his own men, Jim Murphy, and when the Bass gang rode into Round Rock, Texas, July 21, 1878, expecting to rob a bank, they ran smack dab into a posse packing lead. One of Sam's boys was Jim Jackson, Murphy's cousin. Some called him Frank. He had trailed with Sam Bass for a short while. Jim helped get the wounded Sam out of town. Sam couldn't stand riding, and he had Jim take him from the saddle and stash him away in some brush. Then he urged Jim to save his own skin.

Jim Jackson got out of there *pronto*, and he never went back.[4] He changed his name, and he is today more than seventy years of age. He has raised a good family that is a credit to his community, yet his own family doesn't know his right name! Jim once wrote a letter to the editor of a Williamson County, Texas, newspaper, offering to give himself up if the Governor would pardon him for his past deeds. His friends also petitioned for him, but nothing ever came of it.

One good friend of mine that rode with me on the roundup

176

many times in No Man's Land and north Texas was the foreman of a large ranch near Meade, Kansas. He had a strange background, and had changed his name. In the late Seventies he was a partner in a good ranch in Texas, but he had a dispute over range with another cowman and killed the man. He had to get out of there fast. Neither he nor his pardner had enough money to buy the other's share, but they concocted this deal: his pardner borrowed all the cash he could lay hands on and gave it to my friend. Then his pardner *traded his name* for the balance of the cattle. That way the man who had committed the murder could carry a good Texas name never associated with crime. My friend came north with a trail herd, about the time I came to Ogalallie, and worked and lived there on Crooked Creek for many years. He raised a good family, was a top cowman, and was highly respected. He and his wife separated later. His three children, two boys and a girl, bear his partner's name and probably never learned his real name.[5] But my friend made his partner's name a respected one in the Strip, both as cattleman and man.

Back in them days I knew quite a few of the boys who had a price on their heads. Word gets around among you when they know that you, too, are riding the Owl Hoot Trail. You always seem to be striking up an acquaintance with a stranger who will mention that he knows what you did, and then he reveals that the law is after him, too. I knew some of the western gunmen of my time, but the "two-gun" bit has been exaggerated. The Texas Hill Kid was the only real two-gun man I ever saw, with one exception, one of the Christian brothers whom I shall tell you about later. I knew the Dalton boys, Burt Alvord, Billy Stiles, Temple Houston, the Jennings boys, Bravo Juan, and an assortment of others less well-known, both in Arizona and Oklahoma Territories. Earlier there were such gunmen as Wild Bill Hickock, Billy the Kid, and John Wesley Hardin who flattered themselves at how many notches they put on their guns. They actually didn't notch their guns, just talked about it. Men who knew Billy the Kid told me that he had only one desire at the end of his short career and that was to kill another man. Some men who didn't have the faintest idea of what they were talking about said Billy killed thirty men.

177

That was nonsense, for I have been told by men who rode with Billy that he only shot five or six men, and some of them store clerks and barbers who were unarmed. He bushwhacked and shot others in the back.

Wild Bill Hickock was a peace officer in the cow towns of the Seventies in Kansas. Men told me that he had an overweening desire to kill, just to maintain his sorry reputation. The story I heard of him was this: he would shoot first, then tell a man to hold up his hands. If he missed the man, which he did at times, he could still arrest him. If he hit him, his problem was solved. Bill cashed in his checks when shot in the back of the head at Deadwood by another no-good named Jack McColl. Bill was playing poker and was holding a hand of aces and eights, two pair, with a queen kicker. That hand was always afterward called "The Dead Man's Hand." I have held it many times, and I expect I have seen a hundred framed sets of these aces and eights in saloons all over the country, each set said to be the original hand held by Wild Bill. I even had a set framed and hung on the wall of my Cow Ranch Saloon at Naco, Arizona, later. It was a good come-on for visitors who never tired of looking at the hand, listening to some barfly tell of Wild Bill's death and speculating on just what spiritual significance, if any, the cards had. For most people are superstitious.

Another fancy gunman was John Wesley Hardin, a preacher's son from El Paso. I saw him but once, in a saloon on Red River. He was about thirty then, had a terrible reputation. I do not know how many notches he had on his gun, but I looked at the butt of it and saw none. He did wear his suit coat so the butt of the gun stuck out. I believe he was the real McCoy, for every one I ever talked to who knew him, or knew about him, classed him as a killer. He drank plenty, and was mean and dangerous then. I heard once that he shot a man who snored in the room next to him at a hotel where he put up. Well, this may be stretching the rawhide too thin, and I don't guarantee the story, for I stayed in the same hotel he did that night and the way I snore he would surely have plugged me!

178

The old stories about these men grow wilder every year. I doubt the truth of many of them. Yet these men did exist, they did shoot and kill one another, and many of them were just ordinary boys like Billy Hill, kind and sympathetic to their friends and families, mean and spiteful to the lawmen who tried to kill them. Some of them worked both sides of the street, a lawman for a time, an outlaw for a time. I had done that trick myself.

Well, a man can get ornery when they keep him on the dodge year after year and he has no hope of getting back on the straight and narrow again. That is the thing he must guard against most of all when he finds himself riding the Owl Hoot Trail. A man doesn't have to turn himself into an animal just because he is chased like one. I always remembered that.

chapter XI

1894-1899

PAYSON, ARIZONA • PEARCE, ARIZONA
LA MORITA AND NACO, MEXICO
HERRON CHARGED WITH HORSE SMUGGLING

From Luna Valley, where May and I were married and where we parted from Scott Reed and the Texas Hill Kid, it was 150 miles over rugged mountain and hill country to Payson, Arizona. This was a long and trying trip, but with the aid of faithful Gene Hopper, who took care of the horses and helped me with the wagon through the roughest places, May and I arrived safely at Payson. We remembered that trip many years, and always spoke of it as our "Honeymoon Trail." For a while we stayed at the hotel which my cousins ran, until I found a small irrigated ranch, "The Strawberry Hill," two miles from town. There we hoped to settle down for good.

Since Payson, in Gila County, was within the domain of Sheriff Henry Thompson, my brother Frank's friend, I felt a security there I had not felt elsewhere, for I knew that if bounty men came looking for me the Sheriff would probably relay the information to Frank. Well, we lived at Payson nearly two years when Sheriff Thompson came up there in a buggy one day, bringing his wife along. He frequently would leave her at our home while he transacted his business there, and she and May had become good friends. This day he waited until the womenfolk had gone into the house, then handed me a letter he had received from a man in Oklahoma, a cook that I had met on the roundup the previous spring, while helping my brother.

"You might want to read this, Jim," was all he said.

I scanned it, then read it out loud. In the letter this cook revealed to the Sheriff that he had created quite a bit of excitement back in Oklahoma when he told some of my friends where

I was living. He had since learned that there was a reward for my apprehension, he related, and if the Sheriff "wanted to make some easy money" all he needed to do was to bring me in. "We can split the reward," the cook wrote, "and nobody will be the wiser."

After I had read it, both the Sheriff and I laughed at the greedy galoot. Then the Sheriff looked serious.

"You remember Jim, what I told you and Frank when you landed here. I am still not looking for blood or bounty money. But this man is." And he pointed to the letter. "He, or someone like him, will eventually betray you for that reward, for they know now where you are living. Now if you want to return, stand trial, or take your punishment, I will accept this reward money—for you. I will hand it over to Frank, and you will have it to fight your case. Otherwise, I advise you to look for a safer place than Payson, for this rascal has you fingered now and will point you out for other officers here or for a bounty hunter who wants the money."

The Sheriff was giving it to me straight from the shoulder, I knew that, for I had to do the same with a fellow one time that I knew was not guilty but who was about to get himself a life sentence for murder. So I explained my position to him.

"Sheriff," I said, "that money will no longer help me, for the Judge has refused to give me another trial. If there had been a chance, I would not have returned to Arizona. But thanks for being honest with me. You have been a true friend."

May and I had been blessed with a baby boy, Thomas Darrel, born May 28, 1895. Later a Chinaman gave him a nickname, "Sam," and it stuck for life.[1] I now had the boy to think of as well as May, and I told Sheriff Thompson how I felt. He was sympathetic.

"You're well liked here, Jim," he told me. "You folks have been good citizens, the kind this land needs. My advice is to locate another spot here in the Territory and try again. But don't make friends with a greedy cook on the roundup again!" He laughed, but I found it hard to even grin.

It was true that I was a natural-born mixer, liked most every man I ever met, but I couldn't sort out a Judas from another. It was just my nature to like human beings, men, women, and children, especially children. I never cared for bores, and there was always plenty of them among the barflies at my saloons I ran later. But I didn't actually dislike even them fellers, just thought them mighty poor entertainers.

After Sheriff Thompson and his missus departed that day, I told May what he had said, and told her of the cook's letter to him. As was her manner she asked no foolish questions and expressed no disappointment at leaving Payson, which she liked very well. She just asked, "Where do we go, Jim?"

I had begun to think of Old Mexico, for I realized that so long as I rode the Owl Hoot Trail as a wanted man there would be no peace for me in any of the States or Territories. The country was settling up, and I knew that if I bought a small ranch or a farm, soon I would be surrounded by other people, and there was always the possibility of drawing another neighbor like the roundup cook. So I decided to head south.

We cleaned up our property there at Payson and left with a buggy, two wagons, and the ten good saddle horses I had brought from No Man's Land. Gene Hopper had left Payson the year before to work for the Greene interests in Cochise County, but I found two other boys who wanted to move south, Bob Clayton and Harry Ramsey. We had to go through Globe, so I had an opportunity to visit with brother Frank before I left. We also spent an hour with Sheriff Thompson and his wife. I never told either Frank or the Sheriff where we were going, and they didn't ask, for we all preferred to keep my whereabouts unknown, and that way they could honestly tell any peace officers or bounty hunters that they did not know where I had gone. I told Frank I would write him, which I did, but only after we reached Mexico.

From Globe we went on southeast, up the Gila River, to Safford, skirting the Pinaleno mountain range to the west of us. Willcox was an important trading town in southern Arizona, so we passed through there and picked up some supplies at the general store, where I met Mr. Soto, who I was to later know at Pearce. He told me of this mining boom near Bisbee, and we decided to drive on down that way.

The Sulphur Springs Valley, down which we passed, was a hot, dry land of detached mountains, rolling *lomas* and *mesas,* and cloud-filled skies from which no rain seemed to ever fall. To our left lay the hazy-blue crest of the Chirachua Mountains, which the natives called "Cherry Cows." On the right were the ridges of the Dragoons. In this area the country was so dry that about all that grew there was a tall manzanita brush, mesquite, and cactus.

"All this country needs is rain and a better class of people," Harry Ramsey remarked one day. Bob Clayton, my wrangler, who had the answer to every joke I ever heard, replied, "Sure, Harry, and that's all they need in Hell!" This was about the truth, for a man looking for Hell, I told them, would have been satisfied anywhere in Cochise County. Yet I learned to like that region, and there were many big cattle spreads already in there.

When we got nearly to Pearce, a small village northeast from Tombstone about fifteen miles, we camped near the Kansas Settlement, at a ranch owned by an elderly couple, Mr. and Mrs. "Muley" Johnson. I never did learn his first name. They gave us permission to water our stock at their place. Mr. Johnson was six feet two, had graying sandy hair, and was a sociable old fellow. He told me that he owned most of the townsite of Pearce. Of course I thought he was stuffing me, for there was a big gold mining boom on at that town and they were drilling ore out of a big hole in the side of a small mountain right near the town. Muley told us how a cowboy-prospector, Johnny Pearce, had discovered this mine, and it was one of the best in the Southwest.[2] Pearce and his family made their claims on the mountain side, but the surrounding land was Government land, subject to other "squatter claims," all but this land Muley owned. Ore samples from the mine assayed $20,000 or more in silver per ton, and $5,000 in gold. That following year a 200-stamp mill was erected, and in three years more than a million dollars in ore was taken out of that Glory Hole on the hill!

We camped with Muley two days, and he studied me all the time. One day he told me that I appeared to be a fellow who could be trusted. He wanted a partner, and he thought me and my boys

183

could "help hold down my townsite." Others were pushing to get into the action in real estate, he said, and he couldn't stand them off alone.

The two boys with me were well-armed, and this impressed him, so he thought we three could stand off a whole passel of town boomers who were crowding in without so much as a howdy-do. Muley invited me to throw in with him.

Well, this Muley loaded me so full that I nearly lost confidence in him those first two days. But I needed to rest our stock and fill them up as well as to give May and the boy a decent bed to sleep in and this seemed to be the place. So I agreed to stay and see his hand out. Then he told me his full proposition.

Tombstone, Muley said, was the county seat of Cochise County, and from 1880 to 1886 had experienced the greatest mining boom Arizona had seen. Now the town was dead, almost deserted. Many houses and commercial buildings that remained there had the windows broken out and the lumber was weathering fast. His plan, Muley said, was to go there and buy up some of the better homes for a song that we could sing ourselves. Then we would use my horses and wagons and haul this lumber from Tombstone to help build this new town here at Pearce. Muley offered to go 50-50 with me. He would pay half the cost of the buildings, we would haul them over with my outfits and rebuild them on his Pearce town lots. The deal looked good and I agreed to it.

After my stock was rested, I hitched up a fast team to Muley's old phaeton that stood in his front yard with an inch coat of dust on its plush seats and he and I drove over to Pearce to view this burgeoning city.

The "town" was actually just a handful of adobe and frame shacks with one or two respectable buildings, such as the mercantile store of Mr. Soto's. The main street ran north and south and another street, almost as well-developed, cut through east and west. The town lay on the road to Tombstone. The big hill upon which the gold mine was being worked was southeast from the town, and I could see there was a lot of action up there, for they were digging the ore right out of the side of the hill in a sort of open pit mine. The country around was flat and dry, just desert country, and I wondered if May, the boy, and I wanted to spend a lifetime at this place. But it was the best offer I had at the time, so I looked the place over carefully.

I mingled with the miners and townspeople, and though it was still just a tent, wagon train, and adobe town, the atmosphere was good, for like any place where a mining boom has started, the men had money. I felt that I could get my share.

I talked with Mr. Chatman, who was the manager of Soto's store. I had met one of the Soto brothers at Willcox, and met the other one here. I learned from Mr. Chatman and others that a lot of what old Muley Johnson had told me was the real truth after all. Folks were arriving daily from other places and settling here at Pearce. If a man moved on to a piece of land, he had only what was called Squatter's Rights, like we had in No Man's Land, and that was the way it would be until a Government survey was made and a townsite platted.

While I was absorbing information, my friend Muley proceeded to get hog drunk at Gentry's Saloon. By the time I connected with him again he was well-organized, and to hear him tell it he owned not only the townsite but the whole damned country from Cochise to the border. I managed to get him back in the phaeton and we drove back to his ranch. But I had determined that he did have a good claim on much of the land that was right where the town of Pearce was beginning.

The following morning we hitched up to the phaeton again and drove down to Tombstone. There Muley showed me the houses he had talked so much about. There were scores of them that had been vacated, for Tombstone, everyone thought, was plumb dead. Most of the houses in the town were unoccupied, and ready to be moved to our townsite, but many of them were weathered and in very bad condition. Tombstone had hit the doldrums when the gold-silver mines had flooded at the 500-foot level in March of 1881. At the time, they thought they had hit a "water strike" that would aid the town and the surrounding arid country. But as time passed and other mines were flooded, the truth was becoming apparent. They had lifted five million dollars worth of ore out of them hills in 1881. But the water meant that mining days were over there. They kept pumping and trying, but by 1888 Tombstone had almost died, and the great boom was ended forever. This had happened six or seven years before Muley and I rode into the town, and the buildings showed it, for no one had put on a shingle or driven a nail there in ten years.

Martin Costello, a saloonkeeper at Tombstone, owned a block or two of the buildings. We bought a number of them from him, had a few sociable drinks, and played a few hands of poker. Then Muley and I drove back to his ranch the following day. I told May and Harry Ramsey and Bob Clayton that I felt it would be wise for all of us to stop there for the time and see if we could make some money from the mining boom, maybe help build a town. They agreed.

Muley had two large hay frames, or racks. These we put on the running gears of my wagons, after setting off our boxes. We hitched four mules to one and a four-horse team of mine to the other and with my men driving the wagons and Muley and I riding ahead in the phaeton like two squires, we set off for Tombstone.

We took the first house, on Toughnut Street, apart in sections. It was a small house. We loaded the walls, roof, and floor, and headed back to Pearce over the old trail Chief Cochise had used. About half way back, we camped at night near the Turquoise mine, where Gleeson was built, and arrived at the Pearce townsite the next morning.[3] We selected choice lots on the west side of the road, north of Soto's Store, and unloaded the lumber and the walls.

We built a second small building near the general merchandise store. This building was actually just two small homes, connected together, and within its walls I set up my first saloon. I had bought a portion of the old Crystal Palace bar, for I knew there was more money in selling booze in a boom town than in trying any sort of honest toil. In them days all that was necessary to open a saloon in Arizona Territory was to lay in a stock of liquor, register, and send in an application for a Government license, together with the fee. You were then in business. The Tombstone Sheriff's office collected county fees for the Territorial Government then. I built a fifteen-foot backbar: had an old Finnish cabinetmaker construct it from an earlier backbar with a wide mirror I picked up from Martin Costello.[4] The wood was a deep red mahogany, and it would shine like the seat of a cowboy's saddle at roundup time. I placed four card tables down one side of the room, opposite the bar. Then I got some galvanized pig-wire fence at Muley's place and constructed a bullpen at the rear of the building, where I could throw the sick or obstreperous drunks. There was good attendance the day I opened, and I never closed except for a few hours in the early morning. Harry Ramsey became my bartender, and a better man for it never lived, for Harry never drank on the job and little when off work. Later I opened a larger and better-equipped saloon for my trade, getting the good equipment from the defunct saloons in Tombstone.

After I finished the saloon building I built a nice little home for May and the boy. It was two blocks east from the main street, a quiet place where other folks lived whose men worked at the Johnny Pearce mine. There May, "Sam," and I were happy together. My saloon business was extra good, and I continued to pull over houses from Tombstone as the population increased. I had no trouble selling the homes so I put up three or four for rentals to catch that money, too, from the boys who couldn't pay cash. I fixed up one larger place for a widow woman who boarded miners, and all this built up our savings fund.

By the time we had been at Pearce a year we had established a good home and a good business and had made many friends. It was just too good to last. One day two men came to my saloon, took a few drinks, and played cards for an hour or two. While there were many strangers coming and going through that boom town at all times, this pair aroused my suspicions, for they didn't keep their lips buttoned like most unknown men do, and when they left my place they went to another saloon down the street that a friend of mine run, Joe Bignon by name, and Joe overheard scraps of their conversation. Joe sent a Mexican boy to me to tell me about their talk. These men had told our local constable, Billy Stiles, that he must go and place me under arrest, for I was wanted in Oklahoma, the Mexican boy told me.

187

I gave the boy a coin and told him to thank Joe for me. Then I got a horse and rode right out of town. I stayed away all day; no one knew where I was, not even May. Early the following morning I had a rancher named Gentry bring me to town in a light rig that would not be suspected. We drove to my home and I held the team and saddle horse for a quick get-away while Gentry went into the house and got May and the boy. The next morning when the sun lit up the east face of the San Jose mountains we were at the Customs House at La Morita, Sonora, Mexico, about eight miles south of the border! We ate breakfast there at the hotel, safe for the time.

This region of northern Sonora, along the international border, had a good cover of grass, better than at Pearce. The plains, though rough and poorly watered, were interspersed with clumps of palo verde brush, a green-trunked tree of great beauty, and clumps of the impressive *ocotillo* cactus, a plant that resembled nothing so much as a container in a hardware store filled with buggy whips, tasseled with red in the spring. There was prickly pear all over the range, but not like in the south of Texas. This was a land of real beauty, once a person learned to read it, especially in the spring when the wild flowers came in bloom and the yucca spruced up its stalks, but by summer time it was hot like a furnace, dry and dusty. The only relief from the heat was to be found in the higher altitudes in the mountain ranges.

Shortly after we arrived, I sold my interests at Pearce and acquired a cattle ranch and some horses in the Huachuca Mountains. I later sold this property to a Mr. Roberts who was ranching on the San Pedro River.[5]

When May and I first went to Mexico, neither of us could speak or understand Spanish. The proprietor of the hotel at La Morita was a Frenchman, Mons. Mille, who spoke Spanish as well as English and French. He started to teach us Spanish. By the time we had lived there a year, May could speak the language like a native and I could understand it and speak it rather poorly. Her activity in social affairs helped her learn proper conduct, and she taught me. At that time Mons. Mille purchased the general merchandise store at Naco, Arizona, a town that was booming on the border, and he induced May and me to buy his hotel. May then took complete charge of the La Morita Hotel, for I was busy buying and selling livestock. She had a cook and two girls to help her.

Most of the folks in this little community were educated people, for they were principally customs officers and Government representatives from the U.S. and Mexico, and there were lawyers and brokers and cattle buyers among them. We found them to be good neighbors and made many friends among them.

Running the hotel was good for May, for she had felt isolated at both Payson and Pearce, since she was away from her own folks and not living close neighbor to others either at Payson or Pearce. She now had a variety of people coming and going at our hotel, for the Mexican Customs House at La Morita funneled everyone coming into the country or leaving it through the town. Travelers were there from a day to sometimes a week or more. There were miners, cowboys, prospectors, engineers, surveyors, ranchers, geologists, sight-seers, con men, smugglers, card sharks, bull fighters, freighters, gamblers, race horse men, and what not. Some were dead honest; some were dead shots; some were dead-beats. May certainly learned a lot about human nature while running that hotel!

During the Republican administration of Benjamin Harrison, 1888-1891, the duty on Mexican import cattle had been so high that it was almost prohibitive to buy cattle in Mexico and ship them into the United States and make a profit on them. This left Mexico without her major beef market. As a consequence, Mexican and American companies in Mexico held a lot of big, rough steers in Mexico, some of them seven and eight years old, without a market to sell them to in that country.

At the time we went to live in Mexico, a Democratic administration under Grover Cleveland had changed this law, taken off the high duty, or greatly reduced it. It now cost only $1.75 a head to bring a big steer into the United States from Mexico, so there was a brisk business of importing beef into the U.S. I decided that I would buy and sell some of these cattle, for I had a little money and was beginning to make the acquaintance of many Mexican

189

and American growers south of the border. I recall that in 1899 there were reported to be 40,000 head of cattle on the San Pedro River which headed in Mexico and flowed across the border into and across western Cochise County. Buyers like Col. W. C. Land, J. N. Vaughn, Burt Dunlap, and others were buying there.

I began my venture by making short trips into northern Sonora and purchasing direct from the growers. Then my boys and I would drive the herds to the Customs House at La Morita. There the cattle underwent a health inspection and were authorized to enter the U.S., passing Mexican customs. By 1900 they had installed a dipping vat at Naco, Arizona, and there were plenty of buyers there and at La Morita, Sonora, Mexico, too.

The Customs House was moved from La Morita to Naco, Sonora, across from Naco, Arizona, about that time. There, on the U.S. side of the border, I would close my sales, frequently doubling my money on a herd! It was truly a good and profitable business in them earlier years, and with small chance of loss since the entire transaction from buying to selling would often require less than a month, sometimes as little as a week, depending on how far from the border I went to buy the herds.

I usually hired *vaqueros*, Mexican cowboys, that I paid good wages to, and I learned to trust them boys like my own Harry Ramsey and Bob Clayton, who had followed me to the border. I found ample financial backing to take on the biggest deals when I had my money tied up in other herds. I built a good reputation among the Mexican growers, for it was my policy to meet obligations promptly, and on the date specified, not earlier nor later. And I paid in gold and silver when they demanded metals. It was a bother to carry heavy metal coins, but it produced the best results, for everyone preferred hard metal cash to a bank draft of jawbone.

At this time I studied the Mexican people and learned to understand some of their characteristics. By treating them all well, I managed to do well for myself. I learned to trust and depend on the established working ranchers of any range to protect my herds while I was in their vicinity, and until Revolution came I was never disappointed in them.

190

It was not long until I had accumulated a nice herd of she stock and a good *remuda* of 200 head of saddle horses, which still included the good horses I had brought with me to Arizona.

During these years there was a great mining boom in Cochise County, Arizona, centering around the productive copper mines at Bisbee and Warren and at Cananea, in Sonora. About sixty percent of the taxable wealth of Cochise County was found in the seven-mile area surrounding Warren. These Arizona copper mines of the Kennicott Company and later of Phelps-Dodge produced millions of dollars in wealth for their stockholders, and some of it found its way into the pockets of the miners, the stockmen, farmers, town workers, and businessmen. Bisbee had been founded in 1877, about the time that silver and gold made Tombstone. But unlike Tombstone, the copper never ran out, nor could the mines flood for they were mostly the great, open-pit type. So Bisbee, Warren, and points south drew many of the people who had helped make Tombstone famous for its deviltry. I tell you, that whole country was a lively place in those years of the Nineties, and the boom reached down into and below the border country, and to La Morita, where we lived.

Back in Beaver County, Oklahoma Territory, my little daughter Ollie Dot, my first wife's child, was living with her grandmother Mrs. Ansel Groves. I wanted very much to see Dot, so May and I wrote Mrs. Groves and invited her to bring Dot and pay us a visit, since we had plenty of room at the hotel. She replied, agreeing to come, and we sent her money for the fare and met them when they arrived at Bisbee.

We all thoroughly enjoyed that visit, for May and Mrs. Groves' daughter Alice, my first wife, had been fast friends and she and Mrs. Groves felt like mother and daughter. Ollie Dot was now a beautiful child, about nine or ten. She enjoyed going on rides with me on the spotted Indian pony I had borrowed from a friend for this visit. Mrs. Groves fell in love with the hot, dry climate of our warm, Mexican winter, as well as becoming attached to our children, Sam and our baby 'Rita, who was born at La Morita, Sonora, Mexico April 14, 1897, and was named after the town of her birth.[6]

191

Some time after Mrs. Groves and Dot returned to Oklahoma, I was passing a herd of cattle through the American Customs, which was now on the border line, at the new town of Naco, Arizona, when I saw Scott White and his wife drive up to the Customs House. Scott was at that time Sheriff of Cochise County, Arizona, just the other side of the international line. Not knowing what Scott's business might be there at the line, I immediately returned to La Morita. I had sold my herd of cattle to an American buyer at Naco, but he could not move them across the line without my signed release. When this buyer learned that he could not move the stock without my signature, and that I had returned to La Morita he became very hostile about it. Sheriff White heard him bellering around the Naco Hotel, so he talked with the buyer and told him not to worry, that he would cross over the line and locate me.

When Scott appeared at our hotel, he asked me why I had left the yards without releasing the herd with my signature.

"I'll be frank, Sheriff," I said, "I didn't know exactly what your business was there at the Naco Customs Office, and I didn't care to find out."

Scott chuckled. "I thought so," he said. "But Jim, you take my rig and drive up there and sign those releases. Mrs. White and I will remain here and visit with your wife while you're gone." He handed me his buggy whip, which he was carrying. Then he added, "When you get back, we'll talk."

I drove to Naco and signed the papers and returned in time to enjoy a good supper with the Sheriff and his wife and May. After we had eaten, Scott and I sat on the veranda of the hotel and he explained the purpose of his visit.

"I had no intention of bothering you about that old Kansas case, Jim. But I wanted you to know that there is real danger to you from some of these strangers that come here—like the two that visited Pearce," Scott said.

I was surprised that the Sheriff seemed to know as much about me as I did about myself, for I had never mentioned the two men at Pearce to him. He mentioned two more he had seen.

192

Jim Herron and his second wife, May Goddard, in a photo taken shortly after their marriage in 1894.

The La Morita-Nacozari Stage, July 1900, at the Customs House at La Morita, Sonora, Mexico. It was at this Customs House, as a result of the Mexican official's impounding Jim Herron's horses, that all the troubles began which came to be called "The Naco War."

Naco, Sonora, Mexico, about 1923. Customs buildings straddle the gateway entrance. San Jose Mountain in background.

The Naco, Arizona office of the Greene Consolidated Copper Company, about 1900. William Cornell Greene was a mining king and a big rancher in Sonora, Mexico and in Arizona. His copper enterprise was in large part responsible for boom conditions in and around Naco.

William Greene's house, Hereford, Arizona, 1920. Used as office and head-quarters for his Cananea Cattle Company in Sonora, Mexico and for his Greene Cattle Company on the San Pedro River in southern Arizona, near where Jim Herron had a ranch.

195

Jim Herron's big Cow Ranch Saloon sign dominates the town of Naco,
Arizona in this photo taken about 1903, shortly before he moved to Tombstone, Arizona. Naco, Sonora, Mexico in background.

In front of Jim Herron's Cow Ranch Saloon. Herron (on white horse,
right) and Charley Sanders (on other white horse) with pack outfit headed
for the San Jose mine. Herron held a small interest in Sander's mine,
though he never worked at the mining business.

196

Colonel Emilio Kosterlitzky, about 1898-1900. He was in charge of the Rurales and border law forces of northern Sonora, under the Diaz administration, Republic of Mexico. Jim Herron always claimed that "Kosterlitzky saved my life."

Left to right: Arizona Rangers Lieutenant Brooks, Sergeant Hopkins, Captain Tom Rynning; Colonel Kosterlitzky, his trumpeter, Sergeant O'Jada of the Mexican *cordada*. About 1911.

Colonel Kosterlitzky's *cordada*, while campaigning against the Yaquis in Sonora, Mexico. Kosterlitzky is in white uniform. Colonel (later General) Fenokio is in center, wearing white coat.

William (Black Jack) Christian, outlaw in the Southwest. The Christian family was neighbor to the Herron family in Texas and as children Bill and Jim Herron's brother, Frank, played together. Jim Herron tells of meeting Black Jack in Sonora, Mexico shortly before Christian was killed in April 1897. Although this photo has often been identified as that of Black Jack, some authorities have their doubts because he was in his twenties when killed and this seems to be the photo of a man older than that.

Burt Alvord, leader of the Alvord-Stiles outlaw gang. Alvord earlier was a County Sheriff in Arizona.

Billy Stiles of the Alvord-Stiles gang. On one of Jim Herron's cattle-buying trips in Sonora, he met Stiles, and Billy came out of Mexico with Herron when he returned, but Stiles was caught. He escaped and later returned to his pre-outlaw profession—a lawman.

199

The Hotel Nobles, Tombstone, Arizona. The hotel was the stage stop for the Modoc Stage.

Hotel La Rita, about 1906. An early "Helldorado" celebration in progress. Standing on the balcony (left to right) are Lucy Spindles and Mrs. Barry, close friends of the Herrons, Jim Herron, and his daughter, Rita, then about nine years old. Newspaper offices of *The Tombstone Epitaph* and *The Tombstone Prospector* are at the left.

The Hotel Nobles became the Hotel La Rita in 1904, after Jim Herron bought it and moved to Tombstone. Here a visiting Lodge group poses in front of the hotel, about 1905. Fifth man from left (front row, squatting) is James H. Macia, father of Mrs. Burton Devere of Tombstone; to his left is his brother, Harry Macia. Rita, Herron's daughter, stands on the balcony. The building in the background is Schlieffen Hall.

Grave marker for Anna May Herron, Jim Herron's second wife, Tombstone Cemetery. Died November 17, 1904.

Jim Herron is seated at right. Thomas D. (Sam) Herron, his son, eleven, stands at left. Courtland, Arizona, about 1906.

Captain Francisco (Pancho) Villa, 1910, shortly after emerging from the hills to join the Madero Revolution. Villa was at this time thirty-three years old.

General Pancho Villa and one of his raiding columns pass through a Mexican village. Jim Herron had to pay Villa $5 gold (U.S.A.) per head of cattle to assure "safe" passage of the herds Herron bought and drove out of Sonora and Chihuahua, Mexico.

203

Traveling "first class" to war: men on top and horses inside gave Mexican rebel armies good mobility. The Revolution caused many American railroad men working in Mexico to return to the U.S.A. This curtailed much train transportation, and remaining railroads and workers were assigned only to military purposes; thus cattle, such as Jim Herron bought and sold, had to be driven long distances to border markets.

These are the type of Mexican soldiers, both Federal and Revolutionary, that Jim Herron had to get along with while bringing cattle out of Mexico, 1911-17.

Mexican General Jose Inez Salazar, center. Salazar and General Pascual Orozco were responsible for driving the Mormon colonists from Sonora and Chihuahua in 1913-14.

"Red Flaggers" on the move. Their flag, rarely photographed, gave these Orozco forces, or Government guerrillas, their nickname. The flag's white lettering reads (translated): Reform, Liberty and Country.

205

Thomas Darrell (Sam) Herron and his sister, Mrs. Rita Herron McGrew —son and daughter of Jim Herron and May Goddard Herron.

Mrs. Millie Herron Borba, Jim Herron's daughter by his third wife, Mary Valencia Herron.

The Jim Herron-May Goddard family. Standing, l to r: Jim Herron, jr.; grandmother (A. K. Goddard) Jackson; Jim Herron, sr.; Rita May, daughter of Sam Herron; Nell Herron, Sam's wife; Thomas D. (Sam) Herron; Rita (Herron) McGrew; Elmer McGrew. Next row, l to r: Jim Herron III, son of Jim, jr.; Jean McGrew, daughter of Rita; Bessie Herron, daughter of Sam; Emma McGrew, daughter of Rita; Albert Herron, son of Jim, jr.; Ruby Herron, daughter of Sam. Front row, l to r: Norma Mc-Grew, daughter of Rita; Billie Herron, daughter of Sam; Dorothy (?). Photo taken about 1930 at Herron's ranch near Payson, Arizona.

206

Jim Herron in 1940, after the loss of his eyesight.

Pioneers of No Man's Land, 1946. Standing, l to r: Con Jackson, former bronc rider; Burris Wright, old friend of Herron; Boss Neff, pioneer cowman; Jim Herron; C. R. Miller, old Cimarron cowboy; Bertha Loofbourrow, widow of Judge Loofbourrow and sister-in-law of Herron; Charles Hitch, large landowner and cowman; Curt Reichart, cowman. Squatting, l to r: Bill George, cowboy; H. S. Judy, banker-cowboy; Lee Larrabee, cowman and businessman; Bill Ewing, rancher, former Kramer cowboy; Jim England, pioneer cowboy.

207

They dug him a grave, at the set of the sun,
  His riding was over, his ropin' was done;
Brown-featured and bonny and strong were those brave
  Rough cowboys who gathered around Jim's lonely grave.
from the cowboy song, "Jim the Roper"

"Once that pair finds that you are in Mexico, and this close to the border, they'll make an attempt to get you out of here. I learned from a friend in Tombstone that they're after another fellow, too, so they may stay in this vicinty for a while. I saw them at Warren less than a week ago."

I found it difficult from Scott White's words to know whether he was advising me to move on or just letting me know I should be on the alert for bounty men.

"Now I mean to let sleeping dogs lie, Jim," he told me, and that reassured me. Scott had a reputation for being four-square with all men who were trying to do right, so we were good friends after that. I decided to remain at La Morita, for I knew of no better place from which I could watch both sides of the border.

When we first moved there, Mexico was under the administration of *Presidente* Porfirio Diaz. He was a regular dictator, but friendly to American businessmen. His regime was certainly a corrupt one, but to those of us who had investments down there he was our best bet. Toward the end of the century there was great agitation among the peons and the little people of Mexico for a change. They finally overthrew Diaz, but they had a hard time making the new government stick. There were a half dozen factions that moved in and out of power, and it was mighty rough going to buy and sell cattle or do any business there at that time while the Revolution was going. You just had to get along with whatever group held power at a given time, especially if you were moving cattle across their State lines, and across deserts and mountains, trying to get them to the border.

I shall not attempt to tell about the Mexican Revolution, for it was too tangled up for me to understand. I could hardly keep track of what was happening in northern Chihuahua and Sonora, but I did see that the bulk of the Mexican people were supporting or favoring Madero, and he had some tough supporters like Generals Obregon and Pancho Villa, who were great heroes for a while. After Madero was assassinated, everything seemed to go to pot and some of the men who supported him became little more than bandits. The big mining interests and big ranchers like Don Luis

209

Terrazas, who owned hundreds of thousands of cattle and millions of acres of land, were all for putting Diaz back in power. But they couldn't make it stick. The corruptness of the old fox poisoned the people against him, and most of the population had no land and owned only the rags on their backs and were crawling in poverty and anxious to take Terrazas' land for their own use. They wanted to upset everything associated with the old Diaz system, and many of them talked Socialism.

The Mexican laws at that time relating to smuggled goods were much like our own, that is, if the officials of the Mexican Customs House found smuggled goods they were, by law, supposed to confiscate them, sell the goods, and turn the money into the Mexican treasury. Now it was a long, long way from La Morita to Mexico City, and in them days there were few enough railroads, or even roads, to travel there on. There were no telephones, no automobiles, and travel was mostly by horseback or with a team and buggy. So that made it extremely easy for the Mexican Customs officers at La Morita to act about as they pleased. Their Government would likely never know what they seized and held and sold. Most of the Mexican Federal job positions were political plums anyway, and this was sort of what was expected of them.

As I came to know these officers it was not long until I understood how they prospered. I could see that nearly all of them inspectors and officials owned ranches nearby and had them heavily stocked with cattle and horses. I would see those crooked officers take horses, saddles, guns, and the like from American citizens, stuff they had no right to touch, claim it was contraband smuggled into their country, then "sell" it to themselves.

While I knew what was going on, I never interfered with their business. Some one said "Don't worry about the other fellow's graft as long as your own is working." That's about the policy I had adopted, though I did occasionally tip off our American friends when I knew they were about to be swindled or robbed by the officials. I advised them to see the American Consul at Bisbee, and he usually got their stuff back. A Señor Mora was in charge of the Mexican Customs. I seldom saw him. Their Señor Cuen was a cattle inspector, and he was a real petty tyrant and thief, but could be placated with a few gold coins, I soon learned.

210

These Mexican officials would run a bluff on you about as far as it would go, and we all had trouble getting our herds through Mexican Customs without them cutting a slice for themselves by means of an "inspection for health," a "quarantine," etc., etc. They were good at cutting back a few "diseased" cattle, like the Indians did when we crossed the Cheyenne-Arapahoe lands in 1880. The "diseased" cattle were always the biggest, fattest, youngest stuff in the herd! I had learned that a little U.S. gold coin called a Double Eagle was protection against most diseases they would find. That coin kept more cattle healthy on those border crossings for me than all the veterinarians and dipping vats combined!

When the El Paso and Southwestern Railroad built through that country via Benson and Fairbank in 1894, they established a line to Naco, Sonora, and later to Cananea, Sonora, called the Cananea-Yaqui River & Pacific Railroad. An old miner there at Naco who had once met President Cleveland sent him a wire: "The Southern Pacific has reached Naco!" A wire came back from the President to him: "Dear Charley: I'm happy to learn the S.P.R.R. has reached Naco. But just where in the hell *is* Naco?"

At that point the two towns of Naco burgeoned on the border, one on the U.S. side, the other in Mexico, but joined into one town. Then about 1898 we moved from La Morita to Naco, Sonora and built ourselves a nice little home there. These were lively towns, with twenty *cantinas* south of the border and half as many saloons north.

Right after we moved we had another addition to our family, a bright-eyed, dark-haired little son whom we named James Herron, jr., but who, like his father, was always called "Jim" Herron.[7] He was born August 7, 1899, near Naco, Arizona. This little fellow grew up to be a Pinal County, Arizona, Supervisor and Sheriff and later a State Senator from that district.

At that time Naco—both Nacos—had a terrific boom, and the sight of ox teams of thirty head to a wagon pulling heavy mine machinery and supplies from the railroad junction to the mines in Sonora was not unusual. There were thousands of teamsters passing through on the freight wagons and hundreds of cowboys from the nearby cattle range. It was almost impossible to find

211

a man who was not doing well there at that time. Money was loose, and the gambling tables and games in the saloons did a wonderful business. Fortunes were being made on the cattle range and in the mines in a few days or months, and booze flowed like water. There were border bandits of all kinds coming and going and the Mexican *vaqueros* with their gayly decorated sombreros and chaps made a truly picturesque sight. As a gateway to the richest mines and the finest pastures of northern Sonora, and situated so close to the booming mines of the Mule Mountains of Arizona, Naco appeared the brightest star in the Southwest firmament. And I noticed that Joe Wagner's Cow Yard Saloon did one of the largest *cash* businesses in the town.

There was a story told there of a townsman who found a corpse on the street one morning.

"Get shot?" he asked a nearby bartender.

"No," answered the bartender.

"Then he must have drank too much whiskey?" the townsman observed.

"No," the bartender answered, "not that."

The townsman walked over, turned the body over again and carefully studied it, taking the pulse.

"Then this man must be alive," he said, "for that's the only way men die here in Naco."

The story was apocryphal, but about right, for that place was surely as tough as ever Dodge or Tombstone dared to be. And I knew that with Joe Wagner's success selling booze another good saloon north of the border would make out all right, too. So I built a nice new corner lot building at Naco, Arizona, put in a good cowman's saloon there—though I never discouraged freighters and miners from patronizing me! I named it the Cow Ranch Saloon, and did a tremendous business from the start. On the south side of the line I had already become interested in a *cantina*. I liked to have it this way, for as a businessman on both sides of the border I was free to come and go past the Customs Houses without so much as a how-de-doo.

We had lived at Naco, Sonora, only a short time when the Mexican Customs officials at La Morita decided to deal me some

212

grief. This all happened in 1898-99. As I have mentioned, they were a predatory outfit. I kept a number of my best saddle horses close to Naco, for the good, grassy range on the Mexican side of the border was free and I used the horses to drive my herds up from the Sonora ranches. Bob Clayton worked for me then, and he would ride out in the early morning and gather the horses and bring them to my corrals, a little west of the town. One Sunday as Bob was bringing the horses in, a dozen Mexican soldiers rode up to him and their lieutenant informed him that the officials at the Mexican Customs House at La Morita had ordered my horses impounded. Bob asked what the reason could be for such action and the lieutenant told him the horses had been smuggled into Mexico.

Now Bob was excited, and he was the kind of boy that would start shooting and ask questions later, so when he told me what had happened I talked pretty straight to him to keep him from attempting to make a settlement with a gun with those officials. I saddled another horse and got down to La Morita as fast as the horse could travel, but I went alone, telling Bob to stay there at my house until he heard from me.

I went at once to see Señor Savarzo, one of the head men at the Mexican Customs House. He was a slight man, wore a scraggly black mustache and had a pair of shifty eyes, but he was polite as a schoolma'am at a parents meeting. I asked what he meant by seizing my horses and telling Bob they were smuggled into Mexico. He replied that he did not know for certain whether my animals had been smuggled in, but that if I pestered him about the affair, and tried to get them back, then the Customs officers at La Morita would look upon the matter with extreme disfavor and it could cause me a lot of trouble—*muy incómodo*.

This smuggling talk was, of course, nonsense. When I entered Mexico I declared everything I owned, for at that time I thought Mexico might become my permanent home. The ten saddle horses that I brought to Arizona from No Man's Land were a part of this band they impounded, but I had other horses I had bought, and held bills of sale on, in Sonora. All forty head they now held in the yards at La Morita.

213

I protested the action, of course, and Savarzo tried to make me believe they were going to keep my horses whatever I did, and that I would just have to like it. I really did not care to have trouble with them, yet I knew that they well understood what they were doing and that they were making a bold attempt to relieve me of these good saddle horses that were clear and free of any strings to the U.S. or Mexican governments. It riled me.

In my *remuda* there were many other animals wearing those same brands, so if I permitted them to take the ten best horses, which Savarzo indicated it would cost me if I accepted their terms and backed down, then the next raid they made might cost me the rest of my property. Nor would there be any way of preventing them from cutting deeply into every herd of cattle I brought across the border and ran through the Mexican Customs. The bribe they expected me to pay was just too high, for it meant they would be running my business for me, just as they had done others who had opposed them. If I permitted them to take ten head without a knock-down, drag-out fight, the next time I dealt with them they would be assured of my weakness.

Savarzo had stated that it was Captain Angula who had signed the order, seizing my horses, and this soldier worked closely with the Mexican Customs House, so here I was, at loggerheads with men who took their orders directly from the Mexican Government. Captain Angula commanded several hundred soldiers in and near La Morita. So I went to see him.

Captain Angula commented that he only took orders from his superiors, then carried them out to the letter. I haggled with him for nearly an hour, but received no satisfaction, so I rode back to Naco that evening without my horses. As I crossed that grassy plain, thinking about those smug thieves at La Morita, I determined that I would not let them fleece me without a fight. I would try to prevent their theft legally, if possible. If that proved to be impossible—well, I would wait then and see.

But I had no idea of the terrible price my friends would be forced to pay to help me see that justice prevailed.

chapter XII

1899

"THE NACO WAR"

During this time of my troubles with the Mexican Customs officials, we had a visit from my old friends Bud Powers, his wife, and small son, Jack, who lived near Canadian, Texas. Bud had sold his ranch in the Texas Panhandle to Frank Trammell and was looking for some good range land near Naco to lease. I wanted to go down to Arizpe, Sonora, and talk with the old Judge there about my impounded horses, for I knew and respected this old official. Bud and I decided to kill two birds with one stone and make the trip together. Arizpe was about a hundred miles south from Naco, so we planned on a trip that would take at least a week or two. I had bought cattle in that area, and south of there, and knew the roads and trails, so just the two of us made the trip together, driving a good team hitched to my sturdy spring wagon over which I fixed a jet top to break the rays of the sun.

Bud and I enjoyed the trip, arriving at Arizpe late one morning where we went directly to the Judge's home. I related to him the actions of the Mexican Customs officers at La Morita who had impounded my horses. The old Judge took notes, and when we left he advised me to leave everything to him. He had counseled with others concerning the activities of the Customs officers at La Morita, he said, and if they were not abiding by Mexican law, he would see that his Government made amends. If my horses were found to be clean, and not smuggled goods, they would be promptly returned to me, he said.

I rode back to Naco with Bud, greatly relieved of the pressure of having to conduct a fight against such people, personally and alone, in their own courts. Yet I wondered if Señor Savarzo, Captain Angula and Co., would take this lying down?

No sooner had I returned from Arizpe than they sent for me. I rode over to La Morita horseback. Again the officials tried their bluff, this time with open threats that they would force me into a Federal Court at Nogales, one not of my own choosing, if I did not yield to their pressure.

"Go on home, señor," Savarzo said in his wheedling tone, tinged with sarcasm and irony. "Queet worry about dees horsas. You haff many, many horsas. These horsas cause you *muy incómodo* eef you perseest in quarreling weeth us!"

It was becoming most difficult, but I tried to be civil in my talk. But such two-bit horse-thieves masquerading as Government officials under Mexican Law angered me. They still had the notion that they could scare me with "legal" talk of getting me in court until I broke and ran, leaving them in possession of the best saddle horses in northern Sonora, mine, with my legal brand on them.[1] Well, I decided not to play the game to their liking but to quit them cold turkey and carry the fight over their heads.

"I'm sorry, Señor Savarzo," I said, "and if this causes me to lose your friendship, which I have valued highly, so be it. But I am determined not to lose my horses, so I am going to meet your challenge. I am ready to go now to your Federal Court, with which you have threatened me. Please set your date."

I feel sure that this knocked Savarzo back on his heels, but he tried to act free and easy about it and began to make a counter offer "eef you weel just forget about thees horsas." But I was determined to see his hole card, so he finally set a date two days ahead when we would leave for Nogales, Saturday, September 9.

When I reached home that Friday night I told May about the outcome of my talks and told her when I would leave for Nogales. She had taken many trips with me both on horseback and in the buggy and enjoyed getting away from the house, so she asked to go along with me. The Bud Powers were still visiting us, so we invited them to come along. Bud was eager to see the area west of Naco and his wife and little boy, Jack, also came along.

"You may have to give bond, Jim, and I'm sure I'll make a favorable character witness for you," Bud joked me.

The next morning as we prepared to leave, there were quite a few folks standing around watching us including Captain Angula and about fifty of his soldiers. Harry Ramsey, my bartender at the Cow Ranch Saloon, was there. Also Bob Clayton and another young fellow, Franco, a U.S. citizen of Mexican parentage who was to act as my interpreter, for he was well educated and spoke English and Spanish. I wanted no misunderstanding when I got into that Mexican Federal Court.

Since we were to be accompanied by a group of Mexican soldiers, I asked Bob and Franco to follow us shortly after we left. Bob had been with me at the Rancho Escondido down near Magdalena when I bought some of the impounded horses. About sixty head of them had been purchased from Mr. F. Morgan. After I bought the horses, Bob, who was my foreman, and two of Morgan's *vaqueros* moved the horse herd from the Escondido to La Morita, where I was then living. So I needed Bob's testimony to back my own. May had also been along with me in the buggy on that trip and I felt that in a pinch I might need her testimony, too.

I had already instructed Bob and Franco that no matter what happened, they were to follow us on horseback just as soon as we passed through Customs and were on our way, staying at a respectful distance from the soldiers who would accompany us as guards. We planned to be at San Pedro, a small village on the San Pedro River, that night. It was about four miles from the border, in Mexico. We would proceed from there the following morning to Nogales, fifty to sixty miles west. As we left Naco, I asked Captain Angula if it would be permissable for Mr. Clayton and Mr. Franco to follow our party.

"Sí," the captain responded. "Take all the friends you want with you. If you weesh to go back across the border, that weel be all right, too—for it may be a long, long time before you have another chance!" He grinned knowingly at his lieutenants.

I thought his remark peculiar at the time, but made no issue of it, for I decided he might just be chiding me with the idea that I was certain to be convicted and thrown in the Mexican prison. But his high-pitched laugh that accompanied the remark, and the laughter of his officers and men standing nearby sounded to me like coyotes about to begin a feast on carrion. Later, that remark gave me something solid to think about.

The carriage in which we rode was a three-seated hack with a

217

cover, one that could carry nine passengers. My wife and I, our three children, Bud Powers, his wife and son all rode in comfort with our baggage piled behind the seat in a leather boot. The morning was cool, but as the sun rose higher it became quite warm. After we had traveled about ten miles I began to glance back toward Naco to see if Bob and Franco were following, for I had requested them to stay within a few hundred yards of the hack. They were nowhere to be seen. I sensed that something had gone wrong. May felt this too, for we both knew that Bob would never fail to appear unless something beyond his control had happened to him.

The Yaqui Indian lieutenant, who was in charge of the guard, rode alongside the buggy while one soldier rode ahead and the other five behind. May turned in her seat and asked him in Spanish if the soldiers were along to protect us and assure our safe arrival at Nogales. He replied, "Sí," that was true. He was a soldier of the Republic of Mexico, he said, and true to his oath as a soldier. If anyone attempted to molest us, he explained, or stop us, then he would fight for us, for it was his sworn duty to protect us. We knew by the strange way this officer talked that he suspected something and that everything was not all right. Since my family, and Bud's wife and boy were along, it worried me, for I had expected no trouble en route to Nogales. If the Yaqui lieutenant knew something that we didn't, then it didn't look good for us. The fact that neither Bob nor Franco had shown up made me doubly concerned about the trip and how it might end. I wanted to talk to Bud about it but he was sound asleep and I decided not to awaken him.

We had gotten within three miles of San Pedro when I looked back and saw three men riding toward us. The Yaqui lieutenant told May that he thought it was the party of Bob Clayton and Franco. We looked carefully at the three as they approached within 300 yards of us, where two of them dismounted. The third started riding at a slow trot towards us, and I could see then it was neither Bob nor Franco. As the rider drew closer I was surprised to see it was my bartender, Harry Ramsey.

218

Harry rode up smiling and said, "Got anything to drink, Jim?" I took a bottle of beer from a case we had been drinking from, pulled off the cap, and handed it to him. Harry tipped the bottle to his lips. As he lowered the bottle, he stepped his horse up closer to our rig and hurriedly whispered in English, "Something's happened at Naco. Be on the lookout, but don't move until we see how things turn out."

The lieutenant rode in closer and asked May what Harry had said. She smiled at him, but said nothing. Ramsey took his time, calmly drinking the beer, apparently stalling for time for some reason or other. I noted that Harry had our double-barrel, sawed-off backbar shotgun tied to his saddlehorn with a thong, ready for business. He also carried two six-shooters under his coat, but I didn't see them at the time. When he had finished his beer, Harry made his play. Turning to the lieutenant, he spoke in Spanish.

"Lieutenant, there's been trouble at Naco, and I'm obliged to arrest all of you. Order your men to toss their guns in the hack." At this point Harry swung the shotgun on the thong and covered the lieutenant and his men. I could understand now that Harry was trying to free our party from the guard for some yet unknown reason.

Mrs. Powers started crying and Harry quickly said, "My dear lady, don't cry; if these men do as I tell them there will be no trouble." But it was already too late for that, for the lieutenant barked an order in Spanish and started to draw his revolver. Harry's shotgun roared and the lieutenant dropped from the saddle, dead. The sergeant had ridden up with his rifle drawn, and Harry cut him down with the other barrel, blowing a big hole in his hand and arm which sent the sergeant riding away as fast as his horse could carry him. As the soldier in the lead rode back and saw what had happened he cried out, "No! Not me—not me!" and rode away at a gallop, his chaps flapping in the breeze. The remaining soldiers turned tail and fled, just as Harry's two friends rode up, their rifles drawn.[2]

I knew we had better get out of there fast, so I grabbed the whip and headed the team north to the border, about four miles

219

distant. The three men on horseback came galloping along behind us. Before we had gone two miles my team was breathing so hard I slowed down. One of the three men, a complete stranger to me, said "Let them stop and rest, Mista Jim." I pulled up the team. Looking back I could see a long column of Captain Angula's Mexican troopers that had evidently followed Ramsey and his two friends out of Naco. In the distance the six remaining guards now spurred their horses over to join the column. I yelled, starting the team again, but the stranger said to me, "Don't get excited, just walk the team for a spell. As soon as those soldiers get within range I'll turn them back for you." I observed that he carried a very highpowered rifle, and as we pulled away he stepped down from his horse and laid the rifle across his saddle to get a better aim at the soldiers, apparently taking a bead on the officer at the head of the column.

About the time we expected him to fire, the column of troopers turned away from our trail and started back in the direction of Naco. As we rode on north, Harry Ramsey rode alongside the hack and introduced the stranger by the name of Burr. The other man I had already noticed was an old friend of mine, George Astin.[3] We shook hands all around and I handed George and Burr a beer each.

We drove back across the international border and stopped at the ranch of George Spindles, where we posted a guard, for I thought the troops might follow us in the darkness. That evening, as we ate supper, Harry Ramsey enlightened us as to what had brought on this shooting. This was his story:

A few minutes after we left Naco, Bob Clayton and Franco, who were waiting on the American side of the line, started after us as we had planned. When they reached the international line, two Custom officers, backed by a dozen soldiers, stopped them and asked for their revolvers. Now this was a time when everyone who went anywhere carried a weapon of some sort for self-defense, even if it was technically against the law to take them into Mexico. The officers were completely within Mexican law in asking for their guns, but Bob refused to surrender his six-shooters.

"I'm holding you to your promise that Jim can take along all the friends and protection he needs," Bob told Savarzo and Angula.

At this point one of the Mexicans reached out and grabbed Bob's bridle rein. Bob, who was dismounted and holding the rein, snatched it back from the soldier. Bob was about ten feet over the line into Mexico when this happened, and now he jerked the bridle rein and started backing his horse across the line. At the same time he pulled out his revolver, and as the Mexican grabbed for the reins again Bob shot the Mexican and killed him, and also wounded the Captain—Molino. The Mexican soldiers then started firing at Bob, and several of their bullets struck him. He dropped the rein and staggered back across the line and into an adobe building in Naco where there was a little store. He died there on the dirt floor, and that is where Ramsey found him a few seconds later when he heard the shooting and came running from the saloon.

The same blast that killed Bob Clayton wounded Franco who was beside him. They took Franco prisoner and tossed him in their jail. That was the reason, said Harry, that the two men had failed to follow us.

Harry sensed that there was more behind Bob's murder than a spite killing of the moment, for he had already heard it whispered in Naco among the Mexicans that "Jim Herron's party will never reach Nogales alive." Harry reasoned that Bud's family and mine were now in grave danger, as was the unknowing Yaqui lieutenant and his guards, though just what had been planned for us had not yet been revealed.

"I didn't think much about Captain Angula's remark about you being gone 'a long, long time,' " he told me, "until I saw Bob murdered in cold blood there on the street and Franco shot down for no reason at all. If they could shoot men down on the street like dogs, then I knew they had plans to follow you up and murder everyone in your party. That would keep you from appearing against them in Federal Court. They had no intention of seeing you reach there." Harry was never more sincere than when he told us this.

"When I talked with George, he saw it exactly like I did,"

Harry continued. "I told the boys there at the bar that you and your family and the Powers, too, were in danger, Jim, and that I was going to do something about it, no matter how damned many Mexican soldiers were guarding you. George agreed to come along. Burr, here, didn't know you, but he said to me, 'I don't know this fellow, Jim Herron, but I'll tag along to keep you company. This is the sort of amusement I like, anyway.' "

Harry Ramsey looked at me from under his bushy eyebrows. He was a sober, reliable, and kindly man, not given to violence—the sort who would never make an offense against another person unless pressed to do so. I knew he didn't feel very good about this when I told him we were surely in for a lot of trouble over it.

"If I hadn't done what I did, Jim, I'm absolutely certain that none of you would have come out of there alive. I don't know what that lieutenant's orders were, but I'm satisfied all the arrangements had been made to see that you didn't reach Nogales. Bob's murder, and the attempt to kill Franco with him, was just a preliminary for what they had in store for you. That'll teach them Mexicans a lesson about shooting down American citizens on the main street, too," Harry said bitterly. He and Bob Clayton had been together for several years and were the best of friends, so I knew how badly he felt over Bob's death, for I, too, felt it sharply.

I knew that Harry was undoubtedly right about the whole matter. I had been too trusting with them fellers whose careers and fortunes were at stake should I win this case and prove them to be the thieves they were. It was impossible to figure out just what they had planned for us, but that was a hard country at the time and killing a *Gringo* or two was very lightly done, and with no apologies.

It was still my hope to reach the Federal Court at Nogales and tell my side of the story. So I asked Harry, George, and the new man, Burr, to stay away from Naco for a while until things cooled down. Nearly everything I owned was in Mexico at this time, all but my Cow Ranch Saloon, and I had three big herds gathered and paid for that I would have to move out of Sonora or lose them, and I wanted to take no chance of that.

222

The next morning as I was harnessing a fresh team, Burr walked out of the bunkhouse and started helping me with the horses. Since he had no special business, he said, he would like to stick around close to me and see that nothing happened to our families and the children. Harry Ramsey and George Astin were riding on west, he told me, but he had no reason to accompany them. I accepted his offer, so he stayed as a sort of bodyguard.

I didn't want to return to Naco until I had received word of what to expect there, so we drove into the Huachuca Mountains, on the Arizona side of the border, and stopped at the Tom York ranch for a few days. Burr left us there. He didn't say where he was going, or why, and I never asked him. I offered to pay him for his services to me and our families, but he wouldn't accept a cent, so all I could do was to thank him. I later learned that he was one of Black Jack Christian's boys—George Musgrave, I believe.

When we returned to Naco a few days later, hell was popping. At the time the wounded Franco had been arrested and Bob Clayton killed, the Mexican officials had pressed into services as "guards" several young Mexicans who had been standing on the street at the time. When they did this they made the mistake of drafting one boy who had been born in the United States, Jerrado Acado, from Tucson. He was a young cowboy who had just accidently been there at the time, and strangely enough was Franco's brother-in-law. That night, Acado and another guard liberated Franco and, wounded as he was, got him safely back across the border. Everyone now was praising Acado's grit, though unfortunately the other boy who was helping him was killed by the Rurales in the escape. This brought the total casualties in this attempt to keep me away from Federal Court to four dead and several wounded. They had begun to call it "The Naco War."

The Arizona Daily Citizen of September 16, 1899, saw the danger of all this conflict and killing along the international border, and reported the story this way:

OUTLOOK SERIOUS—MORE BORDER TROUBLE
FEARED—PLUCKY ACT OF TUCSON BOY
Bisbee, Ariz.; Sept. 15: Among the Mexicans at Naco pressed into service by the Mexican guards was Jerrado Acado, an American, born in Tucson.

223

Acado was a brother-in-law of Franco, an American cowboy who was arrested at the time of the killing of Clayton. Early yesterday morning Acado liberated Franco. The Mexican on guard with Acado was shot dead while trying to escape past the other guards. Acado and Franco are here. The outlook is serious. Seventy-five American cowboys are camped at Naco and are threatening trouble.

The newspapers weren't stretching it, for the murder of Bob Clayton and the previous shootings and difficulties between Mexicans and citizens of the United States had created an atmosphere of great tension between the two countries at this point.[4]

Though Ramsey explained what had happened at the border, I never got a real picture of it in my mind until I talked to Charley Sanders, an old friend of mine who owned some mining properties in the San Jose Mountains in Sonora. That day he came into the Cow Ranch Saloon as usual and ordered drinks for himself and me. Though I seldom drank with customers, I did treat old friends, so we walked to a table at the rear. I had loaned Charley a saddle horse a year before this and told him he could return him when he didn't need him any longer. For the first six months Charley would come in, buy drinks for the house, and tell me he still needed the horse. Now it was a year later, and he still had my horse! It had become a standard joke in Naco, Charley's borrowing my horse for such a long spell, but the good publicity was worth far more than the horse to me, so Charley and I had a silent understanding that he just keep the horse, reporting periodically to me, which he did.

Well, this day we passed our customary joke about Old Clover, which was the horse's name, then Charley began to tell me of the murder of Bob Clayton. Charley had been in the saloon south from my place, and heard all the wild talk at the border. He carried his beer to the doorway and looked out on the street. At the Mexican Guard House, south and across the street, Bob Clayton and Franco stood talking with these Customs officers. Some of the officials were the same that I had my quarrel with. The talk was pretty violent, Charley said, and Bob was less than ten feet from the international line, but on the Mexican side.

It looked to Charley like there was going to be some gunplay, so he set his beer down and went into the Mille Store, where the

224

walls were thick adobe and not the thin frame walls he had been leaning against. At that time Charley heard the Mexican guards' high-pitched voices demanding that Bob give up his guns, and he heard Bob answer them, "What do you take me for, a damned fool?"

After that Bob started backing his horse with the reins as a guard ran out from the bunch and grabbed his horse's bit. The guard shouted "Geev up your guns or go back!"

Bob was trying to back out of Mexico as the guard grabbed his horse. That was when Bob grabbed his six-shooter and shot the guard. Then the Mexicans shot a score of bullets at Bob, at least two striking him in the stomach.

"I'll never forget that," Charley said, wiping the sweat from his face with his bandana. "Bob just dropped the reins and his revolver in the street. He had a look of surprise on his face as he turned around. Then he started off toward the side of his horse in a little-bitty trot, like he was paralyzed, couldn't hardly walk. The saloonkeeper had a room there at one side of the building and Bob tottered into that door, the Frenchman helping him. A doc came from Bisbee, but he was too late; Bob was dead by that time."

This was the first I heard of Bob's murder from an eyewitness, and Charley's description was so graphic that I could almost see it. Franco, he said, went down a second or two after the firing started, when he tried to grab the gun of one of the Mexicans who was still shooting at Bob after he had been hit.

Within twenty minutes after the shooting, Charley said, Harry Ramsey came to him and asked to borrow Old Clover. Charley asked where he was going and Harry said "I'm going down into Mexico and fetch Jim Herron and his family and friends out before they murder all of them." Since Harry worked for me, and the horse was mine, Charley said he felt he should not only lend the horse but go along, but he didn't like Harry's looks, for he was then carrying the double-barreled shotgun by the thong he had tied to it to carry it on the saddle.

"I knew, Jim, that if Harry went down there and started shooting, the whole family might get killed," Charley said. "But what was I to do. I tried to talk Harry into waiting, but he was

225

determined to go, and he had gathered up two other men to go with him, George Astin and a feller I never saw before. Why was he taking him, I wondered. Well, I wouldn't loan him Old Clover, so he left, angry-like. He borrowed a horse from the Dutchman up the street."

I asked Charley just where Bob was when he was killed. "Was he on the American side of the line or in Mexico?"

"He was just about a yard from the line when the shooting started, when he killed the Mexican," Charley said. "He had backed his horse ten feet or so when the damned fool Mexican grabbed at the reins. But when Bob was hit he just turned and sort of trotted away, like he was paralyzed—with Mille helping him."

The fact that Bob had been killed practically on U.S. soil by a Mexican soldier turned this shooting into an international incident. When it became known that Mexican guards had crossed the line *after* shooting him, feelings ran high. Miners, cowboys, and others poured into town with rifles and revolvers and wanted to make their own settlement with the Mexicans: the customs people, the Rurales, the guards, the soldiers at the border.

The U.S. Army at that time ordered Captain Henry H. Wright down from Fort Huachuca with fifty Negro cavalrymen to keep the peace at Naco and see that no Mexican soldiers crossed the international border again. I believe this is all that stopped a genuine international fight, for our people north of the border were ready to set forth into Mexico.

chapter XIII

1899

THE TROUBLES AND THE TRIAL • NACO, ARIZONA

By this time the town was so hot that I decided I had better depart, after leaving my wife and children and the Powers family at my home. I warned them to burn the lamps low and to stay out of sight for a few days, for I had no idea what was going to happen. I had been the center of much of this controversy, and I did not want my presence there to cause more violence. I knew that if I could reach the Mexican Federal court Judge and give him my story it might allay much of the suspicion held by the Mexican Government officials—not the Customs people at Naco, Sonora, and those who were engaged in frauds and horse stealing, but the more responsible elements in their Sonoran Government. So I saddled a horse and rode back to the ranch home of Mr. and Mrs. T. I. York. Mr. York was an old friend, and one of the Cochise County Supervisors.

"I don't like to leave this country," I told Mr. York, "but by Ned I'll quit it if I have to do so to protect my property. I can't believe there is no law whatever in Mexico, or that there *is* a law that will protect those thieves at the Customs House, just because they are Mexican Nationals. Will you come with me, to see that I get a fair hearing and trial?"

Mr. York had his doubts, but he agreed to accompany me to Nogales. "We will take our saddle horses, ride to the Huachuca Siding, and board the train there. We'll pick up the horses at the Siding on our return," he said.

When we boarded the train at Huachuca Siding, we both bought copies of the *San Francisco Examiner*. On the front page, in bold headlines, was the account of the killing of the Yaqui lieutenant by Harry Ramsey and our delivery from the Mexican soldiers. The only thing missing was Harry's name, for it had not been let out yet just who did the shooting. But the name of Jim Herron was prominently featured in the story with a complete background story of my escape from the authorities at Meade, Kansas. The story went on that "Jim Herron, when interviewed by a reporter on the Mexican side of the border" etc., etc. and went on to say that Herron had stated that "he was safer in Mexico than in the United States."

This statement was, of course, absolutely false, for I had been interviewed by no one and had not been back into Mexico since our escape. It was another example of the yellow journalism of that time, when newspapers made up the news if there was nothing truthful to report, and where these "headline trials" convicted men long before their trial dates had ever been set.

Nevertheless, I observed the impression that had been made on Mr. York by the half-truth and exaggerations, for he peered over his spectacles at me as though he was seeing me for the first time. When he had finished the story, he asked if I had read it.

"I'm the man who made it, remember?" I said to him. "I glanced at the headlines, that's enough for me."

"If there's anything at all to this story, Jim," he said to me, looking very worried, "then we had better get off the train at Patagonia and not go on to Nogales. I started with you, and I'm no quitter, but this Oklahoma story makes it look very bad for you."

I explained to him as best I could that the old story had nothing to do with my present trouble. "I am not the man who is going to be charged this time," I said. "I am going to accuse the Mexican Customs officers. Now I prefer to go on and see it through. But you may turn back if you prefer."

Well, we went on to Nogales together.

Nogales, like Naco, lies on both sides of the border. The towns are actually a single town, but they lie in the two different countries. We went to John Gates' Saloon, on the U.S. side, and while I stayed there and visited with John, Mr. York looked over the town and felt out the public sentiment. When he returned he said he was happy to report that although nearly everyone had read the San Francisco newspaper story, most of them sympathized with me. I might add that Arizona Territory was made up of broad-minded people, most of whom would overlook anything in a man but hypocrisy. Many of them old-timers were, like myself, wanted elsewhere for one reason or another, and they never felt too warmly toward courts and Judges but believed that every man deserved another chance.

Mr. York suggested that I meet and talk with the U.S. Consul, which we did. I asked the Consul to accompany me to the Federal Court across the border, for I wanted him to see that I had a fair hearing. I then asked Mr. York to locate the Santa Cruz County Sheriff, for I wanted him to know about this hearing.

When the Sheriff came to the saloon he said he had read the newspaper story. I told him I was having enough trouble with the corrupt Mexican officials, and that I would appreciate it if he would let sleeping dogs lie for the present. He told me he would have the old Oklahoma charges thoroughly investigated before calling on me, and that this would give me time to clear away my present troubles. I expressed my gratitude to him.

"If you don't have any better sense than to run the risk of being backed up against a 'dobe wall and shot, I would be doing you a favor to arrest you and throw you in my nice, clean jail," he said in a good-natured way. I told him it was my hope to win in the Mexican court, since my business was dealing with cattle on both sides of the border and anything that put a crimp in that would ruin me.

Meanwhile, the U.S. Attorney had been to Naco and investigated the murder of Bob Clayton. He now came to Nogales to interview me. In a deposition, I told of the murder of the Mexican lieutenant and the wounding of his sergeant. Neither I nor anyone in my immediate party played any part in the hostilities, I said. I did not say who did the killing, nor who the two other men were, though the Attorney named Harry Ramsey as the murderer, for he had heard this from those in Naco who knew. I advised the Attorney that I had no intention of fleeing from the United States.

The Mexican Government, the U.S. Attorney said, had asked that I be held in custody until they could get extradition papers to take me across the border. He had turned them down, he said,

229

because of my otherwise good record as a citizen and businessman. But he counseled me not to cross the border until he had investigated the affair more fully. Later, he brought the Mexican Consul with an interpreter to see me. They asked if I would make another full statement of all the facts leading up to the murder of the Yaqui lieutenant and the wounding of the soldier. I agreed to do so.

We met that evening in a hall above the Consulate building. The room was filled with people, including the Sheriff, the U.S. Attorney, many lawyers, and officials for the two Customs Houses. Again I related all the facts I knew, going back to the theft of my horses by the Customs officials at La Morita under the pretense they were impounding "smuggled goods." When I concluded, the Mexican Consul asked me to go over to Nogales, Sonora, with him the following morning, and promised a fair hearing in the Mexican Federal Court. After consulting with the U.S. Attorney, I agreed to go.

When the meeting was over, the U.S. Attorney came over to me and said that he had been re-considering the matter of my going to Mexico the next day and had changed his opinion. He advised me not to go. So when I met the Mexican Consul that next morning I told him I had changed my mind, and that he had a full transcription of my remarks about the case which he could read to the court, and that I had nothing to add to it. It didn't set well with the old fellow.

The next day I received a communication from the Judge of the Mexican Federal Court at Nogales, Sonora, inviting me to cross over into Mexico and assuring me of a fair hearing before him. The document bore his official seal, and the old Mexican Consul had told me that I would receive every consideration before this man.

I was torn between two thoughts: I felt that I actually had less to fear in the Mexican courts than in our own, for I well knew that my fellow Americans frequently paid more attention to getting a conviction than they did to the evidence presented before them. I knew the Mexican people much better than most Americans did, who only crossed the border on occasions to pay a short visit in that country. I had hired many *vaqueros*, and they had served me loyally, and I had made hundreds of good friends among their people, particularly the *rancheros*, with whom I did business for many years. I felt that I was among friends when in their land, and I knew in my heart that the crooked officials at La Morita did no more represent the Mexican Government or the Mexican people than our border outlaws who robbed, killed, and made themselves a nuisance to both the United States and Mexico represented the United States and its people. On the other hand, I had been advised by everyone who pretended to know anything about the Mexican laws to stay on the U.S. side of the border. I considered what it would mean not only to myself but to May and the children if something untoward happened to me while I was down there, so I decided to remain in this country.

That evening Mr. York and I took the train back to Huachuca Siding, disregarding the old Mexican Judge's communication.

At that time I clipped this news story from *The Nogales Oasis*, Saturday, September 16, 1899, and I give it in full for it seems to sum up what had happened:

THE NACO TROUBLE—WEDNESDAY

Mr. James Herron and his friend, T. I. York, of Huachuca, visited Nogales, Mr. Herron coming to lay before the American Consul the particulars of the present bloody tragedy at and near Naco, and to ask the good offices of the Consulate in adjusting the difficulty. Mr. Albert Morawitz, U.S. Vice-Consul, in charge at Nogales, Sonora, took the statement of Mr. Herron and forwarded the same to Washington. The account of the matter given by Mr. Herron is about as follows:

Some time ago, Mexican Customs officials at La Morita, seized a half dozen horses, a part in a brand numbering about seventy, which Mr. Herron bought from Mr. F. Morgan. The allegation of the officials was that the animals were smuggled. Mr. Herron claimed that if the six seized were smuggled, the entire herd came within the same category.

Mr. Herron therewith went to Arizpe and there secured an order from the Judge of the District for the release of the stock. Even upon that order, as a condition precedent to release and delivery, the Mexican officials demanded from Herron repayment of the amount expended in caring for the

231

animals. This, Herron refused. It was finally arranged that Mr. Herron should come to Nogales, Sonora, under guard, to lay the matter before the Federal authorities here. Herron was to be accompanied by his foreman, Robert Clayton, and a Mexican in his employe, Franco, to interpret for him.

The party started from Naco Saturday, September 9th, in the morning. Just as they were leaving, the interpreter was arrested upon some charge. The Mexican guards continued on their way, taking Herron with them. Clayton remained with the interpreter and became engaged in an altercation with the officials in charge, who proceeded to arrest him. He declared he would not submit to arrest, and when one of the officers took hold of his bridle rein, Clayton ordered him to drop it. Upon refusal, Clayton fired, killing the officer.

Clayton immediately crossed the line (close at hand) amid a shower of bullets and entered a house where he died in a very short time from the effect of the wounds received during his retreat. Next upon the program, three of Herron's cowboy friends saddled up and started in pursuit of the guards who were traveling toward Nogales with Herron. They overtook the party 15 miles out, killed two of the three guards, put the other one to flight and released Herron to return to Naco with them.

Excitement ran high for a time at Naco. A number of armed cowboys gathered on the American side, and the Mexican guards were reinforced by a body of 25 Gendarmes under command of Col. Kosterlitzky. But when the two men, Herron and York, left there Monday, everything had quieted down.

When Colonel Kosterlitzky and General Fenokio appeared on the Mexican side of the border, they brought up about 200-300 soldiers with them as well as Colonel Kosterlitzky's *cordada* of twenty-five or thirty men. They set up a headquarters east of town, just across the border fence. There was a natural hostility between some of the Mexicans and Americans along the border, and the fact that my case had been largely responsible for the appearance of the troops and police didn't give me less anxiety, for most anything could now set off an explosion and I, of course, would be blamed for it.

On October 14, 1899, the *Bisbee Orb*, ran this story:

> James Herron, who was arrested by the Mexican
> authorities and taken to Nogales on the charge of
> stealing horses, and over whose arrest two deaths
> occurred, has returned to his ranch near Naco,
> having been released by the Nogales authorities.

This sort of reporting was not helping my reputation in Naco, but there had been such a rash of false rumors along the border that even that was fairly good reporting. On October 28, *The Nogales Oasis* ran the following:

> **ANOTHER FIGHT AT NACO REPORTED BETWEEN COWBOYS AND MEXICAN GUARDS**
>
> A freighter, Ryan by name, was killed, and
> guards riddled his body with bullets. He was a
> British subject. Dan Burgess, an onlooker. was shot
> in the left leg. Joe Rhodes and George Marts,
> American cowboys, were arrested and placed in
> the Mexican jail. A messenger was sent to the
> Mexican judge at La Morita, demanding that the
> Americans be given a hearing or released at once.

This story continued, stating that the cowboys on the American side would not let the prisoners be taken from the jail at Naco, Sonora, "as it means almost certain death to them as has been proven in previous cases when the prisoners are started from one place to another." This latter meant, of course, my particular case, and there had been other such incidents preceding it. The story continued, and I publish it as it was written, for it reveals the tension as well as the facts that occurred at the time:

> The American guards have been reinforced by a
> number of *rurales* and *cordados*, while a body of
> 50 Mexican cavalrymen are now on the way from
> La Morita to Naco. Col. Kosterlitzky and Col.
> Fenokio left Magdalena this afternoon with an-
> other body of cavalrymen. They expect to arrive
> at Naco tomorrow. Cowboys are being reinforced
> from all parts of the country. Over 100 well-armed
> men are now there. Thousands of rounds of ammu-
> nition and numbers of rifles were brought here to-
> day, the stores being nearly cleared out. An order
> for a box of Winchesters was received here from
> the Mexican Customs House and the rifles were
> sent down by wagon, but it is doubtful if they reach

their destination, as two well-armed cowboys left shortly afterwards to overtake the teamster and capture the rifles.

Wednesday, Gov. Murphy had wired Washington, advising the dispatch of troops to Naco. Thursday, under orders from the War Department, Capt. Wright was dispatched from Fort Huachuca with a troop of Cavalry. Capt. Wright wired the Fort from Naco that night that everything was quiet again.

At this time I learned from a friend, the Deputy Sheriff at Naco, that my trials were not over by any means. The arrangements were being completed, he said, to have me extradited to the Federal Court in Mexico.

I should have known that the Mexican Customs officers were not to give up so easy, for by this time it meant their jobs. I had been advised by the U.S. Attorney to not get caught in a Mexican Federal Court without plenty of legal help. So when the deputy told me the papers were ready to be served, I just rode out of town. I needed time to think. I was on the Owl Hoot Trail anyway, so why get gathered up in this extradition process?

As soon as Col. Kosterlitzky and Gen. Fenokio learned that I had returned to Naco and then left again, they sent a friend of mine with a note for me. Their note asked that I come and see them on the U.S. side of the border. I was assured that no extradition papers would be served, no trap laid for me, and no effort to apprehend me would be made.

Although I had never met Gen. Fenokio at this time, I knew Col. Kosterlitzky quite well. I had met him many times in Mexico while bringing out cattle from the interior, and I had been able to do him and his *cordada* small favors at times, once by allowing them a beef from a herd when they had not eaten for several days and had been after some bandits in the mountains. I had a genuine respect for Kosterlitzky, for he had a tough job dealing with some of the meanest outlaws on the border. So I felt I could trust him, and agreed to a meeting. We met at the appointed time at the first white monument east of Naco on the international border, at three o'clock the following afternoon. Col. Kosterlitzky spoke several languages so it was not difficult for the three of us to talk, with him translating. The Colonel explained to me that the Mexican courts would feel much better if I came over of my own free will, than if they had to extradite me, which, he pointed out, they could legally do.

I told them that I was sorry but I had not been able to see my way clear to do this previously. However, I had seriously re-considered and might change my mind; I would like to get everything straightened out and make my peace with the Governments on both sides of the border. Kosterlitzky and I had once talked of my Oklahoma troubles, for he knew everybody and everything that happened in northern Sonora and southern Arizona, and no one fooled him very much. I expressed my regret to Gen. Fenokio that the lieutenant accompanying us had been killed by a man whom I regarded as a faithful friend.

"Had I known what he intended to do, I would have persuaded him not to do it," I told the two men. "But he is *mi amigo*, and he felt responsible for the safety of our wives and families," I explained to them.

Both Kosterlitzky and Fenokio knew that prisoners had been "lost" while making such trips in Mexico, and they nodded their understanding. I previously had the feeling that they, as army men, would want to retaliate for the murder of the officer, of which I, of course, was entirely innocent. Now Gen. Fenokio said that he had thoroughly investigated the matter of the proper ownership of the horses and was in perfect agreement with me about the entire matter. His aide had been to the Rancho Escondido and verified my purchases, he said.

"Now," he said, "my Government does not want to engage in a war with the United States of America. My position here is only to maintain Law and Order, to keep peace and tranquility along the border."

I began to realize that these two officers cared little whether I was guilty or not guilty, free or in jail. Their great interest was in maintaining good relations with the Big Fellow north of the border. If I could help them resolve this friction that my trouble had generated all along the international line, then their support in any Mexican court would make my way much easier.

"Let me think the matter over one night," I told them as we parted. We all shook hands, and Gen. Fenokio invited me to be his personal guest at his camp, just across the border, the next morning for breakfast in event I decided to accompany them to Magdalena, where the troop was moving the following day.

In town the extradition was awaiting me, so I turned and rode over to a goat ranch, kept by an old German fellow I knew by the name of Heinz. I told Heinz I was a wanted man, wanted on both sides of the border now and that he could turn me in if he wished. But I was tired, I said, and needed a place to sleep. He invited me in to his humble quarters of adobe and told me that he wouldn't think of turning me over to the law, for I had always been a good friend. His warmth and friendliness made me feel better, and his humble supper of bread, cheese, and goat's milk was a bracer to me.

But I slept poorly that night. Here you are, I said to myself; you have gone the full trip down the Owl Hoot Trail. Now you are here, a proud cowman bedded down with the goats, and that only by the graciousness and kindness of an old German who is too good to turn you in and receive more money as a reward than he will ever have in his life. Thinking along this line, I reached a clean-cut decision by morning. I would go with Col. Kosterlitzky and Gen. Fenokio in the morning. All I would ask was for fair play.

I was up early and arrived at the sentry post in a short time. The guard accompanied me to the ranch house where Gen. Fenokio had his quarters. Both he and the Colonel were there, together with several staff officers. Both acted as though they were pleased to see me and invited me in for breakfast. I put on my best manners, for I had the feeling that the Colonel would have put me in chains, under a heavy guard, had it not been for the General's presence. We ate breakfast and within an hour were prepared to leave. I had left my revolver at the goat ranch, though I was still wearing my belt and holster. Since we were going overland, I suggested to General Fenokio that it would be a great favor to me if he would permit me to return and pick up my revolver. "We might see some deer or antelope along the road," I suggested. He nodded and smiled.

"Men who carry arms always feel more secure with them," he said. For the first time I began to feel like I would get an honest hearing in Mexico, and I was back in fifteen minutes with my gun. It was the one given me at Wild Horse Lake, years earlier.

About fifty of the soldiers were left at Naco, then the next day we set out for Magdalena, Sonora, with the troop of cavalry. The General and Colonel rode at the lead and I rode with some of the staff officers behind them. We went by way of Cananea, where we camped that night.

The next morning early, before we mounted up, General Fenokio rode by my tent and stopped. He showed me a telegram which an interpreter read to me. It was to the General from *Presidente* Diaz, and it stated something to the effect that "since the man from across the border has surrendered to you voluntarily, it may well be that he is innocent of the charges made by the *aduanero* and should be treated accordingly . . ." The *Presidente* suggested that the Federal Court make a thorough investigation before setting any trial date.

Both the General and the Colonel were pleased at this turn of events, and I was absolutely astounded that this case of horse-stealing, so far from the capital, had reached the *Presidente's* ears. I knew that had not Harry Ramsey taken the law into his own hands and helped blow the matter up into an international incident, Diaz certainly would never have learned of it, and my chances would have been slim. But the policy of the Diaz regime, however corrupt it may have become, was to avoid trouble with the United States and to encourage capital investments in Mexico by the hated Yanqui, even if his own people lacked land, property, or even food on the table.

That evening, following our arrival at Magdalena, Col. Kosterlitzky and I took the train to Nogales, Sonora. On the trip we had a long and friendly visit. My judgment of his character seemed confirmed, for he proved to be a man of wide experience and knowledge, and he became quite friendly in talking about his experiences. I had heard that he was hard on criminals, but I was never treated with more courtesy or consideration.[1] He was curious about my experiences in Oklahoma and expressed great interest in the life I had led, so I found myself practically telling him

237

the story of my life since I was fourteen and became a trail hand. I made it clear to him that I had never seen the inside of a jail, and didn't want to start in a Mexican 'dobe. He said I was fortunate, for he had undergone that experience in his youth, and he told me of jumping ship in South American waters to avoid being impressed as a seaman.

This Kosterlitzky was a Russian or a Pole and had come to the United States years before, then moved to Mexico. He had built a reputation as a policeman, and he now commanded all the Rurales in northern Sonora. What with cattle rustlers, dope smugglers, and outlaws coming and going across the line, he had a time. This was a prime spot for border smuggling, and goods from China, South America—from all over the world—came into the United States through Old Mexico and its ports.

When we arrived at Nogales and reported to the Judge, Col. Kosterlitzky asked that I have a free rein to come and go as I pleased, since I was a voluntary prisoner. The Judge agreed to that. When we made our appearance before the Judge it was at his own home, about nine o'clock in the morning. The Colonel did all of the interpreting, for the Judge spoke only Spanish. The Judge asked if I had not been in Nogales, Arizona, about a week or ten days before and declined his kind invitation to appear before him at that time. I had to admit that it had been so, but I explained my reasons for not appearing at that time.

"It is occasionally the custom in your country, when dealing with prisoners and those charged with crimes, to stand them up before an adobe wall and shoot them first, and to ask them the questions later." I smiled, and tried not to be offensive when I made this remark. "So many of my friends, and my legal advisors, feared for my safety. I personally did not have such fears, at least not while in your hands, but some of the soldiers may have been bitter about the needless murder of the army officer, and taken the matter into their own hands before I reached your court."

The Judge looked at the Colonel and they both smiled as my words were interpreted. The Judge was then read the telegram that had been received from Diaz. He said for translation, "Mr.

238

Herron, I would not want your friends to give you another scare and prevent the natural unfolding of justice in your case."

We were in his court the next day at ten o'clock in the morning. I recognized several friends from each side of the border, there to hear the court's decision. But I made no move to talk with any of them, for I was depending entirely on the Mexican Judge and his sense of Mexican justice to end my worries.

I was kept on the stand more than an hour and again related the background for the trouble. I was then asked many questions, such as whether I had killed any Mexican soldiers and so forth. I replied that I had not, and that the intelligence shown by the remaining soldiers who left the scene probably saved my life and the lives of the others with me. I was asked who killed the Yaqui lieutenant, and here I feared I might not pass their inspection. I told the court that the man was a close friend of mine, but that I did not feel that I could reveal his name, for he showed up at that time and risked his own life in what he believed was a long chance at saving the lives of my family and friends. I felt that if the Judge didn't know it was Harry Ramsey, all he would have had to do was ask Col. Kosterlitzky, because he knew everything that had happened, though not from my lips.

"Do you sincerely believe that?" the Judge asked me.

"I swear I do," I answered him. "I believe this friend was thinking only of saving our lives, and did not want to take the life of any of the guards had they obeyed him."

The Judge pondered a moment or two and ruled that I need not reveal the man's name who had shot the lieutenant. After more testimony that took most of the day, we were all called into the courtroom where the hearing had been underway and I was asked to stand before the bench.

"This court cannot see its way to do anything but give you your freedom and dismiss all charges against you," an interpreter intoned after the Judge. "It is not the purpose or intent of the Republic of Mexico to discourage foreigners from visiting us or to drive them from our land when they try to do business here, especially the good neighbors from the United States of America. I shall issue an order instructing the La Morita Collector of Customs to forthwith return the horses they have impounded."

I was handed an order, and told to report any further trouble to the court at Nogales, Sonora, before taking any action whatever with the officials at Naco or La Morita.

"This does not mean that you may return and start trouble or disturb the peace," the old Judge warned. "The tranquility of relations between our two countries at this time is extremely important, and we wish to remain a friend and good neighbor of your country. I urge all in this court to do whatever is in his power to maintain these good relations."

I bowed, and assured the Judge of my help in this respect.

My affairs had already attracted so much attention that it was not wise to cross the border here and take the train home, so I hired a buggy and a Mexican driver and we drove back across northern Sonora to Naco. When we reached there, all had quieted down. Captain Wright and the U.S. Cavalry had departed. The Mexican army had left only a token force of twenty-five to fifty soldiers. Col. Kosterlitzky and his *cordada* had returned to Magdalena to stay. I was happy to see things quiet down at Naco, for the events had focused a lot of unfavorable attention on the two little Naco towns. By November 4 *The Nogales Oasis* was playing the affair down as much as it had previously been built up in other newspapers:

> The Bisbee correspondent of *The Prospector* says: Judging from the *L.A. Times'* editorial of October 25, our little Naco disturbance has assumed the dignity of actual warfare and is sufficient to demand the serious attention of the Government not only of the United States but of Great Britain as well . . . Such sentiments are laughable.

Actually, the events were not at all laughable. There had been several deaths, and the murder of Ryan, the British subject, had made the situation more international than originally. These tragedies were being referred to as "The Naco War," and they almost led to a settlement by arms which would have been a genuine catastrophe. Most of us wanted peace along the border, and when the changes were made in the Mexican Customs offices things quieted down, the cowboys went back to the range, and the

240

Mexican Government returned its soldiers and policemen to their stations.[2] We all lived to fight another day—all, that is, except Bob Clayton, the Mexican guard he killed, the Yaqui lieutenant, Acado's helper, the British teamster, Ryan, and a few others. Those deaths seemed to me to be pretty senseless when the show was all over. But isn't any man's death a senseless one when brought about by anger and violence?

It was difficult to do business at my saloons, for feelings still were strained on both sides of the border. There was bitterness on the American side over Bob's murder, and though Harry Ramsey had "evened the score," as some put it, by murdering the lieutenant, that only brought a reciprocal toughness from the good Mexican people. For we never would know if Harry had murdered an innocent man. The Yaqui lieutenant, so far as I ever learned, was performing his duty as a soldier of the Republic of Mexico. I always recalled his words "I will fight anyone who attempts to molest you." He was probably no part of the conspiracy framed by the Customs officials and had drawn against Harry Ramsey only in the line of duty. I would never know just what was the truth about that officer's death. That he was a Yaqui Indian, and the Mexicans cared little for Yaquis, I knew.

Because of this whole sad episode in our lives, my wife and I decided to move back to the United States. It would be a safer place to raise our family. The lawmen of southern Arizona had made no effort to bring up the old issue of my flight from Kansas law, even after all the bad publicity that attended my border troubles, so I felt reasonably safe again, which meant a lot to me. I had given as much attention to saving my own hide over a period of nearly ten years as most men have to devote to saving their souls.

We built a nice home in Naco, Arizona, and moved across the border. I sold the home in Mexico, but I kept both the *cantina* there and the Cow Ranch Saloon north of the border. My bartenders in both places spoke Spanish and English, and that gave me an edge on my competition. The Mexican *cantina* faced the international line, being about a hundred feet south from it. The Cow Ranch Saloon was a couple of blocks north. This gave me the

241

privilege of stepping back and forth across the border without challenge from either Port of Entry, since most businessmen who owned places in both countries were allowed to come and go as they pleased. Both my places were clean and well-ordered, and I made them headquarters for cowman, miners, and businessmen from both countries, so long as they behaved themselves. Dealing, as I was, in cattle, I also opened a meat market operation north of the border. This proved to be a most lucrative business.

So May and I now looked forward to a peaceful and happy life for ourselves and our children there.

chapter XIV

1897-1901

ENTERTAINMENT ALONG THE BORDER
OUTLAW GANGS IN SOUTHERN ARIZONA

The Republic of Mexico holds an annual celebration similar to our Fourth of July. Their founding celebration falls on September 16. These are colorful spectacles, with all the natives in their gay holiday dress. But the biggest spectacle I witnessed there was the opening of the Bull Ring, on December 27, 1901.

At Naco, Sonora, they had erected a gigantic adobe Bull Ring. The year they opened the ring the railroad offered excursion rates from California, Texas, and New Mexico. The event brought thousands to Naco.

That day was an extremely hot one—and dusty! The folks from the American side came over for curios and the women to buy silk stockings, for they sold on the Mexican side as cheaply as did cotton stockings in the United States. My wife and I had discussed the advisability of keeping the children on the American side all day, for as the people poured into the little border towns by the thousands I could see that there was going to be every possibility for trouble. Yet, strangely, the day went on quite peacefully—for Naco—with a single exception.

I was just stepping from my *cantina* into the street, where the crowd was milling around in the sweltering heat, when I saw an American, a hobo from all appearances, and a Mexican of about the same quality, fighting in the street. Just at that time two cowboys whom I knew well, Cole Powell and Joe Rhodes, and who were pretty well liquored up on tiger milk, came up alongside me.

"Jim," Cole said to me, "Joe and I can lick any two men on God's green earth. We'll toss that Gringo hobo across the line if you say so." I could see Cole would have enjoyed such fun.

243

"You'd better leave that pair alone," I advised them, "for the way people feel today you might start more trouble than you can finish. Better let the Rurales handle them."

As I turned back into my *cantina*, the two cowboys grabbed the hobo, one by the arms, the other by his feet, and walking over the few steps to the international border marker they tossed him the few remaining feet into the United States. A Rurale quickly ran up, his pistol in his hand, and told the cowboys to throw up their hands. Cole grabbed the policeman and Joe quickly took his gun away from him. The Rurale started hollering for help in Spanish and the ball was on!

Three Mexican soldiers, off duty and unarmed, ran in to help the policeman. Then four or five cowboys from north of the line piled in to help Cole and Joe. I saw a couple of revolvers glisten in the sun and thought the "Naco War" had broken out again, for there was the damnedest clamor you ever heard as fifty or sixty men started fighting in the inch-deep dust in the street right in front of my place!

I quickly ran inside and gathered up my wife and children, who were next door to the *cantina*, and hurried them across the border just as I heard some firing start in the mob. As we crossed over the border with the tourists who were fleeing northward, each trying to reach the United States first, a stream of Mexicans were fighting to get back to their country, looking very much like fish fighting their way up the rapids in a stream. And this torrent of people were streaming right through my *cantina!*

For a few minutes I feared for the building itself as the maddened throng dashed through my doors, from back to front and from front to back, men, women, and children shrieking and squealing.

As I reached the building on my return from the border, a fat woman approached me, panting heavily. She was heading north, carrying a small child on her left arm and hip and dragging a boy of about six with her right arm. She must have weighed 300 pounds, and the perspiration was streaming down her face, making muddy trails on her cheeks where the dust of Mexico was being washed away. She dodged, ran, twisted, and finally made it to where I stood, sheltered by a pillar on the adobe *portico*. As she hesitated beside me for an instant, she looked directly at me. I smiled, and tried to be pleasant.

"Are you enjoying the celebration?" I asked, tipping my hat. She looked at me, her eyebrows almost in vertical positions on her forehead.

"I've had one hell of a day!" she retorted, jerking the boy's arm and re-positioning the baby on her hip-curve, preparatory to her final dash for liberty and freedom on the Arizona side. "Good-bye!" I doubt that that lady ever returned to the Republic of Mexico again!

There was one man, an American, but a citizen of Mexico, killed in the street brawl that day, certainly a low figure for the numbers of fighters involved. Several were injured. But that wasn't as bad as what happened after the Fiesta at Prietas, in 1897, which left four dead men in its wake. Two of those men were *suicides*, who *lost* at the gaming tables that day. The other two, the *winners* in that game, were waylaid and *murdered* that night for their winnings!

My *cantina* suffered enough damage to convince me that riots were unprofitable. For that fleeing mob who passed through it was not so excited that its members forgot to snatch up bottles of whiskey and other souvenirs of their trip. There wasn't a deck of cards left on the backbar where I kept the new decks, and one dealer said a woman snatched a deck right out of his hands! All my poker chips were gone, except those spilled on the floor. I had a dance hall at the rear of the *cantina*, and the girls back there screamed like banshees when that mob surged through there. A late count showed, however, that none of the girls was missing!

There has been a lot said and written about the dance hall girls of them days, but I can say this: those girls made a living as best they could. Many of the girls were orphans, or from broken homes, and all were from poverty-stricken families. I knew scores of them girls personally in my years in the saloon business, and my association with them made me well-acquainted with their problems. I can recall many of them who later made good marriages, and they were faithful wives and made good mothers for their

245

children. Some of Arizona's first families have one or more dance hall girls in their background, and they shouldn't be ashamed of it. I know that several years after this, when I lost my wife and had three small children to care for, the girls from the back room dance hall came to my aid and mothered those tots, as though they were their own, until I could get a full-time housekeeper to care for them.

I know that the real old-timers of Arizona's Territorial Days will agree with me that it took all kinds to make Arizona the great state she is today, and we surely had "all kinds" in them days. My experiences as a saloon man and cattle buyer made me acquainted with both the good and the bad. And like the old saying, I found so much good in the "worst of us" that I never felt it behooved most of us "to talk about the rest of us." Take for example Black Jack Christian. Now this is not the man called Black Jack, whose last name was Ketchum and whose head was pulled off his body when they hung him at Clayton, New Mexico. They were no relation.

Shortly after I came to Arizona Territory, this Black Jack Christian and his gang were well-known along the border. His men had all worked at times as cowboys. They were pretty good fellows. But all of them had, at some time, decided to live easily by going wrong. The gang consisted of Black Jack and his brother, Bob Christian; George Musgrave, who as I mentioned was the fellow "Burr" who accompanied Ramsey into Mexico after me; and Cole Young and Bob Hayes. There were always two or three coming and going, but these were the regulars.

In the spring of 1897 I had gone down onto the Sonora River on a trip and was bringing out a herd of Meskin cattle. On the way back we reached the HC Ranch, which was American-owned. None of the hands was there when we rode in. There was plenty of grub in the kitchen, so I had the boys put my cattle in the corrals and the horses in the pasture. I cooked them up some supper and we all bedded down, as was the custom.

The next morning we turned the cattle out to graze, moving them about a half mile toward the Bull Springs Ranch. I went on ahead of the herd and when I rode up to the corrals I found all the boys from both of the ranches gathered there. Since it was

246

not roundup time, and the boys had nothing special to do, I presumed there was a big poker game or some other amusement going on. I noticed one American I did not recall seeing when I was there before, when I bought cattle. I liked his appearance, for he was neatly dressed and had a clean-cut look about him. He had two six-shooters strapped on and a full belt of cartridges, which made him appear business-like, for most men didn't like to carry the weight of all that ammunition and only had a few rounds stuck in their belts. My first impression was that he might be a lawman, probably looking for Black Jack or other outlaws. He was standing at the kitchen door at this time, munching a piece of dark bread wrapped around a slice of beef.

When I had spoken to the other boys, this stranger walked toward me, leading his saddle horse. "Hello, Jim," he said to me, showing a row of white teeth. He stuck out his hand and I reached down and shook it. "I know you, don't you know me?" he asked. His voice was that of a Texas man.

"I'm sorry, but I just can't call your name," I answered. "Have we met?"

"I'll ride back to the herd with you," he said, not answering my question and mounting his horse.

As we rode back down the trail he told me his people had lived at Round Timbers on the Brazos in north Texas for years. Their family name was Christian, he said. "And I'm Black Jack."

His easy manner and the way he identified himself sort of took me back for a moment. But after we talked a while, and I saw he knew all about me, I allowed that he accorded me the same trust one outlaw always has to give another. He had lots of friends, he told me, on both sides of the border, but none knew his real name. "I'm just Black Jack to them," he said.

His family had lived neighbor to mine on the Brazos. There were eight in his family, and he said he knew my brother Frank quite well, and told me of incidents in their childhood. Since I had left there as a small boy, I could not recall Black Jack at all. I asked what his given name was.

"William," he said. "They all called me Bill." His brother, Bob, was with him in Arizona, he said, had come out with him from Oklahoma a few years earlier. Their family was now living

247

at Wichita Falls, he said, but his folks knew nothing of their escapades, for they had kept their mouths shut about their family name.

"I sure don't want them to ever know what happened to Bob and me," he said, grinning at me. He mentioned the post office robbery at Separ, New Mexico that previous fall of '96. They had to scatter after that. He and Bob Hayes hid out on a horse ranch on Deer Creek. Musgrave and the others took off in different directions, after planning a meeting near Bisbee for the future. After a month of hiding there at Deer Creek, the U.S. Marshal and posse got wind of their location and worked their way up for an ambush. As Black Jack and Bob rode in for breakfast at the ranch house one morning the posse fired on them.

"They shot my horse from under me," Black Jack said, "but I finally got away on foot. I was lame from the horse falling on me, but hid in the brush. Bob and I had ridden in separately, and I heard them shooting at him after I hid out, but I never learned for a month or more that he got killed in that ambush."

I asked Black Jack if he ever tired of running from the law, and acknowledged that I would give a little to be clean and not have the old Kansas case hanging around my neck.

"Yeah, that deal soured me on this business, Jim," he said. "I'm ready to go straight, but it's too late now. We made some good money, like at that store in Cliff, New Mexico. But we had some failures. And I never saved a penny of the money I made." Black Jack acted like a legitimate businessman who had taken bankruptcy. But I knew what he meant, for my own experience had about convinced me there was no road back, once a man had hit the Owl Hoot Trail, and therefore little reason to save and worship money like a free man can do.

Black Jack asked about Frank, and I told him that my brother had a good ranch under the Mogollon Rim, near Payson. Black Jack's ears pricked up at this, for he was looking for a hide-out at the time.

"I'll dodge through the country and get up there," he said. "If I can quiet down, maybe I can outlive it all," he reflected.

I couldn't help but think how "hope rises eternal in the human breast." But I wouldn't have given a plugged nickel for his chances, for I knew how far down the trail he'd gone.

I gave him Frank's location, told him how best to get in there without being seen. I also told him I thought Frank would help him if he was serious and wanted to go straight, but to stay away from Frank's if all he was looking for was a hide-out, for Frank wouldn't stand for that nonsense.

Black Jack rode with us until we got the herd close to the border. I sent one of my boys into Bisbee to buy some clothes for him. When Black Jack had changed clothes he looked like another person, handsome and well-groomed. As soon as we crossed the border he headed for the Mogollon Rim. Later I learned that a posse headed by Ben Clark, the Graham County deputy, had crossed Black Jack's trail near Clifton, April 28, 1897, and had killed him. This was away off his route to Payson, and I never knew why he went that way. The newspaper clipping I read described his clothing, and it matched what we had picked up for him at Bisbee. I knew it was Black Jack, for Tol Bell, a friend of mine, happened to be in that country and saw the body and identified it as that of Black Jack Christian. Sid Moore, who was with Black Jack, was killed later.

The fellow Musgrave dropped out of sight. Cole (Estes) Young was killed in the hold-up attempt on a train near Rio Puerco. Bob Christian reached Frank's ranch, hired on there under another name, and set it out for a spell. And that's about all I learned of the Black Jack gang.

No sooner had the Black Jack gang been shot up and broken up than another outfit took the lamplight. This was the Stiles-Alvord gang. Burt Alvord and Billy Stiles were the principals, and by 1898-1903 they were at the peak of their short careers as bank, train, and post office robbers.

Burt Alvord had been Sheriff of Cochise County at Willcox. At this time I believe he was the constable there. Billy Stiles was a sometime policeman at Pearce when I first met him. I heard that when the Arizona Rangers were first organized he served under Captain Burton C. Mossman. "Bravo Juan," as he was called, was another member of the gang, but he didn't join them until the robbery at Fairbanks Station. Several writers have shown him as a Mexican, but actually he was not of Spanish blood at all but a U.S. citizen. My wife and I both knew him well, for he was working for me at that time when he was persuaded to help in the holdup at Fairbanks. His real name was Tom Yoas.

That fall Tom had been riding the range for me, gathering strays and branding what stock showed up without brands among my cattle. He would be gone two and three days on these trips, for most of my stock was on the range around and south of Naco, in Sonora. On one of these trips Tom met up with Alvord and Stiles and others of their gang—George and Lewis Owints and Matt Burts. He later met Three-Fingered-Jack Stilwell or Dunlap. They told him how easy it was for a small group to hold up a train, take off a bag of gold coins, and be rich men forever. Tom was about nineteen, and swallowed this stuff. He was impressed by their talk of having a hide-out near where Chief Cochise ranged in the earlier times. I never knew what Tom was doing at that time or I would have talked him out of it. But he fell for them get-rich-quick schemes because he was an adventurous boy by nature.

Alvord and Stiles made their headquarters at Pearce, where I had lived and worked with old "Muley" Johnson in the building business. One night Alvord and Stiles and their boys rode into Cochise and held up the train late that following night.

The Pinkertons were at this time investigating the train robberies in southern Arizona, so anyone known to have come into money was suspected by them. In October of 1899, Cristy Robertson, who ran a restaurant at Pearce, was shot to death in cold blood on the main street, just south of the Soto store, by Sid Paige. No one pretended to know why Paige killed him. But there was a background to that killing that later came out. It seemed that Robertson's wife, Alice, had died a few years earlier. Their daughter, Edith, grieved so much over her mother's death that Cristy feared for her and sent her to live at a convent in Tucson. But her grief was so great that the Mother Superior recommended that she return to her family. Unfortunately, the girl picked the same date that the Cochise robbery took place to return home and her train, a Southern Pacific passenger running to Cochise station, was delayed because of that robbery.

When her father took her from the train, she was filled with excitement about the train robbery and started talking to him about it. As they walked toward his buggy, near the station, who should appear but some of the Alvord-Stiles gang, just which ones has never been known, but as these men came around the station one of them who knew Robertson spoke to him.

Cris Robertson must have suspicioned it was these men who pulled the robbery, for he was troubled all the way back to Pearce, and he cautioned his daughter Edith never, under any circumstances, to say anything to anyone about the train robbery or who she had seen that night. The girl may never have connected those men with the robbery, but the family members later put two and two together and realized what had caused their father's warning to his daughter.

Anyway, a day or two later, Matt Burts came and asked Cris if he could deposit a large sum of money in his restaurant safe, which wasn't an unusual request for there was no bank in the town then. Cris asked how much money, and Matt said "around ten thousand dollars." Cris turned him down, for he knew if Matt had that kind of money it could only have come from a bank or train robbery. Matt rode on out of town. Robertson's refusal to take the money seemed proof to the gang that he knew too much about the robbery.

Sid Paige, a young button about twenty then, was trying to make a big name for himself and was running favors for the Alvord-Stiles gang. He owed Cris some money himself, and that made it easy for him to do. So upon Alvord's and Stiles' nods, Sid rode into town a day or two later and shot Cris Robertson to death on the main street, as cold-blooded a murder as was ever committed anywhere.[1]

Cris had another daughter, Ethel, who was about eighteen at that time. It had been just four years since their mother died and it was a hard thing to lose their father, too. But Ethel pitched in and raised that family of younger ones. She was later Mrs. H. E. Macia of Tombstone, when I lived there, a fine woman.

The following February, after the holdup at the Fairbank

Station, I awoke to hear Tom Yoas and the girl who worked for us laughing and talking in the kitchen. That was their habit, and I thought nothing more of it. But when I went to the corral and saw the condition of Tom's horse, I knew he had ridden him hard all night. But it was his own animal, and not from my *remuda,* so I said nothing to him, for that would have been contrary to custom.

After breakfast Tom took his horse across the range several miles and turned him loose, after catching one of my horses to ride that day. That was perfectly natural, for Tom worked for me. Then he used my fresh horse to catch another fresh horse that he owned, and then rode off, tending to business as usual, at least that's what I assumed.

But neither Tom nor his friends of that night suspected that the law officers already had learned who pulled the robbery and were on their trail. The officers had closed in, and Three-Fingered-Jack, who had been so badly wounded that they abandoned him on the trail, was captured. Before Jack cashed in his chips, the officers wormed out of him the names of the others who had been with him in the robbery. They were named by Jack as Bill Downing, a cowman, later thought to be the boy Jackson, who rode with Sam Bass; Matt Burts; Burt Alvord; Billy Stiles; and Bravo Juan, who was my wrangler, real name Tom Yoas. The officers followed their lead and arrested the boys when they least suspected it.

All of them boys were in the Tombstone jail over a month without bond, until their trial in the spring of 1900. About that time, my wife and I attended a dance at Naco, Arizona.[2] Late in the evening a boy came in and told me he had a message for me to meet someone at the pump station, nearby. When I walked down there to see who it was, there stood Tom Yoas. He and Stiles and Alvord had broken jail at Tombstone and escaped, he told me. Billy had turned state's witness and was already free at that time. Alvord had talked Billy into helping them, and Billy drew a revolver on George Bravin, the jailer, who was later the Cochise County Sheriff. Stiles offered all their release, but several of the prisoners declined to join in the break. Downing was one, and the Owints brothers stayed with Downing, or Jackson.

252

Tom was nervous and I could see he hardly knew which way to turn. "You know this is the first time I was ever in real trouble, Jim, trouble like this anyway," he told me. "It was so easy to break out, I came with Burt and Billy. But now I wish I had stayed in jail with the others." I warned him what he would get now, if caught. I asked him if he wanted to surrender to the Sheriff.

"Burt and Billy made plans for us to meet and frame another job," Tom told me, "a really big train or bank job. But Jim, I've learned my lesson. I'm heading for Mexico right now."

Tom said his plan was to ride down the Sonora River to where it empties into the Gulf of California at Bahia Kino. When he got there, he said, if he didn't find a ship he could leave on, he might build a small boat to take him down the coast and out of Mexico. Tom knew the Sonora country pretty well, for he had made many trips down with me and with others to bring out cattle and horses in the Hermosillo and Cerro Cuevas country.

When Tom left he took one of my horses until he could catch a couple of his own. I gave him some food and clothing. He didn't plan for anyone to see him for a long time, he said, and rode away that very night.

Three or four years passed. One day I received a letter in a plain envelope from South America. I opened it, and noticed the letterhead. It read:

BLANK, BLANK AND BLANK CATTLE CO.,
TOM YOAS, General Manager

Bravo Juan was no more. Tom had managed to keep his own name and identity and make it an honored one among the businessmen and cattlemen of South America. There were a hundred tales told later of many "Bravo Juans," but none of them was the real Tom Yoas.

Before Burt Alvord left Arizona, from what I read and heard, he helped Cap Mossman of the Rangers capture the outlaws Chacon and his one-time friend, Billy Stiles. This was the price, so the story said, that was exacted from Alvord for his own free-

253

dom. I cannot guarantee it, but it sounds about right. The role of Judas is one I always connect with bounty hunters, informers, and deliverers. Chacon was hung.

Alvord drifted down into the Canal Zone. The fact that he was fluent in the Spanish tongue no doubt helped him a lot. I learned that he landed a good job bossing Mexican nationals on the construction work on the Panama Canal. While there he met and married a wealthy Spanish lady.

Billy Stiles had turned state's witness and been captured and escaped so many times that we all suspected him. I met him one time in Mexico under unusual circumstances. The Mexican *rancheros* all spoke of the place called the Rancho Escondido, meaning in our language, The Hidden Ranch. This place was in very rough and almost inaccessible mountain country. I had never ridden into this roughest section, though I had bought horses and cattle that had been brought out from there. But I had been told there was some places so rugged and dangerous that even the *vaqueros* could not bring cattle out, even under the best of circumstances.

Several of the *vaqueros* I had hired at times told me that there were big, rough steers in there that could be bought at genuine bargain prices, for no one had gone in after them. I got to thinking on it and decided I could make some real fast and good money by going in there, so I hired some of these *vaqueros* who agreed, for an extra share in the cattle, to bring them out with me. One day when I was having difficulty getting good big steers near the border I rode down there and gathered up my riders. I took Johnny Ragsdale, a top cowboy who had been in there before. He picked a Mexican boy, Pancho, who he said knew all the trails. There were two others.

Well, before we found that ranch we knew they had named it right —The Hidden Ranch. There were places along that mountain trail that Pancho led us where our horses had to walk single file and, if crowded, would have been pushed off into an abyss a thousand feet deep. I knew it would be even more treacherous coming out, for them Longhorn Meskin cattle would have to hold their heads sidewise to pass along them rocky ledges.

We arrived at the Rancho Econdido late one evening, and it did not take long to realize that we were not welcome. The men at the rock house gave us no invite to come in and eat, and I knew that we were under suspicion. Pancho knew the customs of these people better than Johnny and I, so I asked him what he thought was wrong. He told me that they probably thought we were outlaws. If not that, then they thought we were law officers looking for outlaws among them. In either case, he said, he believed they would wait until they had talked it over among themselves, then kill us. It was that simple. Since there were twelve or fifteen of them *hombres* at the house, I had little doubt they could do it, since there were but five of us, all cowboys, not gunmen.

I had been sizing up the other bunch and soon picked out the man I felt would be their leader. I called him off to the front steps of the rock house, and away from my companions. I told him I thought he could speak or understand English, but if he could not, that my boy Pancho could interpret for us. He just nodded and said, "Sí, señor, go ahead." I told him we were neither outlaws nor lawmen. That we came here to buy cattle.

"Do you own any cattle, or know who owns the big steers in this area. I hear there are many for sale." Then I mentioned the names of some of my *vaqueros* who had told me about the cattle in this mountain country. "If we cannot buy cattle here, then we shall return down the mountain in the morning," I told him.

As I spoke, I happened to remember that I had an envelope from a well-known Commission firm in my pocket, addressed to me. I had kept a tally on it the week before. I took out the envelope and handed it to this man, whose name I learned was Manuel. He scanned the envelope, then called two of his men and they whispered in Spanish for a moment. Then one of them mounted a horse and dashed off bareback across the rocks. Within ten minutes he was back, another rider alongside him. When they rode in close to the fire I saw that the second man was Billy Stiles!

Billy dismounted and came over and shook hands. He acted glad to see me, especially since he inquired about his wife who was then living not far from my place, about two miles from the border, on the San Pedro River. She was living there on a homestead, try-

255

ing to prove up on it, I told him. He had not seen her for nearly a year, he said, and was anxious to see her. I related all the little things that I had known or heard of her, and Billy seemed pleased.

From Billy I learned that Rancho Escondido had thousands of cattle, and wanted to sell, for no buyers had been in there for a year or two. The trails were so dangerous that even the *vaqueros* didn't like to move the cattle out. Billy asked me what I would pay, and when I told him I expected to get them very cheap he asked me to please offer a little more, for they were his friends and he wanted them to get the best deal possible, since they had helped conceal him when he needed a friend badly. If I made a good offer, he said, he would even help move the cattle out and see that we had reliable *vaqueros* to trail out with us.

I knew that I could pay a good price, or what they would feel was one, and still almost double my money on a big herd, so I promised Billy to make a good deal for everyone, including himself. Billy talked at length with Manuel, their boss man, and we then all shook hands on a good bargain, after I had stated my price, and the type of animals I must have. Everyone was smiles. Manuel agreed to gather and deliver to the trail 600 steers of the kind I wanted and help us off the mountain with his own men. Billy Stiles decided to come with us, so with three of Manuel's riders we would have enough help to reach the border.

That night, and it was quite late when we had finished bargaining, they brought out the *mezcal* and the *tequila* and we had a good supper of roast ribs of beef with *frijoles* and *tortillas*, and hot sauce called *chili*. After we had eaten, both the men and their women played guitars, danced, and sang the *jácara*, or native songs. It was a beautiful, moonlit night there on the mountainside, and the stars twinkled like the candles on a Christmas tree. We drank several mugs of the strong Mexican coffee, mixed with a very sweet wine, and when I turned in I felt that my trip would be successful, but my stomach would suffer all the next day as a result of the *fiesta* we had enjoyed.

We left eleven days later, and with the kind of steers I wanted. Billy Stiles came along as he had promised, and the *vaqueros* made the trip down the mountainside on the narrow trails much easier than I had anticipated. The cattle were mountain-bred and had the agility of goats. Dizzy heights had always affected me, and mountain trailing is much different than trail driving on the plains. I followed at the rear of the procession which stretched along the rocky cliffs for several miles. Manuel's *vaqueros* established themselves at intervals on the trail with the cattle and encouraged them with low singing and little shouting. On that long and perilous descent, we lost but four head from that herd of 600, and all of our riders came through safely.

When we neared La Morita, Billy told me he was going to see his wife. I warned him to be careful, for I knew he was wanted, yet he appeared unconcerned and said he was going to see his wife "come hell or high water." Someone with our outfit must have told the authorities Billy was there, for that night when he reached his home the place was surrounded by officers and Billy was taken.

Billy had lots of enemies and almost anyone could have turned him in. But I was sorry it happened to him when he had been with me. If I ever knew how he got out of the hands of the law that time, I have forgotten. But he did make the scratch someway, for I heard of his death in a Nevada mining camp sometime later. I believe he had turned lawman again, at the time.

Billy earned the name of being a good law officer, when he worked at it, and he was a lucky cuss as an outlaw. So what more could a man ask after following the Owl Hoot Trail for many years?

chapter XV

1900-1913

RETURN TO NO MAN'S LAND • TOMBSTONE, ARIZONA
MAY HERRON'S DEATH • HERRON'S THIRD MARRIAGE
COURTLAND, ARIZONA
HERRON CHARGED WITH CATTLE THEFT
THE TRIAL AND SENTENCE

In April, 1900, our good friend Bud Powers died. Bud had been with us through the thick and thin of our Mexican troubles, and it grieved us to see him go, for he was a loyal and kind friend. After he was laid away, his wife decided to return to her home in Canadian City, Texas, not far south from our old home in No Man's Land. Both Bud and his wife had been such good friends, and we regarded them so highly, that my wife decided to accompany Mrs. Powers and little Jack back to Texas.

I had not planned to go, at first, but as the time drew near I made the decision to accompany them, though I knew it was risky business, since I was still wanted on a fugitive warrant in Kansas. But I felt that if I stayed in Oklahoma Territory, where we had many friends, I could always fight extradition to Kansas. Furthermore, I wanted to visit my first wife's family, Mr. and Mrs. Ansel Groves, and see my daughter, Ollie Dot. There was always the pleasure of meeting the old friends of my youth and recapturing that feeling of companionship and camaraderie that neither time nor distance can erase or dim in our consciousness. So the prospect of a return visit to the Strip was a bright one.

The four of us went by train, and when the boy and Mrs. Powers left us at Canadian City, where her people met her at the station, May and I continued on to Higgins, Texas after a touching goodbye between my wife and Bud's widow. May and I rented a light buggy and drove north that night to the Goddard Ranch in the Oklahoma Panhandle.

May's parents were most happy to see her, for we had made no mention of this trip in letters home and they had not expected us. Her father at once warned us of the chances we were taking, but I was pleased to hear him say that he would stand by me in any court action that came up. I felt good to know he would stand by me, after the manner in which I had spirited his daughter away from her home.

At Beaver City, my old home, we had a wonderful visit. After Benton folded as a town, my first wife's parents, Mr. and Mrs. Groves, had moved to Beaver, where I had bought the hotel. At this time Grandmother Groves was still living and my first daughter, Ollie Dot, lived there with her. Dot was now a youngster of twelve years, and a lovelier child one seldom sees.

In those years the annual pioneer celebration was held at Beaver, since it was the largest town in the Strip. The celebration was on in full swing when we arrived, and the local authorities paid no attention to me except to welcome me as a pioneer and to tell me that anything I needed they would find for me. I met and visited with many old cattlemen I knew and the cowboys with whom I had rubbed stirrups on the roundups of the Eighties. It was so enjoyable that I was loathe to leave when the celebration ended.

We returned to the Goddard Ranch for a few more days, then my wife's folks accompanied May and the children back to Higgins, where they took the train west. I rode across country with one of the boys from the ranch to Canadian City, where I boarded the train to join my family. Being on the run was always distasteful, but never more so than when I could not properly escort my wife or family and had to dodge around the law and depend on others.

Back at Naco we resumed our life. My Cow Ranch Saloon prospered, and I continued to buy cattle in Mexico for a while despite the fact that the Mexican Customs officials now had marked me and I was watched like a hawk over a henyard. I had sold the *cantina* across the border, for it was not wise to invite more trouble there. May's health had not been good, but as she had no other duties now than raising the family I felt that she would soon get rested up and feel better.

Tombstone, though it was hit hard when the mines flooded and stopped the silver and gold boom, was still a town "too tough to die" as they told it. At this time the Tombstone Consolidated Mining Company was planning big things and there appeared to be some life there again at the mines. I learned in 1903 that Mr. Nobles, who had bought the old hotel there west from Schieffelin Hall, was in bad health and wanted to sell, so I drove up to Tombstone with May and the children to take a look at the old town from which I had helped move the buildings when it looked like it had completely died.

This old Nobles Hotel building had been the stopping place for the Modoc Stage Line and was located across the street and east from the OK Corral, where Tombstone's most famous gun battle had occurred between the Clantons and the Earps. Judge Spicer, that first week in November, 1881, had held court in this old adobe and frame building when the warrants were issued against Marshal Virgil Earp, his brothers, Wyatt and Morgan, and Doc Holliday, for the murders of the Clantons and the Mc-Lowery brothers. At that hearing they were freed, but lots of trouble dogged them afterward. Virgil was bushwhacked on the corner of Allen and Fifth Streets and badly wounded; Morgan was killed at Bob Hatch's saloon; Wyatt and Doc found it to their advantage to clear out of the Territory, and fled to Colorado. Doc died there at Glenwood Springs, years later, and Wyatt lived out his last years in California. Neither came back to Tombstone, at least while I was there.

This street had two newspapers, *The Tombstone Prospector* and *The Tombstone Epitaph*, the latter still published today. This was a good location for a hotel business, so we bought the Nobles Hotel,[1] and put in a good lobby and office downstairs where they had kept a showroom for buggies. We did some remodeling, and a lot of cleaning. There were twenty-eight rooms, twenty-three of which were upstairs. I wanted to change the name, so May named it the La Rita Hotel, after our little seven-year-old Morita, or 'Rita, as we called her, who was named after her birthplace, La Morita, Sonora, Mexico. Over on Allen Street I opened a saloon,[2] two doors west of the old Crystal Palace, and two doors east of Hatch's, where Morgan Earp was shot.

May had always enjoyed the hotel business, and we found it interesting and profitable here, though there is always much work connected with such an enterprise. I have always felt that it may have been this extra burden that played a part in bringing on May's final illness. For on November 17, 1904, after a sickness of a few weeks, my wife died. May's mother and sister came from Oklahoma to nurse her and to help out through this last illness. On a cloudy November we laid her away in the Tombstone Cemetery among the *ocotillo* and the prickly pear. May was but twenty-eight years of age at death, having been born February 27, 1876; she was ten years my junior. Over her grave I had an enduring metal marker placed, and on it this fitting inscription:

> Unto us a few short years,
> Her loving smile was given;
> And then she bade farewell to Earth,
> And went to live in Heaven.

With my beloved little May's death it seemed that another era of my life had ended. Once again I was a widower, after enjoying ten joyful years with her and the three fine children she had given me: "Sam," now nine; Jim, five; and our impish little daughter Rita, now seven. In the following months I do not know what I would have done without the help of May's good friends, Lucy Spindles and Mrs. Barry, and others. They were the greatest comfort to both myself and the children, and much of the work of the hotel was left in their hands. Under the supervision of Miss Mary Valencia, who had worked at the hotel before, we managed to carry on, though I had to make two trips into Mexico that year.

When I lost my first wife, I vowed I could never marry again. In the grief over the loss of May, I again felt that I could never marry for a third time. However, I was now in my thirty-eighth year, robust, virile, and a man with three small children to think about. Mary Valencia was a most attractive Spanish girl, and her work at the hotel in Tombstone had brought her into a friendly relationship with both May and me. As my need for her grew, and as she filled every want for me and the children, our loyalty to one another ripened into love, and in 1906 we were married. Mary had been a tower of strength to me in helping with my family, and our children were very fond of her. To this union was born, on April 15, 1908, a dark-eyed and dark-haired little daughter whom we named Millie.[3]

Mary continued to manage the hotel and I maintained the bar on Allen Street. Following the spring and fall beef roundups, I would make trips into Mexico and bring out cattle for the shippers and feeders. It was beginning to be more difficult to find cattle, and much more difficult to move them out of Mexico. But while I did have trouble getting my herds out of the country, I would not want anything in my writings to make it appear that I am critical of either the Mexican people or their Government. I was generally given every consideration, both in their commercial world and in their courts. The La Morita Customs officials were a part of the Mexican Government, but they did not truly represent it, and while I encountered others of a like cut, they were not representative of the Mexican Government nor its people. If I was occasionally asked how I felt about the new Revolutionary ideas, or of my opinion of the Diaz Government, I would hedge and say, "If I learn which side is right in your disputes over government, I will take sides. So please do not tell me what is right or wrong. I am here only to buy your cattle, and that alone, not to make trouble with anyone over politics. I will not take any side in your Government's problems." That usually calmed them down, whichever side they were on. And so passed those years of 1908 and 1909, the hotel bringing in some money, my cattle operations becoming more difficult.

In 1910 a mining boom had started at Courtland, a few miles south of Pearce, and between that town and Tombstone. The Calumet & Arizona Company and the Great Western Mining Company held high hopes for their investments there. A newspaper, *The Courtland Arizonian*, had convinced me the previous year that there was going to be a big city there as a result of the new strikes, so I began to think of moving. The La Rita Hotel was no longer making money, and Tombstone had lapsed into another slump after the pumping projects failed to empty the mine shafts of the water that had collected there over the years. So we packed up and moved to Courtland. There was quite a bit of construction going on and a good brick block was then being built.

I first opened a small saloon, which I called The Pastime Pool Hall, for liquor selling was not legal at that time and was frowned on. I had some of my cattle moved over there as well as my horse herd. I found such a demand for beef that I opened a slaughtering plant and butcher shop, and I found it easy to buy beef on the hoof as well as kill my own stuff which I ran on the High Lonesome range nearby, with other cattle.

The butcher business paid well, and I opened a second shop at Pearce, though I did all the killing at Courtland. We constructed a good adobe building with slaughter pen and adjacent corrals. I would have half a dozen beeves killed and cut up, then take a few sides and quarters to my Pearce market to sell. This business was in the same building as the Pearce post office, on the west side of the street, a block above the big Soto & Renaud Mercantile Company building. Later I sold this market to Harrison & Drew, and for a good reason—I got into trouble with a cowman over the matter of beef.[4]

Up at Pearce they had dug a lot of gold out of that hill, and now that the boom was over I someway thought Courtland was where the next big strike would be made. I had so much confidence in that country at that time that even the newspapers quoted me, as this old clipping from *The Tombstone Prospector*, March 3, 1910, will show:

HAS GREAT FAITH IN RECENT GOLD STRIKE

Jim Herron, one of the pioneers of the Courtland-Pearce district, was in the city today on a brief business trip. He arranged to take up and settle the case recently filed against him involving $500, thereby releasing the attachment proceedings instituted. Mr. Herron is an enthusiastic believer in the events of the gold strike near Courtland and thinks a bonanza will result with the development of that section.

The lawsuit mentioned arose over the sale of the La Rita Hotel, but was soon cleaned up. My faith in that area was solid, though I later wondered why. Yet the Montana-Tonapah Mining interests made money there and later, after World War I, my son

Sam went up there to Pearce, found some valuable chemicals in the mine tailings, and took a small fortune out for himself. He drove a Cadillac, lived good, and cut quite a figure there and in Arizona mining circles.

But this cattle trouble I have mentioned came on me about that time and was certainly a blow I had never expected, for I did well while at Courtland and Pearce and had no reason to suspect what was in store for me in the future.

By that time I had made many friends in and around Courtland—cattlemen; buyers such as B. A. Packard, Bill Cowman; the Renauds and Soto brothers; the Cartmell brothers, who had recently come there from Oregon and California; Mr. Washington, the postmaster; R. B. S. Clark, an old soldier who later lived at Tombstone; Muley Johnson; and the cattlemen of the CCC's, the Coronados, the Chiricahua, and other ranches in the Sulphur Springs valley and the mountains adjoining. But there was one man who, for some reason, held a grudge against me. That was Charley McKinney. Charley was an arrogant but likeable fellow who had a place south of Pearce and who run cattle on the High Lonesome as I did, that range near Courtland and Pearce. I had never harmed Charley to the best of my knowledge, at least not intentionally. Some of the stocker cattle I brought on to the range were branded with my old brand MAY, a brand that was, in some ways, similar to a brand that Charley held on that range which he had acquired a year or so before, M Bar T. My brand was one I had used to honor my second wife, and to assure her of some property if anything happened to me in Mexico. I had no knowledge of this similar brand when I moved my cattle from near Tombstone to the new range. But I was suspected: a friend told me that Charley McKinney believed I was *changing his brand!*

Now a man who deals in cattle year in and year out, buying thousands of head and trading with anyone who has stock to sell, cannot help but make a mistake in buying once in a while. I had bought brands before that did not belong to the seller, and did it as innocently as any man could do. I have seen other buyers make that same mistake. Wherever possible, we always made restitution if shown the proper owner, or if the cattle were claimed by him. That is the old-time cattleman's way of doing, for we all make mistakes and we intend to pay later for any animal that is inadvertently picked up in a herd or bought with other cattle.

The Sulphur Springs Valley Cattle Company had many cattle there on and near that range, though I bought none from them. I had a rider, John Oldham, a good and honest boy who frequently gathered my cattle that I had bought and brought them in bunches of ten or fifteen head to Courtland to be butchered. In some manner, John picked up four head of Sulphur Springs Valley Cattle Company cows mixed in my bunch and brought them into Courtland. They were killed and butchered by my men at the slaughterhouse, their hides stacked as usual behind the adobe wall, out of the sun, awaiting the hide buyer from Tombstone to whom I sold hides. Well, Charley McKinney happened by that day, studied those hides, read the brands, and brought about my arrest for cattle theft, even though I was not there when the stock was brought in.

When John Oldham told me of gathering the cattle, I told him to plead innocent, for he did not know but what the cattle were some I had bought, since they were grazing in the same area as my stock. I immediately offered to make restitution, to pay for the company's cattle. But neither the company officials nor the county attorney would listen to my pleas. The result was that they scared John into making a plea of guilty, which made it certain I would be convicted whatever I pled. Though I stoutly maintained my innocence, the court gave me five years. John was given the same. This was in October, 1912.

My trial at Tombstone lasted only two days, and fortunately it was overshadowed by a suit in equity well-known to Arizonians of that time as the Cunnigham-Costello case. It was a busy docket that term, and more business was said to have been disposed of than at any court term since that of 1882. Because of the publicity given the equity case, many of my personal friends never knew, even years later, that I had been sentenced as a common cow thief. I was fortunate in another way: I had good, loyal, and true friends in many businesses. Some of these men, like Governor Hunt, had known me since I came to Arizona Territory. Most of them knew all about my Kansas trial and conviction, for I made no excuses nor did I ever try to conceal the facts. Those who knew me best, and who were acquainted with my character, stood by me.[5] Several of my influential friends held high political offices and were in responsible commercial and ranching enterprises. The Arizona people of Territorial Days were different than many of today. Even at that time the Territorial Spirit was still flowing strongly in men's veins. There was little hypocrisy, and the thought of an old friend being in prison galled a man, unless he knew well that his friend deserved his punishment. The men of that time valued their freedom above all things, just as I did. So my friends didn't let me down.

At the end of the first year in the penitentiary, I was asked to appear before the Board of Pardons. I was given my freedom again, and no man ever appreciated it as much as I did, even though I had never felt a moment's guilt over the charges that had been leveled against me.

chapter XVI

1913-1915

MEXICAN CATTLE BUYING AND THE REVOLUTION

When I returned from Florence in October, 1913, I again wanted to take up cattle buying, for livestock was my great interest in life and the business kept me out in the wide open spaces where a man could get a big lungful of fresh air. I had been watching the newspapers and could see that there was to be a boom in the cattle trade if a man knew where to buy the big beefy steers right. So I decided to go down into Mexico and bring out some herds for the sale rings and for feeders. I was through as a small-town butcher, with all the problems attendant to that trade.

In going down into Sonora and Chihuahua, I always obtained a permit from the military faction that was in control at the time, be it Federal or Revolutionary. At this time the Revolution was on in full-swing. All of the Mormon colonists had fled, leaving their farms and villages behind. The "Mexico for Mexicans" policy had brought about strikes by the American railroad engineers and conductors who operated most of the country's northern railroads; because there was little chance of shipping cattle out, I planned to trail all I bought, from the ranches north to El Paso, Texas, or Douglas or Naco, Arizona. There were inspection stations at these points, and I was acquainted with the Customs people there on both sides of the line.[1]

The newspaper headlines at this time excited my imagination with their big headlines, "DEMAND FOR SONORA CATTLE IS HEAVY AND THE PRICE IS HIGH," for I knew some of the more remote ranches down there and how to get to them, besides having a wide acquaintance among the *rancheros*.

In April, 1913, a plot to assassinate Madero was uncovered and Alfredo Robles Dominguez was arrested. Generals Salazar

267

and Orozco, who backed Huerta, had 4,000 men south of Jiminez, and Orozco's wife was reported to have deposited $200,000 in an El Paso bank before leaving for Los Angeles with her children. The rebel generals, del Toro and Rojas, had confiscated Don Luis Terrazas' land and his enormous cattle herds in northern Chihuahua, adding millions, it was said, to the depleted treasury of the Revolutionary armies. But such wealth was a great temptation to the victors, and some of those Mexican generals looked upon such loot as a personal possession once they had it in their hands.

There were the "Red Flaggers," a revolutionary outsprout of some sort, who had just completed raids on the ranches south of Douglas, near the Malabi Ranch, and I knew that Bill Nolan and the other cowmen down there would be getting gray hairs in their mustaches thinking about what could happen to them and their herds. So it was the logical time to get in there, buying.

In Sonora a real civil war was taking place, with fifteen or twenty rival generals and their armies moving back and forth across the mountains and plains seeking advantages. Troops A, B, C, and D of the 4th U.S. Cavalry under Major Tom Dugan were watching along the border and moved to Fort Huachuca that summer. "Poor Mexico," old Diaz had lamented, "so far from God and so near to the United States!" He was about right.

I talked with J. E. Kenney, a buyer and drover I knew quite well. He was making an occasional foray across the border and he filled me in on what to expect of the revolutionary elements and the prospects in Mexico at the time. The lifting of the Quarantine, he said, and the removal of the tariff on Mexican cattle that had taken place in October of that year was responsible for much of this activity at the Port of Naco, for I saw a dozen big herds waiting there at the dipping vats. From January 1 to August 17, 1913, only 16,000 head of cattle had entered this country. The Quarantine was slapped on briefly August 17, but it had been taken off again.

The duty on horses and mules, which had formerly been $30 a head, regardless of size or quality, was now reduced to ten percent of actual value, or about $3 a head. This was more like it!

The cattle duty, twenty-seven percent of their value before, was now taken clear off and the herds could walk into the United States free, a real incentive for us buyers to get in there, despite the risks involved, and start buying cattle early in 1914.

I was interested in doing business with cattle owners only, not being stopped two or three times a day en route to the border by soldiers, policemen, regulars, and irregulars who would go over all the brands, and also look through your stuff for contraband—and any silver or gold you carried. Under these conditions it was most dangerous to carry metal coins. I could do some business with checks with *rancheros* that I knew quite well, but even they preferred gold or silver, something they could bury, to any nation's paper money. So I just loaded my saddle bags with gold coins, for silver was too heavy to carry, and also loaded my Winchester rifle and Colt .45 with bullets, and hoped for the best. I liked to take along one or two of my own boys I could trust in a fight, and I paid them well for their extra risk.

Mr. L. E. Booker[2] of El Paso, who was associated with me at this time, cautioned me not to brag on Diaz very much, for there were many Mexicans in high positions in his own Government who could now see his defeat coming as well as others who hated him.

"Don't take too many chances, Jim," he warned me. "We can make good money if our luck holds, but money isn't everything. This is still a very dangerous project to consider as a routine business venture. Keep out of their politics, and don't worry if you get robbed—just try and save your own necks."[3]

Mr. Booker had had a deal with Señor Luis Terrazas, prior to this time, but when Terrazas fled, he left a big vacuum in Chihuahua. At this time General Pancho Villa was in charge of what was loosely called the Villa Government. I visited him and received a permit to travel and do business in Chihuahua. I agreed to pay the Villa Government $5 (U.S. gold) for every animal I brought out of Mexico at El Paso. This included animals I bought in other provinces, for as Villa told me when I asked about continuing over into Sonora, "You take your own chances there." I was not required to pay anything on animals that failed to pass their health inspection, which was such an easy test, so loosely administered and poorly enforced, that I rarely failed to get an animal by that I myself thought healthy. In return for my permit to travel and do business I agreed to take no part in their revolutionary quarrels, particularly agreeing not to provide beef for their enemy, the Federal armies or garrisons that might still be in Chihuahua.

Before leaving Villa's headquarters, I mentioned the hope that we all held north of the border that Mexico would eventually have a stable government, but I finished by adding "such as once existed under Diaz." I could see Villa's mustache bristle up. "Mexico," he said haughtily, "is a rich prize for the *Gringo*. But it is one fruit he will not pluck soon." He made plain to me that the only businessmen from north of the international line that would be sheltered under his umbrella of protection were those who opposed Huerta. I made every effort to convince him that I favored no faction, just wanted to buy cattle and make money.

"That is easy to understand in all Yanquis," he said. "Money up there is your god."

From Casas Grande I went south with only one boy, Ed Grant, to help me. We headed for a ranch on the San Pedro, near Madero. There I received 879 big steers that I had bought in the Rio Popigochic area and which were brought up this far to meet me. I managed to hire some of the *vaqueros* who had started with the herd, and agreed to pay them double their present wage, which was little enough, if they would see me through to the border. This meeting was in the vicinity of *Colonia* Chuichupa.

In bringing these cattle to El Paso, it was necessary to pass through some country that had been controlled by the Orozco and Salazar faction, the "Red Flag" Government. These generals had opposed Madero in 1912-13 and had been defeated and their armies scattered at that time. But small bands remained as brigands, stealing everything that was loose and not nailed down, such as food, clothing, guns, ammunition, and such.

A few days after we had received the herd, we neared *Colonia* Garcia, which was a Mormon settlement near the Sonora-Chihuahua border. Sonora at that time was controlled by the armies of General Carranza and the Calles Military Government. Villa, of

270

course, controlled Chihuahua. The Mormon settlements in that area were made as early as 1885, when Utah people went down there and organized the Mexican Colonization and Agricultural Company. They held large acreages by purchase in northeastern Sonora and northwestern Chihuahua. In Sonora there were *Colonias* Morelos, San Jose, and Oxaca; and in Chihuahua there were *Colonias* Dublan, Juarez, Diaz, Pacheco, Chuichupa, Guadalupe, and Garcia, the latter of which we would learn more about on this trip, though I had already visited many of the others on previous trips.

Orazco and Salazar had raided these settlements and driven the Mormon colonists out. During the Huerta regime those generals were incorporated into the Federal army forces and given commissions, and that is why Villa hated Huerta so bitterly and fought them fellows tooth and toe-nail.

When we sighted the little village of *Colonia* Garcia I rode ahead to locate a campsite and bedground. Imagine my surprise when I came to the town, which had once held 300 people, to find it abandoned. I felt like a ghost as I rode down through the deserted streets, shouting. But I could raise no one, and only silence greeted me. The town was well-built of good adobe and much frame construction, with fine homes, church and school, and a neat lay-out that would have been a credit to any American community north of the border. After searching around I located a large, community corral where we could pen the cattle for the night. This would relieve us of putting on a full night guard and give my men a little rest. We patched the fences up a bit and turned the herd into the corral at dark, after grazing them in a nearby meadow. I put one *vaquero* on early watch, just to warn us if thieves or wolves showed up in the night.

We had located a clean adobe home with a corner fireplace where we cooked supper and there we bedded for the night. About nine o'clock, while we were just dropping off to sleep, we heard rifle fire at the corrals. There must have been fifty or a hundred shots and we heard shouting down there. I crept outside with my Winchester to see what had happened just in time to see them big wild steers hit the fence gate and tear it off its hinges. No sooner

271

had the gate gone than the rush of the stampeding cattle tore off a forty-foot section of fence beside the gate and the herd busted out of the corral and headed southward like a clap of thunder. When the roar of hooves died away I heard a Mexican's voice shout, "All you *Gringos* who are here in the morning weel be keeled!" Another of the men who had stampeded the cattle cried out, "Take warneeng!"

Ed Grant, the American boy with me, had run out of the house with his rifle and squatted beside me. Now he whispered to me, "What in hell did that Mex say, Jim?"

I repeated the warning to Ed.

"That Mex is crazy if he thinks he'll find this Irishman here at sunrise," Ed grinned at me.

I knew how Ed felt, for I was uneasy for the lives of all of us now. But I had nearly a thousand head of big steers out there scattering all over the hills, and I knew the Mexican outlaws or irregulars who had stampeded them would now give us a fight before handing them back.

It was pretty dark by this time, but I ordered Ed and the nine *vaqueros* with us to saddle up. We packed up and rode out of *Colonia* Garcia that night. I was of the opinion, and hope, that the Mexican outlaws would stay holed up at some nearby building, ranch, or village; and I entertained the hope that we might dislodge them later, though I held no hope of recovering the herd that night. We made a dark and dry camp three miles from the village in the hills and I spent the rest of the night mulling around in my mind plans for getting my herd back.

It would not be easy, I knew.

Pearson, Chihuahua, was a day's ride from our camp. I decided to go there, for the town was occupied by Pancho Villa and his General, Ochoa. The town of Pearson was a lumber town, owned by an English company. This firm bought many miles of fine timber throughout that area and had two of the largest sawmills in the country, one at Pearson and the other at San Pedro Madero. Pearson was a railroad town and they were still receiving freight there in spite of the Revolution and occupation of the town. Although both of these towns were now abandoned by the lumber interests and were occupied by thousands of Villistas, the soldiers of the ragtag army of Villa, and the hundreds of camp-followers, both men and women, I had little fear of them since both Mr. Booker and I had our agreements with the Villa forces to move out cattle.

After a good night's rest in a *cantina*, run by a Mexican I knew, I walked down to the *Villa Quartel*, the headquarters where General Ochoa reigned supreme. I presented myself to his aid-de-camp, and after passing through several doors guarded by a score of black-eyed and swarthy sentries in their big straw hats I was taken into a large room with a desk at one end, behind which sat Ochoa, scowling at a puzzle he was trying to solve with several wooden blocks. He nodded as I drew near the desk and introduced myself, the aide interpreting for us. Then I stated my sad tale of woe. The General listened without so much as batting an eye. Then he arose and stepped out from behind his walnut desk. He was somewhat shorter than I, so I drew up to full height to force him to stand up straight and look me in the face if he was going to tell me to go back, without his help, and try to recover those steers.

"You Americans are crazier than hell to try to take cattle out of those danger zones," he said to me, his fat lips in a pout. "If you expect General Ochoa to pull Yankee chestnuts out of the fires of revolutionary Mexico, you had better reconsider. I shall not lend one soldier to such folly, just so a Yankee can make more dollars." With that he flounced back to his chair and the wooden puzzle.

Though he seemd to pay no attention to my words, I reminded him that Francisco Villa himself had guaranteed my cattle a safe trip to the border, and that General Villa would not feel well to lose the gold coin I would pay him there for the safe delivery, for gold bought guns and food for the Revolution. But all my talk did not change him, so I bid him *adiós*.

I had only the ten men besides myself, and I now had to turn to their loyalty. The *vaqueros* owed me nothing, and Ed Grant had never given me any reason to believe he would risk his own life so I could make money in cattle. But I gave them a talk and

273

told them of my plan to buy a fresh horse for each of us to ride, two packhorses to carry our gear, more supplies, and we would return to *Colonia* Garcia and try to find and gather what was left of my herd. We might have to fight off some of the Mexicans, I told them, but we would all have rifles with plenty of ammunition to do this as well as six-shooters. And since I had my agreement with Villa, we would have his support, even if Ochoa wouldn't back us. I agreed to pay them double, in gold coin, when we reached the border, with or without the cattle, for I knew the risk we would be taking. Following my talk the *vaqueros* walked to one side and whispered among themselves. Only four agreed to go back with us; some declined because of their political feelings about the Revolution, some out of fear.

When Ed, the four Mexican riders, and I reached the crest of the hills that overlooked the beautiful valley where *Colonia* Garcia lay, I studied the land with my field glasses. I could not see a single human being. In the valley, toward the lower end, I saw a good bunch of my steers peacefully grazing in the old Mormon fields that were growing up into weeds and grass. I needed more time to assess the possibilities, and determine if the raiders were down there in hiding, so we made camp outside the village.

The next morning Ed and I rode into the town, taking along one other man, Pedro, who spoke good English as well as Spanish. It was understood that if we encountered the raiders, the others, at the first sound of gunfire, would ride in to help us break away from any fight we couldn't win. For I felt that a show of reinforcements, however small, would make the raiders think twice before following us back into the hills where we might have more men. However, luck was with us. We searched through the village, cautiously at first, later shouting and hurling insults and daring any bandit to show his face and fight. But none was there.

We then rode into the meadows and rounded up what steers we could find, 366 head. We held them in the meadow that night, and the following day made a search of the area around. I picked up the trail of the herd where they had gathered them about three miles from the village, in the hills. But they could have taken all of the cattle had they wished, and I presumed they left what they had to compromise me and make me keep off their trail. I deliberated following them, but reasoned that they would have as many or more men than I. They might ambush us in the hills as we followed them. So I decided a half-loaf was better than none at all, and we headed the herd up to Pearson.

That evening General Ochoa rode out to inspect the cattle, accompanied by five members of his staff, as ugly Revolutionaries as I ever saw, each loaded down with knife and gun and a long bandolier of ammunition strung around his neck as though entering a battle. While his aides counted the herd, Ochoa stood around our campfire making a great show before some of the townspeople who had also ridden out to see the herd that had caused so much controversy. The General, in his way, was making it appear that he and his soldiers had, in some mysterious way, helped us get the cattle away from the raiders. I was requested to sign his report that "with the aid of Gen. Ochoa" we had gathered the remnant of the herd. And I had to pay this extortionist $5 gold for every animal I had recovered! The General and fifty of his cavalrymen accompanied us to the border at El Paso as an escort for our safety!

I had lost 513 head of big steers to the outlaws.[4] It seemed possible that the bandit gang that raided the corrals that night might try to pass or sell some of those cattle at some point along the international line, for there was no market for them in Mexico at the time. However, if the bandits that stole them were from some revolutionary group, and living off the country, the animals could very well have been consumed. I watched all along the border from El Paso to Naco, but saw no herd of that size and none bearing the brands I had bought.

After a few weeks I had decided that none of my cattle had been brought across the border. I felt there was a chance I might learn something of the herd if I rode down to the Yaqui River in Sonora, then controlled by the Calles and Carranza forces. This trip I took Walter Huett with me as a guide, for Walter knew that particular part of the country and its people better than I did.

We first went to Bacadehuachi, on the Yaqui River, then north to Baceroc. There we located Colonel Antonio Lorreto with his command. Col. Lorretto told me that inasmuch as we friends and

275

Americans were so esteemed by the Carranza Government, he could not, for our own sake and safety, permit us to pass over into the danger zone looking for cattle. Then he proceeded to give me a polite bawling out for buying cattle in Mexico at that perilous time. He ended by telling us that while much of the territory was controlled by General Villa, his command would give me every protection, so long as I remained clear of the danger zone.

I was convinced only in part of his desire to protect us, as I knew that he was afraid for his own sake and didn't want to provide men for an escort. I felt that he thought I might learn something about my lost herd that he didn't want known or have come to light at this time. It was probable that his own command was eating my beef, which they had stolen or bought from the raiders. But without his permission I couldn't go into that zone, even if I rode in alone. So we left Lorretto's headquarters without satisfaction. I returned to El Paso.

A few months later I bought a good herd of fat steers from among those little villages in that area and agreed to pay the Calles-Carranza Government $5 gold per head. I planned to take this herd to the border and cross at Douglas, Arizona. When we reached the Gyalla Ranch on the return trip with the herd, about fifteen miles south of the border, General Calles refused to allow me to go farther and for all purposes impounded my cattle at the Gyalla Ranch. At this particular time there was great excitement along the border for there was the possibility of U.S. intervention in the Mexican Revolution.

This was about 1914-15, and the Revolution was on in full swing. Francisco Madero, the Revolutionary *Presidente* had been assassinated by this time and the northern states had been held by various generals such as Huerta, Obregon, Carranza, and Villa. Each man was a single force, as I understood it, more than a member of a body or representative of an idea. These men would install their favorites wherever they ruled. Huerta about this time was elected *Presidente*, but the United States wouldn't recognize him, so he quit. Then Carranza became *Presidente*, and Villa broke with him and raided Columbus, New Mexico, to show his disgust with all *Gringos*. Carranza established his rule pretty firmly and

276

was *Presidente* for several more years but was eventually killed, and Pancho Villa then accepted a big country estate and joined up with the Huerta-Obregon-Calles clique and retired. But he, too, was shot a few years later by some of the old revolutionary boys. But I am running ahead of my story.

When I found out I could not get this herd out of Mexico by fair means, even though it was paid for, I was stuck there with them on the Gyalla Ranch. A month had passed, and I was tired of watching the herd graze on leased land, for the feed bill would soon eat up all the profit. I had not yet decided on any particular course to take to get them out of there and to the border, but the Calles government saved me from further meditation on the matter. One morning a lieutenant and ten Mexican soldiers rode out to the ranch and served an order on my boys to move the cattle to the Quarantine Corrals at Agua Prieta. I happened to be in Douglas at the time, but rode right out there when I was advised of what had happened. I called at the offices of General Calles. He was a handsome man with the overall appearance of a Mexican *ranchero, mucho urbano.* I asked what his purpose might be in moving my herd into the yards at Agua Prieta. "Is this preliminary to seizing possession of my cattle?" I inquired.

"No," he answered, "it is not my purpose to injure you personally in any manner, financially or otherwise. But your country is on the threshold of intervention in our national affairs. We will use every means at our disposal to discourage your Government from this course, and to make it realize the consequences of its acts. There will be more and more need for beef in your country as the great war in Europe spreads and as your Government attempts to support its friends with exports of foodstuffs. But there will be no more beef imported into your country from Mexico so long as the threat of intervention in our national affairs exists.

"I am a Mexican," the general continued, "but I am still a good friend of your people. My wife was born in your land. She and I have many friends there. But if the worst happens, I shall remain faithful to my people and their Government, even as you will remain faithful to yours. You will certainly lose, should intervention occur."

277

This all came to me through an interpreter, for as the general had previously explained, he wanted no misunderstanding. I replied, in part, that there was yet no intervention, hence no need for him to seize my herd. I suggested that the herd could be held at the Gyalla Ranch, where it would be separated from other Mexican cattle that might be diseased in the Nationale Corrals. If anything happened between our two Governments, I said, he would know of it sooner than I and he could send immediately for the cattle and horses and impound them.

My argument and suggestions seemed to change his mind. He consented to allow the herd to remain at the ranch, and provided me with a signed order to that fact that I might present to the lieutenant in charge of moving the herd. Within fifteen minutes he handed me the order, stamped with his official waxed seal. I pocketed the paper and rode as fast as I could toward the Gyalla Ranch, where I met the lieutenant and his soldiers driving the herd, my three boys following along behind at a short distance.

The lieutenant, who spoke very broken English, took the note and carefully studied it. He asked me a few questions about the general, which I answered as best possible, for my visit had been very brief at his offices. After a few moments the lieutenant called his soldiers, arranged them in military order before him, and read them the order. Then he turned, saluted smartly, and rode away toward Agua Prieta.

Bob Lee, who was working for me at this time, and the two *vaqueros*, started to turn the herd back toward the ranch. I rode alongside Bob and instructed him to just graze them back alongside the trail, and "take your time."

"I don't know what you're planning, Jim," Bob grinned, "but I wouldn't do it!"

I turned my horse back to Douglas, where I looked up Kickapoo John, a boy who had ridden for me at various times. Over a glass of beer I told him my plan for bringing the herd up across the border. "I'll need help, John, and it may get you a jail term," was all I offered him. He knew me well, and offered to rustle up two Mormon boys in town who would help us, for they had been among those who had been run out of Mexico a year or two before and their people owned land at *Colonia* Morales.

It was about ten miles to where my men had bedded down the herd, and as we rode down there the Mormon boys related their troubles. Their families had been victimized by the Orozco and Salazar faction and had fled when thier lives were threatened. The boys were anxious to do anything to balance the scale with the Mexicans, and getting my herd out appealed to them. When we reached the herd I ordered the boys to get it moving straight on toward Douglas, then to hold the cattle a mile or two south of the town while I rode in and figured out someway of crossing the border in the night. Then I headed back to Douglas.

When I reached town I located Luke Short, the line rider for Uncle Sam. This was not the Luke Short who was a Texas gambler, for he had died of dropsy at Gueda Springs, Kansas, in '93. This other Luke Short I had known for several years, and as a line rider he was honest and dependable.[5] He understood the problems we cowmen faced doing business in Mexico, and he was always anxious to help us. I told Luke what had happened, that I must cross this herd at once or lose them. I told him I would rather Uncle Sam impounded them than to give them to the Mexicans.

Luke remembered the big loss I had taken a few months previously, and he said he didn't blame me, and doubted if anyone north of the border would hold it against me. But he gave me a warning.

"You may not only lose your cattle this time, Jim," he said, "but you may also get a jolt yourself." He was referring to the old charges against me in Kansas.

"I'll have to chance that," I said. "You meet me at the border, near Niggerhead Mountain. Then you take personal charge of my herd yourself."

I returned to the herd. That night, as we approached within a short distance of the international fence, I rode ahead to see what was going to happen. Only Luke Short was there, sitting his horse in the dusk. I figured that was good, and rode up beside him.

"Jim," he said to me, "it's neither my business to help you get this herd out of Mexico or to let the Mexicans take it away from you. You know that, don't you?" I could see he was unhappy with this business I had thrust upon him.

279

"You can tell me all about this when I get the herd across the border, Luke," I answered him, opening the gate wide.

Luke then appointed Kickapoo John to set one side of the gate while he set the other to count the cattle that came through. An hour later, when the last steer walked through, Luke and Kickapoo John compared their tallies. Each had come up with the same figure, 610 head.

"That's damn good counting in the dark," Bob Lee said to me, in front of Luke and John. "Only a border policeman and a rustler could ever have done it." I agreed. Then, making a little joke on their names, I said, "I doubt that Matthew and Mark could have counted any better than Luke and John." They all laughed, even Kickapoo, who I never thought knew enough about the Bible to know of them names in it.

Luke said to me, "Jim, I don't like to arrest all of you boys and take this herd away from you, for when the cattle get rested they'll drift out of the country."

"Remember this," I said, "these boys are just working for me. If anything done tonight is wrong, Luke, I alone am responsible."

Luke called to Kickapoo John. "Head these cattle for Douglas just as soon as they're rested up," he said. "Put them in the Quarantine Corral there. If anyone asks you who is your boss, tell them you're working for Uncle Sam."

Luke and I started back to Douglas. Before we had ridden far he pulled a pint whiskey bottle from his boot top. It was about half full. "I didn't mention this before your men," he said, "for I only had this much, and it wouldn't go around." He handed me the bottle and I took a healthy belt of the fiery stuff. I can't remember when I needed a drink more, for I was about ready to drop from fatigue. But I was jubilant within that I had foxed old General Calles and got this herd of mine out of Mexico without the loss of a single cow—and through his grasping and conniving way he had even lost the saddlebag of $5 gold pieces which he would have been paid at the border. But I knew that it might cost me that, and more, to now come clean with the United States Government, for my herd was impounded as soon as it reached Douglas.

We put our horses up at the stable near the International Hotel, where we stayed that night, or what was left of it. The next morning I reported to the U.S. Customs officials. They indicated they would cause me no trouble, but would report the case. I was asked to keep in touch with them, and I told them I would not leave town until I knew what disposition would be made of the cattle. They could reach me at the White House Saloon, and I arranged there with the bartender to notify me if they called.

On the street of Douglas that morning I met Governor Hunt, who was in town on a political tour. We were old friends from the Payson days so we stopped there and had a good chat. He told me that Carl Hayden was also in town. Hayden was then a Congressman, later a U.S. Senator, and he had many connections in Washington at that time. Both men were slated to deliver speeches that night. When the Governor learned of my predicament with my cattle he said, "Let's go and talk with Carl about it."

When we found Carl Hayden, the Governor said, "Carl, this is Government business, and perhaps you can be of service to Jim in this matter." I had previously met Carl Hayden and supported his candidacy on the Democratic ticket. He had heard of my trouble, he said, and was particularly interested in my talk with General Calles and the Mexican fear of intervention by the United States. He asked me several questions about the cattle business and the problems facing us as importers of Mexican beeves.[6]

I told Mr. Hayden that my cattle were all clean and in good health, as an inspection would show. That seemed to reassure him.

"Well, if you want some quick action," he said to Governor Hunt, "let's all walk down to the telegraph office." There he composed and sent a telegram to, I believe, William Gibbs McAdoo, who was then Secretary of the Treasury and had great influence in political affairs, particularly in the fields of agriculture, stock raising, and importing.

"I'll have an answer to this within a few hours," Hayden said as we parted. "Come by the Custom House later and we'll find out what is going to happen in the meanwhile."

Congressman Hayden's reference was to the talk on the streets that the Mexican Army might just come over and take my herd back across the border. I was concerned about that, too.

On the street I met the Mexican Consul, Señor Lilliyvier. He greeted me cordially, but I knew there was a lot on his mind.

"I have been looking for you, Señor Herron," he addressed me, "for I have talked with General Calles and he has requested me to invite you to his headquarters to talk with him again."

I was polite but firm, and I told the elderly Consul that I would be most pleased to meet with the general anywhere but on the south side of the border.

"Oh, the general has given me his word of honor that if you return with me for just a brief visit, then I shall accompany you back across the line again," the Consul said. But I was not buying such talk, for I knew where the danger lay.

"Sir," I said to him, "the general's word has already caused me to commit acts that may get me into great trouble with my own Government. So I believe it best to decline his kind invitation. Please extend my best wishes to him when you talk with him." I was trying to be as diplomatic and polite as the occasion permitted, but the old Consul showed in every way his disappointment with me and my attitude.

The following day I had a call from the U.S. Customs House, asking me to call upon them. When I arrived, I was introduced to a gentleman who said he had been ordered by Washington to make an investigation of "the smuggling of a herd of Mexican cattle into the United States."

"I shall want you to tell me, Mr. Herron, just why you drove this herd of cattle out of Mexico without passing through the Mexican Customs and without health papers on them. You are aware that this is illegal, I presume?" This man was direct in his questioning, yet I sensed that he was fair and that he wanted only the facts of the matter upon which our people could base their decision on just how wrong or right I had really been in shaking loose from the Calles Government.

We sat at a desk and he took my name, address, birthplace, and other pertinent data that his task required. I suggested that we get a stenographer who could take down my testimony exactly as I gave it, and he agreed, so we walked to the Don & Don Law Office. These attorneys were among the best in Douglas at that time. Frank Don was there and permitted his secretary to help us. She was speedy and accurate, I knew, for she had helped me before in my cattle deals. It took about an hour to put my facts on record and as I related the incidents that had led up to my action I watched the agent from Washington, wide-awake and weighing my every statement, like a circuit Judge. The agent asked the secretary to type up three copies and as we left the office he remarked, "We've had a pretty rough day, Mr. Herron. Now where can we get a drink to finish it."

We walked to the White House Saloon. Arizona was "dry" in them days, like Kansas was in the Eighties, but if you knew a bartender or druggist he would serve you and any friend you brought in. We had two drinks at the bar, then the investigator asked if we could get a pint to take to the hotel. I got the bottle and we went up to his room at the hotel. There we sat and visited for two hours, talking about everything except what I wanted to know. He asked me many questions about my experiences in Mexico, about their feelings south of the border, about the various generals and soldiers I had talked with, for there were not many Americans down there after the Mormons and the railroad men left, and it seemed to me that he was pumping me for information that would help my Government understand better what was happening down there. But I learned nothing from him about my cattle deal.

We breakfasted together the following morning, and as we walked to the depot so he could get on the train he suddenly said to me, "Jim, you haven't asked me anything about your case. Don't you care to know?"

"I had decided not to be too inquisitive," I replied, "but if you have any factual information you are free to give me, then I will appreciate hearing it."

He shook my hand as the train approached and said, "My report isn't going to hurt you, Jim. And it's been a real pleasure to meet you."

I expressed a mutual sentiment as he picked up his bag and

stepped onto the platform of the coach. I liked that man, for he gave me every opportunity to present my side of the story without trying to twist my facts like the lawyers do, and he permitted me to give the background for the action, that is, my previous experiences with the Customs people at La Morita. We had taken several drinks together, enough to free our spirits from mundane affairs, and I noted how well he carried his liquor. I had worked behind the bar in my saloons, so I could appreciate a man who could rightly judge his capacity for drink and quit before he was drenched. The liquor had loosened his tongue, as it had my own, but he was not full of "brag" as many drunks get when in their cups. I knew well that there is no death worse than being talked to death by a souse. The good bourbon had warmed him as good whiskey should, and we had both enjoyed the feeling of comfort and sociability that is lost to so many men while in "dry" business dealings. I recalled what a Tombstone gambler had once said, that there were three degrees of drunkenness: the social degree, the lion degree, and the hog degree. I always stuck to, and preferred, the first.

I never saw this agent of the Federal Government from Washington again. I have not mentioned his name for obvious reasons. But I have recalled him and the pleasant evening we spent together many times. For he was my type of man, even though he wasn't a cowman.

A few days later I received another call from the U.S. Custom House. They had instructions, so they said, to release my cattle to me. But I would be required to dip the herd, for there was fear of cattle ticks.

Once more I had weathered a cattle dispute where the two Governments, the Republic of Mexico and the United States of America, were involved.

I traded less in cattle as the years went by, but I have related these experiences in some detail because they paint a fairly representative picture of what the problems of the cattleman and importer were in that day, and this applied in some degree to all traders from San Diego, California to Brownsville, Texas, in them

284

tempestuous Territorial Days and later when the Mexican Revolution attracted all eyes to the border.

The buying and selling of livestock had become more and more involved now as both Governments stepped in with all sorts of new regulations and restrictions. I pined for them old days when all a cowman had to worry about was tick fever, screwworm, and rustlers, for we knew how to deal with those problems. But a cowman hasn't a chance when international politics breaks out in his herds.

chapter XVII

1915-1949

RETURN TO NO MAN'S LAND
HERRON'S FINAL ATTEMPTS TO CLEAR HIS NAME

During much of the period 1918 to 1928, I lived at Courtland, Arizona. That town one year would appear to have good prospects, the next year be in a slump. It kept all of us guessing, afraid to leave for fear we would miss something, yet scared to stay. About 1916 the Guggenheims opened a mine there on the hill to the north. It looked like a sure thing. But this Needles Mining Company thing lasted just a few years, then the ore petered out.

My son Sam came back from the war, and was working with Mr. Furnace who was working the Johnny Pearce mine up at Pearce. Sam was a skilled hard rock miner and got Furnace out of debt, so Furnace turned the work over to Sam and gave him a half-interest in the company. Eventually Sam took over all of the company interests when Furnace left there. Sam had two of his war-time buddies there with him for a while, Albert Snyder and Blackie Griffin.

At this time my eyesight had begun to fail me. I had been blessed with eyes that could distinguish a brand on a horse or cow as far as any range man. With my sight failing, I told Mary that I would like to return to the Oklahoma Panhandle country and see the land and the people while my eyes were good enough to help me enjoy the sights. Mary showed little interest in going, for she was a girl born and bred to the Southwest and knew no one back there, but she gave me encouragement to go, so I planned the trip by myself. Of all the hard lessons that had been mine to learn while "seeing the elephant and hearing the owl holler," the chief one was that your old friends are the best ones after all—and you will never forget them, wherever you roam. That's really what made me want to return to No Man's Land.

The day I arrived a friend, Mr. Wells, met me at the station at Forgan, a town northwest of Beaver. We drove in his car down into the lovely Beaver River valley. As we made the drive along what had been the old Jones and Plummer Trail, I asked about the matter closest to my heart at that time, my chance to get a new trial at Meade, Kansas. Mr. Wells was hopeful that something could be arranged, for he assured me that I still had many friends both in southwest Kansas and in the Strip who would testify as character witnesses for me. The Oklahoma Panhandle was now a part of the State of Oklahoma. In 1890 it had been included in Oklahoma Territory, then when the old Indian Territory was given statehood as Oklahoma, in 1907, the Panhandle was taken into the State. The Panhandle strip was now divided into three counties, named, from east to west, Beaver, Texas, and Cimarron. When the railroad built through in 1902-03, Guymon had become the leading town, for it was several more years until Beaver City got a railroad. Kenton, which had been important in the west end, had dried up and Boise City was now the leading village out there.

When we arrived at Beaver, Mr. Wells dropped me off at the home of Judge Robert H. Loofbourrow. The Judge was married to the former Bertha Groves, my first wife's sister. Bertha and I had aways been close friends. Her husband had made an excellent record as a jurist, serving a term on the Oklahoma Supreme Court, 1912 to 1915. Because of his great judicial experience, I was anxious to learn what he thought of my chances for a new trial. The Judge was rather non-committal, but we talked at length about the case.

While I waited for Judge Loofbourrow to study my possibilities more carefully, I attended the Pioneer Reunion at Beaver, which had now grown into an annual celebration. The range cattle business as I had known it had come and gone. The land was rapidly being settled by new farmers, wheat and maize growers, and their motorized machinery was replacing the horse as farm power. A few smaller and substantial ranches remained along the water courses, but the whole country was under barbed wire. Old outfits like Kramer's, Healy's, Hardesty's, Taintor's, Over's, and the YL had withdrawn from the range. Many went north to

Wyoming, Colorado, Montana, and Canada. The rest had shrunk up within their barbed wire fences. Only the Hitches, Neffs, Judys, Barbys, John George, and a few more remained. But it was a great experience to meet some of them old boys of my youth, now wearing gray in their hair—and a few of them talking like they were preachers! But I shook the hands of many friends of old—Boss Neff, Burris Wright, who had been with me in Arizona for a few years, Bernie Lemert, Doc Anschutz, Lee Larrabee, and kinfolks. The Schmokers, Judys, and Barbys were there, and many folks came from the west end of the Strip for this big event and I visited with the Ballards, the Dacys, the Cochrans, the Potters, the Lynchs, and the Easelys. North Texas was well-represented, but I missed seeing my old friend Charlie Hitch, who I had rubbed stirrups with on many an old cattle trail and roundup circle. Oddly enough, I was not treated as a "wanted" man, but like a celebrity was shown around town, introduced to everyone we met, and invited by them to return and spend more time.[1]

Both Ray and Burris Wright had been with me in Arizona, and they had filled in many of my old friends on the years I spent out there and on the Mexican troubles, so everywhere I went folks asked me to recount some of those experiences, which I did of course. As I went from one old friend's company to that of another I could see that, like myself, they were getting gray and wrinkled by the Oklahoma sun, as I had been by the desert sun of Arizona and Mexico. But we verbally rode the old trails again, fought broncs, and recited the cowboy verses and songs we had learned in youth. This proved to be one of the happiest times of my life, for when you are the center of attraction among old friends, time goes only too fast.

I cannot help but recall and tell one of the jokes that was told me by one old cowman there in the Strip. It was about a very religious lady whom I shall call Mrs. Jessamine Johnifer, though of course that was not her real name at all. One day she knelt to pray at church. Mrs. Johnifer was an extremely large woman, weighing in the neighborhood of 300 pounds, though she had not been on a scale for years. It was an extremely hot day, and we must presume that that was the reason why she was wearing her usual two pettiskirts but had on no drawers. In some manner, as she knelt in her pew, the back of her dress caught on the arm of the pew behind her, exposing much pink flesh.

Now it so happened that three indolent youths, Jake and Rance Little and Charlie Ward, by name, were standing just outside the open window listening to the services. It was the season of the year when the sunflowers were tall and in firm stalk, so one of these boys seized a tall sunflower stalk with a beautiful yellow flower at its top, reached through the window and tickled Jessamine on her exposed parts. The startled woman immediately sprang to her feet and screamed, "Christamighty!"

That almost broke up the services. In due time those three boys were arrested and charged with disorderly conduct, as was right and proper to do. When they were brought before the County Judge for their preliminary hearing he deliberated the matter at some length, after hearing all the testimony. With the wisdom given only to Solomon, the Judge convinced the County Attorney of the impossibility of presenting such a case before a jury or any court without completely losing the dignity of that court as well as his case. So the boys were given a sharp lecture by the County Attorney and the Judge, and were dismissed.

After that story was told to a group of us, Judge Loofbourrow came back with another. It dealt with that same congregation.

"That little church was some distance from Beaver," he said, "but there always seemed to be something happening there. I recall the time that the itinerant evangelist who was conducting the services there one Sunday chose for his text, 'Woman, Who Art Thou?'

"While delivering the sermon, this evangelist became very animated and excited, and filled the air with gestures of his arms and hands, pointing at the members of the congregation and thundering for effect, 'Woman—Who Art Thou?' Eventually, his index finger settled upon an elderly woman who was sitting directly in front of the altar, just a few feet from the speaker. As the question fell down upon her from his lips, like the sound of Doom, 'Woman—Who Art *Thou*?,' the timid little lady squeaked up her answer.

289

" 'Why, sir,' she said, 'I'm the dentist's wife, Mrs. Doctor Wislon.' "

Everyone laughed heartily at the Judge's story, for he was not a great hand to tell stories, and if he did, everyone knew that it was the truth.

When the Pioneer Celebration came to an end, I decided to go and pay a visit to my oldest daughter, Ollie Dot. Dot had married Carl H. Stratton, a banker who was affiliated with Pawnee Bill, the well-known Major Gordon Lillie, who was in the Wild West Show business and at one time had been partner to Colonel William F. (Buffalo Bill) Cody. Carl and Dot had married in 1908, at Anadarko, Oklahoma. In their early years they had operated a bank at Kiefer, Oklahoma, where Dot had once been present during a bank holdup by Henry and Belle Starr. Carl and Dot were at this present time living at Pawnee, Oklahoma, and I stayed at their home for a week, meeting many of the old woollies who had spent some part of their youth in No Man's Land or who had made The Run into the Unassigned Land or the Cherokee Strip, in 1889 and 1893. I also had two good talks and several good drinks with Pawnee Bill. Carl and Ollie Dot had lived at his home in earlier years, and I found him a fine gentleman, free talker, and good listener.

From Pawnee I took the train back to the Panhandle and visited the scenes of the old YL Ranch, on Kiowa Creek, where I had gone to work as a fourteen-year old cowboy. Together with a friend, I rode down to the location of Judge Sutter-Hubbard's distillery, where I had seen the two young men's bodies hanging from his ridgelog. There was little here but ruins of his cave.

At the site of old Benton I found little to indicate there had ever been a thriving town at that spot. Now it was open prairie, with the butts of a few soddies showing and the dust-filled cellars of a few of the old homes grown deep in tumbleweeds. The settlers had hauled away most of the frame buildings and the wood roofs to their claims. There was the usual debris of broken glass from the liquor bottles we had emptied in them old days, and I picked up one that was half-embedded in the sod and reflected if perhaps Irish McGovern, Al Dixon, and I hadn't killed that particular "dead soldier." I saw a few rusted wagon tires that had laid behind the old sod blacksmith shop and the adjoining livery stable where Irish worked. And I dug a rusted six-shooter from the dirt and hung it on a weathered cedar post by its triggerguard.

Everything looked smaller to me, and as I wandered back to where we had left the saddle horses I again began to ponder the matter of obtaining a second trial at Meade, Kansas. Many of the ranchers I had met on these trips assured me of their willingness to help me, so I returned to Beaver in good spirits.

Back at Beaver I stayed with Judge Loofbourrow for a day or two. The Loofburrow's gave me a farewell dinner party with a few close friends and relatives invited. When the other guests had departed, I brought up again the matter of a second trial and asked the judge what he had learned during my absence.

"Jim," he said, "I have given your problem considerable thought and attention, but I'm dubious whether any lawyer can ever get you a *new* trial. There are too many factors working against it." He was about to elaborate when the telephone rang. Bertha answered, then called the Judge.

"It's Tom Johnson calling from Meade, dear," she said as he went to the phone.

Tom Johnson was, at the time, the County Clerk at Meade, Kansas. He told the Judge that the mere fact that I was back in the country had disturbed some of them young officials at the county seat. There was now talk at the court house about my old case, and them young lawyers were talking about extradition and its processes. Tom thought that they might like to try it on me to see how them laws worked, and he warned the Judge that it would not be good policy for me to linger longer in the Strip.

Tom was an old friend of mine, so I did not doubt his earnest plea in warning Judge Loofbourrow of the danger I might be in. Both Bertha and the Judge were concerned for my safety, so he suggested that we tarry no longer at his home, where I was known to be staying, but that we go elsewhere until train time where we could visit without danger. So I put my bag in his car and we drove out to a ranch operated by mutual friends, the Robert Mc-Farlands. Bob had been wanting to look at some of his cattle in a

291

pasture west from Beaver, so he and his wife accompanied us as we drove up the river valley. After we had looked at his steers, we were so far west that we decided that I might miss my train if we drove back toward Forgan so I decided to catch a train on the Rock Island at Hooker, and we drove on to that point. The women folks joked the Judge about his compromising situation, acting as the chauffeur for a wanted man during his "get-away," and it gave us all a good laugh.

The Judge told me that if I worked with him closely, there might yet be a way in which we could bring enough influence to bear that I could get some sort of a settlement of my court troubles at Meade.

"You will probably never get another trial, Jim, for you never stayed to have sentence pronounced upon you. But you were convicted, and if you ever go before that court again, it may pronounce sentence upon you. Now you don't want that, for it's too risky at your age.

"My new thought is this: I can write to Governor Capper of Kansas and canvass his opinion on obtaining a pardon for you. In the meanwhile, I want you to get all the letters with good character references you can muster in Arizona. Judge Price is a good friend of mine, and I have discussed your old case with him. He told me recently that the fact that he tried your original case would preclude his acting in any legal manner for you. However, he will assist us to help get this situation ironed out satisfactorily for you."

I asked if I should get a petition signed by my Arizona friends, for I recalled that the signatures of fifty or sixty cattlemen and settlers had, in 1889, made it possible for Bill Eldridge to bring his family back into the Strip after the Vigilantes drove them out, following the shooting of Silas, the oldest Eldridge boy in a gunfight and the killing of one of the Johnson boys.

"No, no," the Judge responded. "That was a different matter. Just get letters written by the highest officials you know and the most important businessmen and cattlemen out there. They will have some influence upon the Governor if a pardon is possible under these circumstances."

I had never told the Judge or any of my Oklahoma friends about my difficulties at Pearce and Courtland, though the cowboys who had returned to the Strip had related the troubles I had been in with the Mexican officials on the border. Now, I felt, I might encounter difficulties, for my Arizona record had not been lily white, and the conviction of six years earlier might now come up to haunt me again. But I resolved to ask for the letters of recommendation and if anyone remembered the old conviction and felt leary providing me with character references, well, the hide would just have to be burned with the wrong brand, that was all.

As I boarded the train, after bidding the Judge and Bertha and our friends goodbye, I picked up a copy of the *Guymon Herald*. When I was settled in my seat and the train had pulled out of the station, I unfolded the paper and, much to my surprise, saw my name under the heading, "The Publisher's Column." I read:

> I just heard a few days ago that Jim Herron had been in Guymon a short time ago. Sorry indeed that Jim did not call me up and give me a chance to visit with him. I heard though that he was on a hurried trip.
>
> Jim Herron was the first sheriff Beaver County had and he presided over what is now Cimarron, Texas, and Beaver counties combined, which at that time was No Man's Land, and he was one of the best sheriffs we ever had. Jim was a kindhearted and brave man, but loved to treat all his friends kindly. I saw a street fight one day in front of Jack Garvey's saloon, along in 1887 or 1888, when 45 Colt bullets were flying everywhere. Jim was several blocks away. Jim came running and jumped into the middle of this war and grabbed the boys' arms and held them high so the bullets would go up in the air. All I heard him say was, "Boys, cut it out! You know the next crack will be mine!"
>
> Jim did not have a gun on him, although he might have thought he had at the time. In less than thirty minutes they were all shaking hands. All went into Jack Garvey's saloon and I think everyone got drunk except Jim. He did not ever drink much, but he was a big hit with the women, for he was a fine-looking chap.
>
> Bob Payne, a good friend of mine, told me he

293

was sick in bed when he learned Jim was in town
and when he was able to be up, Jim had gone. Too
bad we all missed him.
                                        Charlie Hitch

Well, as I read that letter I said to myself, "I've got my first
testimonial letter, and I never even had to ask Charlie Hitch for
it, either!" Charlie's letter brought a warm feeling to my innards,
like the many good drinks of bourbon he and I had shared together at the dances in the old days and at the social gatherings
we held at Beaver City after the roundups. Charlie and his
brother, Jim, were both splendid men, and Charlie's "letter to
the editor" imparted a glow that lasted me during the whole trip
to El Paso.[2]

That fall, after reaching home, I went to the Governor's office
at Phoenix. I knew him and several other State officers, some before they held political offices. I felt that if Governor Tom Campbell (he had defeated Fred Colter in the recent election) would
hand me a testimonial letter, I would be able to get many more
there at the State capitol. I had met Campbell when he was on
his election campaign and he was a jolly fellow. When I was shown
into his office he stepped from behind his desk to shake my hand.

"Jim," he said, to start the conversation, "I've a question I've
always wanted to ask an old cowboy like you. You've punched
cows and you've operated saloons, so you should be able to help
me. Do you mind?"

"Why no, Governor," I answered, "I'll be happy to answer
any question that may help you." I still wasn't on to his tricks
and thought he might want to know something about the Mexican
cattle imports.

"This is the question, then," he said. "Why do you cowboys
always leave on your spurs when you're lined up at the bar in the
saloons?"

His question almost took me off my feet. We did sometimes
have our spurs buckled on to boots so tight and covered with
barnyard manure that it was more trouble than it was worth to
remove them. But I could see from the twinkle in his eyes that he
was joking, so I framed the best answer that I could, on the "spur"
of the moment.

"Why, Governor," I said, "we wear them spurs to make it easy on the bartenders. When a cowpunch' drinks himself stiff, the bartenders can take hold of him from behind and wheel him out the back door on his rowels." I never cracked a smile, but the Governor roared with laughter, and the answer seemed to satisfy his curiosity.

"Now what can I do for you, Jim?" he asked, wiping his eyes with his handkerchief. "You looking for a job?" I expect he had seen his share of job-hunters since his election.

"No sir," I answered him, "I'm looking for something far more difficult for you to give me, Governor. I need a 'good-character' reference from you." He motioned me to a chair, took his seat behind the desk and said, "Tell me about it."

I spilled my story about the old case at Meade, Kansas, and I told how it had kept me on the Owl Hoot Trail now for twenty-five years. I related my recent talks with Judge Loofbourrow, and told of how he was trying to help me.

"You know I'm a Democrat, Governor," I said, "and since you are a good Republican it may sound brassy of me to even ask for your help at this time."

The Governor smiled. "Jim, nearly all the voters in Arizona are Democrats," he answered. "If I hadn't received plenty of Democrats' votes, maybe your own, I would never have been elected." He called in his secretary. "I'll have a letter for you this afternoon, Jim. I'll direct it to the Governor of Kansas, and let's hope that it helps you resolve your troubles." We shook hands and I left. When I called later, the letter was all prepared, in duplicate, so I could keep a copy.

Governor Campbell's letter stated that he hoped that both he and Governor Capper would consider placing a general amnesty on many of the old timers who had done so much to open up the country but who had "also done some wrong." He suggested that "the forgiveness of the sins of youth" would be a good place to start. He told of my long residence in Arizona and my record as cattleman and businessman, and though I had mentioned my conviction in that state, he made no mention of it in the letter. Governor Campbell told that I had been one of the few men "with the courage and the knowledge to travel and do business in Revolutionary Mexico and to bring out many thousands of cattle when beef was so badly needed during our first year in the great World War."

With Governor Campbell's letter in my pocket, I called on my old friend, ex-Governor George Hunt, whom I had known since he was a grocery clerk at Globe and I was a teamster for the mines at Payson. He provided me a fine letter that told of our personal friendship of many years. I next visited the Sanitary Board, where I was well known, then on to a couple of bank presidents, some businessmen, and ranchers. I was not disappointed in a single instance and collected twenty-two letters of recommendation, which I mailed on to Judge Loofbourrow.

But it was no use. Everyone in public office was now tied up in the serious business of war. Governor Capper had gone on to the Senate for the next term, and there was little time for backward looking to the 1890's. However, I did receive news indirectly that if I stayed out of Kansas, no effort would ever be made to extradite me for the old conviction. So I was enabled to return several times and enjoy the Pioneer Day Celebrations at Beaver, and later when they were held at Guymon, Oklahoma.

The years passed. I remained at Courtland and Pearce until 1928, running a small saloon and buying cattle when I had the chance. But I soon found it impossible to bring herds out of Mexico, for my eyesight was going fast. My wives were gone, my families were grown, the children married and with families of their own.[3] I reached seventy years, and an operation for cataracts on my eyes had now left me stone blind, for I had scratched them and let out the fluid one night while under sedation. No one ever told me, but I knew I would never see again. I had yearned so long to clear my name at Meade that I once more planned a trip back for that purpose.

In 1935 I returned for the Pioneer Day Celebration. My old friend, Judge Loofbourrow, had passed from the earthly scene in October, 1926, so I now counseled with his son, Bob, who was a lawyer. Another son, H. J. Loofbourrow, was now County Judge, so he could take no part in my problems. But Bob made a per-

296

sonal trip to Meade to consult the old trial records, if he could find them. But the records had been burned in the court house fire, or lost, and he could unearth no trace of the old trial. Bob had also tried to contact the jurors of that time, and witnesses. All were gone, or moved away. This gave Bob a new approach to the matter.

If there was no legal way by which a District Court Judge could set aside my conviction, my only course would be to return to the Meade District Court and accept whatever sentence might be imposed upon me. The Kansas Governor had no doubt failed to act because I had never been sentenced. Now the old transcripts of the trial could not be found; the court reporter's notes had been either lost or destroyed in the fire; no witnesses could be produced; the present District Court Judge would know nothing of the case. Because of these facts, Bob reasoned, it was possible that should I now appear and plead innocent, the case would be dismissed. My age would be a factor in my favor, he thought, but this would take the full cooperation of the Meade County Attorney to arrange this. There were many old timers like Fred Tracy still living in the Beaver County area who would testify for me, Bob said, summing up the plan. It was risky, but he felt I could win my complete freedom.

I wanted my name clean, above all things, before I died. So I told Bob to go ahead and arrange for a hearing or a new trial, whichever he could get and I would appear and take my chances. He immediately contacted the Meade County Attorney. But this young gentleman thought it would be against his principles—and no doubt poor politics—so he refused to get involved in the case in any way. So Bob advised me that that settled the matter for all time. He counseled me to stay clear of Kansas and said that was all he could do. His efforts in my behalf, like those of his estimable father before him, were wasted.

But life goes on. I have now been on the Owl Hoot Trail the better part of my life, never proud of the fact, always hoping I could clear up my name. This life has brought me into contact with lawmen, outlaws, gamblers, dance hall girls, politicians, miners, lawyers, judges, engineers, and men and women of other trades and professions. Those living a normal, workaday life might never meet such a wide variety of people nor be associated with such an array of characters, both good and bad and everything in between. Dealing with these men and women, who were a normal part of the hotel, saloon, dance hall, and cattle businesses of that time taught me many facts. The men and women of the sporting world were in many instances as decent, as kind, and as true as those of any other profession or trade. It is a case of the individual. I have known gamblers, saloonmen, and outlaws who lived by a personal code of ethics as strict as any deacon of a church might set for himself to follow. I never attempted to change their lives, except as my own personal conduct may have influenced them. But I kept my own self-respect.

I have run across greed and avarice among the richest and most secure people, men and women who have been given the very best this country has to offer. I have seen foolishness and wickedness among the poorest in the land. I have seen the vice and crime of Dodge City in her heyday, of Ogalallie and Camp Supply, of Beer City and old Tombstone and the two Nacos. Though all were small towns, they earned a name and reputation that lives on to this day. I have known many men who fled to No Man's Land for their personal safety and freedom, just as I fled to Arizona for mine. Some of them fellows set themselves up as spiritual and political leaders for the rest of us! I never did that. But I did learn to live in peace among most of them people and to find good qualities and even virtues in them, sometimes buried down within their souls so deep that they didn't know themselves that they possessed them. By looking for that milk of human kindness in others, and having a little bit of it within myself when they needed help, I found a good life among my fellow men, most of which was spent in the saddle making an honorable living for my families. I respected most of the men and women I met on the trail, and I believe most of them respected me.

This much I learned about life and human beings: We are all inclined to want to be good, especially when we are young and unspoiled by life and its burdens. The exceptions to this are generally the mentally irresponsible. We like to live and let live. We

298

treasure friendships. At times, economic circumstances force good people away from the Straight and Narrow Trail they would prefer to follow through life. But that doesn't always make them bad. Some folks are made mean by bitter treatment, just as a young colt may be ruined by an ignorant or cruel and ill-tempered horse-breaker. But the average person, who is not spoiled in youth, learns to treat other folks like he expects to be treated himself. I guess that is what you would call following the Golden Rule.

On the range, we had what we called the Range Law, "You treat me right or we'll have trouble." These two rules are similar, but the Golden Rule recognizes that the other fellow can be just as right as you are, and that he doesn't have to prove himself first. Well, that was the way I tried to live my life, to treat other people of all creeds, kinds, and colors with the same civility and respect that I expected them to use in dealing with me. I am happy to report that after more than eighty years of life, most of the folks I met along both the Owl Hoot Trail and up on the Straight and Narrow Road have treated me with great kindness and respect.

If anything that I have set down in these pages is worth re-membering by the reader, or is suitable to select for guidance in the future, I believe they are these two facts that I have learned in a long and busy life:

First, every man needs a good wife beside him to help shape his life and to influence it for the better. For a good family is indispensable to a good life. Second, friendships are precious, and old friends are valuable assets to have in the Bank of Life as one grows old.

I have been blessed by having many loyal friends, and three of the finest women to help share my fortunes. Those good friends, those good women, and the children we have shared together, have made my life interesting and enjoyable and a most happy one. No man could ask more from life than I have received, and I have enjoyed living every minute of it.

appendix

STORY OF THE ORIGINAL MANUSCRIPT

In June, 1965, the great floods that struck Denver caused many refrigerators and air conditioning systems to fail. In response to this, several firms, such as Westinghouse, sent expert repair and maintenance engineers to Denver to work on their appliances. Among these experts was Mr. Homer C. Jeffrey, Opportunity, Washington. With Mr. Jeffrey came his wife, Jean. Mrs. Jeffrey was the former Jean McGrew, daughter of Rita Herron McGrew of Superior, Arizona, and granddaughter of Jim Herron, the author of this original manuscript.

While in Denver, Mrs. Jeffrey called the undersigned, and was invited to our home to visit with Mrs. Chrisman and me. Mrs. Jeffrey's interest in us, we soon learned, was in the manner in which we had told, in *Lost Trails of the Cimarron*, of her grandfather's escapade at Meade, Kansas, when he had broken away from the law officers and escaped, though his friend, Jack Rhodes, was killed in the escape attempt.

"You handled that so much like grandfather always told it that I wondered where you got all the information," Mrs. Jeffrey said. "Had you ever seen his manuscript that he left?"

At the mention of a *manuscript* by Jim Herron, my ears got big, for though I had talked with many old cattlemen in the Cimarron country who had known him well, I had never met Jim Herron nor read anything from his pen.

"Where is this manuscript now?" I asked Mrs. Jeffrey.

She thought that she could get a copy from her aunt, Millie Borba, who lived at Newman, California, with whom Jim Herron had spent his last days and where he had been laid to rest.

The original manuscript, I learned, had been typed by Jean

301

Jeffrey when she was a high school girl, taking typing in school. Her grandfather was staying at their home at the time, in the early 1940's, and one evening when she was starting to type she had said, "I wish someone would talk, so I could find something to type."

"I'll tell you my life story," her grandfather spoke up, "if you want something to type."

"Go ahead, Grampa," Jean said. And the autobiography had begun.

"I wish now," Jean said to us later, "that I had known and cared more about history—particularly about grandfather's life. But like all young people I couldn't have cared less. I was more interested in learning to type than in what he had to say, and there are so many misspelled names and such that I doubt I was much help to him."

But Jean's efforts were very helpful. For Jim Herron was stone blind at that time and could not write down the adventures that he had lived.

When Jim Herron went back to Beaver, Oklahoma, in 1946, he took with him the typed manuscript, or a copy of it. He knew a man there whom he hoped could find a publisher for it. The man was Fred Tracy, an old pioneer of No Man's Land who was then in the dry goods business. In a letter to James Herron, jr., Superior, Arizona, Fred Tracy wrote, on July 12, 1953:

> The last time your father was here, he brought with him the manuscript of his biography, and left it with me to see if we could find some publishing company who would print it on a commission basis but was unsuccessful. . . . Before sending off the manuscript I made a copy of it in event the original should be lost.
>
> A few years ago I received a letter from Mrs. Millie Borba of Newman, California, stating she had found some of my letters among her father's papers and advising me of his death. We have had an intermittant correspondence ever since, and it is from her that I have your address.
>
> The object of this letter is to advise you that I have a copy of your father's biography and if you would like to have it, I will be pleased to mail it to you. While he was here last I also took his picture with that of the then sheriff, should you wish it.

302

Please excuse misspelled words, as a result of cataract operation, my eyesight is blurred and I frequently strike the wrong keys.

Yours very truly,

(signed) F. C. Tracy

Following the conversation at our home, Jean at once contacted her aunt and obtained a copy of the original Jim Herron manuscript as I asked her to do. Since the copy I would use in rearranging and rewriting the manuscript would be mutilated in the process, I asked that a copy and not the original be sent me.

From this manuscript, from the many letters from old pioneers, from old cattlemen who knew or knew of Jim Herron, from old court records and old newspaper files, this book relating the lifetime experiences of Jim Herron was written.

There is a lesson to be learned from the salvaging of this old cowman's manuscript: Everyone can be a good witness *of their time*. Further, meticulous care should be taken in disposing of old papers, old manuscripts, old letters, old photographs, and other materials that help carry the history of our country and its people from one generation to another. Whenever anything of such nature is to be discarded, call your library or your historical society and turn the materials over to their historians and experts to be checked before being destroyed. Only by doing this can much of our historical record be preserved.

Those who find enjoyment and useful information in the story told by Jim Herron will realize how precarious was the state of his original manuscript during those intervening years after his death in 1949 and the resurrection of the papers in 1965. It has been fortunate that at least one extra copy was made and that at least one survived.

H.E.C.

notes

1. See Appendix for the interesting story of the origin of Jim Herron's manuscript and how it came to the writer's attention.

PART I

CHAPTER I.

1. Herron's gravestone reads "1865-1949." However, he states that he came up the Texas Trail in 1880, aged fourteen, so the year 1866 is established herein as his birth date.
2. A. N. Howe, pioneer of the Neutral Strip, also mentions in his manuscript: "A brother of Phil Sheridan was employed in one of the sutler's stores."
3. The YL Ranch (Cattle Ranche & Land Company) was organized after Webster-Hoare & Company floated a million-dollar stock issue, half in common, half in preferred, in England. Headquarters were on Kiowa Creek, four miles from the eastern end of the Neutral Strip, in the Cherokee Strip. Their range ran over into the Texas Panhandle and the Neutral Strip, and the company, by 1882, claimed 26,000 head of cattle, range count. Rufus Hatch, a Wall Street tycoon, was at the bottom of the stock promotion. Hume Webster, assisted by Spencer and Drew, arranged the stock issue. John Clay played a part as an appraiser of the properties, prior to the issuance of the stock. Clay later reflected upon the audacity of the young men, himself included, who undertook "to give opinions upon a new and unstable business on the western plains where conditions were erratic and the results doubtful. . . . " The YL failed to return the expected profits. Clay said, "There was reckless mismanagement and criminal neglect." Jim Herron makes this

305

same point in his story. After Spencer was replaced by Jim Elliott, a small profit was shown. Charles Rynearson later managed the ranch; he was a man much in the image of Alex Young, whom the new owners had let go. However, said Clay, "As the South Sea Bubble burst, as the Dutch Tulip Craze was dissolved, this Cattle Gold Brick withstood not the snow of winter. It wasted away under the fierce attacks of the sub-arctic season, aided by summer drought. . . . " This, then, was the ranch where Jim Herron learned the cow business.

CHAPTER II.

1. During the nineteenth century, as the United States was expanding westward, creating Territories and States, fixing boundaries, and designating administrative units, this geographical area of almost 5,800 square miles was strangely undefined and overlooked. Boundaries around it were carefully defined, though sometimes hotly contested, but attention was riveted on the Indian problem, on railroad routes, on the slavery issue—and lo and behold a 3,700,000-acre vacuum was created. It became actually, as Carl Rister has dubbed it, a "land-orphan." Legally and administratively it was simply lost between Kansas and Colorado, New Mexico, the Texas Panhandle, and Indian Territory—i.e., parallel of 37° on the north, meridian of 103° on the west, 36° 30' on the south, and 100° on the east.

From the sixteenth to the nineteenth century this Strip had been claimed by Spain, France, Mexico, and Texas—not to mention the Indians; it became part of the United States as a result of the annexation of Texas, but was an unwitting victim of the explosive slavery issue.

The Missouri Compromise of 1820 prohibited slavery in United States federal territory north of 36° 30'. Twenty-five years later when Texas became a State—a "slave state"—about one-sixth of its area was north of 36° 30'. By this time the viability of the earlier and tenuous compromise was failing. The Mexican War, California's appeal for statehood, and the South's threat of secession had tangled and highlighted the slave-state versus free-state controversy. The Compromise of 1850 was, therefore, Congress' attempt to accommodate the problem once again.

It was as part of the 1850 legislation that Texas' northern boundary was drawn at 36° 30′ in deference to the Missouri Compromise and that New Mexico's eastern boundary was set at 103°. The western boundary of Indian Territory, 100°, had been fixed years earlier, though the Cherokees continued to contest it until at least 1890, always unsuccessfully. The Kansas-Nebraska bill of 1854 established 37° as the southern boundary of Kansas. There was an attempt that year to include the Public Land Strip as part of Indian Territory, but the proposal got buried in committee (the Committee on Territories) and was lost in the adjournment of the 33rd Congress. Thus it was that this orphaned rectangle became literally No Man's Land. And would remain so for almost forty years more.

2. The Star Mail Route Frauds of the period 1876-1883 were the biggest scandal produced in Washington at the time. Some Star Routes, such as the Camp Supply to Ft. Elliott and the Camp Supply to Dodge City routes, were contracted for at about $800 per year, but within a year or two were costing the Government six to nine times that much. Other Star Route costs skyrocketed from $8,000 to $75,000 per year and from $2,400 to $70,000! A Congressional investigation revealed fraud on the part of the contractors and a few postal officers, but when trials were held the names of U.S. Senator Stephen W. Dorsey and 2nd Assistant Postmaster General Brady came into the limelight. The frauds ran into the millions before they were stopped.

3. Mrs. Thomas Darrel (Sam) Herron recalls the falling-out between her father-in-law (Jim Herron) and his brothers. The older brother took possession of everything the father owned when he passed away.

4. Herron refers to both Hubbard and Sutter as the same person. It is possible that Sutter was the man's correct name; however, the writer was never able to establish this fact and "the Judge," under either name, was unknown to the legal profes-

307

sion in Ohio—where he presumably came from. In all Oklahoma official records he is referred to as L. M. Hubbard. In the "Journal of Proceedings," the Record Book of the Cimarron Territory Council (cf. Chapter IV, note 1), he is sometimes referred to as Capt. Hubbard.

CHAPTER III.

1. In American legal experience, an "Organic *Act*" has normally meant the act of the U.S. Congress which confers the powers of Government upon a Territory. "Organic *Law*" has usually referred to the fundamental law or constitution, written or unwritten, under which a Territory or a State—or the Nation itself—operates.

Herron seems to use the terms "Organic Act" and "Organic Law" interchangeably. Although more than once he confesses that he was not always clear what Hubbard was talking about when the Judge used these terms, it should be noted that Herron was probably not as confused in his own understanding or usage of the terms as it might appear. The problem lay in the somewhat unusual circumstances of the late 1880's in the Strip, which in turn reflected the peculiar status and history of No Man's Land (cf. Chapter II, note 1).

Many people in the Strip, especially in the eastern end around Beaver City and Benton, felt "a deep interest in the protection of their individual and respective rights to hold all just and lawfully obtained claims upon town lots as well as homesteads" and wanted desperately "to establish and perpetuate judicial, legislative, and executive organization." (from documents of the citizens' mass meeting, November 29, 1886)

This desire led to their attempt to create Cimarron Territory and to get it recognized by the U.S. Government in the form of a Congressional "Organic Act." This was normal procedure. However, when Congress continually turned down their requests, the elected Territorial Council in the Strip proceeded, in December 1888, to draw up their *own* "Organic Act." If Congress would not confer the powers of Government upon them as a Territory, then they would confer the powers of

Government upon themselves until such time as the U.S. Government saw fit to do so. Their own "Organic Act: An Act to Organize the Territory of Cimarron" carried this preamble:

> Whereas, we the people of the Public Land Strip, being as we are virtually debarred from all rights as citizens of the United States, even the elective franchise, in order to establish justice, insure economic tranquility, provide for the common defense, promote the general welfare, and secure the blessings of liberty to ourselves and our posterity, do ordain and establish this Act for our temporary government.

The subsequent history of this action of the Council is too complicated and unrelated to our story to detail here. Suffice it to say that the proposed Organic Act was debated, amendments were introduced, a different version was prepared, and finally on March 15, 1889 the Council signed a revised Organic Act and made provision to submit it to the people on April 23 for ratification.

It should be added that during this 1887-1889 period the Territorial Council of the Strip went ahead and acted as if it were the Government of the Cimarron Territory. It passed bills, held elections, adopted a Territorial Seal, and continually sent memorials and representatives to Washington, D. C. to plead their case.

From this brief sketch it can be seen that during this period the term "Organic Act" applied *both* to the hoped-for action on the part of the U.S. Congress *and* to the action of the Territorial Council whereby they took it upon themselves—in response to Congress' lack of response—to create their own Organic Act in the Strip.

What about the term "Organic Law"? It was probably loosely used by people in the Strip to refer to whatever non-Vigilante Law and Order that they themselves and the Territorial Council at Beaver City were trying to carve out for Cimarron Territory. The term was also employed by those early lawmakers themselves in a more traditional and technical sense. For example, in their first meeting (March 4, 1887, following the February 22 election Herron talks about in Chapter IV) as Territorial Council, in an attempt somehow to organize themselves and to give their Council legitimacy, they adopted the following preamble and resolution:

Whereas; The residents of Cimarron Territory are without the protection of law of any state or recognized Territorial Government, and recognizing the urgent need thereof and desiring to adopt and establish rules and laws for our protection, safety and government, do hereby recognize Almighty God to be the Supreme Ruler of the Universe, the Creator, Preserver and Governor of individuals, communities, states and nations, and recognize the laws of the United States as our *organic law*, and adopt the same with the Constitution of the United States as the foundation and basis of all laws or rules for our government, and insofar as may be execute and enforce the same.

Therefore be it Resolved by the representatives of Cimarron Territory in Territorial Council assembled; That we do hereby declare ourselves the Territorial Council of said Cimarron Territory and do hereby adopt the Constitution of the United States and the laws thereof as the groundwork and foundation for all laws or rules to be adopted for our government. [editor's italics]

The Council also adopted "the Statutes of Colorado as far as applicable to our conditions," but with no treasury from which to make purchases the Council never owned a copy of the Statutes.

Such was the Strip in the 1880's: A land with little if any communciations, without laws, with no land offices, without courts, and even outside the court jurisdiction of any surrounding State or Territory. The Territorial Council Government which emerged in 1886-87 to fill this vacuum was at best only self-authenticating, was powerless to enforce the laws it did create, was without taxing powers, was challenged by other persons and towns in the Strip anxious to share or dominate the leadership, and was virtually ignored both by Washington and by many in the Strip itself. This, then, was the No Man's Land which Jim Herron knew.

CHAPTER IV.

1. For more details about the efforts to establish Cimarron Territory (cf. Chapter III, note 1), the efforts to get some official recognition from Washington, and the vying of personalities and the rivalry between Beaver City and other towns for leadership in these efforts, see Roy Gittinger's *The Formation of the State of Oklahoma* (especially pp. 171-175), Carl Rister's *No Man's Land* (especially Chapter XIII), and George Rainey's *No Man's Land.* Consult also *The Chronicles of Oklahoma,* Spring 1957; and the Record Book of the Cimarron Territorial Council, "Journal of Proceedings," the original copy of which is in the No Man's Land Historical Museum, Goodwell, Oklahoma.

2. Fred Tracy, an old friend of Jim Herron's in No Man's Land, wrote a letter to Herron's son, Jim, jr., July 12, 1953. Here is one portion of Tracy's recollections about his friendship with Herron:

> I have been a resident of this county since 1885 and in mercantile business since 1886. I knew your father and his first wife before their marriage [. . . I knew her well, in fact was going with her older sister at the time . . .], and was one of your father's friends in those days.
>
> With territorial government in May 1890, an election was held the following September [sic] to elect county officials succeeding those appointed. Your father was a candidate for sheriff. My home precinct at Gate City in the east end was 100 percent granger or farmer settlement and there was considerable friction between the homesteaders and the cattlemen. Aware of a resentment against cattlemen, I took an active part in working for your father. I had been in business there then for four years, knew every voter, and I explained your father, though a cowboy, had always been friendly with them. That he had never permitted cattle to eat up their crops, etc. Many would remark that they always liked him when they met him, but he was a dambed cowboy just the same, but I carried the precinct for him by a big vote.
>
> A few days later your father came over and handed me a commission as deputy sheriff. I said I had no time to be one of his deputies, he said that would be all right.

He said during No Man's Land you always liked to tote
a gun and this will give you authority to tote one again
and all he would ask me to do was to keep the woollies
over in the east end to bear in mind we now had laws in
the country and they must observe them.

3. The writer found no written record either through the Federal
Court, Western District of Oklahoma, or through Fort Smith,
Arkansas, stating Jim Herron was a Deputy U.S. Marshal, so
it must be presumed this was a verbal deputyship. Many of
Herron's old friends did, however, speak of him as both
"Sheriff" and "U.S. Marshal."

CHAPTER V.

1. See *Brand Book*, The Western Kansas Cattle Growers Association, 1885. A resolution by W. I. Harwood was certainly offensive to new settlers:

RESOLVED (1): That though we have a kindly feeling to all newcomers, we deem it but just to say that
there is no more room for cattle upon the ranges occupied by the members of this Association, *except such
cattle as the occupants of each range may choose to
introduce.*

RESOLVED (2): That considering the crowded condition of our ranges, parties taking up dry claims on
lakes, dry most of the year, *will be considered intruders,
and treated as such,* as heretofore resolved.
[editor's italics]

1a. The *Benton County Banner* was started in 1888 or 1889 by
Extus Leroy Gay. The weekly had four pages, 22 x 32, and the
price was $1.50 per year. After about fifteen months, Mr. Gay
sold the newspaper and it was moved to Beaver City where its
name was changed to *Beaver City Tribune.* Mr. Gay went
ahead to found and own other newspapers in Oklahoma; he also
became prominent in Oklahoma political circles.

2. Elery Cooper, now deceased, in a letter to the editor, said of
Jim Herron, whom he had known since boyhood: "Jim was a
fearless officer, and was very popular with the public."

3. Herron's unorthodox methods of settling disputes is also suggested in a story related by Mrs. Sam Herron. He told her
once how an accidental murder had been committed. Herron,
the Sheriff, was asked to bring in several men, since they had

312

all been involved in the unfortunate tragedy. Jim Herron went to the ranch and told all the boys but one to get out of the country. "I'll take him back to town. They can't do anything with only one man, and the rest of you can return when things cool off." It worked.

4. Maude Ashcraft was born in a log house in Indiana. She came to the Strip in 1888, taught school at age sixteen. She was later named Poet Laureate of No Man's Land by pioneer editors and teachers. Her married name was Mrs. Mary C. Hanlin.

Jim Herron modestly refrains from mentioning that at their 1890 Wild West Show he himself won the roping contest, the event that range cowboys considered the most important of all in which to display their talent.

5. For a good account of these December storms see John Clay, *My Life on the Range*, pp. 179 ff.

CHAPTER VI.

1. Herron here reveals his innate softness toward lawbreakers, with whom he had so long associated. He appears to feel that if the victim would meekly surrender his purse to the outlaw, all would be well. There is no suggestion in his writings that he felt outlaws might sometimes be just too lazy to work or might possess a mean streak. The Dalton boys paid for their life of crime with their own lives on October 5, 1892 at Coffeyville, Kansas, attempting to rob two banks.

2. This dance, at which the prisoner was honored guest, is typical of frontier tolerance. The event calls to mind Theodore Roosevelt's appreciation of "that delicious sense of equality" which he found characterized the old West. A prisoner Teddy had captured in the Dakota Badlands, and who was sent to prison, wrote him a most sporting letter later: "Should you stop over at Bismarck this fall, make a call to the prison. I shall be glad to meet you." See *Ranch Life and the Hunting Trail*, by Theodore Roosevelt, pp. 128-29.

CHAPTER VII.

1. The Chapman-Tuttle Trail ran north from Mobeetie, crossed Wolf Creek, ran through the YL range, the M Bar, the KK,

313

the Taintor range and north to Dodge City. It was named after Chapman & Tuttle who owned the old Springer Ranch on the old buffalo hide trail. The Jones & Plummer Trail passed to the west, extending from Fort Elliott and Mobeetie to Dodge via Beaver City.

2. *The Territorial Advocate* of March 18, 1891, carried this story:

> County Sheriff James Herron has bought of Mrs. Geo. Z. Wright the Beaver City Hotel, the consideration, we understand, being $800.00. He is to take possession Friday. The house will be thoroughly re-fitted and over-hauled, and will be presided over by Mr. and Mrs. A. Groves, parents of Mrs. Herron, and formerly of Benton. They are well and favorably known throughout this part of the county as excellent hotel people. One of the best recommendations a town can have is a first-class hotel, and such we confidently predict under the new management.

Eleven months later, on February 15, 1892, shortly before Alice Herron's death that winter, Jim and Alice Herron sold the Beaver City Hotel to Ansel Groves for $400.00.

3. An interesting social news item about Alice Herron and her sister appeared in *The Territorial Advocate* (March 25, 1891) during the year prior to Mrs. Herron's death, at the time Jim Herron bought the Beaver City Hotel:

> Mrs. James Herron and sister, Miss Della Groves, leave for their new home in Beaver City, Oklahoma. Miss Della has been attending school here the past winter, and has a host of friends in this city, especially among her schoolmates, with whom she was a favorite.

4. Although Jim Herron saw his daughter very infrequently after he left the Strip, he continued for years to send money for her support.

Ollie Dot Herron married Carleton Herbert Stratton, April 12, 1908, at Anadarko, Oklahoma. Rev. L. Richmond performed the ceremony at the Presbyterian Church. Ollie Dot died at Stillwater, July 16, 1963, aged seventy-five years. Her husband preceded her in death by eight years. Their son, J. L. Stratton, a consulting geologist at Stillwater, wrote the editor of his mother:

314

Mother was an accomplished pianist, enjoyed the study of philosophy, and did some writing under the pen name of Irene Lynd. She had a colorful life with my father in the Oklahoma oil boom. She was in the bank at Kiefer when it was held up by Henry and Belle Starr. Later, my parents moved to Pawnee, and father entered the banking business with Major Gordon Lillie (Pawnee Bill). As a child we lived in the Lillie home while our home was being constructed.

5. Herron's cattle brands:

TK, his personal herd, about 1,500 head mixed stock.

TXA, his wife's (Alice's) cattle; 300 head of she stock.

DOT, Ollie Dot's cattle, about 300 head of she stock.

Bar O, the herd owned with John Over; 2,000 head of mixed cattle.

In addition to the above livestock, Herron owned about fifty head of saddle horses wearing the brands, TK, TXA, and DOT.

6. Edward Sample located in Barber County in 1880. He was a resident of Medicine Lodge for more than twenty years. Born January 1, 1859, in Scott County, Indiana, he studied at DePauw University and was admitted to the bar in 1879. Harry J. Bone (the name is Boone in the Herron ms.,) was born in Illinois, October 7, 1862. He graduated from Lincoln University in 1882 and studied Law at Cumberland University in 1884. He was defeated for nomination to the Legislature in 1892, but the publicity given his name during the Herron trial brought him the nomination on the Republican ticket in 1894.

Chapter VIII.

1. J. H. Abbott, pioneer cowman of the Strip, wrote in his manuscript of the early days:

Dan Keese said that many others did the same [i.e., branded mavericks]. Some bought a few and got off with more. There were many shady deals in the early cowman's time. Charley Parker said it was customary for a cowhand to steal for his boss, but when he started to build a little herd of his own those old thieves made a terrible fuss about it . . . But it was customary, and considered honest, to brand an animal that was weaned and wore no brand.

315

2. Cape B. Willingham, a north Texas cowman and lawman, was earlier involved in some unsavory killings, such as the shotgun murder of Fred Leigh, a cowboy, on the main street of Tascosa, and a posse-murder of an innocent cowboy, John Leverton, who had been framed in a cattle-theft charge on the Backward LX range. It was "four head of cattle, the property of C. B. Willingham," that Jim Herron was convicted of stealing at Meade, Kansas. Mr. P. Doyle was a Livestock Inspector, and later in the livestock commission business.

3. Despite the trial, Herron's manuscript notes speak of Judge Price as "the best friend I ever had."

4. The story of Herron's trial and its aftermath was reported in *The Meade County* (Kansas) *Globe* for September 21, 1893. The newspaper story differs only slightly from Herron's personal account.

A VERDICT OF GUILTY

The big cattle case of the state of Kansas against James Herron is over and a jury of 12 men after hearing the evidence which it took seven days to bring out said he was guilty. The jury was out for about nine hours and reached their verdict in the morning which was read when court opened at 9 o'clock. The verdict was a surprise to many while to others it was expected as the evidence seemed to be clear and that the jury could not do otherwise than convict. A little ripple of excitement seemed to steal over a certain class of our people in a few minutes after the verdict of conviction was read but to many seemed to mean nothing. Mr. Herron was at once placed in charge of deputy Sheriff Givler to be held in custody until the motion for a new trial was disposed of which was set for hearing in the afternoon. Jack Rhodes who was also under bond for his appearance at court for the same offence was ordered by the court to give a new bond and was placed in charge of under Sheriff Buis who turned him over to deputy Givler who had both Herron and Rhodes in his charge. The boys began to look at the matter a little serious—or in other words saw the penitentiary staring them in the face and thought that their only safety was in getting away from Givler. They wanted to see Dr. Button whether he would

316

go on their bond, and while there made a plausible excuse to go to Buis's livery barn which Givler granted and went with them. This is just where they had desired to go as arrangements had there been made for their escape. As soon as they were inside the barn Givler saw that he had made a grave mistake in permitting them to go there but determined to make the best of it. Two horses had been saddled and were ready and in spite of all Givler could do they mounted them. About 11 o'clock, the report of a six shooter was heard twice in quick succession and the clatter of horses feet, and two men going rapidly east. Deputy Givler ran a few yards down the road and again fired at them, and then the crowd began to assemble and excitement ran high. The blood was slowly trickling down Givler's face and at first he said he was shot but the wound was only a small cut near the base of the nose. He was considerably excited and would not say much. Herron and Rhodes was watched as they sped away to the east and none thought that either had been hurt. When about half mile away one of them was seen to weaken and the other ride near to him and hold him on his horse. On the hill near Graceland Cemetery one was seen to take the other from his horse and lay him by the side of the road and again mounting rode rapidly away. A number of people started for the scene and soon found that Jack Rhodes had been fatally shot and was in a dying condition. He was placed in a delivery wagon and brought to the Osgood hotel where he died in about ten minutes. A coroner's inquest was held and it was found that two shots had entered Rhodes body one just below the right shoulder blade and the other just above the right hip coming out near the navel. A number of witnesses were examined at the inquest, Givler testifying that Rhodes held a gun on him while in the barn and shot at him as he (Rhodes) was going out of the door. Peter King also testified that Herron and Rhodes held Givler up in the barn and asked him for his gun and that Givler told them that he had no gun and that Herron told Rhodes to kill the s— of a b——. Robt. Colgan who was in the barn at the time testified that he saw neither Rhodes or Herron have a gun nor saw any of the "holding up" affair. The jury after hearing the evidence returned the following verdict:

We the jury find that Jack Rhodes came to his death

by pistol shot or shots fired from a pistol in the hands of S. B. Givler acting as deputy Sheriff of Meade County, Kansas, while in the line of duty and we also find that he was justified in so doing.

A. H. Heber, Foreman
John Braden,
John Wehrle,
E. A. Twist,
G. H. Losey,
B. F. Cox,
A. Kessler, Coroner.

The funeral was held at 4 o'clock Saturday evening at the Osgood house, Rev. Votaw officiating and burial was made in Graceland Cemetery.

F. M. Rhodes, (Jack as he was known) was born Oct. 1866 in Jack County, Texas, and has for several years resided in Beaver County. He leaves a wife and two children.

[original punctuation and spelling used]

Fred Tracy, an eyewitness to those September events in 1893, tells what he remembers, in a letter to Jim Herron, jr. (cf. Chapter IV, note 2):

> I came to Beaver City in 1892 and I was present at your father's trial at Meade, Kansas in 1893. He received a rotten deal in that trial but was dealing with a powerful organization who were determined to convict him if possible, and did so.
>
> I witnessed his escape and the death of his companion. . . .
>
> The sheriff found it convenient to be called out of town, a deputy was to permit your father and his companion to go into the livery stable before continuing on to dinner, and two saddled horses were in the stable. They were to mount them and escape and the deputy was to fire towards them but not at them as they escaped. The stable doors blew shut and they were delayed forc-ing them open and the deputy fired a shot that killed your father's companion.

PART II

Chapter IX

1. Jim Herron's Homestead Certificate No. 25 is dated July 12, 1894. The Indenture to John Over is dated August 17, 1893. See *Land Records*, Beaver County Court House, Beaver, Oklahoma. Jim received $450 for the SE¼ of NW¼, and ¼ of NE¼ and SE¼ of NE¼, S. 28, T-4, N. Range, 26 E of Cimarron Meridian, Beaver County, Oklahoma. Herron must have received the money from Over *prior* to his Application 201 and Certificate No. 25.

2. A letter written by Lon Ford to Jim Herron's youngest son in 1940, mentions the late Burris Wright of Liberal, Kansas, as well as many other figures of that age. It is herewith reproduced:

OFFICE OF SHERIFF,

CLARK COUNTY, KANSAS

Owen Marshall, Sheriff • Lon Ford, Undersheriff

Ashland, Kansas

Jan. 1, 1940

Mr. James Herron, jr.
Sheriff, Pinal County, Arizona
Florence, Arizona

Friend James:

I received your welcome letter and I am glad your father is well but I am sorry he has lost his eyesight. You may tell him for me that he has a host of old friends in Beaver County yet. Charles Prescott lives at Englewood; an old friend of his, Frank Maple, is Sheriff of Beaver County now. Your father knew him when they were boys. Burris Wright, who was at Naco at the time I was there, lives at Liberal, Kansas. Whatever became of Sherman Crump, Lem Kelley and Eddie O'Larry?

The summer I was there at Naco was the year Bill Stiles and Burt Alvord and the wild bunch broke jail at Tombstone. After I left Naco, and not too slow (!) I went to work for the Harts at the Empire Ranch. Harry Hefner was there at the time; Turner was wagon boss. Your Dad will remember that I gave him the keys to the old Beaver City jail when I left it so fast. Before I came to Naco, he sent the keys back to the Sheriff at Beaver. Those old days are past and gone and I look back over some of our pranks, and find they were not half bad when compared to the deeds of our cold-blooded sluggers and muggers of today. . . .

Ask your Dad if he remembers whatever became of Billy Hill. The last time I saw him he was around Wagon Mound, New Mexico, many years ago. He is a relative to the Brite boys that was in the killing of three men in California. I think they are brothers of Perry Brite who was murdered at a filling station, I believe in your state. I knew this family quite well when I worked on the old Cross L ranch in northeastern New Mexico. In fact I was with the posse that had the battle on Cold Springs Arroyo, and how Billy dodged all that lead that was pumped at him I can't say, but he did, and made his get-away. I do know that some of those cowboys were not trying to take very accurate aim, but Billy was a little more conserving with his ammunition, for he made two direct hits, but they were not fatal. . . .

Yours Respctfy., etc. etc.

LON FORD, Undersheriff

The men mentioned by Ford as "direct hits" were Deputy Sheriff McGill of Clayton, New Mexico and Deputy Sheriff William S. Cochran. The latter admitted *(The West That's Gone*, pp. 102 ff.) that Billy Hill could have killed him, but did not.

When the writer knew Burris Wright, in the 1950's, Wright told him many stories of this interesting period of his life as an Arizona cowboy. Together with Lon Ford and others, Burris witnessed much of the wild life at Naco and in northern Sonora, when he worked for Bill Greene. Speaking of Herron, Burris once said, "A better man never lived than Jim Herron."

3. Cicero Stewart was the fourth Sheriff of Eddy County, New Mexico. He married a Miss Fanning at Hope (old Badger), New Mexico. Stewart had been foreman at the CA Ranch. In 1894 he was beaten for election by Les Dow. Later, Dow was killed by Dave Kemp, the first Sheriff of Eddy county, who was

320

later acquitted. The County Commissioners appointed Stewart to fill out Dow's term. He then was re-elected and held that office eighteen years in all. As Sheriff he helped break up the Black Jack Ketchum gang, in August-September 1899, capturing Ezra Lay (McGinnis) and routing Black Bob McManus. Lay was given a life term for murder, but was pardoned in 1906.

4. Bernard Lemert told the editor of Herron: "He made money and spent it. He was a good feeler. Most everyone liked him."

Chapter X.

1. Billy Hill has been overlooked by western authors. The Hill family was well known, neighbors to Tom Judy. T. A. Judy, his son, recalls that John Hill, a brother, was killed in a jail break at Woodward, O.T., by a posse under Tobe Odom and deputy Love. Alley, another brother, was reported by the late Elery Cooper to have been killed by Mexicans in a horse deal. The elder Tom Judy said that "Billy's reputation was bad, but he was the best shot in the Strip." Irvin Green, pioneer cowman in the Strip, recalled Billy Hill as "Penn" Hill. "He was a Billy The Kid type," wrote Green, "and no good. He aimed to kill a deputy one time, but a chinaberry post deflected the bullet and it only cut a long gash in the lawman's left side." Billy had drawn on Green one time, asking him some pointed questions. Green regarded Hill "as just a rustler."

On August 31, 1895, *The Clayton* (New Mexico) *Enterprise*, had this story on Billy, after he had returned from New Mexico to the Strip:

> Friday, a battle between citizens of the lower Cimarron near the OX ranch and a band of rustlers took place. Sam Smith, Bill Rounds (Rowan), and Arch Bright (Brite) were captured. During the melee 100 rounds of shots were fired. Deputy Sheriff McGill was shot in the arm and Bill Cochran (deputy) received a wound in the leg. Our last account was that the officers were pursuing the Texas Hill Kid, who took off for Colorado.

Previously, on August 16, 1895, *The Enterprise* had indicated in another story that the Texas Hill Kid's gang might have been operating in eastern Colorado:

A slick cattle thief known as Hayes Robbins but who calls himself "Buffalo Bill" has been captured by Constable Titworth of Trinidad and a posse and landed in the Trinidad jail. The prisoner is not more than 18 years old. . . . The Cattlemen's Association in Colorado offered a $375 reward.

Jim Herron regarded Billy Hill as the best gunman he had seen, and Jim Herron has been characterized by many old-timers as himself being "fast and accurate with his Colt .45."

2. According to Bert Laney, pioneer citizen of Luna Valley, there were two Cosper brothers, J. H. T. (Toles) Cosper and John Cosper, both from Texas. Toles was the Justice of the Peace. A man named Hester, unruly and drunk, once fired on Toles' house. Toles shot and killed Hester. Later, said Laney, "Toles Cosper moved down on to the Blue River. He would get drunk and grieve over having killed Hester, though no one ever blamed him." (The name Hester may have been Hesper, thought Laney).

3. See *The Clayton Enterprise*, August 31, 1895.

4. Herron's statement is backed by a similar statement of Jack Thorp, in *Pardner of the Wind* (Caldwell, Idaho, 1945), p. 138: "Jackson did get away, and he came to New Mexico where, in isolated cow camps, under another name, he lived his life out. . . . " Another version of Jackson's life comes from Capt. Tom Rynning, former Arizona Ranger, in *Gun Notches* (New York, 1931), who stated that Downing, the cowman who rode with Alvord and Stiles in the Cochise Station train robbery, *was actually Jackson*. Rynning avers he knew Downing (Jackson), who received ten years in prison. Bill Greene and Sheriff Scott White helped Downing get his freedom after eight years. Downing then worked for Greene in Mexico. This may be where Herron knew him (Jackson), or he may have learned of him through Cicero Stewart.

5. This statement is true and the author knows the man's name, though his daughter, at Liberal, Kansas, has requested it not be used because of her California brothers and their families.

CHAPTER XI.

1. Thomas Darrell Herron received his nickname "Sam" from a

Chinese cook, in a Pearce restaurant, who scolded him for being underfoot while boarders were being served. "Slam! Slam!" the cook would cry out. Sam served with Co. A, 27th Engineers, A.E.F. Returning from France after eighteen months he opened the old Pearce mine with a Mr. Furnace. Sam mined also near Superior and became well fixed and popular in Arizona mining circles. He joined the Knights of Pythias. Sam married Nellie Edna Campbell, who was born on the Choctaw Nation, Indian Territory, Feb. 9, 1900. To this union was born five daughters, Rita May, Bessie Lorraine, Ruby Nell, Dorothy, and Billie. Sam Herron died in 1938.

2. Johnny Pearce was a Cornishman who had been a miner at Tombstone. In 1894, after the Tombstone "bust," he and his wife and two sons settled on a ranch twenty-five miles northeast of Tombstone. Pearce said, "once a miner, always a miner," and while riding the range discovered himself a mine on top of this low hill with surface rocks rich in free gold and a dark chloride of silver. He, his two sons, and a married daughter made claims there. The ore he took to Tombstone for assay was rich, and made him wealthy and famous. The property was later sold to John Brockman, Silver City banker, for a quarter of a million. Pearce's thrifty wife had written into the contract of the sale that she would retain an exclusive contract *to run the boarding house at Pearce's old mine!*

3. Gleeson was named after John Gleeson, an Irish immigrant who came to the Pearce boom in 1895. Gleeson was built near the mining camp called Turquoise which in 1890 had five hotels, three saloons, several restaurants, and a general store. Fine turquoise was mined there, Tiffany & Company of New York having interests; there were also copper mines. A great fire burned the town in 1912.

4. J. Mack Axford, in *Around Western Campfires*, told how Daley, owner of the Irish Mag claims at Lowell, turned them over to Martin Costello to manage, after Daley killed a deputy and had to flee. Costello later sold the claims for $500,000, for they were situated next to the Copper Queen claims, richest property in the region. Costello tried to be fair with the absent Daley and his Mexican wife, but she refused to accept a check for $25,000 in partial payment to bind the agreement. A friend who under-

stood her told Costello to offer her many $1 bills. He counted out 5,000 of these. She accepted!

5. A Mrs. Smith, of Tucson, whose husband operated the bank at Warren, and who had lived at Solomonville, said that when Jim Herron sold his trading post and ranch on the San Pedro his successor went broke. "He didn't know how to deal with the Mexican people like Mr. Herron," she told the editor.

6. Rita Herron was married to Elmer C. (Jake) McGrew, November 10, 1914. They lived at Superior, where McGrew was interested in mining, though he had been a cowboy as a young man and worked for several ranches in the Superstition Mountains. He died in 1961. To this union was born a son, who died in infancy, and five daughters: Mmes. Edith Killion, Jean Jeffrey, Emma Frost, Norma Fegert, and Marian Bryant. Mrs. McGrew still resides at the family home in Superior, Arizona, well-known in the community and surrounded by children, friends, and grandchildren.

7. James Herron, jr. married Mabel Walker. They had two sons, James C. and Albert D. Jim, jr. was Pinal County Supervisor eight years, Pinal County Sheriff eight years, and a State Senator eight years. He later served an appointment as Secretary to the State Highway Commission until his activities were curtailed by ill health. Following a heart attack, he died July 27, 1957. Governor Ernest McFarland and many other noted men and women of the area attended the services and served as pallbearers. He was interred at Superior.

CHAPTER XII.

1. Charley Davis, Prescott, Arizona, the father of Mrs. Ruth Fugate, Leadville, Colorado, punched cows in Cochise County and knew Jim Herron quite well. Davis recalled that Herron used the MAY brand in memory of his wife. Mrs. Fugate has tapes of her father's recollections.

2. Amazingly enough, we have a living eyewitness to this shooting episode in the person of Jack Dempsey Powers, Bud Powers' son, who was then a small boy. Jack was named after a bartender who was a friend of his father, not after the heavyweight

champion. In Jack Powers' memory of the shootings, we have the following description, gleaned from his letters and a personal interview:

> Ramsey approached from the rear, rode up, and talked a few minutes, then turned as though to re-mount his horse but instead grabbed a Winchester rifle from the saddle boot and shot the lead guard, who threw up his hands and called out frantically, "No-no, not me, not me!" but then fell dead from his horse. Ramsey wheeled, shot one of the side guards who was drawing his rifle. The gun flew from the guard's hands and his arms shot upward when Ramsey's bullet struck his shoulder. The other guards and the wounded man galloped away, their hats and chaps flapping in the wind.

Bud Powers, who had been driving, in this version, "jumped from the hack and aimed a six-shooter at the fleeing horsemen, but didn't fire." Jack Powers never knew where his father's revolver came from, as he remembered their being searched at the border before entering Mexico.

3. The name as given by Herron in the original is George Astin; however, it may have been George Aspin, who lived at Naco at the time, or George Ashton, another friend of Herron's.

4. At this time W. E. Pulliam recommended removal of the U.S. Branch Customs House from La Morita to Naco. *The Nogales* (Arizona) *Oasis*, September 30, 1899, reported:

> The Mexican authorities are said to be awaiting such action by the U.S. authorities as a signal for a corresponding removal of their own Customs House.

The killings at the border had the effect of making officials of both Governments see the advisability of locating all inspection offices at one central location on the international line.

CHAPTER XIII.

1. Charles Sanders, ninety-four, Naco, Arizona, stated that his friend, Jim Herron, always said, "Kosterlitzky saved my life," and was a supporter of this stern officer whom many criminals found grim and deadly.

2. Though Jim Herron fails to mention it, the border troubles did not end at this time, for the Mexican Customs officers con-

tinued their thieving practices, as shown in this dispatch from *The Bisbee* (Arizona) *Daily Review*, Sunday, November 17, 1901:

MEXICAN INSPECTOR MAKES TROUBLE FOR AMERICAN CATTLE OWNERS IN MEXICO

Naco, Nov. 10: — (Special Correspondent) There is a good deal of trouble and excitement here in Naco owing to the tyrannical and extraordinary action of Tranquilino Cuen, the Mexican cattle inspector, who is seizing cattle owned by the small American cattlemen in Sonora. Friday, Bob Giles and Joe Rhodes came into Naco complaining that Tranquilino Cuen had seized a number of head owned by them. They begged the Mexican official to explain why this was done. In this they were supported by some of the best cattlemen in the district. The official refused an explanation, blustered and pulled his revolver. Gates [sic] and Rhodes were unarmed. The cowboys came over into Naco and were told that they were virtually outlawed by Mexico. Bert Grover, of the Rangers, got into trouble trying to remove them across the line, and had a tough time of it, getting away free again. The cattle will be driven to Bocachi, many miles to the south, and penned up. The chance of seeing them again is considered small indeed.

The stock are proved the property of the men, the vendors names, brands and money paid being readily shown by them.

CHAPTER XIV.

1. Members of the Robertson family, and others, contended that Robertson was shot not only by Sid Paige but by others. Charley Davis, Prescott, Arizona, in the manuscript taken from his tape recordings, said that Matt Burts, a member of the Stiles-Alvord gang, "had a smoking six-shooter in his hand at the time."

2. Mrs. John J. Newell, Naco, Arizona pioneer, writes of those times:

Mr. Herron built a large home within one block of the Main Street. He put in a butcher shop in a part of it, but before it was finished we had many dances in it. The

326

floor was very good and the Mexican stringed orchestras excellent. There were not too many women and fewer young girls of marriageable age in Naco, so the many cowboys, freighters and miners drew numbers so the men could take their turn dancing with them. Mr. and Mrs. Herron were very fine people. I had a younger sister that played with their daughter, Rita, in the Cow Ranch Saloon before he built this nice home. We really had grand times at these early dances.

Chapter XV.

1. Milton Nobles, Hot Springs, Arkansas, throws the following light upon the old Nobles Hotel that Jim Herron renamed the La Rita Hotel:

> After I was born, July 30, 1888, at Aspen, Colorado, where father, Eugene M. Nobles, worked for the Denver & Rio Grande R.R., we lived at Aspen, Ouray, Pueblo, Denver, Telluride and other western towns. While later working in the electric power business, father was paralyzed from an electric shock. He grew restless, and we moved to Tombstone in 1902 where he bought the hotel, named it the Nobles. Father died in 1905 at Hot Springs, Arkansas, where he had gone for his health after selling the hotel.
>
> We freighted the furniture for the hotel in by wagon train. After the railroad reached there I became a Morse telegrapher. I stayed to graduate from Tombstone High School, May 26, 1904. I came to Hot Springs in 1904 and have been here since.

2. Charley Davis, old Cochise County cowboy, was asked by his daughter in a taped interview to describe Herron's character and personality. He related:

> I used to see Jim often in Tombstone. He was mostly a saloonkeeper there and ran some cattle, too. He branded MAY, his wife's name. One time I went into his saloon. Jim said, "Have a drink?"
> I said, "No, I don't believe I will."
> "What's the matter, Button, are you sick?" he asked me. I was about 14 or 15 then and small for my age, and the people used to call me the OR Button, for I worked on the OR ranch.
> "Yes," I told Herron, "I am sick."

327

"Then you go over to the hotel and tell May I said to give you a bed and something to eat," Jim said to me. That's the kind of man he was.

Somehow Jim Herron had a way of making any gathering or any cow camp more enjoyable. I can see him now, plain as day. One evening we were all gathered around a fire at a cow camp when this big ball of fire went across the sky. It had a long fiery tail behind it, like a comet, for it moved slowly across the heavens in the north, moving from west to east. We were all watching it. Suddenly Jim jumped to his feet like he was all excited and seen something we boys had missed. "Did you all see that?" he exclaimed, pointing. We all laughed.

Since the year was 1910, it may be worth mentioning that these cowboys in their lonely cow camp were probably witnessing Halley's Comet!

3. Millie Herron married Joe Granillo in 1926. To this union were born two sons, Manuel and Fred, and a daughter who became Mrs. Mary Louise Darrow. The Granillos were divorced and in 1940 Millie married Tony Borba, a dairyman who had two sons by a previous marriage, Tony and John. The Borbas adopted a girl, Arlene Borba Chapdelaine and together they raised their four sons and two daughters. They reside today at Newman, California.

4. From this mention of the sale of his market to Harrison and Drew to the part where he returns from Florence (i.e., the remainder of Chapter XV), the material has been written and added by the editor, and was not in Herron's original manuscript notes. What is written in, however, is precisely what occurred as told in old court records and the newspaper files of that day. For example, from the *Bisbee Daily Review*, October 4, 1912:

> Jim Herron, charged with stealing cattle from the Sulphur Springs Valley Cattle Company, was convicted in the Superior Court at Tombstone yesterday, after he had pleaded not guilty, and he will be sentenced this afternoon at one o'clock. There was a great deal of interest in this case among cattlemen. The case was prosecuted by county attorney Alexander Murry [sic]. The trial was started Wednesday and concluded and given to

the jury yesterday afternoon, the jury returning a verdict of guilty last night. Herron was represented by attorney Ross of Douglas. John Oldham, who was arrested at the same time of Herron's arrest, had already entered a plea of guilty and was sentenced to a term of five years in the penitentiary.

5. An old friend told of once mentioning this case where Jim was convicted of stealing "four old cows." The friend said, "When I mentioned it, Jim just snorted and said to me, 'Hell! To think that I, who was charged with stealing trainloads of cattle, would get a term for stealing four damned old milk cows!' "

Charles Sanders, an old friend of Herron's, told the editor how the affair seemed to him:

> Jim Herron was one of the best men I ever knew, honest, straight, friendly, and kind. He moved to Courtland, had a butcher shop. He got hold of some fellow's beef by accident that he didn't pay for, was arrested, and they had the hides with the brand and he couldn't prove he had paid for them. It was just too bad for Jim, and we all felt sorry it happened, even the jurymen who convicted him.

Chapter XVI.

1. L. Rollin Healy, oil man of Los Angeles, and son of George Healy, Jim Herron's old friend and employer in No Man's Land, wrote the editor of meeting Jim Herron in El Paso:

> One day in 1914, Lee Harlan, a pioneer of No Man's Land, brought a man into my office and asked if I knew who he was. I looked at the man and said, "He wears his boots right, his hat, spurs and cowhide vest look like he was a cattleman just out of Mexico and I will say he is Jim Herron." My estimate was correct. Jim had been buying cattle for L. E. Booker and delivering them at Juarez.
>
> Jim knew he was in trouble crossing the border, so he was quiet about it, but always armed with a shoulder holster in which was his Colt .45. Jim made a deal with another fellow to make the border crossings for him. Later Lyman (Savage) and I were on the street at San Antonio, and this partner stopped us and asked what sort of a man Jim Herron was. "You are his partner in Mexico, so you should know," Lyman said. "If you ever

329

steal a dime from him he will kill you." This partner was
later shot on the Rio Grande. What happened though,
I never knew. . . .

When you state that "Jim got in trouble with the
Mexican authorities" you make the understatement of
the century for he was wanted in Mexico as badly as they
wanted him in Kansas, probably more so, for they would
have 'dobe-walled him on sight. But after a lot of people
along the border were killed, those Mexican officials decided it was better to make peace with him—which they
did.

From what my father said, it stands between him and
Ben Medicine (Steadman) as to *who* arranged the Herron-Rhodes escape. My father had great loyalties, and
Jim had been his *segundo* and whatever he did . . . was
for a friend, and friends are hard to find.

In relation to the final paragraph of the above, Burris Wright
once told the author that for the Herron-Rhodes escape it was
John Over "and others" who provided the two horses, through
the colored boy, who was Herron's friend. So it was apparently
the loyal friends Herron speaks of in his story—the Healys and
John Over—who stood by him and helped him at that time.

2. Herron calls this man Hooker, but L. Rollin Healy gives the
   name as Lewis E. Booker. Booker had offices from 1910 to 1920
   in the City National Bank Building in El Paso. He later lived
   at Ysleta, Texas. Old timers there recall that Booker, like
   Herron, "was a loner."

3. Getting out of Revolutionary Mexico with your life, even if you
   lost all your property, was called "a Mexican stand-off," and
   considered almost like winning. Herron's friend, Charley Sanders of Naco, told the editor of losing all of his and Herron's
   Sonora mining properties, valued at $150,000 at the time. "But
   I got out with my life," Sanders said cheerily. He was ninety-
   four when interviewed, so he had been spared fifty more years
   of his life! "Not a bad trade," he said.

4. Herron filed a claim with the Special Mexican Claims Commission, showing the loss of 513 head of cattle. (See Agency
   No. 2594; Docket No. 905 [150]). The amount was eventually
   settled for $2,575, for the Mexican losses were settled on a basis

of funds available. Herron actually received only $1,523 less $150 attorney fees! This decision is found under Doc. No. 80, Decision 3.

5. Luke Short had previously been the Marshal at Paradise, 1902-03.

6. See letter from Senator Carl Hayden to editor, September 8, 1966, in files.

Arizona Territory was organized February 24, 1863. It entered the Union as the forty-eighth State on February 14, 1912. Carl Hayden served as Arizona's Congressman-at-large from 1912 to 1927. He served as Senator from 1927 until his retirement in 1968.

Chapter XVII.

1. Herron made trips back to Oklahoma in 1894, 1900, 1908-09, 1918, 1935, 1938, and 1946. Following his 1935 trip the following story appeared in a Superior, Arizona newspaper, showing how he was received by old friends of his youth:

SUPERIOR MAN TELLS OF ESCAPE 42 YEARS AGO

Beaver, Oklahoma, Aug. 14, 1935 (AP)—Fiction of the old west came alive here today as the many friends of Jim Herron honored the old plainsman for his decision to come back after 42 years and face a cattle rustling penalty he dodged bullets to escape.

Herron, now 70 years old and blind, paused among his panhandle cronies here on his way to Meade, Kansas, to balance the almost forgotten books that show he escaped from the Sheriff there in 1893, after a jury had convicted him of bringing two trainloads of stolen cattle into the state.

The sentence was yet to be passed when an officer took Herron and another cowboy prisoner to an "eating joint." When he and his companion dashed out of the restaurant toward horses their friends had made ready, the officer emptied his pistol. The companion was mortally wounded, but Herron was unscathed and kept going on a long trail that found him, in his declining years, a respected citizen of Superior, Arizona.

But the thought of the conviction has been hanging

331

heavy on his mind and he wants it settled. He knows not what this move will bring him—imprisonment, or freedom of conscience—for the county attorney at Meade (Frank S. Sullivan) had no assurance for him when Herron inquired on this trip.

"I am tired of that deal hanging over me," Herron said, "but my plea is still 'not guilty' ". Herron stoutly maintained his innocence, and he did not propose to go to the penitentiary "on a trumped up charge," as he tells it now.

Because the judge (Judge Carl Miller) is away from Meade on vacation, Herron has decided not to wait any longer for him this trip, but he proposes to return from Arizona again in October and "face the music at Meade." He chose October, he says, because that is when the No Man's Land Historical Society is having its annual convention, and he'll have more sessions with the old- timers, who threw a picnic for him just this week.

When the Judge and Meade County attorney refused to review the case, Herron did not return that October. But on his final visit, in 1946, he made a triumphal return like a conquering general. Aged and stone blind, he was acclaimed at the Pioneers' celebration, was an honored guest in the parade, and was photographed with the surviving pioneers.

2. Years later people would still be recalling Jim Herron favorably. For example, J. J. Ballard, pioneer, writing in the Spring 1961 issue of *Frontier Times* ("When the Law Hit the Strip"), said of Herron: "The first Sheriff elected was a cowman, Jim Herron, a fine man."

3. When Jim Herron was in his mid-seventies, and divorced from his third wife, Mary Valencia (who had later married a Mr. Polti), his daughter Rita Herron McGrew wrote a letter to her daughter, Jean. It read:

"Dear Jean:
"I must tell you what has happened to your grandfather, sad at heart and regretting it as I do . . ."

Jean hurriedly scanned the letter, expecting her mother to relate the details of her grandfather's death. But as she found the words on the paper, her initial sympathy and grief turned to amazement at her mother's revelation:

". . . it has happened to Papa again. He has *remarried*!"

332

This was Jim Herron's fourth—and last—marriage. This time to a pretty widow, a Mrs. Demerick, who had several children of her own. The marriage was of short duration, however, and the problems of detailing the first three marriages and the issues therefrom has been trial enough for both editor and reader, so we mercifully close the book on this final marriage and its aftermath.

Jim Herron died September 4, 1949, aged eighty-three years. The body was interred at Hills Ferry Cemetery, Newman, California, in the Tony and Millie Borba lot.

bibliography and sources

BOOKS

Abbott, E. C. (Teddy Blue) and Smith, H. H. *We Pointed Them North*. New York: Farrar & Rinehart, 1939.

Armstrong, J. B. *The Raw Edge*. Missoula, Montana: Montana State University Press, 1964.

Axford, Joseph Mack. *Around Western Campfires*. New York: Pageant Press, 1964.

Bernstein, Marvin D. *The Mexican Mining Industry*. Albany: The State University of New York, 1964.

Breakenridge, William M. *Helldorado: Bringing the Law to the Mesquite*. Boston: Houghton Mifflin Company, 1928.

Chrisman, Harry E. *The Ladder of Rivers, The Story of I.P. (Print) Olive*. Denver: Sage Books, 1962, 1965.

Chrisman, Harry E. *Lost Trails of the Cimarron*. Denver: Sage Books, 1961, 1964.

Clay, John. *My Life on the Range*. Norman: University of Oklahoma Press, 1962.

Collins, Hubert E. *Warpath and Cattle Trail*. New York: William Morrow & Company, 1928.

Cox, William R. *Luke Short and His Era*. Garden City: Doubleday & Company, 1961.

Dale, Edward E. *Cow Country*. Norman: University of Oklahoma Press, 1965.

Dale, Edward E. *The History of the Ranch Cattle Industry in Oklahoma*. Washington, D. C.: American Historical Association, 1920.

Dale, Edward E. *The Range Cattle Industry*. Norman: University of Oklahoma Press, 1960.

Dobie, J. Frank. *The Longhorns*. Boston: Little, Brown & Company, 1941.

Foreman, Carolyn Thomas. *Oklahoma Imprints 1835-1907*. Norman: University of Oklahoma Press, 1936.

Gard, Wayne. *Sam Bass*. New York: Houghton Mifflin Company, 1936.

Gittinger, Roy. *The Formation of the State of Oklahoma*. Norman: University of Oklahoma Press, 1939.

Gressley, Gene. *Bankers and Cattlemen*. New York: A. Knopf, 1966.

Hamner, Laura V. *Light n' Hitch*. Dallas: American Guild Press, 1958.

Harvey, Clara Toombs. *Not So Wild the Old West*. Denver: Golden Bell Press, 1961.

335

Hasbrouck, Louise S. *Mexico From Cortez to Carranza.* New York: D. Appleton & Company, 1918.

Hendricks, George. *The Bad Man of the West.* San Antonio: Naylor Company, 1959.

Hunter, J. Marvin, compiled by. *The Trail Drivers of Texas.* Nashville: Cokesbury Press, 1925.

Lockwood, Frank C. *Pioneer Days in Arizona.* New York: The Macmillan Company, 1932.

Martin, Charles L. *A Sketch of Sam Bass, The Bandit.* Norman: University of Oklahoma Press, 1956.

Martin, Douglas D. *Tombstone's Epitaph.* Albuquerque: The University of New Mexico Press, 1951.

McCarty, John L. *Maverick Town, The Story of Old Tascosa.* Norman: University of Oklahoma Press, 1946.

McCoy, Joseph G. *Historic Sketches of the Cattle Trade.* Kansas City: Ramsey Millet & Hudson, 1874.

McGinty, Billy and Eyler, Glenn L. *The Old West.* Stillwater, Oklahoma: Redlands Press, 1958.

Meade County, Kansas. *Pioneer Stories,* compiled by City Council of Women's Clubs, 1950.

Miller, Joseph. *Arizona, The Last Frontier.* New York: Hastings House, 1956.

Miller, Joseph. *Arizona, A State Guide.* New York: Hastings House, 1956.

Miller, Joseph. *The Arizona Story.* New York: Hastings House, 1952.

Murbarger, Nell. *Ghosts of the Adobe Walls.* Los Angeles: Westernlore Press.

Myers, John Myers. *The Deaths of the Bravos.* Boston: Little, Brown & Company, 1962.

Myers, John Myers. *The Last Chance, Tombstone's Early Years.* New York: E. P. Dutton & Company, 1950.

Neff, Boss S. *Some Experiences in the Texas and Oklahoma Panhandle.* Amarillo, Texas: The Globe News, 1941.

Nelson, Oliver M. and Debo, A. *The Cowman's Southwest.* Glendale, California: The Arthur H. Clark Company, 1953.

Nordyke, Lewis. *The Great Roundup.* New York: William Morrow & Co., 1955.

Preece, Harold. *The Dalton Gang.* New York: Hastings House, 1963.

Rainey, George. *No Man's Land.* Enid, Oklahoma: author, 1937.

Rath, Ida Ellen. *The Rath Trail.* Wichita, Kansas: McCormick-Armstrong, 1961.

Rayfield, Alma C. *The West That's Gone.* New York: Carleton Press, 1962.

Rister, Carl Coke. *No Man's Land.* Norman: University of Oklahoma Press, 1948.

Rockfellow, John A. *The Log of an Arizona Trailblazer.*
Tucson: Acme Printing Company, 1933.

Ruth, Kent, compiled by. *Oklahoma, A Guide to the Sooner State.*
Norman: University of Oklahoma Press, 1957.

Rynning, Thomas H. *Gun Notches.* New York: Frederick A. Stoles
& Co., 1931.

Schmidt, Heinie. *Ashes of My Campfire.* Dodge City, Kansas:
Journal, Inc., 1952.

Sonnichsen, C. L. *Billy King's Tombstone.* Caldwell, Idaho:
Caxton Printers, 1942.

Spears, J. R. *The Saga of No Man's Land.* Beaver, Oklahoma:
Herald-Democrat, 1956.

Stevenson-McDermott, Myra E. *Lariat Letters.* Liberal, Kansas: np,
1907.

Streeter, Floyd B. *Ben Thompson, Man With a Gun,* New York:
Frederick Fell, Inc., 1957.

Streeter, Floyd B. *Prairie Trails and Cow Towns.* Boston:
Chapman & Grimes, 1936.

Sullivan, Frank S. *A History of Meade County, Kansas.* Topeka:
Crane & Co., 1916.

Thompson, Goldianne. *History of Clayton and Union County, New
Mexico.* Denver: Monitor Publishing Company, 1962.

Thorp, Jack, and Clark, N.M. *Pardner of the Wind.* Caldwell, Idaho:
Caxton Printers, 1945.

Wagoner, J. J. *History of the Cattle Industry.* Tucson:
University of Arizona, 1952.

Webb, Walter Prescott, ed. *The Handbook of Texas,* 2 volumes.
Austin: Texas State Historical Association, 1952.

Westermeier, Clifford P. *Trailing the Cowboy.* Caldwell, Idaho:
Caxton Printers, 1955.

Westerners, The. *Brand Book,* 1947. Los Angeles Corral.

Westerners, The. *The Smoke Signal,* 13 volumes. Tucson Corral.

Western Kansas Cattle Growers Association, The. *Brand Book,*
1882, 1883, 1884, 1885.

Wright, Robert M. *Dodge City, the Cowboy Capital.* Wichita, Kansas:
Wichita Eagle Press, 1917.

Wyllys, Rufus Kay. *Arizona, the History of a Frontier State.*
Phoenix: Hobson & Herr, 1950.

PERIODICALS

Oklahoma Historical Society. *The Chronicles of Oklahoma,* Spring
1957, volume XXXV, number 1. Articles as follows: Morris L.
Wardell, "The History of No-Man's-Land, or Old Beaver
County"; Muriel H. Wright, "The Seal of Cimarron Territory";
Laura V. Hamner, "Shade's Well."

Manuscripts

(Copies or originals in editor's possession).

Abbott, J. H. "Experiences in No Man's Land and the Cherokee Strip."

Cockrum, Richard I. (Red). "My Comrades of the Saddle, 1885-1900."

Cooper, Elery G. "Jim Herron, First Sheriff of No Man's Land."

Cooper, Elery G. "The Story of My Life."

Davis, Charley. "Jim Herron etc. etc." Reminiscences of Cochise County, Arizona, by the OR Button.

Eldridge, Marion, jr. "The Eldridge-Johnson Feud in No Man's Land."

Herron, James (Jim), sr. "My Life in No Man's Land and in Arizona." (The ms. from which this book was written).

Hitch, Charles A. "Cattle Raising in No Man's Land and North Texas."

Howe, A. N. "My Pioneer Experiences in No Man's Land."

Judy, Thomas J. "Reminiscences of Early No Man's Land."

Kinder, D. Ben. "Incidents from My Life and Stories of Old No Man's Land."

Lawson, H. L. "Cimarron Territory Records." The old records as transcribed by Lawson with his daughter, Mrs. M. G. Murphy.

Lemert, Bernard H. "The Roundup of '84: Reminiscences of a Cowman, 1879-1889."

McCoy, A. M. "Reminiscences of Ranch Life," by a member of McCoy Brothers & Summers Ranch, the XI, in southwest Kansas and the Neutral Strip.

Myers, Andrew J. (Andy). "Miscellaneous Writings and Letters by a Pioneer Cowman, Lawman, and Judge."

Nelson, Oliver M. "A Little Bit of the West and No Man's Land." The complete text from which his autobiography, *The Cowman's Southwest*, was published.

Quinn, James R. "The Quinn Family as Pioneers."

Newspapers

Arizona Republic (Phoenix), microfilm at Arizona Pioneer Museum, Tucson.

Arkalon News and Liberal News, The (Kansas), 1888-1920, files at Court House, Liberal, Kansas.

Benton County Banner (Oklahoma)

Beaver Herald-Democrat (Oklahoma), files at Beaver, Oklahoma.

Bisbee Daily Review (Arizona), files at *Review* office in Bisbee.

Dodge City Globe-Livestock Journal (Kansas), files of 1883-1887 at Beeson Museum, Dodge City and at State Historical Society, Topeka.

Fargo Springs News (Kansas), 1885-1888, files in Court House, Liberal Kansas.

Guymon Herald (Oklahoma), files at Guymon and at State Historical Society, Oklahoma City.

Hutchinson News-Herald (Kansas), files at State Historical Society, Topeka.

Kansas Cowboy (Sidney and Dodge City), 1883-1885, files at State Historical Society, Topeka.

Meade County Globe, The (Kansas), files at State Historical Society, Topeka.

Nogales Oasis, The (Arizona), microfilm at Arizona Pioneer Museum, Tucson.

Territorial Advocate, The (Oklahoma), files at State Historical Society, Oklahoma City.

Tombstone Epitaph, The (Arizona), microfilm at Arizona Pioneer Museum, Tucson.

Tombstone Prospector, The (Arizona), microfilm at Arizona Pioneer Museum, Tucson.

Watonga Republican, The (Oklahoma), files at State Historical Society, Oklahoma City.

LETTERS

From members of the Herron families:

Harry C. Ballinger, Miami, Oklahoma
Mrs. Millie Borba, Newman, California
Mrs. T. D. (Sam) Herron, Phoenix, Arizona
Mrs. Jean Jeffrey, Post Falls, Idaho
Mrs. Edith Killion, Georgetown, California
H. F. Loofbourrow, Merced, California
Wade H. Loofbourrow, Boise City, Oklahoma
Mrs. Rita McGrew, Superior, Arizona
Mrs. Bess Groves Morrissey, Fair Oaks, California
Mrs. Billy (Herron) Peper, Phoenix, Arizona
J. L. Stratton, Stillwater, Oklahoma

From others (by states):

ARIZONA

H. S. Copeland (Texas Rangers historian), Tucson
Mrs. Jean Devere (Rose Tree Inn Museum), Tombstone
Mrs. Anna J. Emmons, Sedona
Pecos Higgins, Prescott
Mrs. Walter Hoffman, Phoenix
Mrs. Edna G. Landin, Tombstone
Frank Lea, Bisbee
Mrs. John Newell, Naco
Mrs. Henry Nichols, San Manuel
Margaret Sparks (librarian), Tucson
Harry Stewart, Tombstone
Fred Valenzuela, Naco

339

ARKANSAS
Milton Nobles, sr., Little Rock

CALIFORNIA
Lee M. Cooley, Laguna Beach
Elery G. Cooper, Arroyo Grande
L. Rollin Healy, Los Angeles
J. Manfrini, San Luis Obispo

COLORADO
Mrs. Ruth (Davis) Fugate, Leadville

KANSAS
Mrs. Ernest Dewey, Hutchinson
Ray Over (and sister Lillie), Liberal
Robert W. Richmond (archivist), Topeka
Ira Scott, Meade
Mr. and Mrs. Crompton Tate, Liberal

MISSOURI
Derry Brownfield, Kansas City

NEVADA
Mrs. Charles Ray Wright, Hiko

NEW MEXICO
Ray Anaya (sheriff), Eddy County
Milton R. Smith, Carlsbad

OKLAHOMA
Mrs. M. B. Adams (librarian), Oklahoma City
Hannah D. Atkins (librarian), Oklahoma City
Otto C. Barby, Beaver
Henry C. Hitch, Guymon
T. A. Judy, Forgan
Mrs. Grant Perkins, Laverne
Jack D. Powers, Oklahoma City
Ada Quinn, Beaver
Mrs. Pearl Sharp, Beaver
A. N. Taylor, Laverne
W. H. Wells, Beaver

TEXAS
Mrs. E. T. Barker (librarian), Canadian
Ilerna Friend (librarian), Austin

WASHINGTON, D. C.
Senator Carl Hayden, Arizona
Fabian K. Kwiatek (legal advisor, State Department)

340

ENGLAND
Colin Rickards, London
MEXICO
Gordon McMurray, Yecero, Sonora
Joel C. Terrazas, Nogales, Sonora
WEST GERMANY
Oscar C. (Arizona Jack) Pfaus, Hamburg

photo credits

PART I

Page

73 — Photos courtesy Mrs. Grant Perkins, Laverne, Oklahoma.

74 (top) — Photo courtesy U. S. Department of the Interior, Fort Niobrara Wildlife Refuge, Valentine, Nebraska.

74 (bottom) — Day photo, courtesy Mrs. James C. Banker, Hobbs, New Mexico.

75 (top) — H. M. Steele photo, courtesy Oklahoma Historical Society.

75 (bottom) — Day photo.

76 (top) — Photo courtesy Oklahoma Historical Society.

76 (bottom) — Day photo.

77 (top) — Day photo.

78 (top) — Photo courtesy *Southwest Daily Times,* Liberal, Kansas.

78 (bottom) — Photo courtesy the late Ban Kinder, Beaver, Oklahoma pioneer.

79 (top) — Photo courtesy E. W. McNaghten, Crooked L Ranch, Meade, Kansas.

79 (bottom) — Mensinger photo, courtesy Pearl Sharp, Beaver Museum, Beaver, Oklahoma.

80 (top) — Photo courtesy the late Ban Kinder, Beaver, Oklahoma pioneer.

80 (bottom) — Photo courtesy Marion Eldridge, Jr.

81 — Arnold Ostrom photo.

82 (top) — Harry Chrisman photo.

82 (bottom) — Photo courtesy Paul Custer, Thermopolia, Wyoming.

83 (top) — Day photo.

83 (bottom) — Photo courtesy Mrs. Carrie Cain Ellison.

84 (top) — Photo courtesy Nebraska State Historical Society.

85 — Photocopy courtesy John Jenkin.

86 — Photo courtesy the Herron family.

87 — Photostats from Beaver County, Oklahoma court records, courtesy Lona Neff Graham, Boise City, Oklahoma.

88 (top)   Photo courtesy Beaver Museum, Beaver, Oklahoma.
88 (bottom)   Photo courtesy E. W. McNaghten, Crooked L Ranch, Meade, Kansas.

PART II
————

193   Photo courtesy Mrs. Rita Herron McGrew, Jim Herron's daughter.
194   Photos courtesy Fred Valenzuela, Naco, Arizona.
195 (top)   Photo courtesy Arizona Pioneers' Historical Society, Tucson.
195 (bottom)   Photo courtesy Fred Valenzuela.
196 (top)   Photo courtesy Arizona Pioneers' Historical Society.
196 (bottom)   Photo courtesy Fred Valenzuela.
197   Photo courtesy Arizona Pioneers' Historical Society.
198 (top)   Photo courtesy Arizona Pioneers' Historical Society.
198 (bottom)   Photo courtesy Denver Public Library, Western Collection.
199   Photos courtesy Arizona Pioneers' Historical Society.
200 (top)   Photo courtesy Arizona Pioneers' Historical Society.
200 (bottom)   Photo courtesy Mrs. Rita Herron McGrew.
201   Photo courtesy Rose Tree Inn, Tombstone, Arizona.
202 (top)   Harry Chrisman photo.
202 (bottom)   Photo courtesy Mrs. Thomas D. Herron.
203 (top) &   Photos from the book *Pancho Villa,* by William Doug-
204 (top)   las Lansford, copyright 1965; courtesy the publisher, Sherbourne Press, Los Angeles, California.
204 (bottom)   Photo courtesy Fred Valenzuela.
205 (top)   Photo courtesy Arizona Pioneers' Historical Society.
205 (bottom)   Photo from the book *Pancho Villa,* courtesy Sherbourne Press.
206 (top left) Photo courtesy Mrs. Thomas D. Herron.
206 (top right) Photo courtesy Mrs. Jean McGrew Jeffrey, Jim Herron's granddaughter.
206 (bottom)   Photo courtesy Mrs. Rita Herron McGrew.
207 (top)   Photo courtesy Mrs. Rita Herron McGrew.
207 (bottom)   Photo courtesy Burris Wright and his son, Ray Wright.
208   Photo courtesy Hills Ferry Cemetery, Newman, California.

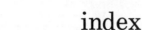

index

The word "Old" following town names indicates abandoned towns and ghost sites. Town of same name may be presently established elsewhere, e.g. Mobeetie, Texas and Hardesty, Oklahoma.
References to photograph illustrations are indicated by italic numerals.

Abbott, J. H., 315n1
Acado, Jerrado, 223, 224
Adobe Walls Battle, 108
Adobe Walls Trail, 146
Allen, L. A., 106
Alpine (Old), Neutral Strip, 27, 43
Alvord, Burt, xviii, 177, *199,* 249-50, 252-54
Alvord-Stiles gang, 199, 249-51, 319n2, 322n4, 326n1
Anadarko, Okla., 314n4
Anchor D Ranch, 115
Angula, Captain, 214, 216-17, 220-21
Antelope Hills, I.T., 9
Aragon, N.M., 173
Artesia, N.M., 155
Arizona Daily Citizen, The, 223
Arizona Rangers, *198,* 249, 253
Arizona Territory, 331n6
Arizpe, Sonora, Mex., 215
Arkansas River, Kan., 31
Ashcraft, Maude (Mrs. Mary C. Hanlin), 92-3, 312n4
Ashland, Kan., 56, 124, 319n2
Aspen, Colo., 327n1
Astin (or Aspin or Ashton), George, 220-23, 226, 325n3
Augustine, N.M., 172
Axford, J. Mack, 323n4

Bacadehuachi, Sonora, Mex., 275
B A D Ranch, 23
Bahia Kino, Sonora, Mex., 253
Ballard family, 288
Ballard, J. J., 332n2
Ballinger, Dyke, 85
Barby family, 288
Barnes, Jim, 166-67
Barry, Mrs., *200,* 261
Bass, Sam, 176
Beaver Advocate, The, 85
Beaver City, Neutral Strip, 27, 39, 41-2, 49, 60, *78, 79, 80, 84, 88,* 110,

120, 156, 259, 287, 291, 294, 296, 301, 308n1, 314n3, 318n4, 320n2, 331n1
Beckham, Joe, xiii
Beer City (Old), Neutral Strip, *82,* 101-02, 298
Beeson, Chalk, 92
Bell, Ham, 10, 13
Bell, Toll, 249
Benson, Ariz., 211
Benton County Banner, 67, 312n1a
Benton (or Groves) Hotel, 68
Benton (Old), Neutral Strip, 28, 37, 41, 43, 46, 49, 53, 56, 61, 67-8, 80, 89, 90, 92, 100, 118, 156, 259, 290, 308n1
Beverly Brothers Ranch, 33
Bignon, Joe, 187
Billy The Kid, 170, 177-78
Bingham, N.M., 172
Bisbee, Ariz., 182, 191, 223, 248-49
Bisbee (Ariz.) *Daily Review,* 325n2, 329n4
Bisbee (Ariz.) *Orb,* 233
Black Kettle (Chief), 10
Black Mesa, Neutral Strip, 150
Blizzards, 65, 93-9, 100
Bocachi, Sonora, Mex., 325n2
Boehler, Louis, 131
Boise City, Okla., 287
Bone, Harry, 128-29, 315n6
Booker, L. E., 269, 273, 330n2
Boone Charlie, 33
Bootleg distilleries, 28, 112-15
Borba, John, 328n3
Borba, Tony, 328n3
Borba, Mrs. Tony (see Millie Herron)
Borba, Tony, jr., 328n3
Box T Ranch, 17
Braden, John, 318n4
Braidwood, Thomas, 52
Bravin, George, 252

"Bravo Juan" (see Tom Yoas)
Brazos River, Tex., 24, 247
Brennan, Matt, 33
Brennan, Tom, 33
Bridgeford, Bill, 42
Brite, Arch, 321n1
Brite, Perry, 320n2
Broadhearst, Mr. 53-9, 60-2, 68, 105
Broadwell, Dick, 108
Brockman, John, 323n2
Brooks, Lt., *198*
Brown, Henry, xviii
Bryant, Mrs. Marian, 324n6
Buffalo bone haulers, 37, 78
Buffalo Soldiers, 9-10
Buis Livery Stable (Meade, Kan.),
   135, 317n4
Buis, Richard (Dick), *88,* 138, 316-
   17n4
Bull Springs Ranch, 246
Burford, Judge John H., 63
Burgess, Dan, 233
"Burr" (see George Musgrave)
Burts, Matt, 250-51-52, 326n1
Bush, Lew, *82,* 102
Button, Dr., 316n4
Byrns, A. J., 110, 124-26

Cain, Zechariah, 83
Calles, General, 276-77, 280-82
Calles Military Government, 270,
   275-76
Calumet & Arizona Mining Co., 262
Campbell, Gov. Tom (Ariz.), 294-96
Camp Supply, I. T., 9, 10, 13, 14, 92,
   298, 307n2
Canadian City, Tex., 160, 258-59
Cananea Cattle Co., 195
Cananea, Sonora, Mex., 191, 211
Cananea-Yaqui River & Pacific
   R.R., 211
Canton, Frank (Joe Horner), xiii
Cantonement, I. T., 30
Capper, Gov. Arthur (Kan.), 292,
   295
CA Ranch, 320n3
Carlsbad, N.M., 155
Carranza, General, 270, 275-76
Carrizozo, N.M., 172
Carter, Mr., 43
Cartmell, brothers, 264
Casas Grande, Chihuahua, Mex., 270

Cattlemen's Association of Colo.,
   321n1
Cattle Ranche & Land Co. (YL
   Ranch), xv, 14, 15, 21, 32, 45, 90,
   99, 134-35, 152, 157, 164, 287, 290,
   305n3, 313n1
Cavius, Ben, 41
Cavius, Bob, 41
CCC Ranch (Ariz.), 264
CCC Ranch (Okla.), 115
Chacon (outlaw), 253-54
Chadwick, Wes, 92
Chama, N.M., 150
Chapdelaine, Arlene Borba, 328n3
Chapman-Tuttle Trail (Tuttle
   Trail), 19, 25, 71, 313n1
Chase, Dr. O. G., 49, 52
Chatman, Mr., 185
Cherokee Strip, xiv, xv, 3, 15, 16, 27,
   52, 118, 137
Cheyenne Indian Reservation, S.D.,
   121, 123, 128-29
Chickasaw Nation, 21
Chitwood, Jim (and brothers), 20, 43
Christian, Bob, 247, 249
Christian, William (Black Jack),
   199, 223, 247-49
Chronicles of Oklahoma, The, 311n1
Cimarron & Crooked Creek Cattle
   Co. (Chain C's), 16
Cimarron River, 30, 66, 101-02, 120,
   122, 150
Cimarron Territory, 29, 49, 52, 308-
   11n1 (see also No Man's Land)
Clanton family, 260
Clark, Ben, 249
Clark, R. B. S., 264
Clay, John, 305-06n3, 313n5
Clayton, Bob, 182-83, 186, 190, 213,
   217-18, 220-22, 224-26, 229, 232,
   241
Clayton (N.M.) *Enterprise, The,*
   321-22n1
Cleveland, President Grover, 189
Cliff, N.M., 248
Clifton, Ariz., 248
Cochise, Ariz., 250
Cochise (Chief), 186, 250
Cochise County, Ariz., 183-84, 190-
   91, 227, 252, 324n1
Cochran family, 288
Cochran, William S., 320n2
Cody, W. F. (Buffalo Bill), 90, 290

Coe gang, 106
Coffeyville, Kan., 313n1
Coldwater River, Neutral Strip, 92, 115
Colgan, Robert, 135, 138-39, 317n4
Collier, Mr., 43
Colonia Chuichupa, Mexico, 270, 271
Colonia Garcia, Mexico, 270-72, 274
Colonia Morales, Mexico, 271, 278
Colorado Rangers, 106
Colter, Fred, 294
Columbus, N.M., 276
Cook, G. W., xiii
Cooper, Elery G., 70, 312n2
Cooper, Frank, 66, 118-19, 122-24, 128
Cooper & Givins Ranch (444), 33
Cosper, J. H. Toles, 174, 322n2
Cosper, Mrs. Toles, 174
Cosper, John, 322n2
Costello, Martin, 186-87, 323n4
Courtland, Ariz., 262-65, 286, 329n5
Courtland Arizonian, The, 262
Cowman, Bill, 264
Cow Ranch Saloon (Naco, Ariz.), 178, 196, 212, 241, 259, 327n2
Cowan, Samuel, 130
Cox, B. F., 318n4
Crooked Creek, Kan., 21, 140
Crooked L Ranch, 79
Crump, Sherman, 319n2
Crystal Palace Saloon (Tombstone), 260
Cuen, Tranquilino, 210, 325n2
Cunningham-Costello lawsuit, 265

Dacy family, 288
Dakota Badlands, 313n2
Dale, John, 52
Daley, Mr. (Irish Mag mine), 323n4
Dalton, Bob, xiii, 106, 108
Dalton, Eva (Mrs. J. N. Whipple), 108
Dalton, Frank, 107-08
Dalton gang, 105-06, 313n1
Dalton, Grat, xiii, 106-08
Daniels, Josh, 41
Davis, Buck, 42
Davis, Charley, 324n1, 327n2
Davis, "Pack Rat," 35
Deerdorf, Mr. (cattleman), 32
DeLong, John, 31

Demerick, Mrs. (see Mrs. James Herron, sr.)
Deming, N.M., 155
Denver, Colo., 301, 327
Devere, Mrs. Burton, 201
Diaz, Presidente Porfirio, 197, 209-10, 237-38, 268-70
Dix, John, 67
Dixon, Al, 67, 73, 290
Dixon, Billy, 115
Doan's Store (Red River), 7
Dobie, Christ, 42
Dodge City, Kan., xiv, 10, 11, 18, 25, 31, 101, 107-08, 156, 212, 298, 313n1
"Dogie John," 54
Dominguez, Alfred R., 267
Dominion Cattle Co. (Box T), 22
Don & Don Attorneys, 283
Don, Frank, 283
Dorsey, Senator Stephen W., 307n2
Douglas, Ariz., 276, 279-80, 283, 329n4
Douglas, Doc, 42
Dow, Les, 320n3
Downing (or Jackson), Bill, 252, 322n4
Doyle, P., 135-37, 316n2
Drew, Mr. (cattleman), 135
Drift fences (danger in blizzards), 94-100
Duck Pond Creek, Neutral Strip, 27-28, 95
Dugan, Major Tom, 268
Dull Knife, 11
Dunlap, Burt, 190

Earp, Marshal Virgil, 260
Earp, Morgan, 260
Earp, Wyatt, 260
Easely family, 288
Eldridge, Bill, 292
Eldridge, Silas, 42, 292
Elephant Saloon (Beer City, Neutral Strip), 82
Elliott, Jim, 306n3
Ellis County, Tex., xiv, 3, 24, 25, 108, 135
Ellis, Smith, 43
Elmer, Mary, 41
El Paso, Tex., 267-70, 275, 294, 329n1
El Paso & Southwestern R.R., 211
Empire Ranch (Ariz.), 319n2

England, Jim, *207*
Englewood, Kan., 28, 125
Evans, Rev. William, 48
Ewing, Bill, *207*

Fanning, Miss (Mrs. Cicero Stewart), 320*n*3
Farwell, Tex., 155
Fairbank, Ariz., 211, 250-51
Fairview (Old), Neutral Strip, 43
Fegert, Mrs. Norma, *206,* 324*n*6
Fenokio, General, *198,* 232-37
Fick, Fred, 131
Fish (or Fisk), Chance, 43
Fisher, John King, 13
Flagstaff, Ariz., 153
Florence, Ariz., 267, 328*n*4
Foltz, Alex, 32, *79*
Ford, Lon (Sheriff), 319*n*2
Forgan, Okla., 287, 292
Fort Elliott, Tex., 16, 118, 173, 307, 313*n*1
Fort Smith, Ark., 108
Fort Worth Livestock Growers Journal, 26, 123
Fort Worth Stock Growers Association, 130
Fowler, Mr., 38
Franco, Señor, 217-18, 220-24, 232
"Fred," (R Bar S cowboy), 110-12
Frost, Mrs. Emma, *206,* 324*n*6
Fugate, Mrs. Ruth, 324*n*1
Fulkerson's Ranch, 146
Furnace, Mr., 286, 323*n*1

Gallinas Peak, N.M., 170
Gamble Ranch, 175
Garden City, Kan., 28
Garth, Major, (cattleman), 5
Garvey, Jack (see Mills and Garvey Saloon)
Gay, E. L., 67, 312*n*1a
Gentry, Mr., 188
Gentry's Saloon (Pearce, Ariz.), 185
George, Bill, *207*
George, John, 92, 117, 288
"Getting good stuff" (early range practice to acquire cattle), 71-72
Gila River, Ariz., 182
Gilbert, Mack, 42
Gilbert, Old Man, (sheepman), 41, 42
Giles, Bob, 325*n*2

Gittenger, Roy, 311*n*1
Givler, Sam (deputy), *88,* 138-41, 316-18*n*4
Gleeson, Ariz., 186
Gleeson, John, 323*n*3
Glenwood Springs, Colo., 260
Globe, Ariz., 150, 153, 155, 182
Goddard, A. K., 46, 47, 48, 51, 146-48
Goddard, Mrs. A. K. (Jackson), 148-49, *206*
Goddard, Belle, 46, 47, 146
Goddard, Bertha, 46, 47
Goddard, John, 46, 47
Goddard, May (see Mrs. James Herron, sr.)
Goddard Ranch, 258-59
Grand Prize mine, 153
Granillo, Fred, 328*n*3
Granillo, Joe, 328*n*3
Granillo, Manuel, 328*n*3
Granillo, Mary Louise (Mrs. Darrow), 328*n*3
Grant, Ed, 270, 272-74
Gray, Zane, 153
Great Western Mining Co., 262
Green, Irvin, 321*n*1
Greene, William (Bill), 182, 195, 322*n*4
Griffin, Blackie, 286
Grover, Bert (Arizona Ranger), 325*n*2
Groves, Alice (see Mrs. James Herron, sr.)
Groves, Ansel, 50, 68, 70, 89, 121, 259, 314*n*2
Groves, Mrs. Ansel, 68, 70, 89, 191, 192, 258, 314*n*2
Groves, Bertha (Mrs. Robert H. Loofbourrow), 68, 70, *207,* 287, 291, 293
Groves, Della (Mrs. Dyke Ballinger), 68, 70, 121, 314*n*3
Groves Hotel (or Beaver City Hotel), *84,* 85, 120
Groves Hotel (at Benton), 44, 50, 68
Gueda Springs, Kan., 279
Guggenheims (Mining Corp.), 286
Guymon, Okla., 287, 296
Guymon (Okla.) *Herald,* 293
Gyalla Ranch, Sonora, Mex., 276-78

Haggenbach, Charley, 32
Halford, John (Lengthy), 33

Hanlin, Mrs. Mary C. (see Maude Ashcraft)
Hardesty, Ed., 18
Hardesty, Col. Richard J., 18
Hardesty (Old), Neutral Strip, 92
Hardesty Brothers Ranch (Quartercircle S), 77, 115
Hardin, John Wesley, 177-78
Harlan, Lee, 329n1
Harrison & Drew Butcher Shop, 263, 328n4
Harrison, President Benjamin, 62, 189
Hart Ranch, 319n2
Harvey, Fred, 33
Harwood, W. I. Ranch (O Bar L), 30, 31, 312n1
Hatch, Bob Saloon (Tombstone), 260
Hatch, Rufus, 305n3
Hayden, Carl (Congressman and Senator), 281, 331n6
Hayes, Bob, 246, 248
Hay Meadow massacre, 102
HC Ranch, 246
Healey Brothers Ranch (KK), 26, 33, 36, 48, 56, 66, 72, 82, 97, 99, 117, 148, 156, 168, 287, 313n1, 330n1
Healey, Frank, 26, 27
Healey, George, 26, 27, 66-69, 72, 89, 95, 96
Healey, L. Rollin, 329n1
Heber, A. H., 318n4
Hefner, Harry, 319n2
Heinz, Mr. (goat ranch), 236
Herring, C. T., 16
Herron, Albert D., 206, 324n7
Herron, Bessie Lorraine, 206, 323n1
Herron, Billie, 206, 323n1
Herron, Dorothy, 206, 323n1
Herron, Francis, 153
Herron, Frank, 150-51, 154, 180-82, 199, 248-49
Herron, Mrs. Frank (Molly), 153
Herron, James (Jim), sr., birth, 3-4; youth, 4; homestead, 87, 116-17, 319n1; rodeo, 90-93; blizzard of 1888, 93-100; prank with Bat Masterson, 109-10; hotel owner, 120, 189, 200, 201, 260, 262, 313n2; brands, 121, 169, 264, 315n5, 324n1; flees to Arizona, 150; returns to No Man's Land, 154-64,

207, 258-59, 286-88, 290-94, 296-97, 331n1; saloon owner, 186-87, 196, 212, 241-45, 259, 262, 263; mine owner, 196, 330n3; meets Col. Kosterlitzky, 234-38; meets Black Jack Christian, Bravo Juan, Billy Stiles, 246-57; meets Pancho Villa, 269-70; his summation of life, general philosophy, 297-99; death, 333n3; tombstone, 208; photos of, 73, 86, 88, 193, 196, 200, 202, 206, 207

COWBOY AND CATTLEMAN: Texas Trail, 6-12; YL Ranch, 14-15; The Association, 19-23; KK Ranch, 26-27, 30-36, 66, 72, 89; M Bar Ranch, 117-18; Texas beef purchase, 118-20; U. S. Government contract, 121-22; Mexican imports, 189-92, 246, 254-57, 259, 262, 267-85; Courtland, Ariz., 263

SHERIFF: No Man's Land, 50-61; Oklahoma Territory, 63-64, 103-06, 110-15, 311n2

CATTLE RUSTLING: informal charges by The Association, 23; formal charges, trial, escape, O.T. and Kansas, 123-42, 316n4; formal charges, trial, Ariz., 263-66, 328n4

HORSE SMUGGLING: charges by Mexican customs, 213-14; "Naco War," 223-34, 240-41; trial, 238-40

MARRIAGES AND CHILDREN: Alice Groves (first wife): wedding, 68-69; child (see Olive Dorothy Herron); death, 120-21. Anna May Goddard (second wife): wedding, 174; children (see Thomas D., Rita, Jim, jr. Herron); death, 261. Mary Valencia (third wife): wedding, 261; child (see Millie Herron); divorce, 332n3. Mrs. Demerick (fourth wife), 332n3

TOWNS LIVED IN AFTER NO MAN'S LAND: Globe, Ariz., 150-53; Payson, Ariz., 153-54, 180-82; Pearce, Ariz., 184-88; La Morita, Sonora, Mex., 188-92, 209-210; Naco, Sonora, Mex., 211-41; Naco, Ariz., 241-59; Tombstone, Ariz., 260-62; Courtland, Ariz., 262-85

Herron, Mrs. James, sr. (nee Alice Groves, first wife), 68, 70, 86, 89, 120, 147, 314n3
Herron, Mrs. James, sr. (nee Anna May Goddard, second wife), 46, 146-49, 151-52, 154, 164, 168, 170, 172, 174, 180-81, 184-89, 191, *193*, 202, 206, 216, 218, 258, 260-61, 328n2
Herron, Mrs. James, sr. (nee Mary Valencia, third wife), 206, 261, 286, 332n3
Herron, Mrs. James, sr. (former Mrs. Demerick, fourth wife), 333n3
Herron, James, jr. (Jim Herron's son), *206*, 211, 311n2, 319n2, 324n7
Herron, Mrs. James, jr., 324n7
Herron, James C., *206*, 324n7
Herron, May (Mrs. John Lazar), 153
Herron, Millie (Jim Herron's daughter) (Mrs. Tony Borba), *206*, 262, 301, 328n3
Herron, Morita (Rita, Jim Herron's daughter) (Mrs. Elmer C. Mc-Grew), 191, *200, 201, 206*, 260, 301, 324n6, 326n2, 332n3
Herron, Olive Dorothy (Ollie Dot, Jim Herron's daughter) (Mrs. Carleton H. Stratton), *86, 88*, 100, 121, 191-92, 259, 290, 314n4
Herron, Rita May, *206*, 323n1
Herron, Ruby Nell, *206*, 323n1
Herron, Thomas Darrel (Sam, Jim Herron's son), 181, 184, 187, 191, *202, 206*, 264, 286, 322n1
Herron, Mrs. Thomas Darrel, *206*, 307n3, 312n3, 323n1
Hester (or Hesper), Mr., 322n2
Hickock, "Wild Bill," 177-78
Higgins, Tex., 119, 157, 165-66, 258-59
Hill, Billy (The Texas Hill Kid), 159-61, 164-65, 169-75, 180, 320-22
Hill, Alley, 160, 321n1
Hill, John, 160, 321n1
Hitch, Charlie, *207*, 288, 294
Hitch family, 288
Hitch, Jim, 294
Hodge, Joe, *80*
Holliday, Doc, 260
Holstein, Sim, 18, 31, 32

Hooker, Okla., 36, 292
Hopkins, Sgt. *198*
Hopper, Gene, 168-70, 180, 182
Hot Springs, Ark., 327n1
Houston, Temple, 152, 162, 177
Houston, General Sam, 152
Huachuca Siding, 227, 231
Hubbard (Sutter), Judge L. M., 28, 29, 39, 40, 44, 49, 50, 52, 56-58, 112-13, 290, 307n4
Hudson, Mr. (horse thief), 21
Huerta, General, 268, 270-71, 276-77
Huett, Walter, 275
Hugoton (Hugo), Kan., 103
Hungate, Bake, 18, 35
Hungate, Tom, 18, 26, 31, 33
Hunt, Gov. George W. P. (Ariz.), 153, 266, 281, 296

International Hotel (Douglas, Ariz.), 281

Jackson, Con, *207*
Jackson, Jim (or Frank), 176
James Brothers, 106
James, Frank, 106
Jeffrey, Homer C., 301
Jeffrey, Mrs. Homer C. (Jean Mc-Grew), *206*, 301-02, 324n6, 332n3
Jennings, Al, 152-53
Jennings brothers, 152-53
Jennings, Ed, 152-53, 177
Jennings, John, 152-53, 177
Jiminez, Chihuahua, Mex., 268
JJ Ranch, *75, 76*
Johns, D. S., 42
Johnson, Charlie, 42
Johnson family, 292
Johnson, Mr. and Mrs. "Muley", 184, 264
Johnson, "Sandhill," *78*
Johnson, Tom, 291
Johnny Pearce mine, 183, 286
Jones & Plummer Trail, 25, 27, 33, 37, 80, 140, 287, 313n1
Jones, Seab, 157, 160-61, 165, 167
Judy family, 288
Judy, H. S,, *207*
Judy, T. A., 321n1
Judy, Tom, 11, 50, 321n1

Kansas City, Mo., 122, 124
Keese, Dan, 315n1

350

Kelley, Lem, 319n2
Kemp, Dave, 320n3
Kenney, J. E., 268
Kennicott Copper Co., 191
Kenton, Neutral Strip, 115, 150, 287
Kessler, A., 318n4
Ketchum, Black Jack, 321n3
KH Ranch, 17, 22
Killion, Mrs. (Edith McGrew),
    324n6
Kinder, Ban, 78
King, Peter, 317n4
Kingfisher, Okla., 60
Kingston, Mr., 43
Kinsley, Mr., 41
Kiowa Creek, Neutral Strip, 15
Koller, Hi (C Y Ranch), 22
Kosterlitzky, Col. Emilio, 197, 198,
    232-39, 240, 325n1
Kramer, Charley, 95
Kramer, Frank, 95
Kramer, Ludwig (Lu), 95, 99, 100

Land, Col. W. C., 190
Lapham, Al, 33
La Rita Hotel (Tombstone), 189,
    200, 201, 260, 262-63
La Morita (Sonora, Mex.) Customs
    House, 194
La Morita-Nacozari Stage, 194
La Morita, Sonora, Mex., 188, 191,
    210-13, 215, 217, 230-32, 239-40,
    256, 260, 262, 284
Laney, Bert, 322
Larrabee, Lee, 207, 288
Larsman (or Landsman), Jack, 68
Lay (or McGinnis), Ezra, 321n3
Lazar, John, 153
Lee, Bob, 278, 280
Lee & Reynolds Co., 10
Leigh, Fred, 315n2
Lemert, Bernard H., 32, 288, 321
Leverton, John, 315n2
LFD Ranch, 156
Liberal, Kan., 101, 319n2
Light, Zack Ranch, 155
Lillie, Gordon W. (Pawnee Bill), 61,
    290, 314n4
Lilliyvier, Señor, 282
"Little Dick" (outlaw), 152
Little, Jake, 289
Little, Rance, 289
Little Wolf Creek, Tex., 17

Littlefield, George Ranch (LIT), 76
Loofbourrow, H. J., 296
Loofbourrow, Robert, 296-97
Loofbourrow, Judge Robert H., 287,
    289, 291, 293, 296
Loofbourrow, Mrs. R. H. (see
    Bertha Groves)
Lorreto, Col. Antonio, 275-76
Los Angeles Times, 240
Las Cruces, N.M., 155
Losey, G. H., 318n4
Lost Trails of the Cimarron, 301
Love, Mr. (deputy), 321n1
Love, Jack, 152
Lowell, Ariz., 323n4
Luna Valley, N.M., 173, 180
Lute, John, 33
Lynch family, 288
"Lynd, Irene," (pen name of Ollie
    Dot Herron Stratton), 314n4
Lyons, Mr. (inspector), 125-26
LX Ranch (Backward LX), 315n2

Macia, Harry, 201
Macia, Mrs. H. E., 251
Macia, James H., 201
Mackey, Dave, 32
Madero, Presidente Francisco, 203,
    209, 267, 270
Madsen, Chris, 63
Magdalena, N.M., 172
Magdalena, Sonora, Mex., 237
Maine, Bill, 53-59, 62
Malabi Ranch, 268
Maple, Frank, 319n2
Marshall, Owen (Sheriff), 319n2
Marts, George, 233
Martz, Jim, 32
Mason, Joe, 23, 116
Masterson, W. B. (Bat), 108-10
Morawitz, Albert (Vice Consul), 231
McAdoo, William Gibbs, 281
McCaire, Alex, 33
McColl, Jack, 178
McCord, Sam, 23
McCoy, A. H., 18
McCoy Brothers Ranch (XI 11), 33
McFarland, Gov. Ernest (Ariz.),
    324n7
McFarland, Robert, 291
McGill, Mr. (deputy), 321n1
McGovern, John (Irish), 67, 73, 92,
    156-57, 168, 290-91

351

McGrew, Elmer C. (Jake), 324n6
McGrew, Mrs. Elmer C. (see Morita Herron)
McKenney, C. F., 116
McKenney, Over & Co. (M Bar Ranch), 23
McKinney, Charley, 264-65
McLane, Sam, 79
McLowery brothers, 260
McManus, Black Bob, 321n3
Meade County (Kan.) Globe, The, 316n4
Meade, Kan., 68, 108, 110, 120, 122, 126, 130, 132, 140-41, 147, 151, 287, 291-92, 297, 301, 316n4, 331n1
Medicine Lodge, Kan., 315n6
Merchant, George Ranch, 115
Mexican Claims Commission (Special), 330n4
Mexican soldiers, 204
Mexican War, 306n1
Mexico City, Mex., 210
Mille, Mons., 188
Mille Store (Naco, Ariz.), 224
Miller, C. R., 207
Miller, Judge Carl, 332n1
Mills and Garvey Saloon (Beaver City), 78, 293
Minneapolis, Minn., 151
Missouri Compromise, 306n1
Mobeetie, Texas, 313n1
Modoc Stage Line, 200, 260
Mogollon Rim (Ariz.), 150, 153-55, 248
Molino, Captain, 221
Montana-Tonapah Mining Co., 263
Moore, Sid, 249
Mora, Señor, 210
Morgan, F., 231
Morman colonists (in Mex.), 267, 283
Mossman, Captain Burton C., 250, 253
Mussett, Wash, 18, 31
Musgrave, George (Burr), 220, 222, 223, 245-46, 248
Muscatine Cattle Co., (ZH), 104
Murry, Alexander (attorney), 329
Murphy, Gov. N. O. (Ariz.), 234
Murphy, Jim, 176

Naco, Ariz., 152, 178, 188, 190, 192-93, 215, 223, 227, 229, 232, 241, 250,
252, 259, 268, 275, 298, 319n2, 330n3
Naco (Ariz.) Customs Office, 192
Naco (Sonora, Mex.) Customs Office, 194
Naco Hotel, 192
Naco, Sonora, Mex., 190, 193, 194, 211-12, 214, 218, 223, 227-29, 232-34, 240, 243, 298
"Naco War, The", 223-24, 232-34, 240, 244
Nave, Dick, 33
Needles Mining Co., 286
Neff, Boss Sebastian, 35, 92, 93, 115, 207, 288
Nelson, Oliver M. (O1), 42
Neutral City (Old), Neutral Strip, 42
Neutral Strip (see No Man's Land)
Newell, Mrs. John J., 326n2
Newman, Calif., 301, 328n3

New York Cattle Co. (see KH Ranch)
Niles Post Office (Old), Neutral Strip, 120
Nobles, Eugene M., 327n1
Nobles Hotel (Tombstone), 200, 260, 327n1
Nobles, Milton, 327n1
Nogales, Ariz., 229, 238
Nogales (Ariz.) Oasis, 231, 233, 240, 325n4
Nogales, Sonora, Mex., 216-18, 226, 228-30, 232-33, 237, 238, 240
Nolan, Bill, 268
No Man's Land (or Neutral Strip or Public Land Strip), 15, 16, 18, 28-29, 62, 305n3, 306n1, 308n1, 310n1
No Man's Land Historical Museum, Goodwell, Okla., 311n1
North Canadian River (or Beaver Creek or River), 9, 15, 20, 26, 30, 97, 102, 104, 115, 118, 120, 122

Obregon General, 209, 276
Ochoa, General, 272-75
Odem, Tobe (Red), 21, 321n1
Offett, Elmore & Cooper Co., 66
Ogallala, Nebr., xiv, 11, 12, 13, 298
O'Herron, 4
O'Jada, Sgt., 198

OK Corral (Tombstone), 260
Oldham, John, 265, 329n4
O'Larry (or O'Leary), Eddie, 319n2
O'Loughlin, John (Pigpen Ranch), 33
Omaha, Nebr., 122
Ong, Maggie (Mrs. Harry Reas), 22
Optima, Neutral Strip, 115
Organic Act, 45, 81, 308n1
Organic Law, 28, 45, 49, 61, 308n1
Orozco, General Pascual, 205, 268, 270-71, 279
Osgood Hotel (Meade, Kan.), 85, 131, 140
Ouray, Colo., 327
Over, John (M Bar Ranch), 23, 26, 27, 66, 72, 82, 87, 116-18, 141, 146, 148, 150, 156, 164-65, 167, 287, 313n1, 330n1
Owints, George, 250, 252
Owints, Lewis, 250, 252
"Owl Hoot Trail," xvii, 11, 151, 155, 177, 179, 182, 236, 248, 257, 286, 295, 297, 299

Packard, B. A., 264
Paige, Sid, 250-51, 326n1
Panhandle City, Tex., 157
Parker, Bill, 67
Parker, Charley, 43, 315n1
Parker, Tom, 67
Parson, Lyman, 43
Pastime Pool Hall (Courtland), 263
Patagonia, Ariz., 228
Pawnee, Okla., 290
Payne, Bob, 293
Payne, Capt. David L., 61
Payson, Ariz., 150, 153, 155-56, 174, 180, 182, 189, 248
Pearce, Ariz., 182-89, 192, 249-51, 262-64, 286, 293, 296, 323n3
Pearce, Johnny mine, 183, 286
Pearson, Chihuahua, Mex., 272
Perkins, Belle, 67
Perkins, Mr. and Mrs. Grant, 27
Peters, Adolf, 33
Phelps-Dodge Mining Corp., 191
Pine, Ariz., 150
Pinos Wells, N.M., 172
"Playing Even," (an early range practice for acquiring maverick cattle), 70-72

Polti, Mrs. (former Mrs. Mary Valencia Herron), 332n3
Potter family, 288
Powell, Cole, 243-44
Powers, Mr. and Mrs. Bud, 215-16, 218-19, 221-22, 227, 258, 324n2
Powers, Emmet, 33
Powers, Jack Dempsey, 215, 218-19, 221-22, 227, 258, 324n2
Prairie Cattle Co., 16
Prescott, Ariz., 324n1
Prescott, Charles, 319n2
Price, Judge Francis C., 130, 133, 137-38, 141, 162-63, 316n3
Public Land Strip (see No Man's Land)
Pueblo, Colo., 327n1
Pulliam, W. E., 325n4
"Pussy Cat Nell" (Madam), 82, 102

Quinlan, Mr. (trail boss), 5, 6, 7, 11

Ragsdale, Johnny, 254-55
Rainey, George, 311n1
Ramsey, Harry, 182-83, 186-87, 190, 216, 218-20, 222-25, 227, 239, 241, 324n2
Rancho Escondido, 217, 235, 254-57
Reas, Harry, 20-23
"Red Flaggers" (Mexican Revolutionaries), 205, 268, 270
Red River, Tex., 20, 107
Reed, Scott, 173-74, 180
Reichart, Curt, 207
Reynolds Cattle Co., 117
Rhodes, F. M. (Jack), 67, 73, 85, 88, 124, 126-27, 131, 138-42, 316-18
Rhodes, Mrs. F. M., 141, 158-59
Rhodes, Joe, 233, 244-45, 325n2
Rice, Mr. (a granger), 41
Richmond, Rev. L., 314n4
Rio Grande River, N.M., 172
Rio Popigochic, Chihuahua, Mex., 270
Rister, Carl Coke, 306n1, 311n1
Robertson, Cristy, 250-51, 326n1
Robertson, Mrs. Cristy (Alice), 250
Robertson, Edith, 250-51
Robertson, Ethel (Mrs. H. E. Macia), 251-52
Roberts, Mr. (rancher), 188
Rock Island R.R., 101

Rocknole (or Rockford), Charlie, 42, 43
Rodeos (early days), 93
Rojas, General, 268
Rome Hotel (Omaha), 129
Roosevelt, Theodore, 313n2
Rosebud Reservation (S.D.), 74, *84*, 121, 123, 128-29
Ross, Mr. (attorney), 329n4
Ross, Old Doc, 33
Roswell, N.M., 155
Rothwell (Old), Neutral Strip, 52
Round Rock, Tex., 176
Round Timbers, Tex., 247
Rowan, Bill, 321n1
Runyon, Tom, 141
Rupe, Steve, 33
Rynearson, Charley, 157-58, 164, 306n3
Ryan, Mr. (murdered freighter), 233, 240
Ryan, Pat, 31
Rynning, Capt. Tom, xviii, *198*, 322n4

Safford, Ariz., 155, 182
Salazar, General, *205*, 267, 270, 271, 279
Sample, Edward, 128-29, 133-34, 137, 160-63, 315n6
San Antonio, N.M., 168, 172
San Antonio, Tex., 25
Sanders, Charley, *196*, 224-26, 325n1, 329n5, 330n3
Sandiford, "Shy," 35
San Francisco Examiner, 175, 227
San Pedro River, Ariz., 188, 190, 217, 255, 324n5
San Pedro, Sonora, Mex., 217
Santa Rosa, N.M., 172
Santa Rosa (N.M.) Star, 70
Savage, Judge John, 49-51, 55-60, 62, 68
Savage, Lyman, 329n1
Savage, Lydia (Mrs. George Healey), 68
Savarzo, Señor, 213-16, 221
Schieffelin Hall (Tombstone), *201*, 260
Schmoker family, 288
Sebra, Charley (Sugarfoot), 43, 44
Secoro Ranch, *83*
Separ, N.M., 248

Shade's Well, Neutral Strip, *83*
Sharps Creek, Neutral Strip, 146
Sheridan, General Phil, 10, 305n2
Short, Luke (gunfighter), 279, 331n5
Short, Luke (U.S. cattle inspector), 279-80, 331n5
Shouse, Bill, 32
Slapout, Okla., 43
Smith, Bob, 43
Smith, Charley, 27
Smith, G. C., 17
Smith, Sam, 321n1
Smith, Mrs. (Solomonville, Ariz.), 324n5
Smokie, Mr. (bondsman), 139
Snyder, Albert, 286
Socorro, N.M., 168, 172, 174
Sonora, Mexico (Civil War), 268
Sonora River, Mex., 246, 253
Soto & Renaud Merc. Co., 263-64
Soto, Mr., 182
Spencer, Earl, 134-35
Spindles, George, 220
Spindles, Lucy, *200*, 261
Sprowl, George, 23
Spur Ranch, 173
Star Mail Route frauds, 307n2
Star Mail Routes, 16
Starr, Belle, 314n4
Starr gang, 108
Starr, Henry, 290, 314n4
Steadman, Ben, 67, 330n1
Steadman, James, 67
Steadman, Stella, 67
Steele, Bob, 16, 18, 32
Stevens, Charlie (Wash.), 20-21
Stewart, M. C. (Cicero), 155-57, 320n3, 322n4
Stiles, Billy, xiii, 177, 187, *199*, 249-50, 252-56
Stilwell (or Dunlap), Jack, 252
Stratton, Carleton H., 314n4
Stratton, Mrs. C. H. (see **Olive Dorothy Herron**)
Stratton, J. L., 314n4
Strong, Dr. E. B. N., 27
Sullivan, Frank S., 332n1
Sulphur Springs Valley Cattle Co., 265, 328n4
Superior, Ariz., 302, 324n6, 331n1
Sutter, Judge (see **L. M. Hubbard**)

Taintor, Fred, 18, *82,* 313*n*1
Tascosa, Tex., 117, 315*n*2
Telluride, Colo., 327*n*1
Terrazas, Don Luis, 209-10, 268-69
Territorial Council (Cimarron Territory), 81, 308*n*1
Territorial (O.T.) *Advocate, The, 81, 314n3*
Texas Cattle Trail (The Western Trail), 4, 13, 16, 25, 71, 74, 101
Thompson, Ben, 13
Thompson, Henry (Sheriff), 150-51, 180-81, 83
Thompson, "Thunder," 69
Thorp, Jack, 322*n*4
Threlkeld, "Hooker", 35, 36
Thurman, Al, 17
Tiffany & Co., N.Y., 323*n*3
Titworth, George W., 321*n*1
Tombstone, Ariz., 183-86, 191, 212, 252, 260-62, 265, 298, 323*n*2, 327*n*2, 328*n*4
Tombstone Epitaph, The, 200, 260
Tombstone Prospector, The, 200, 240, 260
Tombstone Consolidated Mining Co., 260
Towers & Gudgell Ranch (OX), 106, 115
Tracy, Fred C., 99, 297, 302-03, 311*n*2
Trammel, Frank, 215
Turner, Mr. (wagon boss for Empire Ranch), 319*n*2
Tuttle Trail (see Chapman-Tuttle Trail)
Twist, E. A., 318*n*4
Tyrone (Old), Neutral Strip, 31, 101-02

Valencia, Mary (see Mrs. James Herron, sr.)
Valentine, Nebr., 122, 129
Vanderlip, Frank, 42, 43
Vaughn, J. N., 190
Vigilantes, 28, 37-43, 49, *80*
Villa, General Francisco (Pancho), *203,* 209, 269-70, 272-74, 276-77
Votaw, Rev., 318*n*4

Wagner's Cow Yard Saloon (Naco, Ariz.), 212
Wagon Mound, N.M., 320*n*2

Walker, Mabel (see Mrs. James Herron, jr.)
Ward, Charlie, 289
Warren, Ariz., 190
Washington, Mr., 264
Webster, Hoare & Co., 305*n*3
Webster, Hume, 305*n*3
Wehrle, John, 318*n*4
Wells, W. H., 286
Western Kansas Cattle Growers Association, 18, 19, 25, 26, 32, 66, 72, 95, 115-16, 121-22, 124, 127, 130-34, 145, 148, 151, 164-65, 173, 312*n*1
Westmoreland-Hitch Ranch, 117
Whitcomb, Rance, 12, 13
White House Saloon (Douglas, Ariz.), 283
White Oaks, N.M., 172
White, Scott (Sheriff), 192, 209, 322*n*4
Wichita Falls, Tex., 248
Wichita, Kan., 25
Wild Horse Lake (Neutral Strip), 102-04
Wild West Shows, 90-92, 101
Willcox, Ariz., 182, 249
Willingham, Cape, 135-37, 315*n*2
Winslow, Ariz., 150
Woodsdale (Old), Kan., 103
Woodward, O. T., 152, 160-62, 164, 321*n*1
Word & Byler Ranch (R Bar S), 22
Wright, Robert M. (Bob), 31
Wright, Burris, 152, *207,* 288, 319*n*2, 330*n*1
Wright, Mrs. George Z., 313*n*2
Wright, Capt. Henry H., 226, 240
Wright, Ray, 288

Yaqui River, Sonora, Mex., 275
Yellow Snake Saloon (Beer City, Neutral Strip), 102
YO Ranch, 156
Yoas, Tom (Bravo Juan), 177, 250, 252-53
York, "Kid," 21
York, T. I. (Tom), 223, 227-29, 231
Young, Alex, 14, 20, 22, 23, 26, 32, 33, 45
Young, Cole (Estes), 246, 249
Younger brothers, 106
Ysleta, Tex., 330*n*2

Zulu, Tex., 16